Spons on Carpentry & Joinery

A Manual for Handicraftsmen & Amateurs

CINCINNATI, OHIO
POPULAR WOODWORKING BOOKS, PUBLISHERS

First printed in 1910
by E. & F.N. Spon, Ltd., London and Spon & Chamberlain, New York.

CARPENTRY

The term "carpentry" is here employed in its widest sense, embracing what is more properly known as "joinery." The former is strictly applied to the use of wood in architectural structures, as for instance the joists, flooring, and rafters of a house, while the latter refers to the conversion of wood into articles of utility which are not remarkable for beauty of design or delicacy of finish. It is eminently convenient to discuss the united arts of carpentry and joinery under a single head, as they are really so closely connected as to present no real difference.

The art of the carpenter may be divided into 3 distinct heads—(1) a consideration of the kinds, qualities, and properties of the woods to be worked upon; (2) a description of the tools employed, and how to use them and keep them in order; and (3) the rudimentary principles of constructing fabrics in wood, with examples showing their application in various ways. The subject will be dealt with in this order.

Woods.—It will be well to begin with an enumeration of the woods used in carpentry—(other woods will be found described under the arts in which they are used, e. g. Carving)—leaving such matters as relate to all woods in general till afterwards. They will be arranged in alphabetical order. The terms used in describing the characters of the various woods may be explained once for all. The "cohesive force" is the weight required to pull asunder a bar of the wood in the direction of its length; the figures denoting the strength, toughness, and stiffness, are in comparison with oak, which is taken as the standard, and placed at 100 in each case; the "crushing force" is the resistance to compression; the "breaking-weight" is the weight required to break a bar 1 in. sq. supported at two points 1 ft. apart, with the weight suspended in the middle.

Acacia or American Locust-tree (*Robinia pseudo-acacia*).—This beautiful tree, of considerable size and very rapid growth, inhabits the mountains of America, from Canada to Carolina, its trunk attaining the mean size of 32 ft. long and 23 in. diam. The seasoned wood is much valued for its durability, surpassing oak. It is admirable for building, posts, stakes, palings, treenails for ships, and other purposes. Its weight is 49-56 lb. a cub. ft.; cohesive force, 10,000-13,000 lb.; and the strength, stiffness, and toughness of young unseasoned wood are respectively 95, 98, and 92. The wood is greenish-yellow, with reddish-brown veins. Its structure is alternately nearly compact and very porous, distinctly marking the annual rings; it has no large medullary rays.

Ake (*Dodonea viscosa*).—A small tree, 6–12 ft. high. Wood very hard, variegated black and white; used for native clubs; abundant in dry woods and forests in New Zealand.

Alder (*Alnus glutinosa*).—This small tree inhabits wet grounds and river-banks in Europe and Asia, seldom exceeding 40 ft. high and 24 in. diam. The wood is extremely durable in water and wherever it is constantly wet; but it soon rots on exposure to the weather or to damp, and is much attacked by worms when dry. It is soft, works easily, and carves well; but it is most esteemed for piles, sluices, and pumps, and has been much cultivated in Holland and Flanders for such purposes. Its weight is 34–50 lb. a cub. ft.; cohesive force, 5000–13,900 lb.; strength, 80; stiffness, 63; toughness, 101. The wood is white when first cut, then becomes deep-red on the surface, and eventually fades to reddish-yellow of different shades. The roots and knots are beautifully veined. It is wanting in tenacity, and shrinks considerably. The roots and heart are used for cabinet-work.

Alerce-wood (*Callitris quadrivalvis*).—This is the celebrated citrus-wood of the ancient Romans, the timber of the gum sandarach tree. The wood is esteemed above all others for roofing temples and for tables, and is employed in the cathedral of Cordova. Among the luxurious Romans, the great merit of the tables was to have the veins arranged in waving lines or spirals, the former called " tiger " tables and the latter " panther." Others were marked like the eyes on a peacock's tail, and others again appeared as if covered with dense masses of grain. Some of these tables were 4–4½ ft. diam. The specimens of the tree now existing in S. Morocco resemble small cypresses, and are apparently shoots from the stumps of trees that have been cut or burnt, though possibly their stunted habit may be due to sterility of soil. The largest seen by Hooker and Ball in 1878 were in the Ourika valley, and were about 30 ft. high. The stems of the trees swell out at the very base into roundish masses, half buried in soil, rarely attaining a diameter of 4 ft. It is this basal swelling, whether of natural or artificial origin, which affords the valuable wood, exported in these days from Algiers to Paris, where it is used in the richest and most expensive cabinet-work. The unique beauty of the wood will always command for it a ready market, if it be allowed to attain sufficient size.

Alerse (*Libocedrus tetragona*).—This is a Chilian tree, affording a timber which is largely used on the S. Pacific coast of America, and an important article of commerce. It gives spars 80–90 ft. long, and 800–1500 boards. Its grain is so straight and even that shingles split from it appear to have been planed.

Apple [Australian] (*Angophora subvelutina*).—The so-called apple-tree of Queensland yields planks 20–30 in. in diameter, the wood being very strong and durable, and much used by wheelwrights and for ships' timbers.

Ash (*Fraxinus excelsior*).—The common ash is indigenous to Europe and N. Asia, and found throughout Great Britain. The young wood is more valuable than the old; it is durable in the dry, but soon rots by exposure to damp or alternate wetting, and is very subject to worm when felled in full sap. It is difficult to work and too flexible for building, but valuable in machinery, wheel-carriages, blocks, and handles of tools. The weight is 34–52 lb. a cub. ft.; cohesive force, 6300–17,000 lb.; strength, 119; stiffness, 89; toughness, 160. The colour of the wood is brownish-white, with longitudinal yellow streaks; the annual layers are separated by a ring full of pores. The most striking characteristic possessed by ash is that it has apparently no sapwood at all —that is to say, no difference between the rings can be detected until the tree is very old, when the heart becomes black. The wood is remarkably tough, elastic, flexible, and easily worked. It is economical to convert, in consequence of the absence of sap. Very great advantage is found in reducing ash logs soon after they are felled into plank or board for seasoning, since, if left for only a short time in the round state, deep shakes open from the surface, which involve a very heavy loss when brought on later for conversion. Canadian and American ash, of a reddish-white colour, is imported to this country chiefly for making oars. These varieties have the same characteristics as English ash, but are darker in colour. The Canadian variety is the better of the two.

Assegai-wood or Cape Lancewood (*Curtisia faginea*).—This tree, the *oomhlebe* of the African natives, gives a very tough wood, used for wheel-spokes, shafts, waggon-rails, spears, and turnery, weighing 56 lb. a cub. ft.

Beech (*Fagus sylvatica*).—The common beech inhabits most temperate parts of Europe, from Norway to the Mediterranean, and is plentiful in S. Russia. It is most abundant in the S. and Midland counties of England, growing on chalky soils to 100 ft. high and 4–6 ft. diam. Wood grown in damp valleys becomes brittle on drying; it is very liable to destruction by worms, decays in damp situations, less in a dry state, but least of all when constantly under water. It is thus most useful for piles, and for knees and planking of ships. Its uniform texture and hardness make it very valuable for tools and common furniture. It is also used for carriage-panels and wooden tramways. Its weight is 43–53 lb. a cub. ft.; cohesive force, 6070–17,000 lb.; strength, 103; stiffness, 77; toughness, 138.

Beech [American].—Two species of *Fagus* are common in N. America,—the white (*F. sylvestris*), and the red (*F. ferruginea*). The perfect wood of the former is frequently only 3 in. in a trunk 18 in. diam., and it is of little use except for fuel. The wood of the latter, which is almost exclusively confined to the N.-E. States, Canada, New Brunswick, and Nova Scotia, is stronger, tougher, and more compact, but so liable to insect attacks as to be little used in furniture; yet it is very durable when constantly immersed in water.

Beech [Australian] (*Gmelina Leichhardtii*) attains a height of 80 to 120 ft. and yields planks 24 to 42 in. wide; its wood is valuable for decks of vessels, &c., as it is said neither to expand nor contract, and is exceedingly durable. It is worth 100s. to 120s. per 1000 ft. super.

Birch (*Betula spp.*).—The common birch (*B. alba*) is less important as a source of wood than as affording an empyreumatic oil. Its wood is neither strong nor durable, but is easily worked, moderately hard, and of straight and even grain, rendering it useful for chair-making, cabinet-making, and light turnery. The American red birch (*B. rubra*) has similar uses. The black or cherry birch (*B. lenta* [*nigra*]) of N. America is superior to all others, and imported in logs 6–20 ft. long and 12–30 in. diam. for furniture and turnery. Quebec birch is worth 3*l.* 5s.–4*l.* 15s. a load. There is a so-called " yellow birch " in Newfoundland, known also as " witch-hazel."

Birch [White or Black-heart] (*Fagus solandri*).—A lofty, beautiful evergreen tree 100 ft. high, trunk 4–5 ft. diameter. The heart timber is darker than that of *Fagus fusca* and is very durable. This wood is well adapted for fencing and bridge piles. The tree occurs only in the southern part of the North Island of New Zealand, but is abundant in the South Island up to 5000 ft.

Blackwood (*Acacia melanoxylon*) is one of the most valuable Australian woods. It is extensively used in the construction of railway carriages, and is well adapted for light and heavy framing purposes, gun-stocks, coopers' staves, and turners' work, and in this respect contrasts favourably with most of the English woods; and, from the facility with which it is bent into the most difficult curves, it is highly prized for buggy and gig shafts, &c. Within the last few years it has been introduced extensively into the manufacture of the finer description of furniture, such as drawing-room suites, and is found far superior to walnut, owing to its strength and toughness. Blackwood resembles in figure different woods, such as walnut, mahogany, rosewood, zebrawood, &c. Formerly mahogany was extensively imported for the purpose of manufacturing billiard tables; but at the present time blackwood has taken the place of mahogany in the above-named manufacture. It is pronounced to be far superior to the best Spanish mahogany for this purpose ; owing to its density and resisting qualities, it is acted on very slightly by the changes of weather, and is capable of taking a fine polish. It is named from the dark-brown colour of the mature wood, which becomes black when washed with lime-water. In moist shaded localities, the tree grows more rapidly, and the wood is of a much lighter colour ; hence this variety is called "Lightwood" in Hobart Town, to distinguish it from the other. Diameter, $1\frac{1}{2}$ to 4 ft. ; average, about $2\frac{1}{4}$ ft. ; height, 60 to 130 ft. ; sp. grav., about 0·855. Found throughout Tasmania, but not abundantly in any one locality. Price, about 12s. to 14s. per 100 ft. super., in the log.

Box (*Buxus sempervirens*).—The common evergreen box is a native of Europe as far as 52° N. lat., and is abundant in S. and E. France, Spain, Italy, the Black Sea coast, Persia, N. India, China, and Japan. For some years past the supply of this important wood has diminished in quantity and risen in price. It is mainly derived from the forests of the Caucasus, Armenia, and the Caspian shores. The wood of the best quality comes from the Black Sea forests, and is principally shipped from the port of Poti. The produce of the Caspian forests known in the trade as "Persian," used also to be exported through the Black Sea from Taganrog. This found its way, after the commencement of the Russo-Turkish war, viâ the Volga canal, to St. Petersburg. The produce of the Caspian forests is softer and inferior in quality to that of the Black Sea. It is a large article of trade with Russia, reaching Astrakhan and Nijni-Novgorod in the spring, and being sold during the fair. It recently amounted to 130,000 *poods* (of 36 lb.). True Caucasian boxwood may be said to be commercially non-existent, almost every marketable tree having been exported. The value of the yet unworked Abkhasian forests has been much exaggerated, many of the trees being either knotted or hollow from old age, and most of the good wood having been felled by the Abkhasians previous to Russian occupation. The boxwood at present exported from Rostov, and supposed to be Caucasian, comes from the Persian provinces of Mazanderan and Ghilan, on the Caspian. Boxwood is characterized by excessive hardness, great weight, evenness and closeness of grain, light colour, and capacity for taking a fine polish. Hence it is very valuable for wood-engraving, turning, and instrument-making. The Minorca box (*B. balearica*), found in several of the Mediterranean islands, and in Asia Minor, yields a similar but coarser wood, which probably finds its way into commerce. The approximate value of Turkey box is 6–20*l.* a ton.

Box [Australian] (*Tristania conferta*) grows in Queensland to 10 ft. in height, and 35–50 in. in diameter ; the wood is invaluable for ship-building, ribs of vessels made from it having been known to last unimpaired upwards of 30 years.

Box [Spurious] (*Eucalyptus leucoxylon*) is a valuable Victorian timber, of a light-grey colour and greasy nature, remarkable for the hardness and closeness of its grain, great strength, tenacity, and durability both in the water and when placed on the ground. It is largely used by coachmakers and wheelwrights for the naves of wheels and for heavy framing, and by millwrights for the cogs of their wheels. In ship-building it has numerous and important applications, and forms one of the best materials for treenails, and for working into large screws in this and other mechanical arts.

The Grey Box [*E. dealbata*] is another species, used for similar purposes to the preceding.

Broadleaf (*Griselinia littoralis*).—An erect and thickly branched bush tree, 50–60 ft. high ; trunk 3–10 ft. diam. Wood splits freely, and is valuable for fencing and in ship-building ; some portions make handsome veneers. Grows chiefly in the South Island of New Zealand and near the coasts.

Broadleaf or Almond (*Terminalia latifolia*).—This is a Jamaica tree, growing 60 ft high to the main branches, and $3\frac{1}{2}$–5 ft. diam. It is used for timbers, boards, shingles, and staves. Its weight is 48 lb. a cub. ft. ; crushing-force, 7500 lb. ; breaking-weight, 750 lb.

K

Bullet-tree (*Mimusops Balata*).—This tree is found in the W. Indies and Central America. Its wood is very hard and durable, and fitted for most outside work; it is used principally for posts, sills, and rafters. It warps much in seasoning, splits easily, becomes slippery if used as flooring, and is very liable to attacks of sea-worms. Its weight is $65\frac{1}{2}$ lb. a cub. ft.; crushing-force, 14,330 lb.

Bunya-bunya (*Araucaria Bidwillii*) grows to the height of 100–200 ft., and attains a diameter of 30–48 in. This noble tree inhabits the scrubs in the district between the Brisbane and the Burnett rivers, Queensland, and in the 27th parallel it extends over a tract of country about 30 miles in length and 12 in breadth. The timber is strong and good, and full of beautiful veins, works with facility, and takes a high polish.

Cedar [Australian Red] (*Cedrela australis*).—This tree is a native of Australia, where it has been almost exterminated, the timber being found so useful in house-building (for joinery, doors, and sashes) and boat-building. Its weight is 35 lb. a cub. ft.; breaking-weight, 471 lb.

Cedar [Bermuda] (*Juniperus bermudiana*).—This species is a native of the Bermudas and Bahamas. Its wood much resembles that of Virginian Cedar, and is used for similar purposes, as well as for ship-building. It is extremely durable when ventilated and freed from sapwood. It lasts 150 200 years in houses, and 40 years as outside ship-planking. It is difficult to get above 8 in. sq. Its weight is 46–47 lb. a cub. ft.

Cedar [Lebanon] (*Abies Cedrus* [*Cedrus Libani*]).—This evergreen tree is a native of Syria, and probably Candia and Algeria. The trunk reaches 50 ft. high and 34–39 in. diam. The wood is said to be very durable, and to have been formerly extensively used in the construction of temples. It is straight-grained, easily worked, readily splits, and is not liable to worm. Its weight is 30–38 lb. a cub. ft.; cohesive force, 7400 lb. a sq. in.; strength, 62; stiffness, 28; toughness, 106.

Cedar [New Zealand] (*Libocedrus Doniana* and *L. Bidwillii*).—Of the species, the former, the *kawaka* of the natives, is a fine timber tree 60–100 ft. high, yielding heavy fine-grained wood, useful in fencing, house-blocks, piles, and sleepers. It weighs 30 lb. a cub. ft.; breaking-weight, 400 lb. The wood runs 3 to 5 ft. in diameter, and is reddish in colour; it is used by the Maoris for carving, and is said to be excellent for planks and spars. The second species, called *pahantea* by the natives, reaches 60 to 80 ft. high and 2 to 3 ft. in diameter. In Otago it produces a dark-red free-working timber, rather brittle, chiefly adapted for inside work. The timber has been used for sleepers on the Otago railways of late years, and is largely employed for fencing purposes, being frequently mistaken for Totara.

Cedar [Virginian Red] (*Juniperus virginiana*).—This small tree (45 to 50 ft. high and 8 to 18 in. in diameter) inhabits dry rocky hillsides in Canada, the United States, and W. Indies, and flourishes in Britain. The wood is much used in America for wardrobes, drawers, boxes, and furniture, being avoided by all insects on account of its strong odour and flavour. It is light, brittle, and nearly uniform in texture. It is very extensively employed for covering graphite pencils, being imported in logs 6–10 in. sq. It weighs $40\frac{1}{2}$ lb. a cub. ft. The heartwood is reddish-brown, the sapwood is white, straight-grained, and porous. It possesses about $\frac{3}{4}$ the strength of red pine, is easily worked, shrinks little, and is very durable when well ventilated. A resinous exudation makes freshly-cut timber hard to work.

Cedar [W. Indian or Havanna] (*Cedrela odorata*).—This tree is a native chiefly of Honduras, Jamaica, and Cuba, having a stem 70 to 80 ft. high and 3 to 5 ft. diam., and exported in logs up to 3–4 ft. sq. Its wood is soft, porous, and brittle, and used chiefly for cigar-boxes and the inside of furniture. It makes durable planks and shingles. Its weight is 36 lb. a cub. ft.; crushing-weight, 6600 lb.; breaking-weight, 400 lb. The approximate London market values are $4–5\frac{1}{4}d$. a ft. for Cuba cedar, and $4–6\frac{1}{4}d$. for Honduras, &c.

Ceda Boom (*Widdringtonia juniperoides*).—This tree is found in N. and W. Cape

Colony, and its wood is used for floors, roofs, and other building purposes, but will not stand the weather.

Cherry [Australian] (*Exocarpus cupressiformis*) is a soft, fine-grained timber, and forms the best Australian wood for carving. It reaches a height of 20–30 ft., and a diameter of 9–15 in. ; its sp. gr. is about 0·785. It is used for tool-handles, spokes, gun-stocks, &c.

Chestnut (*Castanea vesca*).—This, the sweet or Spanish chestnut, is said to be a native of Greece and W. Asia, but grows wild also in Italy, France, Spain, N. Africa, and N. America. It lives to 1000 years, but reaches its prime at about 50, when the stem may be 40–60 ft. long and 3–6 ft. diam. The wood is hard and compact: when young, it is tough and flexible, and as durable as oak; when old, it is brittle and shaky. It does not shrink or swell so much as other woods, and is easier to work than oak; but soon rots when built into walls. It is valued for hop-poles, palings, gate-posts, stakes, and similar purposes. Its weight is 43–54 lb. a cub. ft. ; cohesive force, 8100 lb. ; strength, 68; stiffness, 54; toughness, 85. The wood much resembles oak in appearance, but can be distinguished by having no distinct large medullary rays. The annual rings are very distinct; the wood has a dark-brown colour; the timber is slow of growth, and there is no sapwood.

Cypress (*Cupressus sempervirens*).—This tree is abundant in Persia and the Levant, and cultivated in all countries bordering the Mediterranean, thriving best in warm sandy or gravelly soil, and reaching 70–90 ft. high. Its wood is said to be the most durable of all. For furniture, it is stronger than mahogany, and equally repulsive to insects. In Malta and Candia, it is much used for building. It weighs about 40–41 lb. a cub. ft.

Cypress pine (*Callitris columellaris*) is a plentiful tree in Queensland, attaining a diameter of 40 in. It is in great demand for piles and boat-sheathing, as it resists the attacks of cobra and white ants. The wood is worth 120s. per 1000 ft. super. The roots give good veneers.

Dark yellow wood (*Rhus rhodanthema*) grows in Queensland to a moderate size, affording planks up to 24 in. wide; the wood is soft, fine-grained, and beautifully marked, and is highly esteemed for cabinet work, being worth 100 to 120s. per 1000 ft. super.

Deal [White], White Fir, or Norway Spruce (*Abies excelsa*).—This tree inhabits the mountainous districts of Europe, and extends into N. Asia, being especially prevalent in Norway. It runs to 80–100 ft. high, and about 2–3 ft. max. diam. The tree requires 70–80 years to reach perfection, but is equally durable at all ages. It is much imported in spars and deals, the latter about 12 ft. long, 3 in. thick, and 9 in. wide. The wood glues well, and is very durable while dry, but much more knotty than Northern Pine. It is fine-grained and does well for gilding on, also for internal joinery, lining furniture, and packing-cases. A principal use is for scaffolds, ladders, and masts, for which purpose it is largely imported from Norway in entire trunks, 30–60 ft. long, and 6–8 in. max. diam. It is shipped from Christiania, Friedrichstadt, Drontheim, Gottenburg, Riga, Narva, St. Petersburg, &c. Christiania deals and battens are reckoned best for panelling and upper floors; Friedrichstadt have small black knots; lowland Norway split and warp in drying; Gottenburg are stringy and mostly used for packing-cases; Narva are next in quality to Norway, then Riga; St. Petersburg shrink and swell even after painting. The wood is generally light, elastic, tough, easily worked, and extremely durable when properly seasoned. It weighs 28–34 lb. a cub. ft. ; cohesive force, 8000–12,000 lb. a sq. in. ; strength, 104; stiffness, 104; toughness, 104. The wood is yellowish-white or brownish-red, becoming bluish by exposure. The annual rings are clearly defined, the surface has a silky lustre, and the timber contains many hard glossy knots. It is soft, warps much unless restrained while seasoning, and lacks durability ; it is weaker than red and yellow pine, less easily worked, and apt to snap under a sudden load. It is a nice wood for dresser-tops, shelves, and common tables, but should not be less than 1 in. thick, on account of warping. The knots are liable to turn the plane-iron.

Deodar (*Cedrus Deodara*).—This tree is found in the Himálayas at 5000–12,000 ft., and on the higher mountains from Nepal to Kashmir, measuring 150–200 ft. high, and over 30 ft. circ. Its wood is extremely valuable for all carpentry, and most generally used in the Punjab for building. Its weight is 37 lb. a cub. ft.; breaking-weight, 520 lb.

Dogwood.—The American dogwood (*Cornus florida*) is a tree 30 ft. high, common in the woods of many parts of N. America. Its wood is hard, heavy, and close-grained, and largely used locally for tool-handles; it has been imported into England with some success as a substitute for box in making shuttles for textile machinery. The black dogwood or alder buckthorn (*Rhamnus Frangula*) is abundant in Asia Minor, and affords one of the best wood charcoals for gunpowder-making. The principal uses made of Bahama dogwood (*Piscidia Erythrina*) are for fellies for wheels and for ship timber. From its toughness and other properties, it is better adapted to the former purpose than any other of the Bahamian woods. The tree does not attain any considerable size, and is generally crooked; a rather soft, open-grained, but very tough wood.

Doorn or Kameel Boom (*Acacia horrida*).—This tree is a native of S. Africa, and affords small timber used for fencing, spars, fuel, and charcoal.

Ebony (*Diospyros spp.*).—The best and most costly kind of ebony, having the blackest and finest grain, is the wood of *D. reticulata*, of Mauritius. The E. Indian species, *D. Melanoxylon* and *D. Ebenaster*, also contribute commercial supplies, and another kind is obtained from *D. Ebenum*, of Ceylon. The heartwood of the trunk of these trees is very hard and dense, and is largely used for fancy cabinet-making, mosaic work, turnery, and small articles. The approximate London market values are 5–20l. a ton for Ceylon, and 3–12l. for Zanzibar, &c.

Elm (*Ulmus spp.*).—Five species of elm are now grown in Britain:—The common rough-leaved (*U. campestris*) is frequent in scattered woods and hedges in S. England, and in France and Spain, attaining 70–80 ft. high, and 4 ft. diam. Its wood is harder and more durable than the other kinds, and is preferred for coffins, resisting moisture well. The corked-barked (*U. suberosa*) is common in Sussex, but the wood is inferior. The broad-leaved wych-elm or wych-hazel (*U. montana*) is most cultivated in Scotland and Ireland, reaching 70–80 ft. high and 3–4½ ft. diam. The smooth-leaved wych-elm (*U. glabra*) is abundant in Essex, Hertford, the N. and N.-E. counties of England, and in Scotland, growing to a large size. The wood is tough and flexible, and preferred for wheel-naves. The Dutch elm (*U. major*), the smallest of the five, is indigenous to Holland; its wood is very inferior. Elm-trunks average 44 ft. long and 32 in. diam. The wood is very durable when perfectly dry or constantly wet. It is not useful for general building, but makes excellent piles, and is used in wet foundations, waterworks, and pumps; also for wheel-naves, blocks, keels, and gunwales. It twists and warps in drying, shrinks considerably, and is difficult to work; but is not liable to split, and bears the driving of bolts and nails very well. Its weight is 34–50 lb. a cub. ft.; cohesive force, 6070–13,200 lb.; strength, 82; stiffness, 78; toughness, 86. The colour of the heartwood is a reddish-brown. The sapwood is yellowish- or brownish-white, with pores inclined to red. The medullary rays are not visible. The wood is porous and very twisted in grain; is very strong across the grain; bears driving nails very well; is very fibrous, dense, and tough, and offers a great resistance to crushing. It has a peculiar odour, and is very durable if kept constantly under water or constantly dry, but will not bear alternations of wet and dry. Is subject to attacks of worms. None but fresh-cut logs should be used, for after exposure, they become covered with yellow doaty spots, and decay will be found to have set in. The wood warps very much on account of the irregularity of its fibre. For this reason it should be used in large scantling, or smaller pieces should be cut just before they are required; for the same reason it is difficult to work. The sapwood withstands decay as well as the heart. Elm timber should be stored under water to prevent decay. Three species of elm are indigenous to N. America, and have similar uses to the European kinds:—The common American (*U. americana*) grows in low woods from New England to Canada, reaching 80–100 ft. high; its wood is inferior to English. The Canada rock or mountain (*U. racemosa*) is common to Canada and the N. States; the wood is used in boat-building, but is very liable to shrink, and gets shaky by exposure to sun and wind; its weight is 47–55 lb. a cub. ft. The slippery (*U. fulva*) gives an inferior wood, though much used for various purposes. Quebec elm is valued at 4–5*l.* a load.

Eucalyptus.—Besides the chief species which are described separately under their common names, almost all have considerable value as timber trees for building, fencing, and general purposes throughout Australia.

Fir [Silver] (*Picea pectinata*).—This large tree (100 ft. high, and 3–5 ft. diam.) is indigenous to Europe, Asia, and N. America, growing in British plantations. It is said to attain its greatest perfection in this country at 80 years. The wood is of good quality, and much used on the Continent for carpentry and ship-building. Floors of it remain permanently level. It is liable to attacks of the worm, and lasts longer in air than in water. It weighs about 25½ lb. a cub. ft.

Greenheart or Bibiri (*Nectandra Rodiœi* [*leucantha*]).—This celebrated ship-building wood is a native of British Guiana, and has been largely exported from Demerara to English dockyards. It gives balks 50–60 ft. long without a knot, and 18–24 in. sq., of hard, fine-grained, strong, and durable wood. It is reputed proof against sea-worms, and placed in the first class at Lloyd's; it is very difficult to work, on account of its splitting with great force. Its weight is 58–65 lb. a cub. ft.; crushing-weight, 12,000 lb.; breaking-weight, 1424 lb. The section is of fine grain, and very full of fine pores. The annual rings are rarely distinct. The heartwood is dark-green or chestnut-coloured, the centre portion being deep brownish-purple or almost black; the sapwood is green, and often not recognizable from the heart. An essential oil causes it to burn freely. It comes into the market roughly hewn, much bark being left on the angles, and the ends of the butts are not cut off square.

Gum [Blue] (*Eucalyptus Globulus*).—This Australian and Tasmanian tree is of rapid growth, and often reaches 150–300 ft. high and 10–20 ft. diam. Its wood is hard, compact, difficult to work, and liable to split, warp, and shrink in seasoning. It is used for general carpentry and wheel-spokes. Its weight is 60 lb. a cub. ft.; crushing-force, 6700 lb.; breaking-weight, 550–900 lb. It is employed in the erection of buildings, for beams, joists, &c., and for railway sleepers, piers, and bridges. It is also well adapted for ship-building purposes; from the great length in which it can always be procured, it is especially suitable for outside planking, and has been used for masts of vessels, but, owing to its great weight, for the latter purpose has given place to Kaurie; it is also bent and used for street cab shafts, &c.

Gum [Red] (*Eucalyptus rostrata*), of Australia, is a very hard compact wood, possessing a very handsome curly figure; it is of light-red colour, and suitable for veneering purposes for furniture; it is largely used for posts, resembling jarrah in durability. Properly selected and seasoned, it is well adapted for ship-building, culverts, bridges, wharves, railway sleepers, engine buffers, &c.

Gum [White or Swamp] *Eucalyptus viminalis*).—This tree is found chiefly in Tasmania, and a variety called the Tuvart occurs in W. Australia. The wood is valued for its great strength, and is sometimes used in ship-building, but more in house-building, and for purposes where weight is not an objection. It is sound and durable, shrinks little, but has a twisted grain, which makes it difficult to work. Its weight is about 70 lb. a cub. ft.; crushing-force, 10,000 lb.; breaking-weight, 730 lb.

Hickory or White Walnut (*Carya* [*Juglans*] *alba*).—There are about a dozen species of hickory, natives of N. America, forming large forest trees. Their timber is coarse-grained, and very strong, tough, and heavy; but is unsuited for building, as it does not bear exposure to the weather, and is much attacked by insects. It is extensively used where toughness and elasticity are required, such as for barrel-hoops, presses, handles, shafts and poles of wheel carriages, fishing-rods, and even light furniture. The most important is the shell-bark, scaly-bark, or shag-bark (*C. alba*), common throughout the Alleghanies from Carolina to New Hampshire, growing 80–90 ft. high and 2–3 ft. diam.

Hickory [Australian] (*Acacia supporosa*) is a valuable wood for many purposes. It is exceedingly tough and elastic, and would make good gig shafts, handles for tools, gun-stocks, &c. Tall straight spars, fit for masts, can be obtained 50 to 100 ft. long and 18 in. in diam.

Hinau (*Elæocarpus dentatus*).—A small tree, about 50 ft. high, and 18 in. thick in stem. Wood, a yellowish-brown colour and close grained, very durable for fencing and piles. Common throughout New Zealand. Makes a very handsome furniture wood.

Hinoki (*Retinospora obtusa*) enjoys the highest repute in Japan for building purposes. The tree grows with amazing rapidity and vigour, and its wood is used almost exclusively for the structure and furniture of the temples, generally unvarnished. It gives a beautifully white even grain under the plane, and withstands damp so well that thin strips are used for roofing and last a hundred years. The wood is soft enough to take the impression of the finger nail.

Hornbeam (*Carpinus Betulus*).—Notwithstanding that the wood is remarkable for its close grain, even texture, and consequent strength, it is seldom used for structural purposes. To a certain extent this is attributable to the tree not usually growing to a very large size, and also to the fact that when it does it is liable to become shaky. Hornbeam has of late been much more largely used in this country than formerly, it having been found to be peculiarly adapted for making lasts used by bootmakers. This wood being sent to this country in considerable quantities from France, led to the discovery that it was being used almost exclusively for the above purpose, and that it was imported in sacks, each containing a number of small blocks, in shape of the rough outline of a last. The advantage over other woods, and even over beech, which has hitherto been considered the best wood for last-making, is that, after the withdrawal of nails, the holes so made close up, which is not the case with most other woods. The wood is white and close, with the medullary rays well marked, and no sapwood. Under vertical pressure, the fibres double up instead of breaking. It stands exposure well.

Horoeka, or Ivy Tree (*Panax crassifolium*).—An ornamental, slender, and sparingly branched tree. The wood is close-grained and tough. Common in forests throughout New Zealand.

Horopito, Pepper Tree, or Winter's Bark (*Drimys axillaris*).—A small, slender, ever-green tree, very handsome. Wood very ornamental in cabinet-work, making handsome veneers. Grows abundantly in forests throughout New Zealand.

Ironbark (*Eucalyptus resinifera*).—This rugged tree is found in most parts of the Australian continent, frequently reaching 100–150 ft. high and 3–6 ft. diam., the usual market logs being 20–40 ft. long and 12–18 in. sq. Its wood is straight-grained, very dense, heavy, strong, and durable, but very difficult to work. It is liable to be shaky, and can only be employed with advantage in stout planks or large scantlings. Its weight is $64\frac{1}{2}$ lb. a cub. ft.; crushing-force, 9921 lb.; breaking-weight, 1000 lb. It forms one of the hardest and heaviest of the Australian woods, and is highly prized by the coachmaker and wheelwright for the poles and shafts of carriages and the spokes of wheels. Its greasy nature also renders it serviceable for the cogs of heavy wheels, and it is valued for many purposes in ship-building.

Ironwood [Cape] (*Olea undulata*).—This S. African wood, the *tambooti* or *hooshe* of the natives, is very heavy, fine-grained, and durable, and is used for waggon-axles, wheel-cogs, spokes, telegraph-poles, railway-sleepers, and piles. This is the "black" ironwood. The "white" (*Vepris lanceolata*) is used for similar purposes.

Jack, or Ceylon Mahogany (*Artocarpus integrifolia*).—This useful tree is a native of the E. Archipelago, and is widely cultivated in Ceylon, S. India, and all the warm parts of Asia, mainly as a shade-tree for coffee and other crops. Its wood is in very general use locally for making furniture; it is durable, and can be got in logs 21 ft. long and 17 in. diam. Its weight is 42 lb. a cub. ft.; breaking-weight, 600 lb.

Jack [Jungle], or Anjilli (*Artocarpus hirsuta*).—This species is remarkable for size of stem, and is found in Bengal, Malabar, and Burma. Its wood is strong and close-grained, and considered next in value to teak for ship-building. Its weight is 38–49 lb. a cub. ft.; cohesive force, 13,000–15,000 lb.; breaking-weight, 740 lb.

Jaral (*Lagerstræmia reginæ*) is a valuable timber tree of Assam, giving a light salmon-coloured wood, with coarse uneven grain, very hard and durable, and not liable to rot under water. It is used chiefly in boat-building and for house-posts. Full-sized trees run 35 ft. high and 7–8 ft. in girth, fetching 6l.–8l. each.

Jarrah, Australian Mahogany, or Flooded or Red Gum (*Eucalyptus marginata*).—This tree attains greatest perfection in W. Australia, reaching 200 ft. high. Its wood is hard, heavy, close-grained, and very durable in salt and fresh water, if cut before the rising of the sap. It is best grown on the hills. It resists sea-worms and white ants, rendering it specially valuable for ships, jetties, railway-sleepers and telegraph-posts, but shrinks and warps considerably, so that it is unfit for floors or joinery. Logs may be got 20–40 ft. long and 11–24 in. sq. Its weight is 62½ lb. a cub. ft.; crushing-force, 7000 lb.; breaking-weight, 500 lb. The chief objection raised against it is that it is liable to "shakes," the trees being frequently unsound at heart. For piles it should be used whole and unhewn; there is very little sapwood, and the outer portion of the heartwood is by far the harder, hence the desirability of keeping the annular rings intact.

Kaiwhiria (*Hedycarya dentata*).—A small evergreen tree 20–30 ft. high; the wood is finely marked and suitable for veneering. Grows in the North and South Island of New Zealand, as far south as Akaroa.

Kamahi (*Weinmannia racemosa*).—A large tree; trunk 2–4 ft. diam., and 50 ft. high. Wood close-grained and heavy, but rather brittle; might be used for plane-making and other joiners' tools, block-cutting for paper and calico printing, besides various kinds of turnery and wood-engraving. Grows in the middle and southern parts of the Northern Island and throughout the Southern Island of New Zealand. It is chiefly employed for making the staves of barrels.

Kanyin (*Dipterocarpus alatus*).—This magnificent tree is found chiefly in Pegu and the Straits, reaching 250 ft. high. Its wood is hard and close-grained, excellent for all house-building purposes, but not durable in wet. Its weight is 45 lb. a cub. ft.; breaking-weight, 750 lb. Another species (*D. turbinatus*), found in Assam, Burma, and the Andamans, is similar, and much used by the natives in house-building.

Kauri, Cowrie, or Pitch-tree (*Dammara australis*).—This gigantic conifer is a native of New Zealand, growing 80–140 ft. high, with a straight clean stem 4–8 ft. diam. The wood is close, even, fine-grained, and free from knots. It is chiefly used and well adapted for masts and spars; also for joinery, as it stands and glues well, and shrinks less than pine or fir. But it buckles and expands very much when cut to narrow strips for inside mouldings. Its weight is 35–40 lb. a cub. ft. cohesive force, 9600–10,960 lb. a sq. in. The timber is in high repute for deck and other planking of ships. It possesses great durability, logs which had been buried for many years being found in sound condition, and used as railway sleepers. In the Thames goldfield it supplies the mine props, struts, and cap pieces. It is the chief timber exported from New Zealand. Some of the largest and soundest sticks have richly mottled shading, which appears to be an abnormal growth, due to the bark being entangled in the ligneous portion, causing shaded parts, broad and narrow, according as the timber is cut relative to their planes; such examples form a valuable furniture wood. The heartwood is yellowish-white fine and straight in grain, with a silky lustre on the surface.

Kohe-kohe (*Dysoxylum spectabile*).—A large forest tree, 40–50 ft. high. Wood tough, but splits freely, and is considered durable as piles under sea-water. Grows in the North Island of New Zealand.

Kohutuhutu (*Fuchsia excorticata*).—A small and ornamental tree, 10–30 ft. high; trunk sometimes 3 ft. in diameter. It appears to furnish a durable timber. House blocks of this, which have been in use in Dunedin for more than 20 years, are still sound and good. Grows throughout New Zealand.

Kohwai (*Sophora tetraptera*).—A small or middling-sized tree. Wood red; valuable for fencing, being highly durable; it is also adapted for cabinet-work. It is used for piles in bridges, wharves, &c. Abundant throughout New Zealand.

Larch [American Black], Tamarak, or Hackmatack (*Larix pendula*).—This tree ranges from Newfoundland to Virginia, reaching 80–100 ft. high, and 2–3 ft. diam. The wood is said to nearly equal that of the European species.

Larch [Common or European] (*Larix europæa*).—This species is a native of the Swiss and Italian Alps, Germany, and Siberia, but not of the Pyrenees nor of Spain. The Italian is most esteemed, and has been considerably planted in England. The tree grows straight and rapidly to 100 ft. high. The wood is extremely durable in all situations, such as posts, sleepers, &c., and is preferable to pine, pinaster, or fir for wooden bridges. But it is less buoyant and elastic than Northern Pine, and boards of it are more apt to warp. It burns with difficulty, and makes excellent ship-timber, masts, boats, posts, rails, and furniture. It is peculiarly adapted for staircases, doors, and shutters. It is more difficult to work than Northern Pine, but makes a good surface, and takes oil or varnish better than oak. The liability to warp is said to be obviated by barking the trees while growing in spring, and cutting in the following autumn, or next year; this is also said to prevent dry-rot. The wood weighs 34–36 lb. a cub. ft.; cohesive force, 6000 –13,000 lb.; strength, 103: stiffness, 79; toughness, 134. The wood is honey-yellow or brownish-white in colour, the hard part of each ring being of a redder tinge, silky lustre. There are two kinds in this country, one yellowish-white, cross-grained, and knotty; the other (grown generally on a poor soil or in elevated positions) reddish-brown, harder, and of a straighter grain. It is the toughest and most lasting of all the coniferous tribe, very strong and durable, shrinks very much, straight and even in grain, free from large knots, very liable to warp, stands well if thoroughly dry, is harder to work than Baltic fir, but the surface is smoother, when worked. Bears nails driven into it better than any of the pines. Used chiefly for posts and palings exposed to weather, railway sleepers, flooring, stairs, and other positions where it will have to withstand wear.

Lignum-vitæ (*Guaiacum officinale*).—This tree grows chiefly on the south side of Jamaica, and affords one of the hardest and heaviest woods, extremely useful for the sheaves and blocks of pulleys, for which purpose it should be cut with a band of sap-wood all round, to prevent splitting. Its weight is 73 lb. a cub. ft.; crushing-weight, 9900 lb. The approximate London market value is 4–10*l.* a ton. Lignum-vitæ grows on several of the Bahama islands, and is generally exported to Europe and America. The principal use made of it in the Bahamas is for hinges and fastenings for houses situated by the sea shore or in the vicinity of salt ponds on the islands, where, from the quick corrosion of iron hinges, &c., metal is seldom used.

Locust-tree (*Hymenæa Courbaril*).—This tree is a native of S. America, and is found also in Jamaica. Its wood is hard and tough, and useful for house-building. Its weight is 42 lb. a cub. ft.; crushing-force, 7500 lb.; breaking-weight, 750 lb.

Mahogany (*Swietenia Mahogani*).—This tree is indigenous to the W. Indies and Central America. It is of comparatively rapid growth, reaching maturity in about 200 years, and the trunk exceeding 40–50 ft. long and 6–12 ft. diam. The wood is very durable in the dry, and not liable to worms. Its costliness restricts its use chiefly to furniture; it has been extensively employed in machinery for cotton-mills. It shrinks very little, warps and twists less than any other wood, and glues exceedingly well. It is imported in logs: those from Cuba, Jamaica, San Domingo, known as "Spanish," are about 20–26 in. sq. and 10 ft. long; those from Honduras, 2–4 ft. sq. and 12–14 ft. long. The weight is 35–53 lb. a cub. ft.; the cohesive force is 7560 lb. in Spanish, and 11,475 lb. in Honduras; the strength, stiffness, and toughness are respectively 67, 73, and 61 in Spanish, and 96, 93, and 99 in Honduras. The tree attains its greatest development and grows most abundantly between 10° N. lat. and the Tropic of Cancer, flourishing best on the higher crests of the hills, and preferring the lighter soils. It is found in abundance along the banks of the Usumacinta, and other large rivers flowing into the Gulf of Mexico, as well as in the larger islands of the W. Indies. British settlements for cutting and shipping the timber were established so long ago as 1638–40, and the right to the territory has been maintained by Great Britain, chiefly on account of the importance of this branch of industry. The cutting season usually commences about August. It is performed by gangs of men, numbering 20–50, under direction of a "captain" and accompanied by a "huntsman," the duty of the latter being to search out suitable trees, and guide the cutters to them. The felled trees of a season are scattered over a very wide area. All the larger ones are "squared" before being brought away on wheeled trucks along the forest roads made for the purpose. By March–April, felling and trimming are completed; the dry season by that time permits the trucks to be wheeled to the river-banks. A gang of 40 men work 6 trucks, each requiring 7 pair of oxen and 2 drivers. Arrived at the river, the logs, duly initialed, are thrown into the stream; the rainy season follows in May–June, and the rising current carries them seawards, guided by men following in canoes. A boom at the river-mouth stops the timber, and enables each owner to identify his property. They are then made up into rafts, and taken to the wharves for a final trimming before shipment. The cutters often continue their operations far into the interior, and over the borders into Guatemala and Yucatan. Bahama mahogany grows abundantly on Andros Island and others of the Bahama group. It is not exceeded in durability by any of the Bahama woods. It grows to a large size, but is generally cut of small dimensions, owing to the want of proper roads and other means of conveyance. It is principally used for bed-steads, &c., and the crooked trees and branches for ship timber. It is a fine, hard, close-grained, moderately heavy wood, of a fine, rich colour, equal to that of Spanish mahogany, although probably too hard to be well adapted for the purposes to which the latter is usually applied. Honduras is best for strength and stiffness, while Spanish is most valued for ornamental purposes. The Honduras wood is of a golden or red-brown colour, of various shades and degrees of brightness, often very much veined and mottled. The grain is coarser than that of Spanish, and the inferior qualities often contain many grey specks. This timber is very durable when kept dry, but does not stand the weather well. It is seldom attacked by dry-rot, contains a resinous oil which prevents the attacks of insects, and is untouched by worms. It is strong, tough, and flexible when fresh, but becomes brittle when dry. It contains a very small proportion of sap, and is very free from shakes and other defects. The wood requires great care in seasoning, does not shrink or warp much, but if the seasoning process is carried on too rapidly it is liable to split into deep shakes externally. It holds glue very well, has a soft silky grain, contains no acids injurious to metal fastenings, and is less combustible than most timbers. It is generally of a plain straight grain and uniform colour, but is sometimes of wavy grain or figured. Its market forms are logs 2–4 ft. sq. and 12–14 ft. in length. Sometimes planks have been obtained 6–7 ft. wide. Mahogany is known in the market as "plain," "veiny," "watered," "velvet-cowl," "bird's-eye," and "festooned," according to the appearance of the vein-formations. Cuba or Spanish mahogany is distinguished from Honduras by a white, chalk-like substance which fills its pores. The wood is very sound, free from shakes, with a beautiful wavy grain or figure, and capable of receiving a high polish. It is used chiefly for furniture and ornamental purposes, and for ship-building. Mexican shows the characteristics of Honduras.

Some varieties of it arc figured. It may be obtained in very large sizes, but the wood is spongy in the centre, and very liable to starshakes. It is imported in balks 15–36 in. sq., and 18–30 ft. in length. St. Domingo and Nassau are hard, heavy varieties, of deep-red colour, generally well veined or figured, and used for cabinet-works. They are imported in very small logs, 3–10 ft. long and 6–12 in. sq.

Mahogany [African] (*Swietenia senegalensis*). — This hard and durable wood is brought from Sierra Leone, and is much used for purposes requiring strength, hardness, and durability. But it is very liable to premature decay, if the heart is exposed in felling or trimming.

Mahogany [E. Indian].—Two species of *Swietenia* are indigenous to the E. Indies :— *S. febrifuga* is a very large tree of the mountains of Central Hindostan; the wood is less beautiful than true mahogany, but much harder, heavier, and more durable, being considered the most lasting timber in India. *S. chloroxylon* is found chiefly in the Circar mountains, and attains smaller dimensions ; the wood more resembles box.

Maire (*Santalum Cunninghamii*).—A small tree 10–15 ft. high, 6–8 in. diam. ; wood hard, close-grained, heavy. Used by the natives of New Zealand in the manufacture of war implements. Has been used as a substitute for box by wood-engravers.

Maire [Black] (*Olea Cunninghamii*).—Grows 40–50 ft. high, 3–4 ft. diam. ; timber close-grained, heavy, and very durable. Much of this very valuable timber is at present destroyed in clearing the land.

Maire-taw-hake (*Eugenia maire*).—A small tree about 40 ft. high ; trunk 1–2 ft. in diam.; timber compact, heavy, and durable. Used for mooring-posts and jetty-piles on the Waikato, where it has stood well for 7 years. It is highly valued for fencing. Common in swampy land in the North Island of New Zealand.

Mako (*Aristotelia racemosa*).—A small handsome tree 6–20 ft. high, quick growing. Wood very light, and white in colour, and might be applied to the same purposes as the lime tree in Britain; it makes good veneers.

Mango (*Mangifera indica*).—This tree grows abundantly in India, where numerous varieties are cultivated, as also in Mauritius, Brazil, and in other tropical climates. Its wood is generally coarse and open-grained, but is excellent for common doors and door-posts when well seasoned ; it is light and strong, but liable to snap ; it is durable in the dry, but decays rapidly when exposed to weather or water, and is much attacked by worms and ants. Its weight is 41 lb. a cub. ft. ; cohesive force, 7700 lb. ; breaking-weight, 560 lb.

Manuka (*Leptospermum ericoides*).—A small tree 10–80 ft. high, highly ornamental, more especially when less than 20 years old. The timber can be had 28–30 ft. long, and 14 in. diam. at the butt, and 10 in. at the small end. The wood is hard and dark coloured, largely used at present for fuel and fencing, axe-handles and sheaves of blocks, and formerly by the natives for spears and paddles. The old timber, from its dark-coloured markings, might be used with advantage in cabinet-work, and its great durability might recommend it for many other purposes. Highly valued in Otago for jetty and wharf piles, as it resists the marine worm better than any other timber found in the province. It is extensively used for house piles. The lightest coloured wood, called "white manuka," is considered the toughest, and forms an excellent substitute for hornbeam in the cogs of large spur wheels. It is abundant in New Zealand as a scrub, and is found usually on the poorer soils, but is rare as a tree in large tracts to the exclusion of other trees.

Maple (*Acer saccharinum*).—The sugar-maple is liable to a peculiarity of growth, which gives the wood a knotted structure, whence it is called "bird's-eye maple." The cause of this structure has never been satisfactorily explained. The handsome appearance thus given to the wood is the reason of its value in furniture and cabinet making.

Mingi-Mingi or Yellowwood (*Olearia avicenniæfolia*).—An ornamental shrub tree, trunk 2 ft. diam. Wood close-grained, with yellow markings, which render it desirable for cabinet-work; good for veneers. Occurs in South Island of New Zealand.

Miro (*Podocarpus ferruginea*).—This is a New Zealand tree, giving brownish wood 20–30 ft. long and 15–30 in. sq., useful for internal carpentry and joinery, and weighing 46 lb. a cub. ft. It is known as the "bastard black pine" in Otago, the wood being less durable than that of the matai or "true black pine"; it is reddish, close-grained and brittle, the cross section showing the heartwood star-shaped and irregular. The wood is generally thought to be unfitted for piles and marine works, except where only partially exposed to the influence of sea-water, when it is reported durable.

Monoao or Yellow Pine (*Dacrydium Colensoi*) is a very ornamental tree, 20–80 ft. high, giving a light and yellow wood, which is one of the strongest and most durable in New Zealand. Posts of this wood have stood several hundred years' use among the Maoris, and it is greatly valued for furniture.

Mora (*Mora excelsa*).—This tree is a native of British Guiana and Trinidad, growing luxuriantly on sand-reefs and barren clays of the coast regions, reaching 130–150 ft. high, and squaring 18–20 in. Its wood is extremely tough, close, and cross-grained, being one of the most difficult to split. It is one of the eight first-class woods at Lloyd's, making admirable keels, timbers, beams, and knees, and in most respects superior to oak. Its weight is 57 lb. a cub. ft.; crushing-force, 10,000 lb.; breaking-weight, 1212 lb. The wood is of a chestnut-brown colour, sometimes beautifully figured. It is free from dry-rot, but subject to starshake. Its market form is logs 18–35 ft. long and 18–20 in. sq.

Muskwood (*Eurybia argophylla*) grows in densely scrubby places among the mountain ranges of Tasmania, which makes it difficult to get out. This timber never grows very high; it has a pleasant fragrance, is of a beautiful mottled colour, and well adapted for veneering, fancy articles of furniture, pianofortes, &c. Diam. 6–15 in., the butt enlarging towards the ground to 1½, and even 2½ ft.; height, 15–30 ft.; sp. grav., about 0·685. Abundant throughout the island.

Mutti (*Terminalia coriacea*).—This is a common tree of Central and S. India. Its wood is hard, heavy, tough, fibrous, close-grained, rather difficult to work, unaffected by white ants, and considered extremely durable. It is used for beams and telegraph posts. Its weight is 60 lb. a cub. ft.; breaking-weight, 860 lb.

Nageswar (*Mesua ferrea*) is a valuable Assam timber, harder and more durable than Jaral, but not so suitable for boat-building, as it is much heavier, and difficult to work. Grows till 80 years old, when it reaches a height of 45 ft. and a diam. of 6 ft., such trees being worth 3*l.*

Nan-mu (*Persea Nanmu*).—That portion of the Chinese province of Yunnan which lies between 25° and 26° N. lat. produces the famous *nan-mu* tree, which is highly esteemed by the Chinese for building and coffins, on account of its durability and pleasant odour. It is imported into Shanghai in planks measuring 8 ft. long and 13–14 in. wide, for which the highest price is 200 *dol.* (of 4*s.* 2*d.*) a plank.

Naugiia.—This tree is generally found in the Pacific Islands on desert shores, or on the brinks of lagoons, where its roots are bathed by the tide. Its wood has great weight, intense hardness, and closeness of grain. It is considered a valuable substitute for box for wood-engraving. Blocks 18 in. diam. are common.

Neem (*Melia Azadirachta*).—This is a common, hardy, and quick-growing Indian tree, reaching 40–50 ft. high, and 20–24 in. diam. The trunk and branches are cut into short, thick planks, much used for lintels of doors and windows. The wood is hard and durable, but attacked by insects. Its fragrant odour makes it in request by natives for doors and door-frames. It is difficult to work, takes a fine polish, and is good for joinery where strength is not demanded; but becomes brittle and liable to snap when dry. Its weight is 51 lb. a cub. ft.; cohesive force 6940 lb.; breaking-weight, 600 lb.

Nei-nei (*Dacrophyllum longifolium*).—Wood is white, marked with satin-like specks, and is adapted for cabinet-work. Grows in South Island of New Zealand, and in Lord Auckland's group and Campbell's Island. The tree in the vicinity of Dunedin attains a diam. of 10–12 in.

Oak (*Quercus spp.*).—The most common British oak is *Q. pedunculata,* found throughout Europe from Sweden to the Mediterranean, and in N. Africa and Asia. Its wood is tolerably straight and fine in the grain, and generally free from knots. It splits freely, makes good laths for plasterers and slaters, and is esteemed the best kind for joists, rafters, and other purposes where a stiff, straight wood is desirable. The "durmast" oak (*Q. pubescens*) has the same range as the preceding, but predominates in the German forests. Its wood is heavier, harder and more elastic, liable to warp, and difficult to split. Both are equally valuable in ship-building. Quantities of Oak timber are shipped from Norway, Holland, and the Baltic ports, but are inferior to English-grown for ship-building, though useful for other purposes. A third kind is the cluster-fruited or "bay" oak (*Q. sessiliflora*). Of American oaks, the most important are as follows: The chestnut-leaved (*Q. prinos*) gives a coarse-grained wood, very serviceable for wheel-carriages. The red (*Q. rubra*), in Canada and the Alleghanies, affords a light, spongy wood, useful for staves. The wood of the white oak (*Q. alba*), ranging from Canada to Carolina, is tough, pliable, and durable, being the best of the American kinds, but less durable than British. It is exported from Canada to Europe as "American oak." The iron or post oak (*Q. obtusiloba*), found in the forests of Maryland and Virginia, is frequently called the "box white oak," and chiefly used for posts and fencing. The live oak (*Q. virens*) is the best American ship-building kind, inhabiting the Virginian coast. Oak warps, twists, and shrinks much in drying. Its weight is 37–68 lb. a cub. ft., according to the kind ; cohesive force, 7850–17,892 lb. It is valuable for all situations where it is exposed to the weather, and where its warping and flexibility are not objectionable. Quebec oak is worth about 4*l.* 10*s.*–7*l.* a load ; Dantzic and Memel, 3*l.* 10*s.*–5*l.* It is generally considered that the timber from the stalk-fruited oak is superior to that from the bay oak. The respective characteristics of the two varieties are :—The wood of the stalk-fruited oak is lighter in colour than the other. It has a straight grain, is generally free from knots, has numerous and distinct medullary rays, and good silver grain ; it is easy to work and less liable to warp, and is better suited for ornamental work, joists, rafters, and wherever stiffness and accuracy of form are required ; it splits well and makes good laths. The timber of the cluster-fruited oak is darker in colour, more flexible, tougher, heavier, and harder ; it has but few large medullary rays, so that in old buildings it has been mistaken for chestnut ; it is liable to warp, difficult to split, not suited for laths or ornamental purposes, but is better where flexibility or resistance to shocks is required. On the whole they so much resemble each other that few are able to speak positively as to their identity ; but the Durmast oak is decidedly of inferior quality. Oak is sometimes felled in the spring for the sake of the bark (instead of being stripped in the spring and felled in the winter) ; the tree being then full of sap, the timber is not durable. American oak has a pale reddish-brown colour, with a straighter and coarser grain than English. The timber is sound, hard, and tough, very elastic, shrinks very slightly, and is capable of being bent to any form when steamed. It is not so strong or durable as English oak, but is superior to any other foreign oak in those respects. It may be used for ship-building, and for many parts of buildings. It is imported in very large-sized logs varying from 25 to 40 ft. in length, and from 12 to 28 in. in thickness ; also in 2–4 in. planks, and in thick stuff of 4½–10 in. Dantzic oak is grown chiefly in Poland, and shipped also at Memel and Stettin. It is of dark-brown colour, with a close, straight, and compact grain, bright medullary rays, free from knots, very elastic, easily bent when steamed, and moderately durable. It is used for planking, ship-building, &c. It is classified as "crown" and "crown brack" qualities, marked respectively W and WW. It is imported in logs 18–30 ft.

long, 10–16 in. sq., and in planks averaging 32 ft. long, 9–15 in. wide, and 2–8 in. thick. French oak closely resembles British in colour, quality, texture, and general characteristics. Riga oak is grown in Russia, and is like that shipped from Dantzic, but with more numerous and distinct medullary rays. It is valued for its silver grain, and is imported in logs of nearly semicircular section. Italian (Sardinian) oak is from several varieties of the tree. It is of a brown colour, hard, tough, strong, subject to splits and shakes in seasoning, difficult to work, but free from defects, and extensively used for ship-building in her Majesty's dockyards. "Wainscot" is a species of oak, soft and easily worked, not liable to warp or split, and highly figured; it is obtained by converting the timber so as to show the silver grain, which makes the wood very valuable for veneers, and other ornamental work. It is imported chiefly from Holland and Riga, in semicircular logs. "Clap Boarding" is a description of oak imported from Norway, inferior to wainscot, and distinguished from it by being full of white-coloured streaks.

Oak [African], African Teak, or Turtosa (*Oldfieldia africana*).—This important W. African timber has lately been largely imported from Sierra Leone as a substitute for oak and teak. Though stronger than these, its great weight precludes its general use; but it is valuable for certain parts of ships, as beams, keelsons, waterways, and it will stand much heat in the wake of steamer fires, decaying rapidly, however, in confined situations. It warps in planks, swells with wet, and splits in drying again; it is not proof against insects. Its weight is 58–61 lb. a cub. ft.; cohesive force, 17,000–21,000 lb.

Oak [Australian].—Two hard-wooded trees of Australia are the forest-oak (*Casuarina torulosa*) and the forest swamp-oak (*C. paludosa*). They reach 40–60 ft. high and 12–30 in. diam., and are used in house-building, mainly for shingles, as they split almost as neatly as slate. They weigh 50 lb. a cub. ft.; crushing-force, 5500 lb.; breaking-weight, 700 lb. The she-oak (*C. quadrivalvis*) and he-oak (*C. suberosa*) of Tasmania are used mostly for ornamental purposes. *C. leptoclada* and *C. cristata* are other species well adapted for furniture purposes from the singular beauty of their grain. They are used for certain applications in boat-building, but rarely found to exceed 2–3 ft. in diameter. The wood is excellent for turnery purposes and the manufacture of ornamental work.

Pai-ch'ha (*Euonymus sp.*).—The wood of this tree has been proposed as a substitute for boxwood, being extensively produced in China, and largely used at Ningpo and other places for wood-carving. It is very white, of fine grain, cuts easily, and is well suited for carved frames, cabinets, &c.; but it is not at all likely to supersede box-wood, though well fitted for coarser work.

Pear (*Pyrus communis*).—Pear-tree wood is one of the heaviest and hardest of the timbers indigenous to Britain. It has a compact, fine grain, and takes a high polish; it is in great request by millwrights in France for making cog-wheels, rollers, cylinders, blocks, &c., and is preferred before all others for the screws of wine-presses. It ranks second to box for wood-engraving and turnery.

Persimmon (*Diospyros virginiana*).—The Virginian date-palm or persimmon is a native of the United States, growing 50–60 ft. high and 1½ ft. diam. Its heartwood is brown, hard, and elastic, but liable to split; it has been with some success introduced into England as a substitute for boxwood in shuttle-making and wood-engraving.

Pine [Black], or Matai (*Podocarpus spicata*).—This New Zealand timber is much more durable than Miro, and is used for all purposes where strength and solidity are required. Its weight is 40 lb. a cub. ft.; breaking-weight, 420–800 lb. It is a large tree, 80 ft. high and with a trunk 2–4 ft. in diameter. The wood is yellowish, close-grained, and durable; among the various purposes to which it is applied may be mentioned piles for bridges, wharves and jetties, bed-plates for machinery, millwrights' work, flooring, house blocks, railway sleepers, fencing, and bridges. It has been known to resist exposure for over 200 years in a damp situation.

Pine [Cluster], or Pinaster (*Pinus Pinaster*).—This pine inhabits the rocky mountains of Europe, and is cultivated in English plantations; it reaches 50–60 and even 70 ft. in height. It likes deep dry sand, or sandy loam in a dry bottom; but avoids all calcareous soils. The wood is said to be more durable in water than in air. It is much used in France for shipping-packages, piles and props in ship-building, common carpentry and fuel. It weighs 25½ lb. a cub. ft.

Pine [Huon] (*Dacrydium Franklinii*).—This tree is said to be abundant in portions of S.W. Tasmania, growing 50–100 ft. high and 3–8 ft. diam. The wood is clean and fine-grained, being closer and more durable than American White Pine, and can be had in logs 12–20 ft. long and 2 ft. sq. Its weight is 40 lb. a cub. ft. It is considered one of the handsomest and most suitable woods for bedroom furniture, bearing a strong resemblance to satinwood. From its lasting qualities, it is much prized for ship-building.

Pine [Moreton Bay] (*Araucaria Cunninghami*).—This abundant Queensland tree grows over 150 ft. high and 5 ft. diam., giving spars 80–100 ft. long. Its wood is straight-grained, tough, and excellent for joinery; but is not so durable as Yellow Pine, and is liable to attacks of sea-worms and white ants. It is used for flooring and general carpentry, and for shingles; it holds nails and screws well. Its weight is 45 lb. a cub. ft. It is strong and lasting either when dry or actually under water, but will not bear alternations of dryness and damp. When grown on the mountains of the interior, the wood is fine-grained and takes a polish which is described as superior to that of satin-wood or bird's-eye maple. Its average value is 55s.–70s. per 1000 ft. super.

Pine [Norfolk Island] (*Araucaria excelsa*).—This tree inhabits Norfolk Island and Australia, growing 200–250 ft. high and 10–12 ft. diam. Its wood is tough, close-grained, and very durable for indoor work.

Pine [Northern], or Red, Yellow, Scotch, Memel, Riga, or Dantzic Fir (*Pinus sylvestris*).—This tree forms with the spruce fir the great forests of Scandinavia and Russia, and attains considerable size in the highlands of Scotland. The logs shipped from Stettin reach 18–20 in. sq.; those from Dantzic, 14–16 in. and even 21 in. sq. and up to 40–60 ft. long; from Memel, up to 13 in. sq. and 35 ft. long; from Riga, 12 in. sq. and 40 ft. long, and spars 18–25 in. diam. and 70–80 ft. long; Swedish and Norwegian, up to 12 in. sq. It comes also in planks (11 in. wide), deals (9 in.), and battens (7 in.). The best are Christiana yellow deals, but contain much sap; Stockholm and Gefle are more disposed to warp; Gottenburg are strong, but bad for joinery; Archangel and Onega are good for joinery, but not durable in damp; Wiborg are the best Russian, but inclined to sap; Petersburg and Narva yellow are inferior to Arch-angel. Well-seasoned pine is almost as durable as oak. Its lightness and stiffness render it the best timber for beams, girders, joists, rafters, and framing; it is much used for masts, and for joinery is superior to oak on all scores. The hardest comes from the coldest districts. The cohesive force is 7000–14,000 lb. per sq. in.; weight, 29–40 lb. per cub. ft.; strength, 80; stiffness, 114; toughness, 56. The colour of the wood of different varieties is not uniform; it is generally reddish-yellow or honey-yellow of unequal depths of brightness. The section shows alternate hard and soft circles, one part of each annual ring being soft and light-coloured, the other harder and darker. It has a strong resinous odour and flavour, and works easily when not too highly resinous. Foreign wood shrinks about $\frac{1}{30}$ in width in seasoning from the log. In the best timber the annual rings do not exceed $\frac{1}{10}$ in. in thickness, and the dark parts of the rings are bright, reddish, hard, and dry, neither leaving a woolly surface after the saw nor choking the teeth with rosin. Inferior kinds have thick rings, and their dark portion is either more yellow, heavier, and more resinous, or is spongy, less resinous, and leaves a woolly surface after sawing; such is neither strong nor durable. Shavings from good timber will bear curling 2 or 3 times round the finger, those from bad will break off. The best balks come from Dantzic, Memel, and Riga. Dantzic is strong, tough, elastic, easily worked, and durable when seasoned. It contains (especially in small trees) much sapwood, and large and dead knots, while the heart is often loose and cuppy. The balks run 18-45 ft. long and 14-16 in. sq. ; deals, 18-50 ft. long and 2-5 in. thick. Memel is similar to Dantzic, but hardly so strong, and only 13-14 in. sq. Riga is somewhat weaker than Dantzic, but remarkable for straightness, paucity of sapwood, and absence of knots; being often rather shaky at the centre, it is not so good for turning into deals. Norway is small, tough, and durable, but generally contains much sapwood. The balks are only 8-9 in. sq. Swedish resembles Prussian, but the balks are generally tapering, small, of yellowish-white colour, soft, clean, straight in grain, with small knots and very little sap, but generally shaky at heart, and unfit for conversion into deals. It is cheap, suitable for the coarser purposes of carpentry, and used chiefly for scaffolding. Balks are generally 20-35 ft. long, and 10-12 in. sq. Planks, deals, and battens from the Baltic, cut from northern pine, are known as "yellow" or "red" deal; when cut from spruce, they are called "white" deals. Taking deals, battens, &c., in a general way, the order of quality would stand first or best with Prussia; then with Russia, Sweden, and Finland; and lastly with Norway. Prussian (Memel, Dantzic, Stettin) deals are very durable and adapted for external work, but are chiefly used for ship-building, being 2-4 in. thick. The timber from the southern ports, being coarse and wide in the grain, cannot compete in the converted form as deals, &c., with the closer-grained and cleaner exports from the more northern ports. Russian (Petersburg, Onega, Archangel, Narva) are the best deals imported for building purposes. They are very free from sap, knots, shakes, or other imperfections; of a clean grain, and hard, well-wearing surface, which makes them well adapted for flooring, joinery, &c. The lower qualities are of course subject to defects. Petersburg deals are apt to be shaky, having a great many centres in the planks and deals, but the best qualities are very clean and free from knots. They are very subject to dry rot. All Russian deals are unfit for work exposed to damp. In those from Archangel and Onega the knots are often surrounded by dead bark, and drop out when the timber is worked. Wyborg deals are sometimes of very good quality, but often full of sap. Finland and Nyland deals are 14 ft. long, very durable, but fit only for the carpenter. Norwegian (Christiania, Dram) yellow deals and battens used to bear a high character, being clean and carefully converted, but are now very scarce. Much of the Norwegian timber is imported in the shape of prepared flooring and matched boarding. Dram battens often suffer from dry rot, especially when badly stacked. Of Swedish (Gefle, Stockholm, Holmsund, Soderham, Gottenburg, Hernosand, Sundswall) the greater portion is coarse and bad, but some of the very best Baltic deal, both yellow and white, comes from Gefle and Soderham. The best Swedish run more sound and even in quality than Russian, from the different way in which the timber is converted. A balk of Russian timber is all cut into deals of one quality, hence the numerous hearts or centres seen amongst them, which are so liable to shake and split; whereas in Swedish timber the inner and the outer wood are converted into different qualities of deals. Hence the value of first-class Swedish goods. 4-in. deals should never be used for cutting into boards, as they are cut from the centres of the logs. 3-in. deals, the general thickness of Russian goods, are open to the same objection. Swedish 2½- and 2-in. of good quality are to be preferred to 3-in., since they are all cut from the sound outer wood. Swedish deals are fit for ordinary carcase work, but, from their liability to warp, cannot be depended upon for joiners' work. They are commonly used for all purposes connected with building, especially for floors.

Pine [Pitch] (*Pinus rigida* [*resinosa*]).—This species is found throughout Canada and the United States, most abundantly along the Atlantic coast. The wood is heavy, close-grained, elastic, and durable, but very brittle when old or dry, and difficult to plane. The heartwood is good against alternate damp and dryness, but inferior to White Pine underground. Its weight is 41 lb. per cub. ft. ; cohesive force, 9796 lb. per sq. in.; stiffness, 73; strength, 82; toughness, 92. The best comes from the S. States of N. America, chiefly from the ports of Savannah, Ilarien, and Pensacola. The colour is reddish-white or brown; the annual rings are wide, strongly marked, and form beautiful figures after working and varnishing. The timber is very resinous, making it sticky and troublesome to plane, but very durable; it is hard, heavy, very strong, free from knots, but contains much sapwood, is subject to heart and cup shake, and soon rots in damp; it is brittle when dry, and often rendered inferior by the trees having been tapped for turpentine. Its resinous nature prevents its taking paint well. It is used in the heaviest timber structures, for deep planks in ships, and makes very durable flooring. Market forms are logs 11–18 (aver. 16) in. sq., 20–45 ft. long; planks 20–45 ft. long, 10–15 in. wide, 3–5 in. thick.

Pine [Red, Norway, or Yellow] (*Pinus rubra* [*resinosa*]).—This tree grows on dry, stony soils in Canada, Nova Scotia, and the N. United States, reaching 60–70 ft. high, and 15–25 ft. diam. at 5 ft. above ground. The wood weighs 37 lb. per cub. ft.; it is much esteemed in Canada for strength and durability, and, though inferior in these respects to Northern Pine, is preferred by English shipwrights for planks and spars, being soft, pliant, and easily worked. This timber has a reddish-white appearance, with clean, fine grain, much like Memel, but with larger knots. It is small, very solid in the centre, with little sap or pith, tough, elastic, not warping nor splitting, moderately strong, very durable where well ventilated, glues well, and suffers little loss in conversion. Cabinet-makers use it for veneering, and sometimes it is employed for internal house-fittings. Market forms are logs 16–50 ft. long, 10–18 in. sq., 40 cub. ft. in contents, sized as "large," "mixed," and "building."

Pine [Red] or Rimu (*Dacrydium cupressinum*).—This New Zealand wood runs 45 ft. long, and up to 30 in. sq., and is much used in house-framing and carpentry, but is not so well adapted to joinery, as it shrinks irregularly. It weighs 40 lb. a cub. ft. It is an ornamental and useful wood, of red colour, clear-grained, and solid; it is much used for joisting, planking, and general building purposes from Wellington southwards. Its chief drawback is liability to decay under the influence of wet. It is largely employed in the manufacture of furniture, the old wood being handsomely marked like rosewood, but of a lighter brown hue. The best quality comes from the South Island.

Pine [Weymouth or White] (*Pinus strobus*).—This tree inhabits the American continent between 43° and 47° N. lat., occupying almost all soils. The timber is exported in logs over 3 ft. sq. and 30 ft. long; it makes excellent masts; is light, soft, free from knots, easily worked, glues well, and is very durable in dry climates; but is unfit for large timbers, liable to dry-rot, and not durable in damp places, nor does it hold nails well. It is largely employed for wooden houses and timber bridges in America. Its weight is 28¾ lb. per cub. ft.; cohesive force, 11,835 lb.; stiffness, 95; strength, 99; toughness, 103. The wood, when freshly cut, is of a white or pale straw colour, but becomes brownish-yellow when seasoned; the annual rings are not very distinct; the grain is clean and straight; the wood is very light and soft, when planed has a silky surface, and is easily recognized by the short detached dark thin streaks, like short hair-lines, always running in the direction of the grain. The timber is as a rule clean, free from knots, and easily worked, though the top ends of logs are sometimes coarse and knotty; it is also subject to cup and heart shakes, and the older trees to sponginess in the centre. It is much used in America for carpenters' work of all kinds; also for the same purpose in Scotland, and in some English towns, but considered inferior in strength to Baltic timber. The great length of the logs and their freedom from defects causes them to be extensively used for masts and yards whose dimensions cannot be procured from Baltic timber. For joinery this wood is invaluable, being wrought easily and smoothly into mouldings and ornamental work of every description. It is particularly adapted for panels, on account of the great width in which it may be procured; it is also much used for making patterns for castings. Of market forms the best are inch masts roughly hewn to an octagonal form. Next come logs hewn square, 18–60 ft. long, averaging 16 in. sq., and containing 65 cub. ft. in each log. A few pieces are only 14 in. sq.; short logs may be had exceeding even 26 in. sq. Some 3-in. deals vary in width from 9 to 24 and even 32 in. The best are shipped at Quebec. Goods from southern ports, such as Richibucto, Miramichi, Shedac, are inferior. American yellow deals are divided into 3 principal classes—Brights, Dry floated, Floated. Each of these is divided into 3 qualities, according to freedom from sap, knots, &c.; the first quality should be free from defects. First quality brights head the classification, then first quality dry floated, next first quality floated; then come second quality brights, second quality dry floated, and so on. Brights consist of deals sawn from picked logs and shipped straight from the sawmills. Floated deals are floated in rafts down the rivers from the felling grounds to the shipping ports. Dry floated deals are those which, after floating down, have been stacked and dried before shipment. Floating deals damages them considerably, besides discolouring them. The soft and absorbent nature of the wood causes them to warp and shake very much in drying, so that floated deals should never be used for fine work.

Pine [White] or Kahikatea (*Podocarpus dacrydioides*).—This New Zealand timber tree gives wood 40 ft. long and 24–40 in. sq., straight-grained, soft, flexible, warping and shrinking little, and well adapted for flooring and general joinery, though decaying rapidly in damp. Its weight is 30 lb. a cub. ft.; breaking-weight, 620 lb. When grown on dry soil, it is good for the planks of small boats; but when from swamps, it is almost useless. A variety called "yellow pine" is largely sawn in Nelson, and considered to be a durable building timber.

Pine [Yellow, Spruce, or Short-leaved] (*Pinus variabilis* and *P. mitis*).—The former species is found from New England to Georgia, the wood being much used for all carpentry, and esteemed for large masts and yards; it is shipped to England from Quebec. The latter is abundant in the Middle States and throughout N. America, reaching 50–60 ft. high and 18 in. diam. It is much used locally for framework: the heartwood is strong and durable; the sapwood is very inferior.

Plane (*Platanus orientalis* and *P. occidentalis*).—The first species inhabits the Levant and adjoining countries, growing 60–80 ft. high and up to 8 ft. diam. The wood is more figured than beech, and is used in England for furniture; in Persia it is applied to carpentry in general. The second species, sometimes called "water-beech," "button-wood," and "sycamore," is one of the largest N. American trees, reaching 12 ft. diam. on the Ohio and Mississippi, but generally 3–4 ft. The wood is harder than the oriental kind, handsome when cut, works easily, and stands fairly well, but is short-grained and easily broken. It is very durable in water, and preferred in America for quays. Its weight is 40–46 lb. a cub ft.; cohesive force, 11,000 lb.; strength, 92; stiffness, 78; toughness, 108.

Pohutukawa (*Metrosideros tomentosa*).—This tree has numerous massive arms; its height is 30–60 ft.; trunk 2–4 ft. in diam. The timber is specially adapted for the purposes of the ship-builder, and has usually formed the framework of the numerous vessels built in the northern provinces of New Zealand. Grows on rocky coasts, and is almost confined to the province of Auckland.

Poon (*Calophyllum Burmanni*).—This tree is abundant in Burma, S. India, and the E. Archipelago. It is tall and straight, and about 6 ft. circ. It is used for the decks, masts, and yards of ships, being strong and light. Its texture is coarse and porous, but uniform: it is easy to saw and work up, holds nails well, but is not durable in damp. Its weight is 40–55 lb. a cub. ft.; cohesive force, 8000–14,700 lb. Another species (*C. angustifolium*) from the Malabar Hills is said to furnish spars.

Poplar (*Populus spp.*).—Five species of poplar are common in England: the white (*P. alba*), the black (*P. nigra*), the grey (*P. canescens*), the aspen or trembling poplar (*P. tremula*), and the Lombardy (*P. dilatata*); and two in America: the Ontario

(*P. macrophylla*) and the black Italian (*P. acladesca*). They grow rapidly, and their wood is generally soft and light, proving durable in the dry, and not liable to swell or shrink. It makes good flooring for places subject to little wear, and is slow to burn. It is much used for butchers' trays and other purposes where weight is objectionable. The Lombardy is the lightest and least esteemed, but is proof against mice and insects. The weight is 24–33 lb. a cub. ft.; cohesive force, 4596–6641 lb.; strength, 50–86; stiffness, 44–66; toughness, 57–112. Poplar is one of the best woods for paper-making. The colour of the wood is yellowish- or browish-white. The annual rings are a little darker on one side than the other, and therefore distinct. They are of uniform texture, and without large medullary rays. The wood is light and soft, easily worked and carved, only indented, not splintered, by a blow. It should be well seasoned for 2 years before use. When kept dry, it is tolerably durable, and not liable to swell or shrink.

Pukatea (*Laurelia Novæ-Zelandiæ*).—Height, 150 ft., with buttressed trunk 3–7 ft. in diam.; the buttresses 15 ft. thick at the base; wood soft and yellowish, used for small boat planks. A variety of this tree has dark-coloured wood that is very lasting in water, and greatly prized by the natives in making canoes. Grows in the North Island and northern parts of the Middle Island of New Zealand.

Puriri or Ironwood (*Vitex littoralis*).—A large tree, 50–60 ft. high, trunk 20 ft. in girth. Wood hard, dark olive brown, much used; said to be indestructible under all conditions. Grows in the northern parts of the North Island of New Zealand only. It is largely used in the construction of railway waggons, and is said to make excellent furniture, though but little employed in that direction. It splits freely and works easily, and is used wherever durability is essential, as in cart work, bridges, teeth of wheels, and fencing-posts.

Pymma (*Lagerstræmia reginæ*).—The wood of this abundant Indian tree, particularly in S. India, Burma, and Assam, is used more than any except teak, especially in boat-building, and posts, beams and planks in house-building. Its weight is 40 lb. a cub. ft.; cohesive force, 13,000–15,000 lb.; breaking-weight, 640 lb.

Pynkado or Ironwood (*Inga xylocarpa*).—This valuable timber tree is found throughout S. India and Burma. Its wood is hard, close-grained, and durable; but it is heavy, not easily worked, and hard to drive nails into. It is much used in bridge-building, posts, piles, and sleepers. Its weight is 58 lb. a cub. ft.; cohesive force, 16,000 lb.; breaking-weight, 800 lb. Called also erool.

Rata (*Metrosideros lucida*).—This tree is indigenous to New Zealand, giving a hard timber 20–25 ft. long and 12–30 in. sq., very dense and solid, weighing 65 lb. a cub. ft. A valuable cabinet wood; it is of a dark-red colour; splits freely. It has been much used for knees and timbers in ship-building, and would probably answer well for cogs of spur wheels. Grows rarely in the North Island, but is abundant in the South Island, especially on the west coast. In Taranaki it is principally used by mill- and wheelwrights. *M. robusta* grows 50–60 ft. high, diameter of trunk 4 ft., but the descending roots often form a hollow stem 12 ft. in diam. Timber closely resembles the last-named species, and is equally dense and durable, while it can be obtained of much larger dimensions. It is used for ship-building, but for this purpose is inferior to the pohutukawa. On the tramways of the Thames it has been used for sleepers, which are perfectly sound after 5 years' use. Grows in the North Island; usually found in hilly situations from Cape Colville southwards.

Rewarewa (*Knightia excelsa*).—A lofty, slender tree 100 ft. high. Wood handsome, mottled red and brown, used for furniture and shingles, and for fencing, as it splits easily. It is a most valuable veneering wood. Common in the forests of the Northern Island of New Zealand, growing upon the hills in both rich and poor soils.

Rohun (*Soymida febrifuga*).—This large forest tree of Central and S. India affords a close-grained, strong and durable wood, which stands well when underground or buried in masonry, but not so well when exposed to weather. It is useful for palisades, sleepers, and house-work, and is not very difficult to work. Its weight is 66 lb. a cub. ft.; cohesive force, 15,000 lb.; breaking-weight, 1000 lb.

Rosewood.—The term "rosewood" is applied to the timber of a number of trees, but the most important is the Brazilian. This is derived mainly, it would seem, from *Dalbergia nigra*, though it appears equally probable that several species of *Triptolemæa* and *Machærium* contribute to the inferior grades imported thence. The wood is valued for cabinet-making purposes. The approximate London market values are 12–25*l*. a ton for Rio, and 10–22*l*. for Bahia.

Sabicu (*Lysiloma Sabicu*).—This tree is indigenous to Cuba, and found growing in the Bahamas, where it has probably been introduced. Its wood is exceedingly hard and durable, and has been much valued for ship-building. It has been imported from the Bahamas in uncertain quantities for the manufacture of shuttles and bobbins for cotton-mills. It resembles mahogany in appearance, but is darker, and generally well figured. The wood is very heavy, weathers admirably, and is very free from sap and shakes. The fibres are often broken during the early stages of the tree's existence, and the defect is not discovered until the timber is converted, so that it is seldom used for weight-carrying beams.

Sal or Saul (*Shorea robusta*).—This noble tree is found chiefly along the foot of the Himálayas, and on the Vindhyan Hills near Gaya, the best being obtained from Morung. Its wood is strong, durable, and coarse-grained, with particularly straight and even fibre; it dries very slowly, continuing to shrink years after other woods are dry. It is used chiefly for floor-beams, planks, and roof-trusses, and can be had in lengths of 30–40 ft., and 12–24 in. sq. Its weight is 55–61 lb. a cub. ft.; cohesive force, 11,500 lb.; crushing-force, 8500 lb.; breaking-weight, 881 lb.

Satinwood.—The satinwood of the Bahamas is supposed to be the timber of *Maba guianensis*, an almost unknown tree. The Indian kind is derived from *Chloroxylon Swietenia*, a native of Ceylon, the Coromandel coast, and other parts of India. The former comes in square logs or planks 9–20 in. wide; the latter, in circular logs 9–30 in. diam. The chief use of satinwood is for making the backs of hair- and clothes-brushes, turnery, and veneering. The approximate value of San Domingan is 6–18*d*. a ft. Bahama satinwood, also called yellow-wood, grows abundantly on Andros Island and others of the Bahamian group, and to a large size. It is a fine, hard, close-grained wood, showing on its polished surface a beautifully rippled pattern.

Sawara (*Retinospora pissifera*) is used in Japan for the same purposes as hinoki, when that is unprocurable.

She-pine (*Podocarpus elata*) is very common in Queensland, attaining 80 ft. in height and 36 in. in diam.; the timber is free from knots, soft, close-grained, and easily worked. It is used for joinery and spars, and worth 65*s*.–70*s*. per 1000 ft. super.

Sissu or Seesum (*Dalbergia Sissu*).—This tree is met with in many parts of India, being said to attain its greatest size at Chanda. Its wood resembles the finest teak, but is tougher and more elastic. Being usually crooked, it is unsuited for beams, though much used by Bengal ship-builders, and in India generally for joinery and furniture. Its weight is 46½ lb. a cub. ft.; cohesive force, 12,000 lb.; breaking-weight, 700 lb.

Sneezewood or Nies Hout (*Pteroxylon utile*).—This most durable S. African timber, the *oomtata* of the natives, is invaluable for railway-sleepers and piles, being almost imperishable.

Spruce [American White], Epinette, or Sapinette blanche (*Abies alba*).—This white-barked fir is a native of high mountainous tracts in the colder parts of N. America, where it grows 40–50 ft. high. The wood is tougher, lighter, less durable, and more liable to twist in drying than white deal, but is occasionally imported in planks and deals. It weighs 29 lb. a cub. ft.; cohesive force, 8000–10,000 lb.; strength, 86; stiffness, 72; toughness, 102.

Spruce [American Black] (*Abies nigra*).—This tree inhabits Canada and the N.

States, being most abundant in cold-bottomed lands in Lower Canada. It reaches 60–70 and even 100 ft. high, but seldom exceeds 24 in. diam. The wood is much used in America for ships' knees, when oak and larch are not obtainable.

Spruce [Red], or Newfoundland Red Pine (*Abies rubra*).—This species grows in Nova Scotia, and about Hudson's Bay, reaching 70–80 ft. high. It is universally preferred in America for ships' yards, and imported into England for the same purpose. It unites in a higher degree all the good qualities of the Black Spruce.

Stopperwood is principally used for piles and for wheel spokes. It is a very strong and durable wood, and grows from 12 to 16 ft. long and from 6 to 8 in. in diam. It is found on all the Bahamian islands, and is an exceedingly hard, fine, close-grained, and very heavy wood.

Stringy-bark (*Eucalyptus gigantea*).—This tree affords one of the best building woods of Australia, being cleaner and straighter-grained than most of the other species of *Eucalyptus*. It is hard, heavy, strong, close-grained, and works up well for planking, beams, joists, and flooring, but becomes more difficult to work after it dries, and shrinks considerably in drying. The outer wood is better than the heart. Its weight is 56 lb. a cub. ft.; crushing-force, 6700 lb.; breaking-weight, under 500 lb. It is liable to warp or twist, and is susceptible to dry-rot. It splits with facility, forming posts, rails and paling for fences, and shingles for roofing.

Sycamore or Great Maple (*Acer pseudo-platanus*).—This tree, mis-called "plane" in N. England, is indigenous to mountainous Germany, and very common in England. It thrives well near the sea, is of quick growth, and has a trunk averaging 32 ft. long and 29 in. diam. The wood is durable in the dry, but liable to worms; it is chiefly used for furniture, wooden screws, and ornaments. Its weight is 34–42 lb. a cub. ft.; cohesive force, 5000–10,000 lb.; strength, 81; stiffness, 59; toughness, 111. The wood is white when young, but becomes yellow as the tree grows older, and sometimes brown near the heart; the texture is uniform, and the annual rings are not very distinct; it has no large medullary rays, but the smaller rays are distinct.

Tamanu (*Calophyllum sp.*).—This valuable tree of the S. Sea Islands is becoming scarce. It sometimes reaches 200 ft. high and 20 ft. diam. Its timber is very useful for ship-building and ornamental purposes, and is like the best Spanish mahogany.

Tanekaha or Celery-leaved Pine (*Phyllocladus trichomanoides*) is a slender, handsome tree, 60 ft. high, but rarely exceeding 3 ft. in diam., affording a pale, close-grained wood, excellent for planks and spars, and resisting decay in moist positions in a remarkable manner. It grows in the hilly districts of the North Island of New Zealand, and in Tasmania.

Tasmanian Myrtle (*Fagus Cunninghamii*) exists in great abundance throughout the western half of the island, growing in forests to a great size in humid situations. It reaches a height of 60–180 ft., a diam. of 2–9 ft., averaging about 3½ ft., and has a sp. gr. of 0·795. Its price is about 16s. per 100 ft. super. in the log. It is found in considerable quantities in some of the mountainous parts in South Victoria. It is a reddish-coloured wood, and much employed by cabinet-makers for various articles of furniture. Occasionally planks of it are obtained of a beautiful grain and figure, and when polished its highly ornamental character is sure to attract attention. It is also used for the cogs of wheels by millwrights.

Tawa (*Nesodaphne tawa*).—A lofty forest tree, 60–70 ft. high, with slender branches. The wood is light and soft, and is much used for making butter-kegs. Grows in the northern parts of the South Island, and also on the North Island of New Zealand, chiefly on low alluvial grounds; is commonly found forming large forests in river flats. The wood makes fairly durable flooring, but does not last out of doors.

Tawhai or Tawhai-raie-nui (*Fagus fusca*).—Black birch of Auckland and Otago (from colour of bark). Red birch of Wellington and Nelson (from colour of timber). This is a noble tree, 60–90 ft. high, the trunk 5–8 ft. in diam. The timber is excessively tough and hard to cut. It is highly valued in Nelson and Wellington as being both strong and durable in all situations. It is found from Kaitaia in the North Island to Otago in the South Island of New Zealand, but often locally absent from extensive districts, and grows at all heights up to 3000 ft.

Teak (*Tectona grandis*).—This tall, straight, rapidly-growing tree inhabits the dry elevated districts of the Malabar and Coromandel coasts of India, as well as Burma, Pegu, Java, and Ceylon. Its wood is light, easily worked, strong, and durable; it is the best for carpentry where strength and durability are required, and is considered foremost for ship-building. The Moulmein product is much superior to the Malabar, being lighter, more flexible, and freer from knots. The Vindhyan excels that of Pegu in strength, and in beauty for cabinet-making. The Johore is the heaviest and strongest, and is well suited for sleepers, beams, and piles. It is unrivalled for resisting worms and ants. Its weight is 45–62 lb. a cub. ft. ; cohesive force, 13,000–15,000 lb. ; strength, 109 ; stiffness, 126 ; toughness, 94. It contains a resinous aromatic substance, which has a preservative effect on iron. It is subject to heartshake, and is often damaged. The resinous secretion tends to collect and harden in the shakes, and will then destroy the edge of any tool. When the resinous matter is extracted during life by girdling the tree, the timber is much impaired in elasticity and durability. Teak is sorted in the markets according to size, not quality. The logs are 23–40 ft. long, and their width on the larger sides varies according to the class, as follows :—Class A, 15 in. and upwards ; B, 12 and under 15 in. ; C, under 12 in. ; D, damaged logs.

Titoki (*Alectryon excelsum*).—A beautiful tree with trunk 15–20 ft. high and 12–20 in. diam. Wood has similar properties to ash, and is used for similar purposes. Its toughness makes it valuable for wheels, coach-building, &c. Grows in the North and Middle Islands of New Zealand, not uncommon in forests.

Toon, Chittagong-wood, or Red Cedar (*Cedrela Toona*).—This tree is a native of Bengal and other parts of India, where it is highly esteemed for joinery and furniture, measuring sometimes 4 ft. diam., and somewhat resembling mahogany. Its weight is 35 lb. a cub. ft. ; cohesive force, 4992 lb. ; breaking-weight, 560 lb. It is found in abundance in Queensland, on the coast and inland, reaching 100–150 ft. in height, and 24–76 in. in diam. The wood is light and durable; it is largely employed in furniture and joinery-work, and beautiful veneers are obtained from the junctions of the branches with the stem. Its value runs from 150s. to 170s. per 1000 ft. super. In Assam this timber is reckoned one of the most important, and is employed for making canoes and furniture. It is highly spoken of for making tea-chests in India and Ceylon, being light, strong, clean, non-resinous, not attacked by insects, and giving no unpleasant odour or flavour to the tea. It grows to an immense size ; one tree alone has been known to yield 80,000 ft. of fine timber. It stands the test of climate well, and does not require the same amount of seasoning as blackwood; it is of a much softer nature, but takes a very fine polish, and is suitable for dining-room furniture, &c.

Totara (*Podocarpus Totara*).—This tree is fairly abundant in the North and South Islands of New Zealand, reaching 80 ft. high and 2½–3½ ft. diam. Its wood is easily worked, straight and even-grained, warps little, and splits very clean and free; but it is brittle, apt to shrink if not well seasoned, and subject to decay in the heart. It is used generally for joinery and house-building. Its weight is 40 lb. ; breaking-weight, 570 lb. The timber is reddish-coloured, and much employed for telegraph poles ; it is extensively used in Wellington for house-building, piles for marine wharves, bridges, railway sleepers, &c. When felled during the growing season, the wood resists for a longer time the attacks of *teredo* worms. It is durable as fencing and shingles, post and rail fences made of it being expected to last 40–50 years. The Maoris made their largest canoes from this tree, and the palisading of their pahs was constructed almost entirely of it. Timber from trees growing on hills is found to be the more durable.

Towai or Red Birch (*Fagus Menziesii*) is a handsome tree, 80–100 ft. high, trunk

2-3 ft. diam. The timber is chiefly used in the lake district of the South Island of New Zealand. Durable and adapted for mast-making and oars, and for cabinet and cooper's work. Grows in the North Island on the mountain-tops, but abundant in the South Island at all altitudes to 3000 ft.

Tulip (*Harpullia pendula*) grows in Queensland to a height of 50–60 ft., and yields planks 14–24 in. wide, of close-grained and beautifully marked wood, highly esteemed for cabinet-work.

Walnut (*Juglans regia*).—The walnut-tree is a native of Greece, Asia Minor, Persia, along the Hindu Kush to the Himálayas, Kashmir, Kumaon, Nepal, and China, and is cultivated in Europe up to 55° N. lat., thriving best in dry, deep, strong loam. It reaches 60 ft. high and 30–40 in. diam. The young wood is inferior; it is in best condition at about 50–60 years. Its scarcity excludes it from building application, but its beauty, durability, toughness, and other good qualities render it esteemed for cabinet-making and gun-stocks. Its weight is 40–48 lb. a cub. ft.; cohesive force, 5360–8130 lb.; strength, 74; stiffness, 49; toughness, 111—all taken on a green sample. Of the walnut-burrs (or *loupes*), for which the Caucasus was once famous, 90 per cent. now come from Persia. The walnut forests along the Black Sea, which give excellent material for gun-stocks, do not produce burrs, which only occur in the drier climates of Georgia, Daghestan, and Persia. Italian walnut is worth 4–5½d. a ft.

Walnut [Black Virginia] (*Juglans nigra*).—This is a large tree ranging from Pennsylvania to Florida; the wood is heavier, stronger, and more durable than European walnut, and is well adapted for naval purposes, being free from worm attacks in warm latitudes. It is extensively used in America for various purposes, especially cabinet-making.

Willow (*Salix spp.*).—The wood of the willow is soft, smooth, and light, and adapted to many purposes. It is extensively used for the blades of cricket-bats, for building fast-sailing sloops, and in hat-making, and its charcoal is used in gunpowder-making.

Yellow-wood or Geel hout (*Taxus elongatus*).—This is one of the largest trees of the Cape Colony, reaching 6 ft. diam. Its wood is extensively used in building, though it warps much in seasoning, and will not bear exposure.

Yew (*Taxus baccata*).—This long-lived shrubbery tree inhabits Europe, N. America, and Japan, being found in most parts of Europe at 1000–4000 ft., and frequently on the Apennines, Alps, and Pyrenees, and in Greece, Spain, and Great Britain. The stem is short, but reaches a great diameter (up to 20 ft.). The wood is exceedingly durable in flood-gates, and beautiful for cabinet-making. Its weight is 41–42 lb. a cub. ft.; cohesive force, 8000 lb.

As this volume is intended as much for colonial as for home readers, it will be useful to give a brief summary of the woods native to various localities:—

British Guiana Woods.—The only wood from this colony which is known as it deserves is the greenheart, already described at p. 133. Yet there are several other woods equally worthy of being studied and utilized; among them the following were mentioned recently by Dr. Prior at the Linnean Society. "Ducalibolly" is a rare red wood used in the colony for furniture. "Hyawa-bolly" (*Omphalobium Lamberti*) is a rare tree 20 ft. high, known commercially as zebrawood. Lancewood is variously referred to *Duguetia quitarensis, Guatteria virgata, Oxyandra virgata, Xylopia sp.*, and *Rollinia Sieberi*; there seem to be 2 kinds, a "black" called *carisiri*, growing 50 ft. high and 4–8 in. diam., only slightly taper and affording by far the better timber, and a "yellow" called "yari-yari" (*jéjérécou* in French Guiana), 15–20 ft. high and 4–6 in. diam.; the Indians make their arrow points of this wood, and the spars go to America for carriage building. Letter-wood (*Brosimum aubletii*) is useful for inlaying and for making very choice walking-sticks.

Cape, Natal, and Transvaal Woods.—The timber trees of Cape Colony and Natal are chiefly evergreens. Their wood is dry and tough, and worked with more or less difficulty. Owing to the dryness of the soil and climate, it is very liable to warp and twist in seasoning. Some descriptions shrink longitudinally as well as transversely, and with few exceptions the timber is not procurable in logs of more than 12–15 in. diameter. The Cape woods principally used for waggon-making, mill machinery, fences, posts, &c., are assegai wood, essen wood or Cape ash, cedarwood, red and white ironwood (excellent for spokes); and melk wood, red and white, for felloes of wheels. These are principally brought to the market in convenient scantlings for the purposes for which they are required, and are all rather tough than hard to work. They have considerable specific gravity, and at first an English carpenter finds it difficult to do a satisfactory day's work with them. No European wood can stand the heat and dryness of the Cape climate as these woods do.

Assegai-wood, Cape lancewood, or Oomhlebe: weight, 56 lb. per cub. ft.; cost of working 1·5 times as much as fir; colour, light-red; grain, like lancewood; very tough and elastic; used for wheel-spokes, shafts, waggon-rails, assegai-shafts, turnery.

Cedar boom: weight, 41 lb.; cost of working, 1·25; used for floors, roofs, and other building purposes; grain not unlike Havannah cedar, but of a lighter colour; will not stand exposure to the weather.

Doorn boom, Kameel doorn, Makohala or Motootla: weight 40 lb.; cost of working, 1·25; several varieties afford small timber available for fencing, spars, &c., and are also much used for fuel, charcoal, &c.

Els (white) or Alder; weight, 38 lb.; cost of working, 1·25; used for palings, posts, and ordinary carpentry.

Els (red): weight, 47 lb.; cost of working 1·6; grain, colour of red birch; used for waggon-building and farm purposes.

Els (rock): a harder and smaller variety of the last.

Essen hout, Cape ash, or Oomnyamati: weight, 48 lb.; cost of working, 1·30; used for common floors, palings, &c.; is a tough and valuable timber, somewhat resembling elm; can be procured up to 18 in. sq.

Flat crownwood: cost of working, 1·30; grows in Natal to 2 ft. diameter; the wood is similar to elm, but of a bright yellow colour, with a fine and even grain; used for the naves of wheels.

Ironwood (black), Tambooti, or Hooshe: weight, 64 lb.: cost of working, 2·0; the grain fine, like pear tree; used for waggon axles, cogs of machine wheels, spokes, telegraph poles, railway sleepers, piles, &c.; is very durable, and can be obtained in logs up to 18 in. sq.

Ironwood (white), or Oomzimbiti: used for same purposes as black.

Kafir boom, Oomsinsi, or Limsootsi: weight, 38 lb.; wood, soft and light; the grain open and porous; splits easily; and is used principally for roof shingles, owing to its not being liable to take fire.

Mangrove (red): used in Natal for posts and fencing generally.

Melk hout, Milkwood, or Oomtombi: weight, 52 lb.; cost of working, 1·75; colour, white; used in the construction of waggons (wheelwork); there is also a darker variety.

Oliven hout, Wild olive, or Kouka; weight, 60 lb.; cost of working, 2·0; wood of small size, and generally decayed at the heart; used for fancy turnery, furniture, &c.

Pear hout or Kwa: weight, 46 lb.; resembles European pear, but closer in the grain.

Saffraan hout: weight, 54 lb.; wood strong and tough; used for farm purposes.

Sneezewood, Nies hout, or Oomtata: weight, 68 lb.; cost of working, 3·0; most durable and useful timber, resembling satinwood; very full of gum or resin resembling guaiacum; burns like candlewood; invaluable for railway sleepers, piles, &c., as it is almost imperishable, and is very useful for door and sash sills or similar work; difficult to be procured of large scantling.

Stinkwood, Cape mahogany, or Cape walnut: weight, 53 lb.; cost of working, 1·6; resembles dark walnut in grain; is used for furniture, gun-stocks, &c.; while working, it emits a peculiar odour; stands well when seasoned; usually to be obtained in planks 10–16 in. wide and 4 in. thick; there are one or two varieties which are inferior; for furniture, it should be previously seasoned by immersing the scantlings, sawn as small as possible, in a sand bath heated to about 100° F. (38° C.).

Yellow-wood, Geel hout, or Oomkoba: weight, 40 lb.; cost of working, 1·35; one of the largest trees that grows in the Cape, and often found upwards of 6 ft. in diameter; the wood is extensively used for common building purposes; it warps much in seasoning, and will not stand exposure to the weather; the colour is a light-yellow, which, with the grain, resembles lancewood; it shrinks in length about $\frac{1}{60}$ part; it has rather a splintery fracture, which makes it very unsafe for positions where heavy cross strains may be expected; for flooring, it does well, but should be well seasoned and laid in narrow widths; planks up to 24 in. wide can be got, but 12-in. ones are more general; it suffers much loss in conversion, owing to twisting; when very dry, it is apt to split in nailing; and is subject to dry-rot if not freely ventilated.

Willow or Wilge boom: weight, 38 lb.; this wood, which grows along the banks of rivers, is of little value, as it is soon destroyed by worms; but is used where other timber is scarce; makes good charcoal.

Ceylon woods.—In the following list of Ceylon woods, the breaking-weight and the deflection before breaking are taken on a bar 24 in. long and 1 in. square; the absorptive power is calculated on a block measuring 12 in. by 4 in. by 4 in.; and the weight represents 1 cub. ft.

Alubo; weight, 49 lb.; durability, 20 years; use, common house-building.

Aludel: breaking weight, 356 lb.; deflection, 1 in.; absorption, 15 oz.; weight, 51 lb.; durability, 35–70 years; logs average $22\frac{1}{2}$ ft. by 16 in.; uses, fishing boats and house buildings.

Aramana: breaking weight, 297 lb.; deflection, $1\frac{1}{2}$ in.; absorption, 13 oz.; weight, 57 lb.; durability, 50 years; logs average 15 ft. by 13 in.; uses, furniture and house buildings.

Beriya: weight, 57 lb.; durability, 10–30 years: uses, anchors and house-building.

Buruta or Satinwood: breaking-weight, 521 lb.; deflection, 1 in.; absorption, 14 oz.; weight, 55 lb.; durability, 10–80 years; logs average 19 ft. by $20\frac{1}{2}$ in.; uses, oil-presses, waggon-wheels, bullock-carts, bridges, cog-wheels, buildings, and furniture.

Calamander: weight, 57 lb.; durability, 80 years; a scarce and beautiful wood; the most valuable for ornamental purposes in Ceylon.

Daminna: weight, 44 lb.; durability, 40 years; uses, gun-stocks and common house buildings.

Dangaha: weight, 23 lb.; buoys for fishing nets, models for dhonies.

Dawata: weight, 43 lb.; durability, 25 years; uses, roofs of common buildings.

Del: breaking-weight, 264 lb.; deflection, $\frac{7}{8}$ in.; absorption, 17 oz.; weight, 40 lb.; durability, 20–50 years.; logs average $22\frac{1}{4}$ ft. by 16 in.; uses, boats and buildings.

Dun: weight, 29 lb.; durability, 50 years; uses, house buildings.

Ebony: breaking-weight, 360 lb.; deflection, $1\frac{5}{8}$ in.; absorption, 11 oz.; weight, 71 lb.; durability, 80 years; logs average $12\frac{1}{2}$ ft. by 13 in.; a fine black wood, used largely for buildings and furniture.

Gal Mendora: breaking-weight, 370 lb.; deflection, $1\frac{1}{4}$ in.; absorption, 14 oz.; weight, 57 lb.; durability, 15–60 years; logs average $22\frac{1}{2}$ ft. by 13 in.; uses, bridges and buildings; is the best wood for underground purposes; also used for reepers (battens) for tiling.

Gal Mora: weight, 65 lb.; durability, 30 years; uses, house buildings, and gives best firewood for brick- and lime-kilns.

Godapara: weight, 51 lb.; durability, 60 years; use, roofs for houses.

Gorukina: weight, 44 lb.; durability, 25 years; uses, poles for bullock-carts, and house buildings.

Hal: weight, 26 lb.; durability, 10 years; uses, packing cases, ceilings, coffins.

Hal Mendora: weight, 56 lb.; durability, 8–20 years; uses, bridges and house buildings, lasts longer than the preceding for underground purposes.

Hal Milila: breaking-weight, 422 lb.; deflection, $2\frac{1}{4}$ in.; absorption, 6 oz.; weight, 48 lb.; durability, 10–80 years; logs average $20\frac{1}{2}$ ft. by $14\frac{3}{4}$ in.; uses, casks, tubs, carts, waggons, and buildings; is the best wood for oil-casks in the island.

Hirikadol: weight, 49 lb.; durability, 15 years; use, common house buildings.

Hora: weight, 45 lb.; durability, 15 years; use, roofs of common buildings.

Ironwood: breaking-weight, 497 lb.; deflection, 1 in.; absorption 7 oz.; weight, 72 lb.; durability, 10–60 years; logs average $22\frac{1}{2}$ ft. by $14\frac{1}{2}$ in.; uses, bridges and buildings.

Jack: breaking-weight, 306 lb.; deflection, $\frac{7}{8}$ in.; absorption, 17 oz.; weight, 42 lb.; durability, 25–80 years; logs average 21 ft. by 17 in.; in general use for buildings, boats, and all kinds of furniture.

Kadol: weight, 65 lb.; durability, 40 years; use, common house-building.

Kadubberiya or Bastard ebony; weight, 45 lb.; durability, 40 years; use, furniture; the heart of this wood is occasionally of great beauty.

Kaha Milila: breaking-weight, 385 lb.; deflection, 1 in.; absorption, 8 oz.; weight, 56 lb.; durability, 15–80 years; logs average 16 ft. by $18\frac{1}{2}$ in.; uses, water-casks, padé-boats, waggon-wheels, bullock-carts, bridges, and buildings.

Kahata: weight, 38 lb.; durability, 10–20 years; uses, axles for bullock bandies, and buildings.

Kalukela: weight, 38 lb.; durability, 30 years; uses, common house buildings; when variegated, it is a beautiful wood, and is used for furniture and cabinet-work.

Kiripella: weight, 30 lb.; durability, 20–30 years; uses, common furniture and house buildings.

Kiriwalla: weight, 35 lb.; durability, 30 years; uses, principally for inlaying ornamental furniture and cabinet-work.

Kitul: weight, 71 lb.; durability, 30–90 years; uses, reepers (roof battens) and window-bars.

Kokatiya: weight, 56 lb.; durability, 80 years; use, house buildings.

Kon: weight, 49 lb.; durability, 5–10 years; uses, native oil presses and wooden anchors.

Kottamba: weight, 38 lb.; durability, 30 years; use, common house buildings.

Mal Buruta: breaking-weight, 252 lb.; weight, 57 lb.; durability, 80 years; logs average 19 ft. by $20\frac{1}{2}$ in.; use, furniture, being the most valuable Ceylon wood next to Calamander.

Mi: breaking-weight, 362 lb.; deflection, 1 in.; absorption, 15 oz.; weight, 61 lb.; durability, 25–80 years; logs average 25 ft. by 16 in.; uses, keels for dhonies, bridges, and buildings.

Mian Milila: breaking-weight, 394 lb.; deflection, 1 in.; absorption, 8 oz.; weight, 56 lb.; durability, 20–90 years; logs average 16 ft. by $18\frac{1}{2}$ in.; uses, bridges, padé-boats, cart and waggon-wheels, water-tubs, house buildings.

Muruba; weight, 42 lb.; durability, 30–40 years; uses, water and arrack casks, buildings, and underground purposes.

Nedun: breaking-weight, 437 lb.; deflection, 1 in.; absorption, 12 oz.; weight, 56 lb.; durability, 60–80 years; logs average 15 ft. by 16 in.; uses, buildings and furniture.

Nelli: weight, 49 lb.; durability, 30 years; uses, wheels and wells.

Pol or Coconut: weight, 70 lb.; durability, 20–50 years; uses, buildings, fancy boxes, and furniture.

Sapu: weight, 42 lb.; durability, 20–50 years; uses, carriages, palankins, &c.; in buildings it is a very good wood for window-sashes.

Sapu Milila: weight, 49 lb.; durability, 10–40 years; uses, water-casks, cart and waggon wheels, padé-boats, bridges, and house buildings.

Suriya: breaking-weight, 354 lb.; deflection, $1\frac{1}{8}$ in.; absorption, 16 oz.; weight, 49 lb.; durability, 20-40 years; logs average 12 ft. by 16 in.; uses, admirable for carriages, hackeries, gun-stocks, and in buildings.

Tal: breaking-weight, 407 lb.; deflection, $\frac{3}{4}$ in.; absorption, 13 oz.; weight, 65 lb.; durability, 80 years; uses, rafters and reepers (battens for roofs).

Teak: breaking-weight, 336 lb.; deflection, $\frac{7}{8}$ in.; absorption, 13 oz.; weight, 44 lb.; durability, 15-90 years; logs average 23 ft. by $17\frac{1}{2}$ in.; uses, carts, waggons, bridges, buildings, and arrack casks, imparting fine colour and flavour to the liquor.

Ubbariya: breaking-weight, 232 lb.; weight, 51 lb.; durability, 80 years; uses, rafters and reepers.

Velanga: weight, 36 lb.; uses, poles of bullock-carts, betel trays, and gun-stocks.

Walbombu: weight, 36 lb.; durability, 15 years; use, common house buildings.

Waldomba: weight, 39 lb.; durability, 20 years; use, common house buildings.

Walukina: weight, 39 lb.; durability, 10 years; use, masts of dhonies.

Welipenna: weight, 35 lb.; durability, 40 years; use, common house buildings.

Wewarana: weight, 62 lb.; durability, 60 years; uses, house buildings and pestles.

English woods.—The spruce fir of Oxfordshire is used for scaffold-poles, common carpentry, &c.; the maple of the same county is valuable for ornamental work when knotted, it makes the best charcoal and turns well. The Wandsworth sycamore is used in dry carpentry, turns well and takes a fine polish. The Wandsworth horse-chestnut is used for inlaying toys, turnery, and dry carpentry. The Oxfordshire alder for common turnery work, &c., and lasts long under water or buried in the ground. The Killarney arbutus is hard, close-grained, and occasionally used by turners; the Killarney barberry is chiefly used for dyeing. The common birch of Epping is inferior in quality, but much used in the North of England for herring barrels. The Epping hornbeam is very tough, makes excellent cogs for wheels, and is much valued for fuel. Cornwall chestnut is valuable in ship-building, and is much in repute for posts and rails, hop-poles, &c. Cedar of Lebanon makes good furniture, and is sometimes employed for ornamental joinery work. The common cherry is excellent for common furniture, and much in repute; it works easily, and takes a fine polish. The young wood of the common nut is used for fishing rods, walking sticks, &c. The Epping white thorn is hard, firm, and susceptible of a fine polish; that of Mortlake is fine-grained and fragrant, and very durable. Oxfordshire common laburnum is hard and durable, and much used by turners and joiners. Lancewood is hard and fine-grained, and makes excellent skewers. Oxfordshire common beech is much used for common furniture, for handles of tools, wooden vessels, &c., and when kept dry is durable. Oxfordshire common ash is very tough and elastic. It is much used by the coachmaker and wheelwright, and for the making of oars. Holly is the best whitewood for Tunbridge ware, turns well, and takes a very fine polish. The common walnut of Sussex is used for ornamental furniture, is much in repute for gun-stocks, and works easily. Oxfordshire larch is excellent for house carpentry and ship-building; it is durable, strong, and tough. Mortlake common mulberry is sometimes worked up into furniture, and is useful to turners, but is of little durability. Silver fir is used for house carpentry, masts of small vessels, &c. Oxfordshire pine makes good rafters and girders, and supplies wood for house carpentry. The Wandsworth plane is an inferior wood, but is much used in the Levant for furniture. The damson of that part is hard and fine-grained, but not very durable, and is suitable for turning. The laurel is hard and compact, taking a good polish. The Yorkshire mountain ash is fine-grained, hard, and takes a good polish, and is of great value for turnery, and for musical instruments. Yorkshire crab is hard, close-grained, and strong. Epping service-tree, hard, fine-grained, and compact, and much in repute by millwrights for cogs, friction rollers, &c. Wandsworth evergreen oak is very shaky when aged, is strong and durable, and makes an excellent charcoal. Sussex oak is much esteemed for ship-building, and is the strongest and most durable of British woods. Welsh oak is a good wood for ship-building, but is said to be inferior to the common oak. Epping common acacia is much used for treenails in ship-building, and in the United States is much in repute for posts and rails. Surrey white willow is good for toys, and used by the millwright; it is tough, elastic, and durable. Oxfordshire palm willow is tough and elastic, is much used for handles to tools, and makes good hurdles. Oxfordshire crack willow is light, pliant, and tough, and is said to be very durable. The yew is used for making bows, chairs, handles, &c.; the wood is exceedingly durable, very tough, elastic, and fine-grained. Wandsworth common lime is used for cutting blocks, carving, sounding boards, and toys. English elm is used in ship-building, for under-water planking, and a variety of other purposes, being very durable when kept wet, or buried in the earth; and Oxfordshire wych elm is considered better than common elm, and is used in carpentry, ship-building, &c. Specimens of the above were shown at the Great Exhibition of 1862. Of course, the list is far from being exhausted, still sufficient has been said to give an idea of the various uses to which our home-grown wood can be put.

Indian woods.—In the following descriptions of Indian woods, the "weight" denotes that of 1 cub. ft. of seasoned timber, "elasticity" is the coefficient of elasticity, "cohesion" is the constant of direct cohesion in lb. per sq. in., "strength" is the constant of strength in lb. for cross strains.

Abies Smithiana: furnishes a white wood, easily split into planks, but not esteemed as either strong or durable; used as "shingle" for roof coverings.

Acacia arabica: weight 54 lb.; elasticity, 4186; cohesion, 16,815 lb.; strength, 884 lb.; seldom attains a height of 40 ft., or 4 ft. in girth: its wood is close-grained and tough; of a pale-red colour inclining to brown; can never be had of large size, and is generally crooked; used for spokes, naves, and felloes of wheels, ploughshares, tent pegs.

Acacia Catechu: weight, 56–60 lb.; a heavy, close-grained, and brownish-red wood, of great strength and durability; employed for posts and uprights of houses, spear and sword handles, ploughs, pins and treenails of cart-wheels; but rarely available for timber.

Acacia elata: weight, 39 lb.; elasticity, 2926; cohesion, 9518 lb.; strength, 695 lb.; furnishing logs 20–30 ft. long, and 5–6 ft. in girth; wood red, hard, strong, and very durable; used in posts for buildings, and in cabinet-work.

Acacia leucophlœa: weight, 55 lb.; elasticity, 4086; cohesion, 16,288 lb.; strength, 861 lb.; resembles *A. arabica* and has similar uses.

Acacia modesta: very hard and tough timber, suitable for making mills, &c.

Acacia speciosa: weight, 55 lb.; elasticity, 3502; strength, 600 lb.; grows to 40–50 ft. in height and 5–6 ft. in girth: the wood is said by some writers to be hard, strong, and durable, never warping or cracking, and to be used by the natives of South India for naves of wheels, pestles and mortars, and for many other purposes; but in Northern India it is held to be brittle, and fit only for such purposes as box planks and firewood.

Acacia stipulata: weight, 50 lb.; elasticity, 4474; cohesion, 21,416 lb.; strength, 823 lb.; furnishes large, strong, compact, stiff, fibrous, coarse-grained, reddish-brown timber, well suited for wheel naves, furniture, and house-building.

Adenanthera pavonina: weight, 55 lb.; elasticity, 3103 lb.; cohesion, 17,846 lb.; strength, 863–1060 lb.; timber does not enter the market in large quantities; is strong, but not stiff; hard and durable, tolerably close and even-grained, and stands a good polish; when fresh cut, it is of beautiful red coral colour, with a fragrance somewhat resembling sandalwood; after exposure it becomes purple, like rosewood; used sometimes as sandalwood, and adapted for cabinet-making purposes.

Ailanthus excelsa: wood is white, light, and not durable; used for scabbards, &c.

Albizzia elata: weight, 42–55 lb.; used by the Burmese for bridges and house-posts; it has a large proportion of sapwood, but the heartwood is hard and durable; may eventually become a valuable article of trade.

Albizzia stipulata: weight, 66 lb.; has a beautifully streaked brown heartwood, which is much prized for cart-wheels and bells for cattle.

Albizzia sp. (Kokoh): weight, 46 lb.; elasticity, 4123; cohesion, 19,263 lb.; strength, 855 lb.; much valued by the Burmese for cart-wheels, oil-presses, and canoes.

Artocarpus hirsuta (Anjilli): weight, 40 lb.; elasticity, 3905; cohesion, 15,070 lb.; strength, 744 lb.; especially esteemed as a timber bearing submersion in water; durable, and much sought after for dockyards as second only to teak for ship-building; also used for house-building, canoes, &c.

Artocarpus integrifolia (Jack): weight, 44 lb.; elasticity, 4030; cohesion 16,420 lb.; strength, 788 lb.; wood when dry is brittle, and has a coarse and crooked grain; is, however, suitable for some kinds of house carpentry and joinery; tables, musical instruments, cabinet and marquetry work, &c.; wood when first cut is yellow, afterwards changing to various shades of brown.

Artocarpus Lacoocha (Monkey Jack): weight, 40 lb.; wood used in Burma for canoes.

Artocarpus mollis: weight, 30 lb.; used for canoes and cart-wheels.

Azadirachta indica (Neem): weight, 50 lb.; elasticity, 2672–3183; cohesion, 17,450 lb.; strength, 720–752 lb.; wood is hard, fibrous, and durable, except from attacks of insects; it is of a reddish-brown colour, and is used by the natives for agricultural and building purposes; is difficult to work, but is worthy of attention for ornamental woodwork; long beams are seldom obtainable; but the short thick planks are in much request for doors and door-frames for native houses, on account of the fragrant odour of the wood.

Barringtonia acutangula: weight, 56 lb.; elasticity, 4006; cohesion, 19,560 lb.; strength, 863 lb.; wood of a beautifully red colour, tough and strong, with a fine grain, and susceptible of good polish; used in making carts, and is in great request by cabinet-makers.

Barringtonia racemosa; weight, 56 lb.: elasticity, 3845; cohesion, 17,705 lb.; strength, 819 lb.; wood is lighter coloured, and close-grained, but of less strength than that of the last-named species; used for house-building and cart-framing, and has been employed for railway-sleepers.

Bassia latifolia: weight, 66 lb.; elasticity, 3420; cohesion, 20,070 lb.; strength, 760 lb.; wood is sometimes used for doors, windows, and furniture; but it is said to be eagerly devoured by white ants.

Bassia longifolia: weight, 60 lb.; elasticity, 3174; cohesion, 15,070 lb.; strength, 730 lb.; is used for spars in Malabar, and considered nearly equal to teak, though smaller.

Bauhinia variegata: centre wood is hard and dark like ebony, but seldom large enough for building purposes.

Berrya ammonilla (Trincomallie): weight, 50 lb.; elasticity, 3836; cohesion, 26,704 lb.; strength, 784 lb.; most valuable wood in Ceylon for naval purposes, and furnishes the material of the Madras Masoola boats; considered the best wood for capstan bars, crosstrees, and fishes for masts; is light, strong, and flexible, and takes the place of ash in Southern India for shafts, helves, &c.

Bignonia chelonoides: weight, 48 lb.; elasticity, 2804; cohesion, 16,657 lb.; strength, 642 lb.; wood is highly coloured orange-yellow, hard, and durable; a good fancy wood, and suitable for building.

Bignonia stipulata: weight, 64 lb.; elasticity, 5033; cohesion, 28,998 lb.; strength, 1386 lb.: furnishes logs 18 ft. in length and 4 ft. in girth, with strong, fibrous, elastic timber, resembling teak; used in house-building, and for bows and spear-handles; one of the strongest, densest, and most valuable of the Burman woods.

Bombax heptaphyllum : elasticity, 2225 ; cohesion, 6951 lb. ; strength, 678 lb. ; light loose-grained wood, valueless as timber, but extensively used for packing cases, tea-chests, and camel trunks; and as it does not rot in water, it is useful for stakes in canal banks, &c. ; long planks 3 ft. in width can be obtained from old trees.

Borassus flabelliformis: weight, 65 lb. ; elasticity, 4904 ; cohesion, 11,898 lb. ; strength, 944 lb. ; timber is very durable and of great strength to sustain cross strain ; used for rafters, joists, and battens; trees have, however, to attain a considerable age before they are fit for timber.

Briedelia spinosa: weight, 60 lb. ; elasticity, 4132 ; cohesion, 14,801 lb. ; strength, 892 lb. ; strong, tough, durable, close-grained wood, of a copper colour, which, however, is not easily worked ; employed by the natives for cart-building and house-beams, and is also used for railway-sleepers ; lasts under water, and is consequently used for well-curbs.

Butea frondosa : wood is generally small or gnarled, and used only for firewood ; in Guzerat, however, it is extensively used for house purposes, and deemed durable and strong.

Buxus nepalensis : a very valuable wood for engraving, but inferior to the Black Sea kind of box in closeness of grain and in hardness.

Byttneria sp.: weight, 63 lb. ; elasticity, 4284 ; cohesion, 26,571 lb. ; strength, 1012 lb. ; wood of great elasticity and strength, invaluable for gun-carriages ; used by Burmese for axles. cart-poles, and spear-handles.

Cæsalpinia Sappan : weight, 60 lb. ; elasticity, 4790 ; cohesion, 22,578 lb. ; strength, 1540 lb. ; admirably adapted for ornamental work, being of a beautiful " flame " colour, with a smooth glassy surface, easily worked, and neither warping nor cracking.

Calophyllum angustifolium : weight, 45 lb. ; elasticity, 2944 ; cohesion, 15,864 lb. ; strength, 612 lb. ; see Poon, p. 145.

Calophyllum longifolium : weight, 45 lb. ; elasticity, 3491 ; cohesion, 16,388 lb. ; strength, 546 lb. ; a red wood, excellent for masts, helves, &c., and also (when well cleaned and polished) for furniture ; but it does not appear to be abundant.

Careya arborea: weight, 50–56 lb. ; elasticity, 3255 ; cohesion, 14,803 lb. ; strength, 675–870 lb. ; furnishes a tenacious and durable wood, which admits of a fine polish ; does not, however, appear to be much used as timber, except in Pegu, where it grows to a very large size, and is the chief material of which the carts of the country are made, and the red wood is esteemed equivalent to mahogany.

Casuarina muricata: weight, 55 lb. ; elasticity, 4474 ; cohesion, 20,887 lb. ; strength, 920 lb. ; yields a strong, fibrous, stiff timber, of reddish colour.

Cathartocarpus Fistula : weight, 41 lb. ; elasticity, 3153 ; cohesion, 17,705 lb. ; strength, 846 lb. ; generally a small tree, whose close-grained, mottled, dark-brown wood is suited for furniture ; in Malabar, however, it grows large enough to be used for spars of native boats.

Cedrela Toona : weight, 31 lb. ; elasticity, 2684–3568 ; cohesion, 9000 lb. ; strength, 560 lb. ; see Toon, p. 149.

Cedrus Deodara : elasticity, 3205–3925 ; strength, 456–625 lb. ; see Deodar, p. 132.

Chickrassia tabularis : weight, 42 lb. ; elasticity, 2876 ; cohesion, 9943 lb. ; strength, 614 lb. ; stronger and tougher than Toon (p. 149), but very liable to warp ; used as mahogany by cabinet-makers.

Chloroxylon Swietenia : weight, 60 lb. ; elasticity, 4163 ; cohesion, 11,369 lb. ; strength, 870 lb. ; see Satinwood, p. 147.

Cocos nucifera : weight, 70 lb.; elasticity, 3605 ; cohesion, 9150 lb. ; strength, 608 lb. ; gives a hard and durable wood, fitted for ridge-poles, rafters, battens, posts, pipes, boats, &c.

Connarus speciosa: heavy, strong, white timber, adapted to every purpose of house-building.

Conocarpus acuminatus: weight, 59 lb.; elasticity, 4352; cohesion, 20,623 lb.; strength, 880 lb.; heartwood is reddish brown, hard, and durable; used for house and cart building; exposed to water, it soon decays.

Conocarpus latifolius: weight, 65 lb.; elasticity, 5033; cohesion, 21,155 lb.; strength, 1220 lb.; furnishes a hard, durable, chocolate-coloured wood, very strong in sustaining cross strain; in Nagpore 20,000 axletrees are annually made from this wood; it is well suited for carriage shafts.

Dalbergia latifolia; weight, 50 lb.; elasticity, 4053; cohesion, 20,283 lb.; strength, 912 lb.; perhaps the most valuable tree of the Madras Presidency, furnishing the well-known Malabar blackwood; the trunk sometimes measures 15 ft. in girth, and planks 4 ft. broad are often procurable, after the outside white wood has been removed; used for all sorts of furniture, and is especially valued in gun-carriage manufacture.

Dalbergia oojeinensis: centre timber is dark, of great strength and toughness, especially adapted for cart-wheels and ploughs.

Dalbergia Sissu: weight, 50 lb.; elasticity, 3516–4022; cohesion, 12,072–21,257 lb.; strength, 706–807 lb.; see Sissu, p. 147.

Dillenia pentagyna; weight, 70 lb.; elasticity, 3650; cohesion, 17,053 lb.; strength, 907 lb.; furnishing some of the Poon spars of commerce; wood used in house and ship building, being close-grained, tough, durable (even under ground), of a reddish-brown colour, not easily worked, and subject to warp and crack.

Dillenia speciosa: weight, 45 lb.; elasticity, 3355; cohesion, 12,691 lb.; strength, 721 lb.; light, strong, light-brown wood, of the same general characteristics with the preceding tree; used in house-building and for gun-stocks.

Diospyros Ebenum: see Ebony, p. 132.

Diospyros hirsuta: weight, 60 lb.; elasticity, 4296; cohesion, 19,830 lb.; strength, 757 lb.; see Calamander wood, p. 152.

Diospyros melanoxylon: weight, 81 lb.; elasticity, 5058; cohesion, 15,873 lb.; strength, 1180 lb.; furnishing a valuable wood for inlaying and ornamental turnery; the sapwood white, the heartwood even-grained, heavy, close, and black, standing a high polish.

Diospyros tomentosa: furnishing a hard and heavy black wood; young trees are extensively felled by the natives as cart-axles, for which they are well suited from their toughness and strength.

Dipterocarpus alatus: weight, 45 lb.; elasticity, 3247; cohesion, 18,781 lb.; strength, 750 lb. timber is excellent for every purpose of house-building, but if exposed to moisture is not durable; it is hard and coarse-grained, with a powerful odour, and of light-brown colour.

Dipterocarpus turbinatus: weight, 45–49 lb.; elasticity, 3355; cohesion, 15,070 lb.; strength, 762–807 lb.; a coarse-grained timber of a light-brown colour, not easily worked, and not durable; used by the natives for house-building, in sawn planks, which will not stand exposure and moisture.

Emblica officinalis: weight, 46 lb.; elasticity, 2270; cohesion, 16,964 lb.; strength, 562 lb.; furnishing a hard and durable wood, used for gun-stocks, furniture, boxes, and veneering and turning; is suitable for well-curbs, as it does not decay under water.

Erythrina indica: furnishes a soft, white, easily worked wood, being light, but of no strength, and eagerly attacked by white ants; used for scabbards, toys, light boxes and trays, &c.; grows very quickly from cuttings.

Feronia elephantum: weight, 50 lb.; elasticity, 3248; cohesion, 13,909 lb.; strength, 645 lb.; a yellow-coloured, hard, and compact wood, used by the natives in house- and cart-building, and in some places employed as railway sleepers.

Ficus glomerata (Gooler): weight, 40 lb.; elasticity, 2096–2113; cohesion, 12,691 lb.;

strength, 588 lb.; wood is light, tough, coarse-grained, and brittle; used for door-panels, and, being very durable under water, for well-curbs.

Ficus indica (Banyan): weight, 36 lb.; elasticity, 2876; cohesion, 9157 lb.; strength, 600 lb.; wood is brown-coloured, light, brittle, and coarse-grained, neither strong nor durable (except under water, for which cause it is used for well-curbs); the wood, however, of its pendant aërial roots is strong and tough, and used for yokes, tent-poles, &c.

Ficus religiosa: weight, 34 lb.; elasticity, 2371–2454; cohesion, 7535 lb.; strength, 458–584 lb.; similar in appearance, characteristics, and uses to banyan.

Gmelina arborea: weight, 35 lb.; elasticity, 2132; has a pale-yellow wood, light, easily worked, not shrinking or warping, strong and durable, especially under water; it is, however, readily attacked by white ants; used for furniture, carriage panels, palkees, &c.; in Burma, for posts and house-building generally.

Grewia elastica: weight, 34 lb.; elasticity, 2876; cohesion, 17,450 lb.; strength, 565 lb.; wood generally is procured in small scantlings, suitable for spear-shafts, carriage- and dooly-poles, bows, and tool-handles, for which it is admirably adapted, being light, soft, flexible, and fibrous, resembling lancewood or hickory.

Guatteria longifolia: weight, 37 lb.; elasticity, 2860; cohesion, 14,720 lb.; strength, 547 lb.; wood is very light and flexible, but only used for drum cylinders.

Hardwickia binata: weight, 85 lb.; elasticity, 4579; cohesion, 12,016 lb.; strength, 942 lb.; furnishing a red- or dark-coloured, very hard, very strong and heavy wood, useful for posts, pillars, and piles; excellent also for ornamental turnery.

Heritiera minor: weight, 64 lb.; elasticity, 3775–4677; cohesion, 29,112 lb.; strength, 816–1312 lb.; the toughest wood that has been tested in India, and stands without a rival in strength; is used for piles, naves, felloes, spokes, carriage shafts and poles; is, however, a perishable wood, and shrinks much in seasoning.

Hopea odorata: weight, 45–58 lb.; elasticity, 3660; cohesion, 22,209 lb.; strength, 706–800 lb.; one of the finest timber trees of British Burma, sometimes reaching 80 ft. in height to the first branch, and 12 ft. in girth—a large boat of 8 ft. beam, and carrying 4 tons, being sometimes made of a single scooped-out trunk; wood is close, even-grained, of a light-brown colour.

Inga lucida: heartwood is black, and called " ironwood " in Burma.

Inga xylocarpa: weight, 58 lb.; elasticity, 4283; cohesion, 16,657 lb.; strength, 836 lb.; furnishing a wood of very superior quality, heavy, hard, close-grained, and durable, and of a very dark-red colour; it is, however, not easily worked up, and resists nails; is extensively used for bridge-building, posts, piles, &c., and is a good wood for sleepers, lasting (when judiciously selected and thoroughly seasoned) for 6 years.

Juglans regia (walnut): its beautiful wood is used for all sorts of furniture and cabinet work in the bazaars of the Hill stations.

Lagerstræmia reginæ: weight, 40 lb.; elasticity, 3665; cohesion, 15,388 lb.; strength, 637–642 lb.; the wood is used more extensively than any other, except teak, for boat-, cart-, and house-building, and in the Madras Gun-carriage Manufactory for felloes, naves, framings of waggons, &c.

Mangifera indica (mango): weight, 42 lb.; elasticity, 3120–3710; cohesion, 7702–9518 lb.; strength, 560–632 lb.; wood is of inferior quality, coarse, and open-grained, of a deep-grey colour, decaying if exposed to wet, and greedily eaten by white ants; is, however, largely used, being plentiful and cheap, for common doors and door-posts, boards and furniture; also for firewood; should never be used for beams, as it is liable to snap off short.

Melanorhœa usitatissima: weight, 61 lb.; elasticity, 3016; strength, 514 lb.; furnishes a dark-red, hard, heavy, close and even-grained and durable (but brittle) timber; used for helves, sheave-blocks, machinery, railway sleepers, &c.

Melia Azadirach; weight, 30 lb.; elasticity, 2516; cohesion, 14,277 lb.; strength,

596 lb.; soft, red-coloured, loose-textured wood (resembling in appearance cedar), is used only for light furniture.

Michelia Champaca: weight, 42 lb.; in Mysore, trees measuring 50 ft. in girth 3 ft. above ground-level are found, and slabs 6 ft. in breadth can be obtained; as the wood takes a beautiful polish it makes handsome tables; it is of a rich brown colour.

Millingtonia hortensis: wood is white, fine and close-grained, but of little use.

Mimusops elengi: weight, 61 lb.; elasticity, 3653; cohesion, 11,369 lb.; strength, 632 lb.; wood is heavy, close and even-grained, of a pink colour, standing a good polish and is used for cabinet-making purposes, and ordinary house-building.

Mimusops hexandra: weight, 70 lb.; elasticity, 3948; cohesion, 19,036 lb.; strength, 944 lb.; furnishes wood very similar to the last named; used for similar purposes, and for instruments, rulers, and other articles of turnery.

Mimusops indica: weight, 48 lb.; elasticity, 4296; cohesion, 23,824 lb.; strength, 845 lb.; a coarse-grained, but strong, fibrous, durable wood, of a reddish-brown colour; used for house-building and for gun-stocks.

Morus indica (mulberry): wood is yellow, close-grained, very tough, and well suited for turning.

Nauclea Cadumba: a hard, deep-yellow, loose-grained wood, used for furniture; in the Gwalior bazaars it is the commonest building timber, and is much used for rafters on account of cheapness and lightness; but it is obtained there only in small scantlings.

Nauclea cordifolia; weight, 42 lb.; elasticity, 3052–3467; cohesion, 10,431 lb.; strength, 506–664 lb.; a soft, close, even-grained wood, resembling in appearance box, but light and more easily worked, and very susceptible to alternations of temperature; is esteemed as an ornamental wood for cabinet purposes.

Nauclea parviflora: weight, 42 lb.; strength, 400 lb.; a wood of fine grain, easily worked, used for flooring-planks, packing-boxes, and cabinet purposes; much used by the wood-carvers of Saharunpore.

Phœnix sylvestris: weight, 39 lb.; elasticity, 3313; cohesion, 8356 lb.; strength, 512 lb.

Picea webbiana: weight, 88 lb.; wood is white, soft, easily split, and used as shingle for roofing, but is not generally valued as timber.

Pinus excelsa (Silver Fir): furnishing a resinous wood much used for flambeaux; durable and close-grained; much used for burning charcoal in the hills, and also for building.

Pinus longifolia: elasticity, 3672–4668; strength, 582–735 lb.; being common and light, is largely used in house-building; requires, however, to be protected from the weather, and is suitable for only interior work in houses.

Pongamia glabra: weight, 40 lb.; elasticity, 3481; cohesion, 11,104 lb.; strength, 686 lb.; wood is light, tough, and fibrous, but not easily worked, yellowish brown in colour, not taking a smooth surface; solid wheels are made from this wood; it is, however, chiefly used as firewood, and its boughs and leaves as manure.

Prosopis spicigera: a strong, hard, tough wood, easily worked.

Psidium pomiferum (Guava): weight, 47 lb.; elasticity, 2676; cohesion, 13,116 lb.; strength, 618 lb.; furnishes a grey, hard, tough, light, very flexible, but not strong wood, which is very close and fine-grained, and easily and smoothly worked, so that it is fitted for wood-engraving, and for handles of scientific and other instruments.

Pterocarpus dalbergioides: weight, 49–56 lb.; elasticity, 4180; cohesion, 19,036 lb., strength, 864–934 lb.; furnishes a red, mahogany-like timber, prized by the natives above all others for cart-wheels, and extensively used by Government in the construction of ordnance carriages.

Pterocarpus Marsupium: weight, 56 lb.; elasticity, 4132; cohesion, 19,943 lb.; strength, 868 lb.; wood is light-brown, strong, and very durable, close-grained, but not easily worked; it is extensively used for cart-framing and house-building, but should be protected from wet; also well fitted for railway sleepers.

Pterocarpus Santalinus (Red Sandal): weight, 70 lb.; elasticity, 4582: cohesion, 19,036 lb.; strength, 975 lb.; heavy, extremely hard, with a fine grain, and is suitable for turnery, being of a dark-red colour, and taking a good polish.

Pterospermum acerifolium: a dark-brown wood of great value, and as strong as teak; but its durability has not yet been tested.

Putranjiva Roxburghii: wood is white, close-grained, very hard, durable, and suited for turning.

Quercus spp. (Oak): woods are heavy, and do not float for two years after felling, hence they are not sent down the rivers into the plains.

Rhus acuminata: furnishes a wood much valued by cabinet-makers for ornamental furniture: planks 8 × 2½ ft. can be obtained from some trees.

Santalum album (Sandal): weight, 58 lb.; elasticity, 3481; cohesion, 19,461 lb.; strength, 874 lb.; valued for making work-boxes, and small articles of ornament; and for wardrobe-boxes, &c., where its agreeable odour is a preventive against insects.

Sapindus emarginatus: weight, 64 lb.; elasticity, 3965; cohesion, 15,495 lb.; strength, 682 lb.; furnishing a hard wood, which is not durable or easily worked, and is liable to crack if exposed; but is used by natives for posts and door-frames, also for fuel.

Schleichera trijuga: a red, strong, hard, and heavy wood, used for oil-presses, sugar-crushers, and axles; a large and common tree in Burma, where excellent solid cart-wheels are formed from it.

Shorea obtusa: weight, 58 lb.; elasticity, 3500; cohesion, 20,254 lb.; strength, 730 lb.; a heavy and compact wood, closer and darker coloured than ordinary sâl, used for making carts, and oil- and rice-mills.

Shorea robusta (Sâl): weight, 55 lb.; elasticity, 4209–4963; cohesion, 11,521–18,243 lb.; strength, 769–880 lb.; furnishes the best and most extensively used timber in Northern India, and is unquestionably the most useful known Indian timber for engineering purposes; is used for roofs and bridges, ship-building and house-building, sleepers, &c.; timber is straight, strong, and durable, but seasons very slowly, and is for many years liable to warp and shrink.

Sonneratia apetala: yields a strong, hard, red wood of coarse grain, used in Calcutta for packing-cases for beer and wine, and is also adapted for rough house-building purposes.

Soymida febrifuga: weight, 66 lb.; elasticity, 3986; cohesion, 15,070 lb.; strength, 1024 lb.; furnishing a bright-red close-grained wood, of great strength and durability, preferred above all wood by the Southern India Hindus for the woodwork of their houses; though not standing exposure to sun and weather, it never rots under ground or in masonry, and is very well suited for palisades and railway sleepers.

Sterculia foetida: weight, 28 lb.; elasticity, 3349; cohesion, 10,736 lb.; strength, 464 lb.; in Ceylon it is used for house-building, and in Mysore for a variety of purposes, taking the place of the true Poon; wood is light, tough, open-grained, easily worked, not splitting nor warping, in colour yellowish-white.

Syzygium jambolanum: weight, 48 lb.; elasticity, 2746; cohesion, 8840 lb.; strength, 600 lb.; brown wood is not very strong or durable, but is used for door and window-frames of native houses, though more generally as fuel; is, however, suitable for well and canal works, being almost indestructible under water.

Tamarindus indica (Tamarind): weight, 79 lb.; elasticity, 2803–3145; cohesion, 20,623 lb; strength, 816–864 lb.; heartwood is very hard, close-grained, dark-red, very hard to be worked; used for turnery, also for oil-presses and sugar-crushers, mallets, and plane-handles; is a very good brick-burning fuel.

Tectona grandis (Teak): weight, 42–45 lb.; elasticity, 3978; cohesion, 14,498–15,467 lb.; strength, 683–814 lb.; wood is brown, and when fresh cut is fragrant; very hard, yet light, easily worked, and though porous, strong and durable; soon seasoned, and shrinks little; used for every description of house-building, bridges, gun-carriages, ship-building, &c.

Terminalia Arjuna: weight, 54 lb.; elasticity, 4094; cohesion, 16,288 lb.; strength, 820 lb.; furnishes a dark-brown, heavy, very strong wood, suitable for masts and spars, beams and rafters.

Terminalia Belerica: wood is white, soft, and not used in carpentry.

Terminalia Chebula: weight, 32 lb.; elasticity, 3108; cohesion, 7563 lb.; strength, 470 lb.; wood is used in Southern India for common house-building, but it is light and coarse-grained, possessing little strength, and liable to warp. In Burma it is used for yokes and canoes.

Terminalia coriacea: weight, 60 lb.; elasticity, 4043; cohesion, 22,351 lb.; strength, 860 lb.; the heartwood is one of the most durable woods known: reddish-brown, heavy, tough, and durable, very fibrous and elastic, close and even-grained; used for beams and posts, wheels, and cart-building generally, and telegraph-posts; is durable under water, and is not touched by white ants.

Terminalia glabra: weight 55 lb.; elasticity, 3905; cohesion, 20,085 lb.; strength, 840 lb.; furnishing a very hard, durable, strong, close and even-grained wood, of a dark-brown colour, obtainable in large scantling, and available for all purposes of house-building, cart-framing, and furniture.

Terminalia tomentosa: supplies a heavy, strong, durable, and elastic wood; is, however, a difficult timber to work up, and splits freely in exposed situations; good wood for joists, beams, tie-rods, &c., and for railway purposes, and is often sold in the market under the name of sâl, but it is not equal to that wood.

Thespesia populnea: weight, 49 lb.; elasticity, 3294; cohesion, 18,143 lb.; strength, 716 lb.; grows most rapidly from cuttings, but the trees so raised are hollow-centred, and only useful for firewood; seedling trees furnish a pale-red, strong, straight, and even-grained wood, easily worked; used for gun-stocks and furniture.

Trewia nudiflora: a white, soft, but close-grained wood.

Ulmus integrifolia: (Elm): a strong wood, employed for carts, door-frames, &c.

Zizyphus Jujuba: weight, 58 lb.; elasticity, 3584; cohesion, 18,421 lb.; strength, 672 lb.; red dark-brown wood is hard, durable, close and even-grained, and well adapted for cabinet and oriental work.

New Zealand Woods.—The dimensions of the specimens described in the following table were 12 in. long, and 1 in. sq.

Name.	Specific Gravity.	Weight of 1 Cub. Ft.	Greatest Weight Carried with Unimpaired Elasticity.	Transverse Strength.
		lb.	lb.	lb.
Hinau (*Elæocarpus dentatus*)	·562	33·03	94·0	125·0
Kahika, supposed white pine	·502	31·28	57·3	77·5
Kahikatea, white pine (*Podocarpus dacrydioides*),	·488	30·43	57·9	106·0
Kauri (*Dammara australis*)	·623	38·96	97·0	165·5
Kawaka (*Libocedrus Doniana*)	·637	39·69	75·0	120·0
Kohekohe (*Dysoxylum spectabile*)	·678	42·25	92·0	117·4
Kowhai (*Sophora tetraptera*)	·884	55·11	98·0	207·5
Maire, black (*Olea Cunninghamii*)	1·159	72·29	193·0	314·2
Maire (*Eugenia maire*)	·790	49·24	106·0	179·7
Mako (*Aristotelia racemosa*)	·593	33·62	62·0	122·0
Manoao (*Dacrydium colensoi*)	·788	49·1	200·0	230·0
Mangi, or mangeo (*Tetranthera calicaris*)	·621	38·70	109·0	137·8

Name.	Specific Gravity.	Weight of 1 Cub. Ft.	Greatest Weight Carried with Unimpaired Elasticity.	Transverse Strength.
		lb.	lb.	lb.
Manuka (*Leptospermum ericoides*) ..	·943	59·00	115·0	239·0
Mapau, red (*Myrsine urvillei*)	·991	61·82	92·0	192·4
Matapo, black mapau (*Pittospermum tenuifolium*)	·955	60·14	125·0	243·0
Matai (*Podocarpus spicata*)	·787	49·07	133·0	197·2
Miro (*Podocarpus ferruginea*)	·658	40·79	103·0	190·0
Puriri (*Vitex littoralis*)	·959	59·5	175·0	223·0
Rata, or ironwood (*Metrosideros lucida*)	1·045	65·13	93·0	196·0
Rewarewa (*Knightia excelsa*)	·785	48·92	93·0	161·0
Rimu, red pine (*Dacrydium cupressinum*)	·563	36·94	92·8	140·2
Taraire (*Nesodaphne taraire*)	·888	55·34	99·6	112·3
Tawa (*Nesodaphne tawa*)	·761	47·45	142·4	205·5
Tawiri-kohu-kohu, or white mapau (*Carpodetus serratus*)	·822	51·24	80·0	177·6
Titoki (*Alectryon excelsum*)	·916	57·10	116·0	248·0
Totara (*Podocarpus totara*)	·559	35·17	77·0	133·6
Towai, red birch (*Fagus menziesii*) ..	·626	38·99	73·6	158·2
Towai, black birch (*Fagus fusca*) ..	·780	48·62	108·8	202·5

Queensland Woods.—Among the principal are the following:—

Acacia pendula (Weeping Myall): 6–12 in. diam.; 20–30 ft. high; wood is hard, possessing a close texture, and a rich dark colour.

Barklya syringifolia: 12–15 in. diam.; 40–50 ft. high; wood hard and close-grained.

Bauhinia Hookeri: 10–20 in. diam.; 30–40 ft. high; wood is heavy, and of a dark reddish hue.

Bursaria spinosa: 6–9 in. diam.; 20–30 ft. high; timber is hard, of a close texture, and admits of a good polish.

Cargillia Australis: 18–24 in. diam.; 60–80 ft. high; grain is close, very tough and fine, of little beauty, but likely to be useful for many purposes.

Cupania anacardioides: 18–24 in. diam.; 30–50 ft. high; the wood is not appreciated.

Cupania nervosa: 12–20 in. diam.; 30–45 ft. high; wood is nicely grained.

Eremophila Mitchelli (Sandalwood): 9–12 in. diam.; 20–30 ft. high; wood is very hard, beautifully grained, and very fragrant; will turn out handsome veneers for the cabinet-maker.

Erythrina vespertilio (Cork-tree): 12–25 in. diam.; 30–40 ft. high; wood soft, and used by the aborigines for making war-shields.

Excœcaria Agallocha (Poison Tree): 12–14 in. diam.; 40–50 ft. high; wood is hard, and fine-grained.

Exocarpus latifolia (Broad-leaved Cherry): 6–9 in. diam.; 10–16 ft. high; wood very hard and fragrant; excellent for cabinet-work.

Flindersia Schottiana: stem 12–16 in. diam.; 60–70 ft. high; wood is soft, and soon perishes when exposed.

Harpullia pendula (Tulipwood): 14–24 in. diam.; 50–80 ft. high; wood has a firm fine texture, and is curiously veined in colouring; much esteemed for cabinet-work.

Maba obovata: 10–15 in. diam.; 30–50 ft. high; timber is hard, fine-grained, and likely to be useful for cabinet-work.

Melia Azadirach (White Cedar): 24–30 in. diam.; 40–60 ft. high; wood is soft, and not considered of any value.

Owenia venosa (Sour Plum): 8–12 in. diam.; 20–30 ft. high; wood is hard, of a reddish colour, and its great strength renders it fit for wheelwright work.

Podocarpus elata: 24–36 in. diam.; 50–80 ft. high; wood is hard, fine-grained, flexible, and elastic.

Sarcocephalus cordatus (Leichhardt's Tree): 24–36 in. diam.; 60–80 ft. high; wood is soft, but close-grained, of a light colour, and easily worked.

Spondias pleiogyna (Sweet Plum): 20–45 in. diam.; 70–100 ft. high; the wood is hard and heavy, dark-red, finely marked, and susceptible of a high polish.

Stenocarpus sinuosus (Tulip Tree): 18–24 in. diam.; 40–60 ft. high; wood is very nicely marked, and would admit of a good polish.

Straits Settlements Woods.—The specimens experimented on measured 3 ft. by 1½ ft. by 1½ ft.

Name of Wood.	Average weight per cub. ft.	Deflection in in.	Weight producing deflection in lb.	Breaking weight in lb.	Remarks.
Billian Chingy ..	60	$\frac{5}{10}$	408	913	Hard, close-grained, fine-fibred, but very much inferior to Billian Wangy; of a brownish grey colour; readily attacked by insects and dry rot; used for flooring joists.
Billian Wangy ..	72	$\frac{5}{10}$	473	1038	Very hard, durable, heavy, close-grained, fibre long, is not liable to be attacked by worms or white ants; beams of 50 ft. long and 18 in. square can be obtained. Very suitable for roofing timber, girders, joists, and timber bridges.
Darroo	61	$\frac{7}{10}$	840	1300	Much used for beams of houses and door frames; durable, if kept either wet or dry, but rots soon if exposed to sun and rain; colour white, close-grained, fracture long; has an agreeable smell.
Johore Cedar ..	40½	$\frac{5}{8}$	410	616	Well adapted for house-building purposes, as in the manufacture of doors, windows, and flooring planks. Fracture short, timber open-grained, and is not liable to be worm-eaten.
Johore Rosewood, or Kayu Merah.	38	$\frac{5}{8}$	583	952	Resembles rosewood in appearance, and used largely in cabinet-work and household furniture.
Johore Teak, or Ballow.	73	$\frac{5}{8}$	737	1210	Well adapted for permanent sleepers, beams, piles, ship-building, engineering, and general purposes where strength and durability are required. Piles which have been in the ground for 100 years have been found in a good state of preservation. One of the few woods which will really stand the climate of India. Colour dull grey.
Jolotong	29	$\frac{5}{8}$	280	732	Well adapted for patterns and mouldings, excellent for carving purposes; grain very close, scarcely any knots, colour whitish yellow, fracture short, but not very durable.

Name of Wood.	Average Weight per cub. ft.	Deflection in in.	Weight Producing Deflection in lb.	Breaking Weight in lb.	Remarks.
Krangee	77	$\frac{5}{8}$	980	1339	Very hard, close-grained, well adapted for beams of every description. White ants or other insects do not touch it. Well adapted for piles for bridges in fresh or salt water; also used for junks' masts; stands well when sawn, ranks with Tampénis for durability. Fracture long, fibres tough, colour dark red.
Kruen	50	$\frac{5}{8}$	472	$625\frac{1}{3}$	Close-grained, tough fibres, and resembling yellow pine. Used for native boats, planks, &c. Contains a kind of dammar-like oleo-resin.
Kulim, or Johore Ironwood.	73	$\frac{5}{8}$	766	1141	Somewhat similar to Ballow. Used for planking cargo boats; fracture short; makes superior beams and telegraph-posts, as it lasts well in the ground.
Marbow, Murboo, or Marraboo.	61 {	$\frac{5}{10}$ to $\frac{5}{8}$	399 to 578	894 to 987 }	Durable, principally used for furniture, readily worked, and takes polish well; also used for flooring beams, timber bridges, carriage bodies, and framing of vessels; trees 4 ft. diam. are sometimes obtained; not readily attacked by white ants, but is by worms. Colour almost like English oak.
Panaga	72	$\frac{5}{10}$	688	1310	Bright red, very hard and durable, well adapted for roofing timbers, joists, and timber work of bridges; very cross-grained and difficult to work; can be obtained in any quantity to 9 in. square. Fracture short.
Samaran	42	$\frac{5}{8}$	326	532	Well adapted for doors, windows, moulding, and other house-building purposes; close and even grained, dull-red colour, short fracture, but liable to attacks of white ants.
Serian	47	$\frac{5}{8}$	438	$737\frac{1}{3}$	Of a dull-red colour, close-grained, and largely used in house-building, for boxes, boards, &c.
Tampénis	67	$\frac{7}{10}$+	802	1599+	Very hard, close-grained, red-coloured, long-fibred, and tough. Well adapted for beams of every description; white ants and other insects do not touch it. Used largely for bridge piles in fresh or salt water; considered one of the most lasting timbers; warps if cut in planks.
Tumboosoo ..	67	$\frac{5}{10}$	306	548	Capital for piles, or for any wood-work which is exposed to the action of fresh or salt water; not attacked by worms or white ants. Fracture short.

Tasmanian woods.—Ironwood, Tasmanian (Noteloea ligustrina): exceedingly hard, close-grained wood, used for mallets, sheaves of blocks, turnery, &c.; diam., 9--18 in.; height, 20–35 ft.; sp. grav., about ·965. Not uncommon.

Native Box (Bursaria spinosa): diam., 8–12 in.: height, 15–25 ft.; sp. grav., about 825. Used for turnery.

Native Pear (Hakea lissosperma): diam., 8–12 in.; height, 29–30 ft.; sp. grav., about ·675. Fit for turnery.

Pinkwood (Beyeria viscosa): diam., 6–10 in.; height, 15–25 ft.; sp. grav., about 815. Used for sheaves of blocks, and for turnery.

Swamp Tea-tree (Melaleuca ericæfolia): diam., 9–20 in.; height, 20–60 ft.; sp. grav., about ·824. Used for turnery chiefly.

White-wood (Pittosporum bicolor); diam., 8–13 in.; height, 20–35 ft.; sp. grav., about ·875. Used in turnery; probably fit for wood-engraving.

West Indian woods.—Crabwood is mostly used for picture-frames and small ornamented cabinet-work, &c. It seldom grows larger than 3–4 in. in diam., and is a rather hard, fine, cross-grained, moderately heavy wood. The heartwood is of a beautifully veined Vandyke brown, its external edge bright black, and the alburnum of a pure white. In Trinidad, the balata is a timber extensively used for general purposes, and much esteemed. Its diameter is 2–6 ft. The mastic is also held in high estimation, and varies from 2 to 4 ft. in diam. The gru-gru, which is a palm, yields beautiful veneer, as also does the gri-gri. For some of these trees it will be observed there is no vernacular name, consequently the choice lies between the native and the botanical name. The heartwood of the butterwood only is used. The beauty of the wood is well known, but it never attains a large size. Its recent layers are of a uniform yellowish-white colour. The carapa bears a considerable resemblance to cedar, and is extensively used and much esteemed. It is 2–3 ft. in diam. The West Indian cedar of Trinidad is a most useful timber, and is well deserving the attention of consumers, as is also the copai, a beautiful and durable wood. The sepe is a light wood, resembling English elm, impregnated with a bitter principle, which preserves it from the attacks of insects. It is tough, strong, and is used for general purposes. In diameter it ranges from 1 to 2 ft. L'Angleme is a strong, hardy wood, exclusively used for the naves of wheels, &c. Courbaril is a valuable and abundant timber of 2–6 ft. in diam., and may be otherwise described under the name of West India locust. Yorke saran is a very hard and useful wood, and also pearl heart, which has the advantage of being very abundant, and runs from 2 to 4 ft. in diam. Aquatapana is a very durable and curious wood, susceptible of high polish, and 18–36 in. in diam. The green, grey, and black poui furnish the favourite timbers of the colony, and produce the hardest and most durable of wood. Their timber takes a fine polish, has a peculiar odour, and is very abundant. The trees are 3–4 ft. in diam., and proportionately lofty.

Growth of wood.—This may be sufficiently explained in a few words. A cross section of an exogenous ("outward growing") tree, which class includes all timbers used in construction, shows it to be made up of several concentric rings, called "annual," from their being generally deposited at the rate of 1 a year; at or near the centre is a column of pith, whence radiate thin lines called "medullary rays," which, in some woods, when suitably cut, afford a handsome figure termed "silver grain." As the tree increases in age, the inner layers are filled up and hardened, becoming what is called duramen or "heartwood"; the remainder, called alburnum or "sapwood," is softer and lighter in colour, and can generally be easily distinguished. The heartwood is stronger and more lasting than the sapwood, and should alone be used in good work. The annual rings are generally thicker on the side of the tree that has had most sun and air, and the heart is therefore seldom in the centre.

Felling.—While the tree is growing, the heartwood is the strongest; but after the growth has stopped, the heart is the first part to decay. It is important, therefore, that the tree should be felled at the right age. This varies with different trees, and even in the same tree under different circumstances. The induration of the sapwood should have reached its extreme limits before the tree is felled, but the period required for this depends on the soil and climate. Trees cut too soon are full of sapwood, and the heart-wood is not fully hardened. The ages at which the undermentioned trees should be felled are as follows:—Oak, 60–200 years, 100 years the best; Ash, Larch, Elm, 50–100 years; Spruce, Scotch Fir, 70–100 years. Oak bark is sometimes stripped in the spring, when loosened by the rising sap. The tree is felled in winter, at which time the sapwood is hardened like the heart. This practice improves the timber. A healthy tree for felling is one with an abundance of young shoots, and whose topmost branches look strong, pointed, and vigorous. The best season for felling is midsummer or mid-winter in temperate, or the dry season in tropical climates, when the sap is at rest.

Squaring.—Directly the tree is felled it should be squared, or cut into scantling, in order that air may have free access to the interior.

Features.—These depend greatly upon the treatment of the tree, the time of felling it, and the nature of the soil in which it has grown. Good timber should be from the heart of a sound tree, the sapwood being entirely removed, the wood uniform in sub-stance, straight in fibre, free from large or dead knots, flaws, shakes, or blemishes of any kind. If freshly cut, it should smell sweet; the surface should not be woolly, nor clog the teeth of the saw, but firm and bright, with a silky lustre when planed; a disagreeable smell betokens decay, and a dull chalky appearance is a sign of bad timber. The annual rings should be regular in form; sudden swells are caused by rind-galls; closeness and narrowness of the rings indicate slowness of growth, and are generally signs of strength. When the rings are porous and open, the wood is weak, and often decayed. The colour should be uniform throughout; when blotchy, or varying much from the heart outwards, or becoming pale suddenly towards the limit of the sapwood, the wood is probably diseased. Among coloured timbers, darkness of colour is in general a sign of strength and durability. Good timber is sonorous when struck; a dull, heavy sound betokens decay within. Among specimens of the same timber, the heavier are generally the stronger. Timber for important work should be free from defects. The knots should not be large or numerous, and on no account loose. The worst posi-tion for large knots is near the centre of the balk required, more especially if forming a ring round the balk at one or more points. Though the sapwood should be entirely removed, the heart of trees having most sapwood is generally strongest and best. The strongest part of the tree is usually that containing the last-formed rings of heartwood, so that the strongest scantlings are got by removing no more rings than those including the sapwood. Timber that is thoroughly dry weighs less than green; it is also harder and more difficult to work.

Defects.—The principal natural defects in timber, caused by vicissitudes of climate, soil, &c., are:—" Heartshakes ": splits or clefts in the centre of the tree; common in nearly every kind of timber; in some cases hardly visible, in others extending almost across the tree, dividing it into segments; one cleft right across the tree does not occasion much waste, as it divides the squared trunk into 2 substantial balks; 2 clefts crossing one another at right angles, as in Fig. 217, make it impossible to obtain scant-lings larger than $\frac{1}{4}$ the area of the tree; the worst form of heartshake is when the splits twist in the length of the tree, thus preventing its conversion into small scantlings or planks. " Starshakes ": in which several splits radiate from the centre of the timber, as in Fig. 218. " Cupshakes ": curved splits separating the whole or part of one annual ring from another (Fig. 219); when they occupy only a small portion of a ring they do no great harm. " Rind-galls ": peculiar curved swellings, caused generally by the growth of layers over the wound remaining after a branch has been imperfectly lopped off. " Upsets ": portions of the timber in which the fibres have been injured by crushing. " Foxiness ": a yellow or red tinge caused by incipient decay. " Doatiness ": a speckled stain found in beech, American oak, and others. Twisted fibres are caused by the action of a prevalent wind, turning the tree constantly in one direction; timber thus injured is not fit for squaring, as many of the fibres would be cut through.

The large trees of New South Wales, when at full maturity, are rarely sound at heart, and even when they are so, the immediate heartwood is of no value, on account of its extreme brittleness. In sawing up logs into scantlings or boards, the heart is always rejected. The direction in which the larger species split most freely is never from the bark to the heart (technically speaking, the " bursting way "), but in concen-

217.   218.   219.

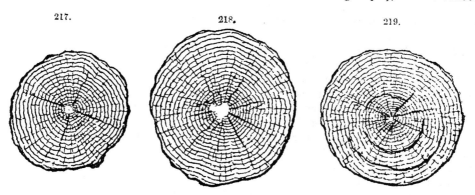

tric circles round the latter. Some few of the smaller species of forest trees are exceptions to this rule; such as the different species of *Casuarina, Banksia,* and others belonging to the natural order *Proteaceæ.* They split most freely the " bursting way," as do the oaks, &c., of Europe and America. A very serious defect prevails amongst a portion of the trees of this class, to such an extent as to demand especial notice here. It is termed " gum-vein," and consists simply in the extravasation, in greater or less quantity, of the gum-resin of the tree, in particular spots, amongst the fibres of woody tissue, and probably where some injury has been sustained; or, which is a much greater evil, in concentric circles between successive layers of the wood. The former is often merely a blemish, affecting the appearance rather than the utility of the timber; but the latter, when occurring frequently in the same section of the trunk, renders it comparatively worthless, excepting for fuel. In the latter case, as the wood dries, the layers with gum veins interposing separate from each other; and it is consequently impracticable to take from trees so affected a sound piece of timber, excepting of very small dimensions. The whole of the species of *Angophora,* or apple-tree, and many of the *Eucalypti,* or gums, are subject to be thus affected; and it is the more to be regretted, because it appears to be the only reason why many of the trees so blemished should not be classed amongst the most useful of the hard woods of the colony.

In selecting balks and deals, it should be remembered that most defects show better when the timber is wet. Balk timber is generally specified to be free from sap, shakes, large or dead knots and other defects, and to be die-square. The best American yellow pine and crown timber from the Baltic have no visible imperfections of any kind. In the lower qualities is either a considerable amount of sap, or the knots are numerous, sometimes very large, or dead. The timber may also be shaken at heart or upon the surface. The wood may be waterlogged, softened, or discoloured by being floated. Wanes also are likely to be found, which spoil the sharp angles of the timber, and reduce its value for many purposes. The interior of the timber may be soft, spongy, or decayed, the surface destroyed by worm holes, or bruised. The heart may be " wandering "—that is, at one part on one side of the balk, at another part on the other side. This interrupts the continuity of the fibre, and detracts from the strength of the balk. Again, the heart may be twisted throughout the length of the tree. In this case, the annual rings which run parallel to 2 sides of the balk at one end run diagonally across the section at the other end. This is a great defect, as the wood is nearly sure to twist in seasoning. Some defects appear to a certain degree in all except the very best quality of timber. The more numerous or aggravated they are, the lower is the quality of the timber. Deals, planks, and battens should be carefully examined for freedom (more or less according to their quality) from sap, large or dead knots, and other defects, also to see that they have been carefully converted, of proper and even thickness, square at the angles, &c. As a rule, well-converted deals are from good timber, for it does not pay to put much labour upon inferior material. The method in which deals have been cut should be noticed, those from the centre of a log, containing the pith, should be avoided, as they are likely to decay.

Classification.—Timber is generally divided into 2 classes, called " pine " woods and " hard " woods. The chief practical bearings of this classification are as follows :—Pine wood (coniferous timber) in most cases contains turpentine ; is distinguished by straightness of fibre and regularity in the figure of the trees, qualities favourable to its use in carpentry, especially where long pieces are required to bear either a direct pull or a transverse load, or for purposes of planking ; the lateral adhesion of the fibres is small, so that it is much more easily shorn and split along the grain than hard wood, and is therefore less fitted to resist thrust or shearing stress, or any kind of stress that does not act along the fibres. In hard wood (non-coniferous timber) is no turpentine ; the degree of distinctness with which the structure is seen depends upon the difference of texture of several parts of the wood, such difference tending to produce unequal shrinking in drying ; consequently those kinds of timber in which the medullary rays and the annual rings are distinctly marked are more liable to warp than those in which the texture is more uniform ; but the former kinds are, on the whole, more flexible, and in many cases very tough and strong, which qualities make them suitable for structures that have to bear shocks. For many practical purposes timber may be divided into two classes :— (*a*) soft wood, including firs, pines, spruce, larch, and all cone-bearing trees ; (*b*) hard wood, including oak, beech, ash, elm, mahogany, &c. Carpenters generally give the name " fir " to all red and yellow timber from the Baltic, " pine " to similar timber from America, and " spruce " to all white wood from either place.

Market Forms.—The chief forms into which timber is converted for the market are as follows :—A " log " is the trunk of a tree with the branches lopped off ; a " balk " is obtained by roughly squaring the log. Fir timber is imported in the subjoined forms : " Hand masts " are the longest, soundest, and straightest trees after being topped and barked ; applied to those of a circumference between 24 and 72 in., measured by the hand of 4 in., there being also a fixed proportion between the number of hands in the length of the mast and those contained in the circumference taken at $\frac{1}{3}$ the length from the butt end ; " spars " or " poles " have a circumference of less than 24 in. at the base ; " inch masts " have a circumference of more than 72 in., and are generally dressed to a square or octagonal form ; " balk timber " consists of the trunk, hewn square, generally with the axe (sometimes with the saw), and is also known as " square timber " ; " planks " are parallel-sided pieces 2–6 in. thick, 11 in. broad, and 8–21 ft. long ; " deals " are similar pieces 9 in. broad and not exceeding 4 in. thick ; " whole deals " is the name sometimes given to deals 2 in. or more thick ; " cut deals " are less than 2 in. thick ; " battens " are similar to deals, but only 7 in. broad ; " ends " are pieces of plank, deal, or batten less than 8 ft. long ; " scaffold " and " ladder poles " are from young trees of larch or spruce, averaging 33 ft. in length, and classed according to the diameter of their butts ; " rickers " are about 22 ft. long, and under $2\frac{1}{2}$ in. diameter at the top end ; smaller sizes are called " spars." Oak is supplied as follows : " rough timber " consists of the trunk and main branches roughly hewn to octagonal section ; " sided timber," the trunk split down and roughly formed to a polygonal section ; " thick stuff," not less than 24 ft. and averaging at least 28 ft. long, 11–18 in. wide between the sap in the middle of its length, and 4½–8½ in. thick; "planks," length not less than 20 ft. and averaging at least 28 ft., thickness 2–4 in., and width (clear of sap) at the middle of the length varying according to the thickness, i. e. between 9 and 15 in. for 3-, 3½-, and 4-in. planks, between 8 and 15 in. for 2- and 2½-in. planks. "Waney" timber. is a term used for logs which are not perfectly square; the balk cut being too large for the size of the tree, the square corners are replaced by flattened or rounded angles, often showing the bark, and called "wanes." "Compass" timber consists of bent pieces, the height of the bend from a straight line joining the ends being at least 5 in. in a length of 12 ft.

The following is an approximate classification of timber according to size, as known to workmen:—

Balk	12 in. × 12 in.	to	18 in. × 18 in.
Whole timber	9 „ 9	„	15 „ 15 .,
Half timber	9 „ 4½	„	18 „ 9 „
Scantling	6 „ 4	„	12 ., 12 „
Quartering	2 „ 2	„	6 „ 6 „
Planks	11 in. to 18 in.	×	3 in. to 6 „
Deals	9 in.	×	2 „ 4½ „
Battens	4½ in. to 7 in.	×	¾ „ 3 „
Strips and laths ..	2 „ 4½	×	½ „ 1½ „

Pieces larger than "planks" are generally called "timber," but, when sawn all round, are called "scantling," and, when sawn to equal dimensions each way, "die-square." The dimensions (width and thickness) of parts in a framing are sometimes called the "scantlings" of the pieces. The term "deal" is also used to distinguish wood in the state ready for the joiner, from "timber," which is wood prepared for the carpenter. A "stick" is a rough whole timber unsawn.

Seasoning.—The object of seasoning timber is to expel or dry up the sap remaining in it, which otherwise putrefies and causes decay. One effect is to reduce the weight. Tredgold calls timber "seasoned" when it has lost ⅕, and considers it then fit for carpenters' work and common purposes; and "dry," fit for joiners' work and framing, when it has lost ⅓. The exact loss of weight depends, however, upon the nature of the timber and its state before seasoning. Timber should be well seasoned before being cut into scantlings; the scantlings should then be further seasoned, and, after conversion, left as long as possible to complete the process of seasoning before being painted or varnished. Logs season better and more quickly if a hole is bored through their centre; this also prevents splitting.

Natural seasoning is carried out by stacking the timber in such a way that the air can circulate freely round each piece, at the same time protecting it by a roof from the sun, rain, draughts, and high winds, and keeping it clear of the ground by bearers. The great object is to ensure regular drying; irregular drying causes the timber to split. Timber should be stacked in a yard, paved if possible, or covered with ashes, and free from vegetation. The bearers should be damp-proof, and keep the timber at least 12 in. off the ground; they should be laid perfectly level and out of winding, otherwise the timber will get a permanent twist. The timber should be turned frequently, so as to ensure equal drying all round the balks. When a permanent shed is not available, temporary roofs should be made over the timber stacks. Logs are stacked with the butts outwards, the inner ends being slightly raised so that the logs may be easily got out; packing pieces are inserted between the tiers of logs, so that by removing them any particular log may be withdrawn. That timber seasons better when stacked on end, seems doubtful, and the plan is practically difficult to carry out. Boards may be laid flat and separated by pieces of dry wood 1 in. or so in thickness and 3–4 in. wide; any that are inclined to warp should be weighted or fixed down to prevent them from twisting; hey are, however, frequently stacked vertically, or inclined at a high angle.

Laslett recommends that they should be seasoned in a dry cool shed, fitted with horizontal beams and vertical iron bars, to prevent the boards, which are placed on edge, from tilting over. The time required for natural seasoning differs with the size of the pieces, the nature of the timber, and its condition before seasoning. Laslett gives the following table of the approximate time required for seasoning timber under cover and protected from wind and weather :—

	Oak. Months.	Fir. Months.
Pieces 24 in. and upward square require about	26	13
„ Under 24 in. to 20 „	22	11
„ „ 20 „ 16 „	18	9
„ „ 16 „ 12 „	14	7
„ „ 12 „ 8 „	10	5
„ „ 8 „ 4 „	6	3

Planks $\frac{1}{2}$–$\frac{2}{3}$ the above time, according to thickness. If the timber is kept longer than the periods above named, the fine shakes which show upon the surface in seasoning open deeper and wider, until they possibly render the logs unfit for conversion. The time required under cover is only $\frac{5}{7}$ of that required in the open.

Water seasoning consists in totally immersing the timber, chaining it down under water, as soon as it is cut, for about a fortnight, by which a great part of the sap is washed out; it is then carefully dried, with free access of air, and turned daily. Timber thus seasoned is less liable to warp and crack, but is rendered brittle and unfit for purposes where strength and elasticity are required. Care must be taken that it is entirely submerged; partial immersion, such as is usual in timber ponds, injures the log along the water line. Timber that has been saturated should be thoroughly dried before use; when taken from a pond, cut up and used wet, dry-rot soon sets in. Salt water makes the wood harder, heavier, and more durable, but should not be applied to timber for use in ordinary buildings, because it gives a permanent tendency to attract moisture.

Boiling water quickens the operation of seasoning, and causes the timber to shrink less, but it is expensive to use, and reduces the strength and elasticity. The time required varies with the size and density of the timber, and according to circumstances; one rule is to allow 1 hour for every inch in thickness.

Steaming has much the same effect as boiling; but the timber is said to dry sooner, and it is by some considered that steaming prevents dry-rot. No doubt boiling and steaming partly remove the ferment spores.

Hot-air seasoning, or desiccation, is effected by exposing the timber in an oven to a current of hot air, which dries up the sap. This process takes only a few weeks, more or less, according to the size of the timber. When the wood is green, the heat should be applied gradually. Great care must be taken to prevent splitting; the heat must not be too high, and the ends should be clamped. Desiccation is useful only for small scantling; the expense of applying it to larger timber is very great; moreover, as wood is one of the worst conductors of heat, if this plan be applied to large logs, the interior fibres still retain their original bulk, while those near the surface have a tendency to shrink, the consequence of which would be cracks and splits of more or less depth. Desiccated wood should not be exposed to damp before use. During this process ordinary woods lose their strength, and coloured woods become pale and wanting in lustre

M'Neile's process consists in exposing the wood to a moderate heat in a moist atmosphere charged with various gases produced by the combustion of fuel. The wood is placed in a brick chamber, in which is a large surface of water to produce vapour. The timber is stacked in the usual way, with free air-space round every piece; about $\frac{1}{3}$ of the whole content of the chamber should be air-space. Under the chamber is a fireplace. The fire having been lighted, the products of combustion (among which is carbonic acid gas) circulate freely in a moist state around the pieces of timber to be seasoned. The time required varies with the nature of the wood. Oak, ash, mahogany, and other hard wood planks 3 in. thick, take about 8 weeks; oak wainscot planks 2 in. thick take 5–6 weeks; deals 3 in. thick, something less than a month; flooring-boards and panelling, about 10 days or a fortnight. The greener the wood when first put into the stove the better. As a rule, if too great heat be not applied, not a piece of sound wood is split, warped, or opened in any way. The wood is rendered harder, denser, and tougher, and dry-rot is entirely prevented. The wood will not absorb by subsequent exposure to the atmosphere nearly so much moisture as does wood dried by exposure in the ordinary way. The process seems to have no injurious effects upon the appearance or strength of the timber.

Gardner's process is said to season timber more rapidly than any other, to preserve it from decay and from the attacks of all kinds of worms and insects, to strengthen the timber, and render it uninflammable; and by it the timber may be permanently coloured to a variety of shades. The process takes 4–14 days, according to the bulk and density of the timber. It consists in dissolving the sap (by chemicals in open tanks), driving out the remaining moisture, leaving the fibre only. A further injection of chemical substances adds to the durability, or will make the timber uninflammable. The process has been satisfactorily tested in mine props, railway sleepers, logs of mahogany for cabinet-work, and in smaller scantlings of fir and pine. Experiments showed that the sap was removed, the resistance of the timber to crushing augmented 40–90 per cent., and its density considerably increased.

René, a pianoforte manufacturer, of Stettin, Germany, has devised a plan by which he utilizes the property of ozonized oxygen, to artificially season timber used for sounding-boards of musical instruments. It is a well-known fact that wood, which has been seasoned for years, is much more suitable for the manufacture of musical instruments than if used soon after it is thoroughly dried only. René claims that instruments made of wood which has been treated by his oxygen process possess a remarkably fine tone, which not only does not decrease with age, but as far as experience teaches, improves with age as does the tone of some famous old violins by Italian masters. Sounding-boards made of wood prepared in this manner have the quality of retaining the sound longer and more powerfully. While other methods of impregnating woods with chemicals generally have a deteriorating influence on the fibre, timber prepared by this method, which is really an artificial ageing, becomes harder and stronger. The process is regularly carried on at René's works, and the apparatus consists of a hermetically closed boiler or tank, in which the wood to be treated is placed on iron gratings; in a retort, by the side of the boiler and connected to it by a pipe with stop-valve, oxygen is developed and admitted into the boiler through the valve. Provision is made in the boiler to ozonize the oxygen by means of an electric current, and the boiler is then gently fired and kept hot for 48–50 hours, after which time the process is complete.

Woods, of Cambridge, Mass., has introduced a method which is spoken of as leaving no room for improvement. The wood is placed in a tight chamber heated by steam, and having one side made into a condenser by means of coils of pipes with cold water continually circulating through them. The surface of these pipes is thus kept so much below the temperature of the chamber that the moisture drawn from the wood is condensed on them, and runs thence into a gutter for carrying it off. In the words of the United States Report on the Vienna Exhibition, "if the temperature of these condensing pipes can be kept at say 40° F., and that of the atmosphere be raised to 90° F., it will not require a long time to reach a degree of 20 per cent. of saturation, when the work of drying is thoroughly completed."

Smoke-drying.—It is said that if timber be smoke-dried over a bonfire of furze, straw, or shavings, it will be rendered harder, more durable, and proof against attacks of worms; to prevent it from splitting, and to ensure the moisture drying out from the interior, the heat should be applied gradually.

Second seasoning.—Many woods require a second seasoning after they have been worked. Floor boards should, if possible, be laid and merely tacked down for several months before they are cramped up and regularly nailed. Doors, sashes, and other articles of joinery should be left as long as possible after being made, before they are wedged up and finished. Very often a board that seems thoroughly seasoned will commence to warp again if merely a shaving is planed off the surface.

Decay.—To preserve wood from decay it should be kept constantly dry and well ventilated; clear of the influence of damp earth or damp walls, and free from contact with mortar, which hastens decomposition. Wood kept constantly submerged is often weakened and rendered brittle, but some timbers are very durable in this state. Wood that is constantly dry is very durable, but also becomes brittle in time, though not for a great number of years. When timber is exposed to alternate moisture and dryness it soonest decays. The general causes of decay are (1) presence of sap, (2) exposure to alternate wet and dryness, or (3) to moisture accompanied by heat and want of ventilation.

"Rot" in timber is decomposition or putrefaction, generally occasioned by damp, and which proceeds by the emission of gases, chiefly carbonic acid and hydrogen; 2 kinds of rot are distinguished—"dry" and "wet." Their chief difference seems to be that wet-rot occurs where the gases evolved can escape; by it, the tissues of the wood, especially the sappy portions, are decomposed. Dry-rot, on the contrary, occurs in confined places, where the gases cannot get away, but enter into new combinations, forming fungi which feed upon and destroy the timber. Wet-rot may take place while the tree is standing; dry-rot occurs only when the wood is dead.

"Dry-rot" is generally caused by want of ventilation; confined air, without much moisture, encourages the growth of the fungus, which eats into the timber, renders it brittle, and so reduces the cohesion of the fibres that they are reduced to powder. It generally commences in the sapwood. Excess of moisture prevents the growth of the fungus, but moderate warmth, combined with damp and want of air, accelerates it. In the first stage of rottenness, the timber swells and changes colour, is often covered with fungus or mouldiness, and emits a musty smell. The principal parts of buildings in which it is found are—warm cellars, under unventilated wooden floors, or in basements particularly in kitchens or rooms where there are constant fires. All kinds of stoves increase the disease if moisture be present. The ends of timbers built into walls are nearly sure to be affected by dry-rot, unless they are protected by iron shoes, lead, or zinc. The same result is produced by fixing joinery and other woodwork to walls before they are dry. Oilcloth, kamptulicon, and other impervious floorcloths, by preventing access of air and retaining dampness, cause decay in the boards they cover · carpets do the same to a certain extent. Painting or tarring cut or unseasoned timber has a like effect.

Sometimes the roots of large trees near a house penetrate below the floors and cause dry-rot. It is said that if two kinds of wood—as, for example, oak and fir—are placed so as to touch end to end, the harder will decay at the point of junction. There is this particular danger about dry-rot, that the germs of the fungi producing it are carried easily, and in all directions, in a building where it once displays itself, without necessity for actual contact between the affected and the sound wood.

"Wet-rot" occurs in the growing tree, and in other positions where the timber may become saturated with rain. If the wood can be thoroughly dried by seasoning, and the access of further moisture can be prevented by painting or sheltering, wet-rot can be prevented. The communication of the disease only takes place by actual contact. To detect dry-rot, in the absence of any outward fungus, or other sign, the best way is to bore into the timber with a gimlet or auger. A log apparently sound, as far as external appearances go, may be full of dry-rot inside, which can be detected by the appearance of the dust extracted by the gimlet, or more especially by its smell. If a piece of sound timber be lightly struck with a key or scratched at one end, the sound can be distinctly heard by a person placing his ear against the other end, even if the balk be 50 ft. long ; but if the timber be decayed, the sound will be very faint, or altogether prevented from passing along. Imported timber, especially fir, is often found to be suffering from incipient dry-rot upon arrival. This may have originated in the wood of the ship itself, or from the timber having been improperly stacked, or shipped in a wet state, or subjected to stagnant, moist, warm air during the voyage. Sometimes the rot appears only in the form of reddish spots, which, upon being scratched, show that the fibres have been reduced to powder. After a long voyage, however, the timber will often be covered with white fibres of fungus. Canadian yellow pine is very often found in this state. The best way of checking the evil is to sweep the fungus off, and restack the timber in such a way that the air can circulate freely round each piece.

Preserving.—The best means for preserving timber from decay are to have it thoroughly seasoned and well ventilated. Painting preserves it if the wood is thoroughly seasoned before the paint is applied ; otherwise, filling up the outer pores only confines the moisture and causes rot. The same may be said of tarring. Sometimes before the paint is dry it is sprinkled with sand, which is said to make it more durable. For timber that is not exposed to the weather, the utility of paint is somewhat doubtful. Wood used in outdoor work should have those parts painted only where moisture is likely to find a lodgment, and all shakes, cracks, and joints should be filled up with white-lead ground in oil, or oil putty, previous to being painted over. The lower ends of posts put into the ground are generally charred with a view of preventing dry-rot and the attacks of worms. Care should be taken that the timber is thoroughly seasoned, otherwise, by confining the moisture, it will induce decay and do more harm than good. Posts should be put in upside down, with regard to the position in which they originally grew ; the sap valves open upwards from the root, and when thus reversed they prevent the ascent of moisture in the wood. Britton recommends charring the embedded portions of beams and joists, joists of stables, wash-houses, &c., wainscoting of ground-floors, flooring beneath parquet work, joints of tongues and rebates, and railway sleepers. Lapparent applied the method on a large scale by the use of a gas jet passed all over the surface of the timber, but Laslett would only advise its use as a possible means of preventing the generation of moisture or fungus where two unseasoned pieces of wood are placed in juxtaposition.

There are some preserving processes of a special character, not available for application by the carpenter. The following will be found a good method of preserving wooden posts, say verandah posts, from decay, and also from the white ant, which is the greatest enemy to carpenters' work in Ceylon. Bore with a $1\frac{1}{4}$-in. auger from the butt-end of the post to a distance that will be 6 in. above the ground-line when the post is set. Then char over a good fire for 15 minutes. This will drive all moisture out of the heart of the butt through the hole bored. Next fill with boiling hot coal-tar, and drive in a well-fitted plug, which will act as a ram, and force the tar into the pores of the wood ; the latter thus becomes thoroughly creosoted, and will last for many years. A post 4 in. × 4 in. may have one hole in its centre ; a post 6 in. × 6 in., 2 holes side by side ; a post 8 in. × 8 in., 3 holes ; and one 12 in. × 12 in., 4 holes. Creosoting timber for sleepers and underground purposes answers very well ; also coal-tar is a great means of preserving timber underground from the effects of the white ant, as they will not touch it as long as there is a smell of tar from it. A method used by the natives to protect timber from white ants is—To every gallon of water add 3 oz. croton tiglium seeds, 3 oz. margosa bark, 3 oz. sulphur, 2 oz. blue vitriol ; immerse the timber until it ceases to absorb the water, and afterwards take out, and dry in an airy situation.

The following table shows the amount of creosote that will be taken up by some of the harder Indian woods:—

	Lb. of Creosote per cub. ft.		Lb. of Creosote per cub. ft.
Sissú	$3\frac{3}{4}$	Sâl	1
Sundri	$2\frac{1}{4}$	Ironwood	1
Teak	$1\frac{3}{4}$	Mahogany	$\frac{3}{4}$
Swan River wood (Australia)	$1\frac{3}{4}$	Jaman	$\frac{2}{4}$

It was thought that the forests of Southern India would furnish numerous timbers suitable for sleepers ; but these hopes have not been fulfilled, no timber used having been found capable of resisting the combined effects of the heat and moisture of Southern India, and only on the woods of 3 trees is any great reliance now placed, viz. the Erool (*Inga xylocarpa*), Karra marda (*Terminalia glabra*), and Vengay (*Pterocarpus Marsupium*). Taking an average of the various native woods used on the Madras railway, the duration of its sleepers has been about $3\frac{1}{4}$ years. Creosoted sleepers of Baltic fir have been found to last nearly $6\frac{1}{2}$ years.

Fireproofing.—The accepted methods for rendering wood incombustible or reducing its inflammability are described in the Second Series of 'Workshop Receipts,' under the head of Fireproofing Timber, pp. 298-9.

Conversion ; Shrinkage.—By the term " conversion " is understood the cutting up of the log or balk timber to dimensions suitable for use, allowance being made for alterations in form due to atmospheric influence, even on well-seasoned wood. While wood is in the living state, a constant passage of sap keeps the whole interior moist and the fibres distended, more especially towards the outside. When the tree is felled and exposed to the air, the internal moisture evaporates gradually, causing a shrinkage and collapse of the fibres according to certain laws, being always greatest in a direction parallel with the medullary rays. In straight-grained woods the changes of length caused by atmospheric effects are slight, but those in width and depth are great, especially in new timber. Ordinary alternations of weather produce expansion and contraction in width in wood of average dryness to the following extent :—fir: $\frac{1}{360}$ to $\frac{1}{75}$, mean $\frac{1}{124}$; oak: $\frac{1}{412}$ to $\frac{1}{80}$, mean $\frac{1}{140}$. A practical allowance for shrinkage in 9-in. deals is $\frac{1}{4}$ in. for northern pine and $\frac{1}{8}$ in. for white.

The subject of shrinkage in timber has been well dealt with by Dr. Anderson, in a Cantor Lecture at the Society of Arts. His observations may be summarized as follows. If Fig. 220 be taken as representing the section of a newly-felled tree, it will be seen that the wood is solid throughout, and on comparing Fig. 221 with this the result of the seasoning will be apparent. The action is exaggerated in the diagrams in order to render it more conspicuous. As the moisture evaporates, the bundles of woody fibres shrink and draw closer together ; but this contraction cannot take place radially, without crushing or tearing the hard plates forming the medullary rays, which are unaffected in size by the seasoning. These plates are generally sufficiently strong to resist the crushing action, and the contraction is therefore compelled to take place in the opposite direction, i.e. circumferentially ; the strain finding relief by splitting the timber in radial lines, allowing the medullary rays in each partially severed portion to approach each other in the same direction as the ribs of a lady's fan when closing. The illustration of a closing fan affords the best example of the principle of shrinking during seasoning, every portion of the wood practically retaining its original distance from the centre. If the tree were sawn down the middle, the cut surfaces, although flat at first, would in time become rounded, as in Fig. 222; the outer portion shrinking more than that nearer the heart on account of the greater mass of woody fibre it contains, and the larger amount of moisture. If cut into quarters, each portion would present a similar result, as shown in Fig. 223. Figs. 224–228 show the same principle applied to sawn timber of various forms, the peculiarities of which are perhaps indicated more clearly in Fig. 230. If we assume the tree to be cut into planks, as shown in Fig. 229, it will be found, after allowing due time for seasoning, that the planks have altered their shape, as in Fig. 230. Taking the centre plank first, it will be observed that the thickness at

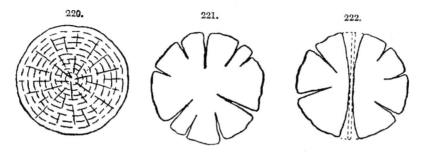

the middle remains unaltered, at the edge it is reduced, and both sides are rounded, while the width remains unchanged. The planks on each side of this are rounded on the heart side, hollow on the other, retain their middle thickness, but are reduced in width in proportion to their distance from the centre of the tree; or, in other words,

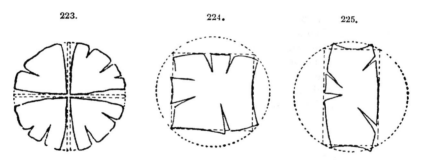

the more nearly the annual rings are parallel to the sides of the planks the greater will be the reduction in width. The most striking result of the shrinkage is shown in Figs. 231–233. Fig. 231 shows a piece of quartering freshly cut from unseasoned timber; in Fig. 232 the part coloured black shows the portion lost by shrinkage, and Fig. 233

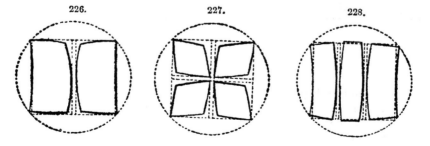

shows the final result. These remarks apply more especially to oak, beech, and the stronger home firs. In the softer woods the medullary rays are more yielding, and this slightly modifies the result; but the same principles must be borne in mind if we wish to avoid the evils of shrinking which may occur from negligence in this respect.

The peculiar direction which " shakes " or natural fractures sometimes take is due to the unequal adhesion of the woody fibres, the weakest part yielding first. In a "cup-shake," which is the separation of a portion of 2 annual rings, the medullary rays are deficient in cohesion. The fault sometimes occurs in Dantzic fir, and has been attributed to the action of lightning and of severe frosts. So far we have considered the shrinking only as regards the cross section of various pieces. Turning now to the effect produced when we look at the timber in the other direction, Fig. 234 represents a piece of timber with the end cut off square; as this shrinks, the end remains square, the width alone being affected. If, however, the end be bevelled as in Fig. 235, we shall find that in

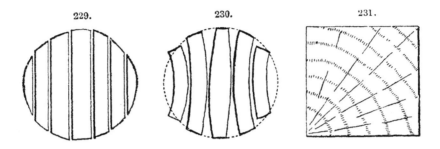

229.   230.   231.

shrinking it assumes a more acute angle, and this should be remembered in framing roofs, arranging the joints for struts, &c., especially by the carpenters who have to do the actual work of fitting the parts. If the angle be an internal one or bird's-mouth, it will in the same way become more acute in seasoning. The transverse shrinkage is here considered to the exclusion of any slight longitudinal alteration which might occur, and which would never be sufficient to affect the angle of the bevel. When seasoned timber is used in positions subject to damp, the wood will swell in exactly the

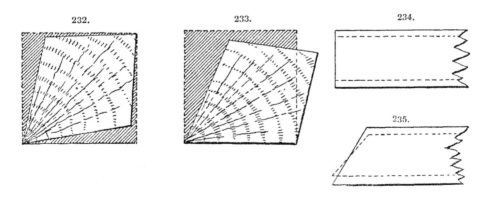

232.   233.   234.

235.

reverse direction to the shrinkage, and induce similar difficulties unless this point has also received due attention. Of course it will be seen from a study of the cross sections illustrated in the diagrams that the pieces might be selected in such a way that the shrinkage and expansion would take place chiefly in the thickness instead of the width, and thus leave the bevel unaltered. In this consists the chief art of selecting pieces for framing; but in many instances motives of economy unfortunately favour the use of pieces on stock, without reference to their suitability for the purpose required.

It has been proved that beams having the annual rings parallel with their depth are stronger than those having them parallel with their breadth. Thus in the log shown in

Fig. 236, the beam cut from A will be stronger than that from B. In preparing floorboards, care should be taken that the heart does not appear on the surface of the finished board, or it will soon become loose and kick up, as in Fig. 237, forming a rough and unpleasant floor. When planks which have curved in shrinking are needed to form a flat surface, they are sometimes sawn down the middle, and the pieces are alternately reversed and glued together, as in Fig. 238, each piece tending to check the curvature of the others.

In converting fir timber in Sweden and Norway, each log is inspected before sawing, to see how many of the most marketable sizes it will cut, and then it is marked out accordingly. The most general arrangement is that shown in Fig. 239, the thicker deals

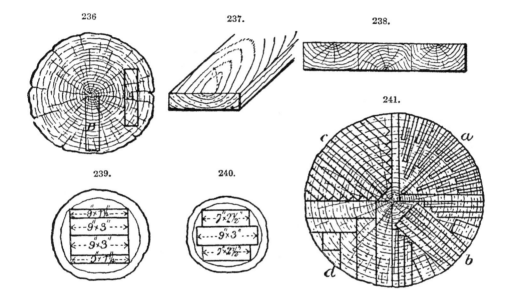

being for the English and the thinner for the French market. Another plan, shown in Fig. 240, has the disadvantage that the central deal embraces all the pith, and is thus rendered more liable to dry-rot.

In converting oak, the log is first cut into 4 quarters, each of which may then be dealt with as shown in Fig. 241. The best method is represented at *a*; it gives no waste, as the triangular portions form feather-edged laths for tiling, &c.; it also shows the silver grain of the wood to the best advantage. *b* is the next in order of merit; *c* is inferior; *d* is most economical for thick stuff.

Composition.—The composition of wood is shown in the following table :—

	Carbon.	Hydrogen.	Oxygen.	Nitrogen.	Ash.
	per cent.	per cent.	per cent.	per cent.	per cent.
Beech	49·36	6·01	42 69	0·91	1·00
Oak	49·64	5·92	41·16	1·29	1·97
Birch	50·20	6·20	41·62	1·15	0·81
Poplar	49·37	6·21	41·60	0·96	1·86
Willow	49·06	5·96	39·56	0·96	3·37
Average	49·70	6·06	41·30	1·05	1·80
Practically ..	50	6	41	1	2

Wood, in its raw state, contains a large amount of water, which holds more or less soluble minerals, and is called sap. By drying wood a great part, but not all, of this water is evaporated. If wood is dried in a closed vessel, and then exposed to the atmosphere, it quickly absorbs moisture; but the moisture thus absorbed is much less than the wood originally contained. The amount of water varies in different kinds of wood. and according to the season. Wood cut in April contains 10–20 per cent. more water than that cut in January. The following table shows the percentage of water in woods, dried as far as possible in the air :—

Beech	.. ..	18·6	Pine, white	37·0
Poplar	.. ..	26·0	Chestnut	38·2
Sugar and common maple		27·0	Pine, red	39·7
Ash ..	.. ..	28·0	Pine, white	45·5
Birch ..	.. ..	30·0	Linden	47·1
Oak, red ..	.. .. ..	34·7	Poplar, Italian	48·2
Oak, white	.. .. ..	35·5	Poplar, black	51·8

Wood cut during December and January is not only more solid, but will dry faster than at any other period of the year, because the sap by that time has incorporated a great part of soluble matter with the woody fibre; what remains is merely water. When the sap, during February, March, and April, rises, it partly dissolves the woody fibre, and the drying of the wood is not only retarded, but the wood is weakened in consequence of the matter thus held in solution.

Suitability.—The properties which render a wood most suitable for one class of purposes may preclude its use in another class. It is therefore useful to have a general idea of the relative order of merit of woods according to the application for which they are destined. The subjoined catalogue is framed after the opinions of the best authorities :—

Elasticity—ash, hickory, hazel, lancewood, chestnut (small), yew, snakewood.

Elasticity and Toughness—oak, beech, elm, lignum-vitæ, walnut, hornbeam.

Even grain (for Carving or Engraving)—pear, pine, box, lime tree.

Durability (in Dry Works)—cedar, oak, yellow pine, chestnut.

Building (Ship-building)—cedar, pine (deal), fir, larch, elm, oak, locust, teak.

Wet construction (as piles, foundations, flumes, &c.)—elm, alder, beech, oak, whitewood, chestnut, ash, spruce, sycamore.

Machinery and millwork (Frames)—ash, beech, birch, pine, elm, oak.

Rollers, &c.—box, lignum-vitæ, mahogany.

Teeth of wheels—crab tree, hornbeam, locust.

Foundry patterns—alder, pine, mahogany.

Furniture (Common)—beech, birch, cedar, cherry, pine, whitewood.

Best furniture—amboyna, black ebony, mahogany, cherry, maple, walnut, oak, rosewood, satinwood, sandalwood, chestnut, cedar, tulip-wood, zebra-wood, ebony.

Piles—oak, beech, elm. Posts—chestnut, acacia, larch. Great Strength in Construction—teak, oak, greenheart, Dantzic fir, pitch pine. Durable in Wet Positions—oak, beech, elm, teak, alder, plane, acacia, greenheart. Large Timbers in Carpentry—Memel, Dantzic, and Riga fir; oak, chestnut, Bay mahogany, pitch pine, or teak, may be used if easily obtainable. Floors—Christiania, St. Petersburg, Onega, Archangel, make the best; Gefle and spruce inferior kinds; Dram battens wear well; pitch pine, oak, or teak, where readily procurable, for floors to withstand great wear. Panelling—American yellow pine for the best; Christiania white deals are also used. Interior Joinery—American red and yellow pine; oak, pitch pine, and mahogany for superior or ornamental work. Window Sills, Sleepers—oak; mahogany where cheaply procurable. Treads of Stairs—oak, teak. Handles—ash, beech. Patterns—American yellow pine, alder, mahogany.

Strength.—The following table shows the results of many experiments :—

Wood seasoned.	Weight of 1 cub. ft. (dry.) Lb.	Tenacity per sq. in., lengthways of the grain. Tons. From.	To.	Modulus of Rupture. 1000 lb.	Modulus of Elasticity. 1000 lb.	Resistance to Crushing in direction of fibres. Tons per sq. in. Moderately dry.	Thoroughly dry.	Comparative Stiffness and Strength. Oak being 100. Stiffness.	Strength.
Acacia..	48	5·0	8·1	..	1152–1687			98	95
Alder	50	4·5	6·3	..	1086			63	80
Ash, English ..	43–53	1·8	7·6	12–14	1525–2290	3·8	4·2	89	119
„ Canadian ..	30	2·45		10	1380		2·5	77	79
Beech..	43–53	2·1	6·6	9–12	1350	3·4	4·2	77	103
Birch	45–49	6·7		11	1645	1·5	2·8		
Cedar	35–47	1·3	5·1	7–8	486	2·5	2·6	28	62
Chestnut	35–41	4·5	5·8	10	1140	..		67	89
Elm, English ..	34–37	2·4	6·3	6–9	700–1340	2·6	4·6	78	82
„ Canadian..	47	4·1		14	2470		4·1	139	114
Fir, Spruce ..	29–32	1·3	4·5	9–12	1400–1800	2·9	3·0	72	86
„ Dantzic ..	36	1·4	4·5	13	2300		3·1	130	108
„ American red pine ..	34	1·2	6·0	7–10	1460–2350		2·1	132	81
„ American yellow pine..	32	0·9		8	1600–2480		1·8	139	66
„ Memel.. ..	34	4·2	4·9	..	1536–1957		6	114	80
„ Kaurie ..	34	2·0		11	2880		2·6	162	89
„ Pitch pine ..	41–58	2·1	4·4	14	1252–3000		3·0	73	82
„ Riga	34–47	1·8	5·5	9	870–3000		2·1	62	83
Greenheart	58–72	3·9	4·1	16–27	1700	5·8	6·8	98	165
Hornbeam.. ..	47·5	9·1		..	..		3·7	..	108
Jarrah	63	1·3		10	1187		3·2	67	85
Larch..	32–38	1·9	5·3	5–10	1360		2·6	79	103
Mahogany, Spanish	53	1·7	7·3	7	1255–3000		3·2	73	67
„ Honduras	35	1·3	8·4	11–12	1596–1970		2·7	93	96
Mora ..	57–68	4·1		21–22	1860	..		105	164
Oak, English ..	49–58	3·4	8·8	10–13	1200–1750	2·9	4·5	100	100
„ American..	61	3·0	4·6	12	2100		3·1	114	86
Plane..	40	5·4		..	1343	..		78	92
Poplar	23–26	2·68		..	763	1·4	2·3	44	50
Sycamore	36–43	4·3	5·8	9	1040		3·1	82	111
Teak	41–52	1·47	6·7	12–19	2167–2414	2·3	5·4	126	109
Willow	24–35	6·25		6	..	1·3	2·7		

Timber when wet has not half the strength of the same when dry. The resistance of wood to a crushing force exerted across the fibres is much less than in the direction of their length. Memel fir is indented with a pressure of 1000 lb. per sq. in., and oak with 1400 lb. The resistance to shearing is nearly twice as great across the fibres as with them.

Measuring.—Following are useful rules for the measurement of timber :—

Standing timber.—In measuring standing timber, the length is taken as high as the tree will measure 24 in. in circumference. At half this height the measurement for the mean girth of the timber in the stem of the tree is taken. One-fourth this girth is assumed to be the side of the equivalent square area. The buyer has generally the option of choosing any spot between the butt-end and the half height of the stem as the girding place. All branches, as far as they measure 24 in. in girth, are measured in with the tree as timber.

Unsquared timber.—In order to ascertain the contents, multiply the square of the quarter girth, or of $\frac{1}{4}$ of the mean circumference, by the length. When the buyer is not allowed his choice of girth in taper trees, he may take the mean dimensions, either by girthing it in the middle for the mean girth, or by girthing it at the two ends, and taking half of their sum. If not, girth the tree in so many places as is thought necessary, then the sum of the several girths divided by their number, will give a mean circumference, the fourth part of which being squared, and multiplied by the length, will give the solid contents.

The superficial ft. in a board or plank are known by multiplying the length by the breadth. If the board be tapering, add the breadth of the two ends together, and take half their sum for the mean breadth, and multiply the length by this mean breadth.

The solid contents of squared timber are found by measuring the mean breadth by the mean thickness, and the product again by the length. Or multiply the square of what is called the quarter girth, in inches by the length in feet, and divide by 144, and you have the contents in feet.

Boughs, the quarter girth of which is less than 6 in., and parts of the trunk less than 2 ft. in circumference, are not reckoned as timber.

$1\frac{1}{2}$ in. in every foot of quarter girth, or $\frac{1}{8}$ of the girth, is allowed for bark, except of elm. 1 in. in the circumference of the tree, or whole girth, or $\frac{1}{12}$ of the quarter girth is the general fair average allowance.

The quarter girth is half the sum of the breadth and depth in the middle.

The nearest approach to truth in the measuring of timber is to multiply the square of $\frac{1}{5}$ of the girth, or circumference, by double the length, and the product will be the contents.

100 superficial feet of planking equals 1 square.
120 deals „ 1 hundred.
50 cub. ft. of squared timber „ 1 load.
40 ft. of unhewn timber „ 1 load.
600 superficial ft. of 1-in. planking „ 1 load.

A fir pole is the trunk of a fir tree, 10–16 ft. long.

Battens, deals, and planks, as imported into this country, are each similar in their various lengths, but differing in their widths and thicknesses, and hence their principal distinction; thus, a batten is 7 in. by $2\frac{1}{2}$ in.

a deal „ 9 „ 3 „
a plank „ 11 „ 3 „

these being what are termed the standard dimensions, by which they are bought and sold, the length of each being taken at 12 ft.; therefore, in estimating for the proper value of any quantity, nothing more is required than their lineal dimensions by which to ascertain the number of times 12 ft. there are in the given whole. Thus—if purchasing deals—

7 of 6 ft.   6 × 7 = 42 ft.
5 „ 14 „   14 × 5 = 70 „
11 „ 19 „   19 × 11 = 209 „
and 6 „ 21 „   21 × 6 = 126 „

12)447(37·25 standard deals.

Prices.—In London, a different system of charging sawing of deals is adopted to that in the provinces, viz. cuts are charged so much per dozen, the price varying with the length; ripping being called flat-cuts in the same way. In the country method, all cuts in the deal or log are charged for at per 100 ft. super, and all rips or flat-cuts under 6 in. are charged at per 100 ft. lineal; herewith are the usual prices for this work, viz.:—

	Per 100 ft. super.	Ripping per 100 ft. run.	× Cuts.
	s. d.	*s. d.*	*d.*
Oak	4 0	1 6	each 4
Mahogany	5 6	1 6	„ 4
Memel	2 6	1 0	„ $2\frac{1}{2}$
Swede and Yellow Pine..	2 3	0 10	„ $2\frac{1}{2}$
Pitch Pine	3 9	1 6	„ 3
Deals..	1 9	0 9	„ $0\frac{3}{4}$
Planing Deals	1 6		
Chipping do.	1 0		

Matching, Rebating, or Grooving for Hoop Iron, 3*d.* per 100 ft. super.

Tools.—Carpenters' tools may conveniently be divided into 7 classes, as follows:—(1) Guiding tools—rules, lines, squares; (2) Holding tools—pincers, vice; (3) Rasping tools—saws, files; (4) Edge tools—chisels, planes; (5) Boring tools—awls, gimlets, bits; (6) Striking tools—hammers, mallets; (7) Chopping tools—axes, adzes.* In an eighth category may be put such important accessories as the carpenter's bench, nails, screws, and various hints and recipes.

GUIDING TOOLS.—These comprise the chalk line, rule, straight-edge, square, spirit level, A-level, plumb level, gauges, bevel, mitre-box, callipers and compasses, trammel, and a few modern contrivances combining two or more of these tools in one.

Chalk line.—The chalk line is used as shown in Fig. 242 for the purpose of marking where cuts have to be made in wood. It consists of several yards of cord wound on a

242.

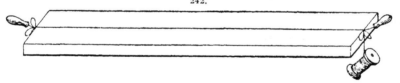

wooden reel, and well rubbed with a piece of chalk (or charcoal when a white line would be invisible) just before use. In applying it, first mark with the carpenter's pencil the exact spots between which the line is to run, then pass a bradawl through a loop near the end of the cord and fix it firmly in the wood at the first point marked, next apply the chalk or charcoal to the cord, or as much of it as will suffice for the length of line to be marked, this done, stretch the cord tightly to the second point marked, and either fasten it by looping it round a second bradawl, or hold it very tightly in the finger and thumb of one hand, whilst with the finger and thumb of the other hand you raise it in the middle as much as it will stretch; on suddenly releasing it, it springs back smartly and leaves a well-defined line between the two points. The novice may find it helpful to mark both sides of his work, which is best done by removing the cord without disturbing the bradawls.

Rule.—The foot rule consists of a thin narrow strip of metal, hard wood, or ivory, generally 2 ft. long, graduated on both sides into inches and fractions of an inch (halves, 4ths, 8ths, 12ths, 16ths, 32ndths), and hinged so as to fold into a shorter compass for convenience in carrying. Superior kinds are fitted with a sliding brass rule adding another foot to the length, and graduated in minute subdivisions which facilitate calculations of dimensions. In the form shown in Fig. 243, known as "Stanley's No. 32," this brass slide is furnished with an elbow at the end, so that it constitutes a combined

* Holtzapffel & Co., 64, Charing Cross, London, are to be recommended for tools of carpentry and other handicrafts.

rule and calliper (see p. 64).   Ordinary prices are 1s. to 5s., according to quality and finish.

Straight-edge.—The nature of this tool is expressed in its name.   It consists of a long (5 or 6 ft.) strip of well-seasoned wood or of bright hardened steel (nickel-plated if preferred), several inches wide, having at least one edge perfectly level and true throughout.   Its use is for ascertaining whether a surface is uniformly even, which is readily done by simply laying the straight-edge on the surface, when irregularities of the surface become apparent by spaces between the two planes in contact.   Steel straight-edges are made with one bevelled edge and with English or French scales graduated on them.

243.

Squares.—The use of these instruments is for marking out work at right angles. The most usual forms are illustrated below.   Fig. 244 is a common brass-mounted square ; Fig. 245 a mitre square.   It consists generally of a wooden stock or back with a steel blade fitted into it at right angles, and secured by 3 screws or rivets; the sizes vary from 3 to 30 in., and the prices from 1s. to 10s.   They are also made of plain or nickel-plated steel, with scales engraved on the edges.   In use, the stock portion of the square is placed tight against the edge which forms the base of the line to be marked, so

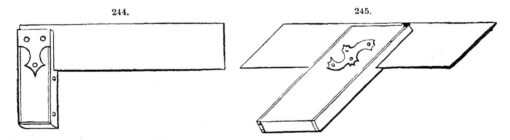

244.   245.

that the blade indicates where the new line is to be drawn.   The making and application of squares have been well described by Lewis F. Lyne in the *American Machinist*.   He remarks that the 2 sides of a square should form an angle of 90°, or the $\frac{1}{4}$ of a circle ; but hundreds of tools resembling squares in appearance, and so named, when the test is applied to them, are found entirely inaccurate : the angle is in some instances more, and in others less, than a right angle.   The way these tools are generally made is by taking a piece of steel for the stock, planing it up to the right size, and squaring up the ends, after which a slot is cut in one end to receive the blade.   The blade is neatly fitted and held securely by 2 or 3 rivets passing through the end of the stock and blade.   It is a very difficult undertaking, with ordinary appliances, to cut this slot precisely at right angles to the sides and ends of the stock ; and, when the blade is finally secured, it will be found that it leans to one side or the other, as shown in Fig. 246, where *a* represents the stock, and *b* the blade ; *c* is an end view, the dotted lines showing the position of blade, as described.

The best way to produce a square without special tools is to make a complete flat square of the size desired out of thin sheet steel, the thickness depending upon the size of square desired.   In almost every instance where squares are made by amateurs at tool-making, the blades are left too thick.   After the square has been trued up and finished upon the sides, 2 pieces of flat steel should be made exactly alike as to size, to be riveted upon the sides of the short arm of the square to form the stock. To properly locate these pieces, the square should be placed upon a surface plate, and the parts clamped in position, care being taken to get them all to bear equally upon the surface plate, after which, holes may be drilled and countersunk, and the rivets inserted. The angle formed by the cutting edges of the drills for countersinking the holes should be about 60°, so that when the rivets are driven, and the sides of the back finished, there will be no trace left of the rivets, which should always be of steel.

Close examination may reveal the fact that the blade is winding, or is slightly inclined to one side. If inclined, as shown at e, in Fig. 246, the end of the blade only will touch a square piece of work when the tool is held in a proper position, as shown in Fig. 247, where i represents the piece of work, and f the square. It is a custom among machinists to tip the stock, as shown at k and l, to enable the workman to see light under the blade. This only aggravates any imperfection in the squareness of the blade, for when the stock is tipped, as shown at k, it will touch

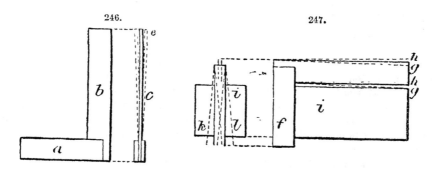

the work at g, occupying the position indicated by the dotted lines g, g; whereas, if the stock be tipped, as shown at l, the blade will assume the position indicated by the dotted lines h, h. These conditions will exist when the blade of the square is inclined, as shown at e, in Fig. 246. If the blade is inclined to the left, a precisely similar condition will exist, except in the reverse order. It is next to an impossibility to perform accurate work, or test the same with a square having a thick edge, because of the reason already stated that the light cannot be seen between the edge of the blade and the work.

The most ingenious tool for overcoming the foregoing difficulties is a sort of self-proving square, made by a machinist in New York. This is shown in Fig. 248, and consists of a steel beam j, shown in bottom view at k. In the end of this beam is a hole for the reception of a screw, with a common bevelled head. A square piece of steel, l, m, forms the blade of this square, n representing the end of the blade. The blade is first planed, then tapped and hardened, after which it is ground to bring the sides exactly parallel and of equal size, which makes the bar perfectly square. The stock is of a rectangular section, and, with this exception, is hardened and ground in the same manner as the blade. The end of the screw is then carefully ground at right angles to the sides, after which the parts are put together and the screw is tightened. If the blade is not precisely at right angles to the stock, it will occupy a position indicated by the dotted line ; then, if the screw be loosened and the blade turned half a revolution, the edge will stand as shown by the dotted line at p.

The end must be so ground that the blade will occupy precisely the same relation to the beam when turned in all positions. When this is accomplished, the square is a very close approximation to perfection. The accuracy of work is tested with one of the corners; when it becomes worn, another may be turned into position; and when all are worn, the blade is removed and trued up by grinding, as at first. In testing the accuracy of the ordinary square, it is usually placed upon a flat surface having a straight edge, as shown in Fig. 249, where *s* represents the surface with the square upon it. The stock is pressed firmly against the edge of the surface, and with a scriber

248.   249.

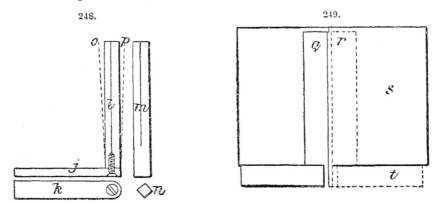

a fine line is drawn along the edge of the blade. The square is then turned to the position *t*, indicated by the dotted lines, and a second line is drawn along the edge of the blade. If the tool is less than a right angle, the line with the square in the former position will incline towards *q*, while in the latter position it will appear as shown at *r*; whereas, if the square be correct, the two lines will exactly coincide with each other. This is not a reliable test for the accuracy of a square, but it answers very well in case of emergency.

It is difficult to draw the lines to exactly represent the edge of the blade, owing to the fact that the slightest inclination of the hand holding the scriber to either side will make a crooked line. The form of square shown in Fig. 248 always presents a fine edge to work to, and may always be relied upon for accuracy when properly fitted up. This square would seem to be quite as easily made as the common one, but the construction of an accurate square with ordinary appliances is a job that tests the skill of a good workman.

Spirit level.—The spirit level consists of a glass tube partially filled with spirit, encased in a framework made of hard wood and protected by metallic facing on the most important sides. The quantity of spirit placed in the glass tube is just insufficient to

250.

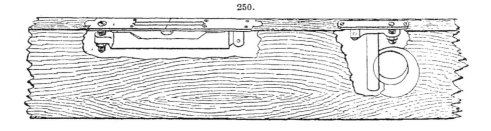

fill it, so that a " bubble " of air perhaps ½ in. long always appears at the surface, being rendered visible by means of a sight-hole in the metallic plate which encloses and secures the glass tube in the wooden block. The ends of the glass tube are hermetically sealed when the proper quantity of spirit has been introduced. The wooden case or block must be perfectly level and true, and of a material that will not change its form by climatic or other influences. Average sizes are 8-14 in. in length and cost 2-10s.

Some are made with the sight-hole at the side instead of the top. Others have both top and side openings. Such is shown in Fig. 250, which represents Stanley's improved adjustable combined spirit and plumb level, by which it is possible to adjust a surface to a position both truly horizontal and truly perpendicular. The principle of action of the spirit level is that the air bubble contained in the glass tube will always travel towards the highest point; when it rests immediately in the centre of the sight-hole, a true level is obtained. It is necessary to remember, however, that it is only a guide to the level of that length of surface on which it lies; and in levelling longer surfaces the spirit level should be placed on a straight-edge instead of directly on the surface to be tested.

Plumb level.—This consists of a straight-edge to which is attached a cord having a weight suspended from the end, as shown in Fig. 251. The top end *a* of the straight-edge has 3 saw-cuts made in it, one being exactly in the centre. From this centre cut a line is drawn perfectly straight to the other end *b*. On this line at *c* a pear-shaped hole is cut out of the straight-edge. A piece of supple cord is next weighted by attaching a pear-shaped lump of lead, and then fastened to the top *a* of the straight-edge by passing it first through the central saw-cut, and then through the others to make it fast, just so that the leaden weight is free to swing in and out of the hole. The law of gravity forces the cord to hang (when free) in a truly upright (perpendicular) position; on

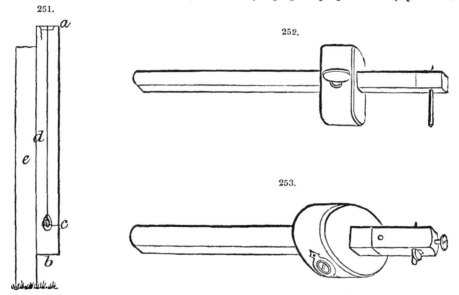

251.

252.

253.

placing the side *d* of the straight-edge against a surface *e*, whose perpendicularity is to be tested, if there is any disagreement between the cord and the line marked on the straight-edge, then the surface is not upright, and it must be altered until the cord exactly corresponds to and covers the line marked down the centre of the straight-edge.

Gauges.—There are 3 kinds of gauge used in carpentry, known respectively as the "marking," the "cutting," and the "mortice" gauge. They are outlined in the annexed illustrations. Fig. 252 is a cutting gauge having the head faced with brass; Fig. 253 is an improved form of cutting gauge; Fig. 254 is a thumb or turn-screw screw-slide mortice gauge; Fig. 255 is an improved mortice gauge with improved stem. The marking gauge has a shank about 9 in. long with a head or block to slide along it; a spike is inserted near the end of the shank, and the movable head is fixed at any required distance from the spike by a screw or wedge; its use is to make a mark on the wood parallel to a previously straightened edge, along which edge the gauge is guided; for dressing up several pieces of wood to exactly the same breadth this gauge is eminently useful. The cutting gauge is similarly composed of a shank and a head, but the spike is replaced by a thin steel plate, passing through the shank and secured by a screw, and sharpened on one edge so as to be capable of making a cut either with or across the grain; its main applications are for gauging dovetailed work and cutting veneers to breadth. The

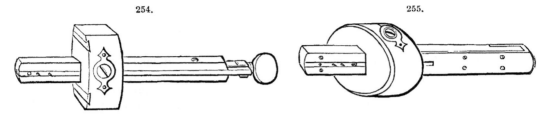

254.   255.

mortice gauge resembles the others in having a shank (about 6 in. long) and a movable brass-shod head, but it has 2 spikes, one fixed and the other arranged to be adjusted by means of a screw at varying distances from the first; it is used for gauging mortice and tenon work. Gauges are generally made of beech, and the shank is often termed the "strig"; compound gauges are now made, consisting of marking and cutting, or marking and mortice appliances combined in one tool. Prices vary from 3d. to 10s., according to finish. In using the gauge, the marking point is first adjusted to the correct distance, then secured by turning the screw, and the mark is made when required by holding the head of the gauge firmly against the edge which forms the basis of the new lines, with the marker resting on the surface to be marked, and passing the instrument to and fro.

Bevels.—These differ from squares, in that they are destined for marking lines at angles to the first side of the work, but not at right angles. Examples are shown in the

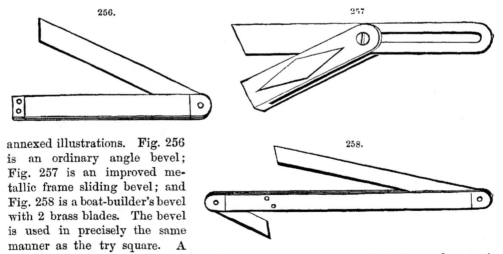

256.   257

258.

annexed illustrations. Fig. 256 is an ordinary angle bevel; Fig. 257 is an improved metallic frame sliding bevel; and Fig. 258 is a boat-builder's bevel with 2 brass blades. The bevel is used in precisely the same manner as the try square. A very useful bevel protractor, with a sliding arm and half circle divided into degrees, is sold by Churchills.

Mitre-box.—The mitre-box is an arrangement for guiding a saw-cut at an angle of 45° exactly, or half the dimensions of a right angle. It is mostly required for cutting mouldings, where the end of one piece of wood meeting the end of another has to form with it a true corner of 90° (a right angle). The best illustration of a mitre is to be seen in either of the 4 corners of a picture frame. In its simplest form the mitre-box may be made out of any piece of good sound plank 1½ ft. long and say 6 in. by 3 in. A rebate is cut lengthwise in this, i.e. half its width and half its thickness is cut away, leaving the slab in the form of 2 steps, thus constituting a rest for any work to be operated upon. Next 2 saw-cuts, one facing each way, are carried down through the top step and about ¼ in. into the lower step, these saw-cuts being exactly at an angle of 45° with the front edge of the "box."

When a mitre has to be cut, the wood to be operated on is laid on the lower step and held firmly into the angle, while a saw is passed down in the old cuts in the box and so through the wood to be mitred.

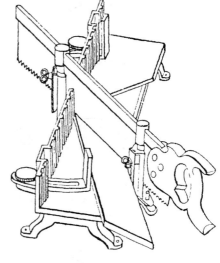

259.

For cutting other angles than 45°, other saw-cuts might be made in the same box; but the most convenient instrument for cutting a wide series of angles is the Langdon mitre-box, sold by Churchills, and illustrated in Fig. 259. Whilst ordinary mitre-boxes range only from right angles (90°) to 45°, this cuts from right angles to 73° on 2½-in. wood, and is the only form adjustable for mitreing circular work in patterns and segments of various kinds. Prices range between 24s. and 70s. without the saw, according to depth and width of cut.

The ordinary mitre-box may also be made in the form of a wide shallow trough, the saw-cuts at an angle of 45° being carried down through the sides to the floor, while the sides and floor combined form the rest for the work in hand.

All the forms of mitre-box described above are intended for use with a saw, the edges of the mitre being left rough from the saw in order to take glue better.

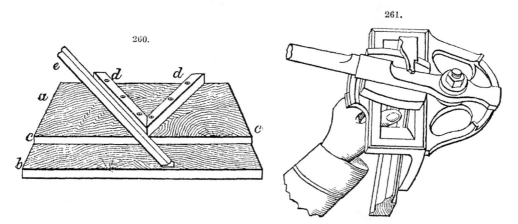

261.

260.

Another form, admitting of the sawed work being planed up, is called a "shooting-board," and is shown in Fig. 260. It consists of 2 slabs, a b, of good sound mahogany, about 30 in. long, 18 in. wide, and 1 in. thick, screwed together so as to form a step c; on the topmost are screwed 2 strips d of hard wood 1½–2 in. wide, at right angles. The piece of moulding e to be mitred is laid against one guide bar, and sawn off on the line c, or laid on the other side against the second guide bar, and similarly cut off. It will be necessary to use both sides in this way, because, although the piece cut off has also an angle of 45°, it would need to be turned over and applied to the other, which could not be done without reversing the moulding. In a plain unmoulded strip, this would not signify. The strip lying close to the step or rebate of the board, can be trimmed by the plane by laying it on its side, but care must be taken not to plane the edge of the step itself. The plane must be set very fine, and must cut keenly. To saw off

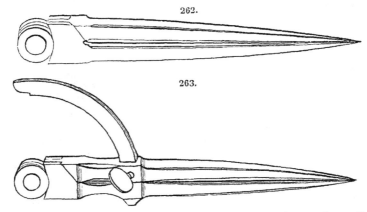

262.

263.

a piece at right angles, and not with a mitre, lay it against the bar, and saw it off in a line with the other, when it cannot fail to be cut correctly, *d d* forming 2 sides of a square.

A handy mitreing tool sold by Melhuish is shown in Fig. 261. It cuts a clean

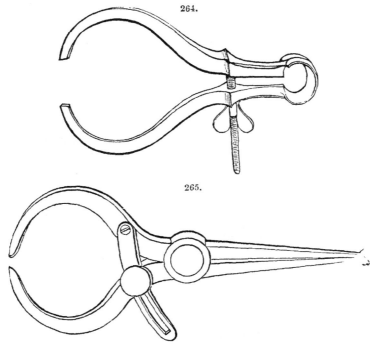

264.

265.

mitre at one thrust of the handle. Its price is 12s. to cut 2-in. mouldings, and 22s. 6d. for 4-in.

Compasses and Callipers.—These implements are used for taking inside and outside dimensions where a rule cannot be employed, and for striking out circular figures. Ordinary forms are shown in the annexed diagrams. Fig. 262 is a pair of ordinary plain compasses; Fig. 263, wing compasses; Fig. 264, spring callipers; Fig. 265, inside and outside callipers; Fig. 266, improved inside and outside callipers. The method of using

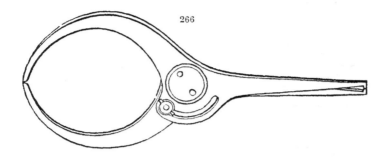

266

these instruments is sufficiently obvious from their shape. Ordinary useful sizes vary in price from 1 to 5s. Churchills have several new forms.

Trammel.—This is employed for drawing elliptic or oval curves, and is represented in Fig. 267. It can be purchased with varying degrees of finish, or may be home made in the following manner:—Two strips of dry hard wood a, 18 in. long, $1\frac{1}{2}$ in. wide, and $\frac{3}{4}$ in. thick, are ploughed down the centre to a depth of $\frac{3}{8}$ in. and a width of $\frac{3}{4}$ in.; one is let into the other at right angles so that the bottoms of the grooves or channels are exactly flush, and the structure is strengthened by having a piece of thin sheet brass cut to the shape and screwed down to its upper surface. Next 2 hard-wood blocks $1\frac{1}{4}$ in. long are cut to slide easily but firmly in these grooves, their surfaces coming barely flush with the face of the instrument. A hole is drilled nearly through the centre of each block and about $\frac{1}{10}$ in. diam., to admit the pins b; and thin strips of brass are then screwed on to the surface of the instrument in such a manner as to secure the blocks from

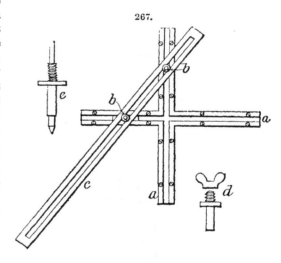

267.

coming out of the grooves while not interfering with the free passage of the pins and blocks along the grooves. To this is added the beam compass c, which consists of a straight mahogany ruler with a narrow slit down the middle permitting it to be adjusted on the pins. These last may be of brass or steel wire with a shoulder and nut, as at d; they are fixed at the required points on the ruler c, and then inserted in the holes in the blocks, where they are free to revolve. A hollow brass socket e fitted with a pencil is also made to screw on to the beam, and forms the delineator.

Shooting-board.—This implement, Fig. 268, is for the purpose of securing a true surface and straight edge on wood when planing. It is generally made by fastening one board on another in such a way as to form a step between them; shooting-boards made by gluing 2 pieces of board together, are very apt to twist and cast through the action of the air, and once out of square, are very hard to set right, generally requiring to be pulled apart, and made again. The following plan renders this unnecessary:—Take 2 boards (of the length you require the board, allowing at least 1 ft. extra for the plane to run;

thus, to plane up 5-ft. stuff, make the board at least 6 ft.) of thoroughly dry pine, 1 in. thick and 11 in. wide, and plane them perfectly true; cut 4 in. off one the whole length of the board; these 2 pieces are for the bottom board, and across these glue about

268.

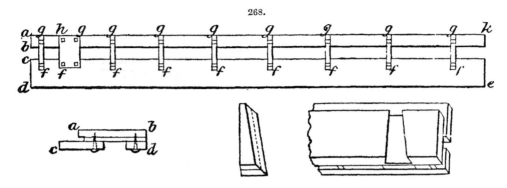

8 pieces of ½-in. pine 1½ in. wide by 10 in. in length and one piece 5 in. in width by 10 in. in length to build up or strengthen the upper board where the groove will come, leaving a gap 4 in. wide between the 2 bottom boards, thus making it 15 in. wide; now glue on the upper board, allowing it to lap 1 in. over the cross-pieces (as in cross section), and screw together with 2 1-in. screws from the bottom. This will allow the top to be planed if it should cast, as the screws do not come through, and the edge being raised and lapping over the cross-pieces, allows the edge to be squared, without parting the boards, while the air having free play all round the boards they are not so likely to cast, and, in shooting an edge, the shavings and dust work away under the top board, so as not to throw the plane out of square. The blocks are generally screwed across the board, but it is better to cut a groove across, wedge-shape, 6 in. from the end, and cut wedges of various thicknesses for planing wood of any substance, so that the plane may run over the block, as in section. The measurements are *a–b*, 4 in.; *b–c*, 4 in.; *c–d*, 7 in.; *d–e*, 6 ft.; *f–g*, 10 in.; *g–h*, 5 in.; *h–k*, 4 in.; and in the section of the boards, *a–b*, 11 in.; *c–d*, 15 in.

269.

Bell centre punch.—This handy little device enables any mechanic instantaneously to centre any round, square, oval, triangular, hexagonal, or octagonal article for the purpose of drilling or turning. In use the punch is held upright (as shown in Fig. 269) over the article to be centred, and the punch centre tapped, when the true centre of any geometrically-shaped article will be found. It will centre any size from ¼ to 1 in. diam., and costs from 3s. upwards.

270.

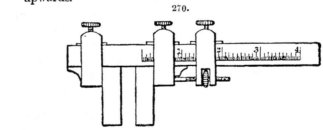

Combinations.—Combination tools are essentially American novelties, and those described here may all be obtained of Churchills, Finsbury.

Starrett's calliper-square is shown in Fig. 270; the jaws are hardened, and, being made independent and accurately ground, can be reversed for an inside calliper of larger scope, or used for depth gauge, &c. The beam is graduated to 64ths in. on one, and 100ths on the other. The 4-in. size costs 18s. with adjusting screw, or 14s. without.

The steel calliper-rule is shown in Fig. 271; when closed it is 3 in. long, and the

271.

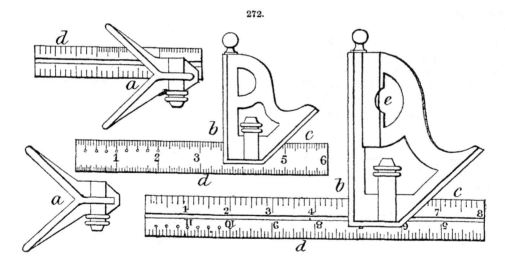

calliper can be drawn out to measure $2\frac{1}{2}$ in. They are accurately graded, and durable; cost, 8s. 6d.

Starrett's combined try-square, level, plumb, rule, and mitre, is shown in Fig. 272; the various parts are: a, centre head forming centre square both inside and outside, one scale fitting both heads; b, square; c, mitre; d, rule; e, plumb level. As a try-square, it is a substitute for every size of the common kind, and more compact; as a centre square, it gives both inside and outside grades; as a mitre, it affords both long

272.

and short tongues; and it can be used as a marking gauge, mortice gauge, or ⊤-square. The 4-in. size without centre head or level costs 4s. 6d., and the complete tool may be had for 11s. 3d. for the 6-in. size to 15s. 9d. for the 12-in.

Ames's universal or centre square is shown in Fig. 273. For finding the centre of a circle, as in A, the instrument is placed with its arms b a e resting against the circumference, in which position one edge of the vertical rule a d will cross the centre. If a line be drawn here, and the instrument be similarly applied to another section of the circumference, and another line be drawn crossing the first, the point of crossing will be the centre of the circle. B illustrates its use as a try-square at n, and as an outside square at *l*. In C it is applied as a mitre, in D as a rule and T-square, in E as an outside square, and in F as a T-square for machinists. The prices range from 8s. 6d. for the 4-in. size to 27s. for the 12-in.

HOLDING-TOOLS.—These are chiefly represented by pincers, vices, and clamps.

Pincers.—This well-known tool is shown in Fig. 274. It is made in various sizes and qualities, the most generally useful being the 5-in. and 8-in. sizes, costing about 3d. per in.

Vices.—The old-fashioned form of hand-vice is shown in Fig. 275; in size and price it ranges from 3-in. and 2s. to 6-in. and 6s. An improved patent hand-vice, as sold by Melhuish, Fetter Lane, is represented in Fig. 276; cost 4s. 6d. The improved American hand-vice, as sold by Churchills (Fig. 277), is of metal throughout, the jaws being of forged steel, and the handle of case-hardened malleable iron; price 6s. 6d. The 2 last forms have a hole through the handle, and screw for holding wire. An ordinary wrought-iron parallel vice is shown in Fig. 278.

Great improvements have been made of late years in vices, more especially in the American forms sold by Churchills. The one shown in Fig. 279 has a 3-in. jaw, with swivel base; and beckhorn and swivel-jaw attachment, allowing it to take hold in any

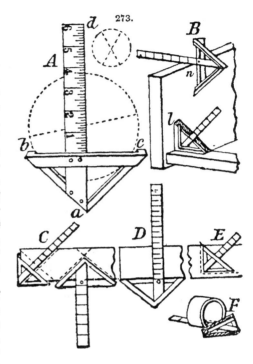

position that may be found convenient; its price is 20s. Fig. 280 illustrates Parker's saw-filer's vice, made with a ball-and-socket joint, by which the jaws may be turned to any position; price 7s. for 9-in. jaws. Hall's patent sudden-grip vice is shown in Fig. 281. To open the jaws, lift the handle to a horizontal position, or as high as it

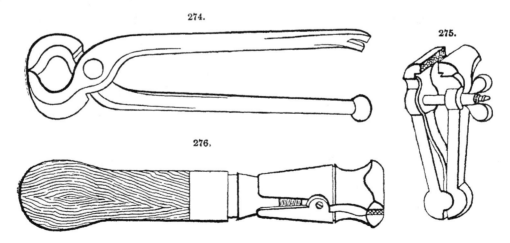

will go, and draw it towards you. In this way the sliding jaw can be moved to any position, and the vice swivelled if desired. In order to grasp the work, push in the sliding jaw till it presses against the work, then depress the handle, which causes the jaws to securely grasp the work and at the same time lock the swivel. If the handle should not go low enough for convenience, it can be made to go lower by depressing it just before it touches the work to be held. If the vice swivels too easily, drive in the key W in the bottom plate; but if it does not turn easily enough, drive out the key a little. If the handle fails to remain in a horizontal position, the screw S can be tightened to hold it. Care should be taken that the screw N is down, so as to keep the rack H from lifting

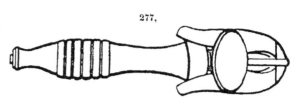

277.

278.

279.

280.

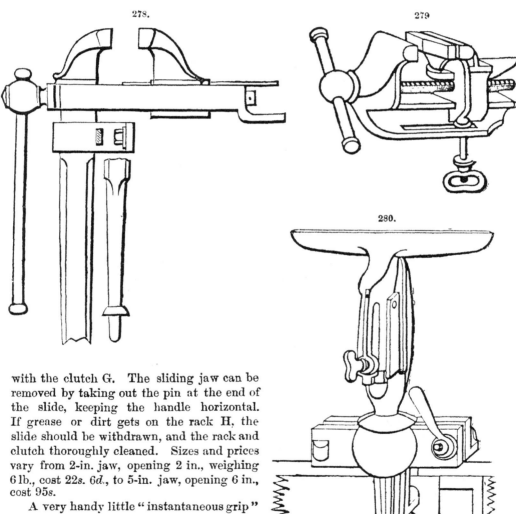

with the clutch G. The sliding jaw can be removed by taking out the pin at the end of the slide, keeping the handle horizontal. If grease or dirt gets on the rack H, the slide should be withdrawn, and the rack and clutch thoroughly cleaned. Sizes and prices vary from 2-in. jaw, opening 2 in., weighing 6 lb., cost 22s. 6d., to 5-in. jaw, opening 6 in., cost 95s.

A very handy little "instantaneous grip" vice, sold by Melhuish, Fetter Lane, is shown in Fig. 282; the size with 9-in. jaws opening 12 in. costs 14s.

The picture-frame vice illustrated in Fig. 283 is a useful novelty, sold by Churchills. It is operated by means of a cam lever attached to a treadle, thus allowing entire freedom to both hands of the workman. It is easily and quickly adjusted of mouldings of any width and frames of all sizes; and holds both pieces, whether twisted or straight, so firmly that perfect joints are made without re-adjusting; price, 22s. 6d.

Stephens' parallel vice, as sold by Churchills, is shown in Fig. 284. The working parts consist simply of a toggle G and toothed bar T, held together by a spring S, and

281.

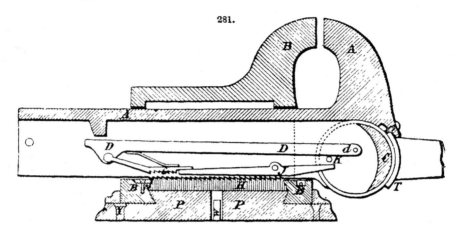

worked by a cam C, and hook M, on the handle H. Pressing the handle hard back, the tooth M is brought to bear under the tooth m, on the left joint of the toggle, thus disengaging the racks by raising the tooth bar t away from the rack T. The movable

282.

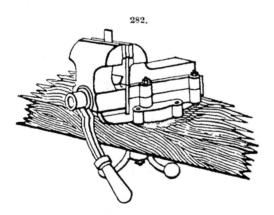

283.

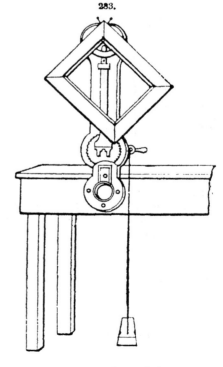

jaw B can now be slid in and out, to its extreme limits, with perfect ease, and an article of any size be held at any point between these limits, simply by placing it between the jaws of the vice, then pressing the movable jaw B against it and pulling the handle out. At the first start of the handle outward, the tooth M slips from under the tooth m, and the spring S draws down and firmly holds the tooth bar t against the rack T; as the handle is pulled farther outward, the cam C is brought to bear against the ridge n, thus straightening the toggle and forcing the movable jaw B against the article to be held. The parts are interchangeable. The racks and all parts where pressure comes are made of steel. There is no wear to the racks, for they merely engage without rubbing. Great solidity and strength are added to the movable jaw by a projection from the stock strengthened by two upright flanges Occasionally put a drop of oil on the cam C and tooth M.

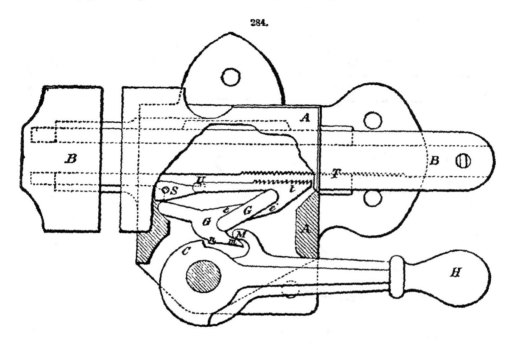

Fig. 285 represents Stephens' adjusting taper attachment, for holding all kinds of taper or irregular work; and Fig. 286 illustrates the pipe attachment for holding gas-pipes or round rods. The width of jaw varies from 2 to 6½ in.; opening, 2¼–11 in.;

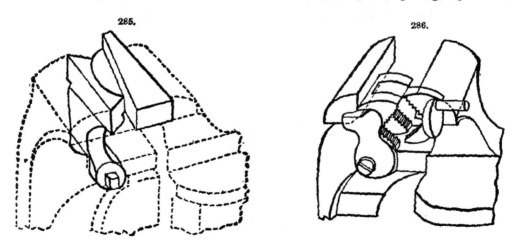

price 14–150s. with plain base, or 18–176s. with swivel base; taper attachment costs 6–32s., and pipe attachment, 12s. 6d.–36s.

Vices also form an essential part of the carpenter's bench, and will be further noticed under that section (p. 136).

Clamps.—The ordinary carpenter's clamp (or cramp), shown in Fig. 287, is employed for tightening up the joints of boards, whether for the purpose of nailing or to allow time for glue to harden.   It is composed of a long iron bar *a* provided with holes *b* at intervals for receiving iron bolts which hold the sliding bracket *c*; the length of slide of the second bracket *d* is limited by the screw *e* which actuates it.   The length of opening varies from 3 to 6 ft., cost 25–38*s.*

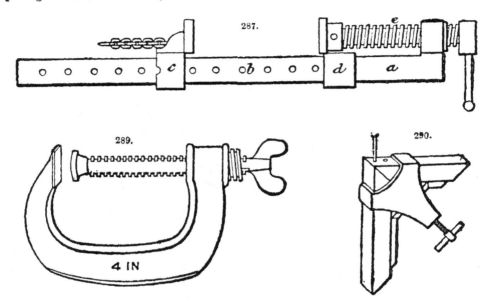

287.

289.

4 IN

290.

Hammer's adjustable clamp, Fig. 289, is a strong tool made of malleable iron; prices range from 22*s.* 6*d.* a doz. for the 3-in. size, to 55*s.* for the 8-in.

For simple rough work a suitable clamp can be made by driving wedges in to tighten up the work laid between stops on a plank.

A very useful corner clamp for securely gripping 2 sides of a picture frame during nailing or gluing together, is shown in Fig. 290.   The two pieces being accurately

291

mitred are placed in close contact and so held while the clamp is being tightened. These clamps are sold by Melhuish at 1*s.* 8*d.* a pair for taking 1¾-in. mouldings, up to 4*s.* for 4-in.

Fig. 291 shows a clamp designed for holding a circular-saw while being filed; *a* has 2 jaws, one of which is seen at *b*; they are of metal lined with wood, and are closed or unclosed by turning the handle c. The temporary mandrel of the saw may be placed in either of the holes of the clamp standards at d, so as to bring the saw to the right height in the jaws.

Bench clamps and holdfasts will be described under another section (p. 134).

RASPING TOOLS.—These comprise the various forms of saw as well as files and rasps.

Saws.—The saw is a tool for cutting and dividing substances, chiefly wood, and consisting of a thin plate or blade of steel with a series of sharp teeth on one edge, which remove successive portions of the material by cutting or tearing. Some representative examples of handsaws are illustrated below: Fig. 292 is a panel and ripping·

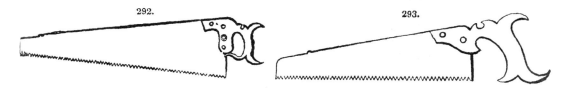

292.   293.

saw; Fig. 293, a grafter saw, Fig. 294, a tenon saw; Fig. 295, a dovetail saw; Fig. 296, an iron bow saw; Fig. 297, a frame turning saw.

Principles.—The saw is essentially a tool for use across or at right angles to the fibres of the wood, although custom and convenience have arranged it for use along the fibres, still not when those fibres are straight and parallel. If in the growth of timber there was not any discontinuity in the straight lines of the fibres, then all longitudinal separation would be accomplished by axes or chisels. It is because this rectilineal continuity is interrupted by branches and other incidents of growth that the saw is used for ripping purposes. Were not some tool substituted for the wedge-like action of the axe,

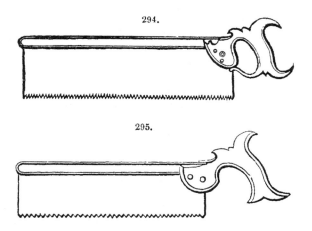

294.

295.

timber could not as a general rule be obtained from the log with flat surfaces. Hence the ripping saw, a tool which is intermediate between an axe and a saw proper. To study the saw as a tool fulfilling its own proper and undisturbed duties, it must be

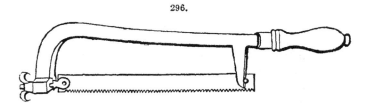

296.

regarded in the character of a cross-cut saw. In this character it is called upon to meet the two opposing elements—cohesion and elasticity of fibre.

To deal with the treatment of fibrous wood at right angles to the length of the fibre is then clearly an operation in which considerations must enter, differing in many respects from those that decide action in direction of the grain. The object now is, as it were, to divide with the least expenditure of power a string which connects two ends of a tensioned bow. If a blow be given in the middle of a bow-string, the elasticity imparted by the bow to the string renders the blow inoperative. The amount of this elasticity is very apparent when one notes the distance it can project an arrow. Indeed, any one who has struck a tensioned cord or a spring is well aware that the recoil throws back the instrument, and by so much abstracts from the intensity of the blow. To separate the string in this experiment even the pressure of a knife blade is insufficient; for a heavy pressure, as manifested by the bending of the string, is borne before separation takes place. It

may be taken for granted that in thus severing the string, the power expended has been employed in two ways; first in bending the string; second in separating it. If the string be supported and prevented from bending, and the same cutting edge be applied, and the power be measured by weights or a spring balance, it will be seen how much of the former was expended in the useless act of bending the string, and therefore quite lost in the separating of it.

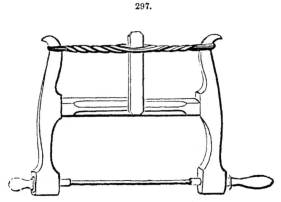

297.

If the cutting instrument were a short narrow edge, or almost a sharpened point, and drawn forward, each fibre would be partially cut. A repetition of this action in the same line would still further deepen the cut. But a cutting edge requires support from a back, i.e. from the thicknessing of the metal, otherwise it would yield. Further, a cutting edge held at right angles to the surface of the fibres may not be the most effective position. Let any one draw the point of a knife across the grain of a smooth pine plank, holding the blade first at right angles to the surface, and, secondly, inclining forward, he will observe that by the first operation the fibres are roughly scratched; by the second they are smoothly divided.

Hence, even where the edge has deepened, this back support or metal strengthening must follow. It cannot do so upon this knife contrivance, because the sharp edge has not prepared a broad way for the thick back, which being of a wedge-like character should be acted upon by impact and not by such tension or thrust as in this case is only available. Therefore simple cutting is insufficient for the purpose of separating the fibres, but it has been suggestive.

If now something must enter the cut thicker than the edge, then it is clear that the edge alone is insufficient for the required purpose, and an edge, as a cutting edge alone, cannot be used for the separation of the fibres cross-wise. Longitudinally it may be, and is used, but in reality what appears to be thus used is a wedge, and not a cutting edge, for in a true cut the draw principle must enter. The axe and chisel do not work upon the cutting "edge," but upon the driven "wedge" principle. They are driven by impact, and not drawn by tension or thrust by pressure.

The consideration now suggested is not simply how to cross-cut the fibres, but, further, how to permit the material on which the edge is formed to follow without involving an inadmissible wedge action. It may be done as in a class of saws called metal saws, viz. making the "edge" the thickest part of the metal of the saw. This however, ignores the true principle of the saw, and introduces the file. It may, in passing, be well to remark that in marble cutting, where the apparent saw is only a blade of metal without teeth, this want of metal teeth is supplied by sharp sand, each grain of which becomes in turn a tooth, all acting in the manner of a file, and not a saw proper. A former method of cutting diamonds was similar to this. Two thin iron wires were twisted, and formed the string of a bow. These were used as a saw, the movable teeth being formed of diamond dust. A similar remark applies to a butcher's saw; its metal teeth really act as files.

For the purpose of separating a bundle of fibres, the "edge" cannot be the edge with which we are familiar in axes and chisels. Such an edge drawn across will cut fibres on a surface only; this is insufficient, for a saw is required to cut fibres below a surface.

The tearing also of upper fibres from lower ones is not consistent with true work. To actually cut or separate these is the question to be considered, and the simple answer is another question. Can a narrow chisel be introduced which shall remove the piece of fibre whose continuity has been destroyed by cutting edges previously alluded to? If so, then an opening or way will have been found along which the back or strengthening part of the cutting edge can be moved. If, however, we look at the work of a single cutting edge, we notice that, although the continuity of the fibre is destroyed, yet the separated ends are still interlaced amongst the other fibres. To obtain a piece removable as by a small narrow chisel, it will be requisite to make a second cut parallel to the first. This being done, there is the short piece, retained in position by adhesion only, which must by some contrivance be removed, for it is in the way, and the room it occupies is that in which the back of the cutting edge must move. To slide, as it were, a narrow chisel along and cut it out is more simple in suggestion than in execution.

There is another defect upon the application of what at first seems sufficient in principle, but only wanting in physical strength—it is the absence of any guide. To draw a pointed cutting edge along the same deepening line needs a very steady hand and eye. This consideration of the problem requires that some guide principle must enter.

To increase the number of cutting edges, and form as it were a linear sequence of them, may give a partial guidance, and if the introduction of our chisel suggestion be impracticable, then another device must be sought. Instead of the 2 parallel cutters, it will be possible to make these externally parallel but internally oblique to the line of cut, in other words to sharpen them as an adze is sharpened and not as an axe, and in doing so one obstacle will be removed, it is true, but a blemish which was non-existent will appear. The combining obliquity of the dividing edges will so press upon the intervening piece of fibre as to press it downwards into and upon the lower fibres, thus solidifying, and, in so far as this is done, increasing the difficulty of progressing through the timber.

Note the mode of operating, as shown by Fig. 298. The portions of wood $a\,b\,d$ and $e\,c\,d$ have been removed by the gradual penetration of the oblique arms—not only have they been cut, but they have been carried forward and backward and removed, leaving a clear space behind them of the width $a\,e$. But how with regard to the portion within the oblique arms? That part would either be left as an impeding hillock, or it would have to be removed by the introduction of such a plan as making rough the insides of these oblique arms. If we consider the nature of the material left, it will be admitted to consist of particles of woody fibre adhering to each other only by the glutinous or gummy matter of the timber, and not cohering. If the breadth $a\,e$ is not too large, the whole of the heap would be rubbed away by the power exerted by the workman. There will therefore be not only economy in power, but economy also in material in narrowing $a\,e$. If attention be given to the form of the pieces bent from the plane of the metal of which this cutting instrument is made. it will be observed that the active portion has 3 edges, of which the lower or horizontal one only is operative, for the tool rides upon the fibres, divides them, and when the dividing has been accomplished, the sloping parts will remove the hillock. To act thus, the lower edges would require to be sharpened at *a* and *e* so as to clear a gate for the metal to follow. The action of the tool as described would require a downward pressure, in order to cause the cutting segments to penetrate vertically. The resistance to this downward entrance is the breadth of the " tooth," for it rides upon a number of fibres and divides them by sliding over ; the complete action requires not only downward pressure for the cut, but also horizontal pressure for the motion, the latter both in the advance and withdrawal of the tool. These 2 pressures being at right angles do not aid each other, and will employ both hands of the workman. It is very obvious that the compounding of these will give freedom to at least one hand.

For the present, assume that the 2 pressures to be compounded are equal, then the simple operation is to employ one pressure making (say) an angle of 45° with the horizontal line of thrust. Although this be done, yet if the saws be any length, clearly the angle will vary, and therefore the effect of the sawyer's labour will be counteracted, either as a consequence of excessive thrust or of excessive pressure at the beginning or ending of the stroke. In fact, not only the position in which the handle is fixed on the saw, but the very handling itself will require those adaptations which experience alone can give.

The effect of this will be to cause the forward points to penetrate, and cross-cut the fibres obliquely. The return action will be altogether lost unless the instrument is arranged accordingly, and sloped in the other direction.

If the tool becomes a single-handed one, and relies for its operation upon thrust or tension in one direction only (say thrust), then cutting edges on the back portions of the teeth are useless, and had better be removed.

The experiment worthy of trial is, can the whole power, or nearly the whole power, be converted into a tension or thrust for cutting purposes. To do this the cutting edge must be so formed as to be almost self-penetrating ; then the cutting edge is no longer a horizontal edge, but it becomes oblique, on the advancing face, and formed thus there is no reason why it should not also be oblique on the back face, and so cut equally in both directions. The inclination of these faces to the path of the saw must be determined by the power—whether it is capable of separating as many fibres as the teeth ride between, and if these are formed to cut each way (as a single-handed tool) whether it could be done ; because it necessitates a construction to which tension and thrust may be alternately applied. The nature of the wood, the power and skill of the workman, and the strength of the metal, must answer this suggestion.

The depth, or rather length, of the cutting face may be decreased, and the number of teeth increased, for the fibres to be cut cannot be more vertically than can be contained between 2 teeth. The operative length of the tool must also be taken into account, for the combined resistance of all the fibres resting within the teeth must be less than the power of the workman. It may be well to remark that this difficulty is generally met in practice by the workman so raising certain teeth out of cut as to leave only so many in operation as the circumstances enable him to work. One advantage results by so doing—the guide principle of a longer blade is gained than could be done had the length been limited by that of the operating teeth, or had there been a prolongation of metal without any teeth upon it. To avoid complicating an attempt to deal progressively with the action of the saw, this, and perhaps other considerations may for a while pass from notice. Considered as hitherto the teeth and tool are planned for operation in both tension and thrust. Now these are of so opposite a nature that a tool perfect under the one is likely to be imperfect under the other. When the necessary thinness of the material and the tenacity of it are taken into account, tension seems the most suitable :

but although the ancients and the workmen in Asia are of this way of thinking, yet in England the opposite practice is adopted. It may be well to give a few minutes to this branch of the subject.

The form of a saw must in one dimension at least be very thin, and that without any opportunity for strengthening any part by means of ribs. When a strengthening bar is introduced at the back as in dovetail saws, the depth of cut is limited. In order, then, to permit the guide principle to operate efficiently, this thin material must be so prolonged as under all circumstances to guide the cutting edge in a straight line. Of course we are dealing with saws to be used by hand, and not with ribbon or machine-driven saws.

If a light saw blade be hooked on an object, or placed against one, then tension causes this straight blade to be more and more straightened. On the contrary, if pressed forward by thrust, the weakness of the blade is evidenced by the bending. Now, formed as saw teeth are, either to cut in both directions, or in the forward direction only, then there is always one direction in which the work to be done is accomplished by a thrust upon this thin metal. Clearly the metal will bend. If, however, the teeth are such as to cut in one direction only, and that when the tension is on the metal, the work tends to preserve that straightness of blade upon which an important quality and use of the tool depends. That this tension system can be efficient with a very narrow blade is clear from the extensive use of ribbon saws. There is, however, a property in the breadth of the blade which applies equally to the tension and thrust systems—it is the guide principle. The breadth of the blade operates by touching the sides of the gateway opened by the teeth. When it is desired to dispense with a straight guide for sawing purposes, it is done by narrowing the blade as in lock saws, tension frame saws, &c.

There is obviously a limit to the required breadth even for the most effectual guidance and movement: this guidance should be uniform through the entire cut; hence upon the guide principle alone, there is required a breadth of saw beyond what is requisite for the teeth. The reasoning hitherto has landed us upon a parallel blade of some (as yet) undecided breadth. When one of our ordinary hand cross-cutting saws is examined, it is observed to be taper and not parallel, the tapering being at the edge or back, where the teeth are not. This has been done to meet our practice of using the saw as an instrument for thrust instead of tension. When the teeth near the end farthest from the handle are to operate, and there is no steadiness obtained from the guidance of the sides of the already separated timber, then the whole of the thrust must be transmitted through the necessarily thin blade. An attempt to compensate for this thinness by increasing the breadth is the only course open. It is one not defensible upon any true principles of constructive mechanism, for it is not in the increased breadth or extension of surface that resistance to bending is wanted, but it is in the thickness, and that is impracticable.

In thrust saws, the hand and the arm of the workman occupy a definite position, and the line of pressure on the saw is thus very much determined by the inclination of the handle (that part grasped in the hand) to the line of teeth prolonged backwards. If the handle be placed at such an angle that a large part of the resolved thrust be perpendicular to the line of teeth, then the "bite" may be greater than the other resolved portion of the power can overcome. At another angle the "bite" may be very little, and although the saw thus constructed would move easily, it would work "sweetly," but slowly. The construction is suitable for saws with fine teeth and for clear cuttings. It will be seen from these considerations that there should be preserved a very carefully considered relationship between the size and angle of the teeth and the position in which the handle is fixed, or rather the varying adaptability of the workman's thrust. Indeed, upon fully developed and accurate principles, the timber to be cut should first be examined, its fibrous texture determined physically, and a saw deduced from these data, having teeth and handle so related as to do the required work with a minimum of power. This multiplicity of saws is not available ; and as in music the multiplicity of notes which only the violin can produce are rejected in other instruments, so here the multiplicity of theoretical saws is rejected, and a kind of rough and ready compromise is effected between the position of the handle and the angle and depths of the teeth. It would, however, well repay those whose works are usually of the same character and of the same class of timber, to consider these points, with a view to the selection of saws and position of handle suitably constructed to do the work with the least expenditure of power.

A few words upon the handles of single-handed saws. Whatever may be the other conditions required in handles, the large majority of saw-handles have the curved hooked projections a and b, Fig. 299; these are connected with the pressure of the sawyer on the teeth. If, in sawing, the hand bears upon the upper hook a, then an increased pressure is given to the forward teeth; if upon the hook b, the pressure on the forward teeth is released, and consequent ease in sawing results, also a pressure may be given to the back teeth. The angle at which direct thrust ought to act upon the line of teeth in the saws is obviously very different. Each material may be said to have its own proper angle. Provision may be made by 2 set screws above a and b for varying the intersection of the line of thrust with the line of teeth. It will be further noticed that in the handle of the " one-man saw," Fig. 301, the upper hook is wanting, and this because under any circumstances the weight of the saw is more

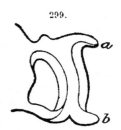

299.

than sufficient, and therefore it is not requisite that any resolved portion of the workman's energy should be compounded with this. Not so with the other hook ; that is retained in order that thus the weight of the saw may be taken from the work. For these reasons the line of direct thrust is nearly parallel with that of the teeth. We seem to be guilty of much inconsistency in the placing as well as in the formation of saw handles.

A brief recapitulation of what has been said may suitably close this far from exhausted branch of the subject.

There have been considered :—

The effect of impact transverse to fibre.

The effect of thrust transverse to fibre.

The passing of a cutting edge transverse to fibre.

The reduction of length of cutting edge transverse to fibre.

The introduction of combined vertical with horizontal cut.

The rounding off the back of cutting edge.

The pressures required in sawing.

Tension compared with thrust.

The angular position of handle.

The resolution of forces operating.

Now may be considered the circumstances which influence the form and position both of the teeth and the edges to be put upon them, in the case of hand-saws operating either by thrust alone, or by thrust and tension combined (as in the 2-handled crosscutting saws used by 2 men, or in the whip and frame saw used in saw pits). Unless specially mentioned the thrust hand-saw for cross-cutting will be the only one considered.

It may be well at the outset to explain that the coarseness and fineness of saws are estimated by the number of teeth points in an inch. The sawmaker uses the term " pitch," but not in the sense as employed in wheels and screws. By pitch he " means the inclination of the face of the teeth up which the shaving ascends." Clearly if the saw is to cut when drawn in both directions, the slope of the teeth from the points must be the same on both sides; indeed, this may be considered the primitive form of saw teeth, and derived as the saw is said to have been from the backbone of a fish, it is the form that would be suggested. To use a saw with such teeth in the most perfect manner would require that the action at each end should be the same; hence, these are the forms of teeth generally met in the ordinary 2-handled saw used for the cross-cutting of timber. The teeth of these saws are generally wide spaced, and the angle included in their point is from 40° to 60°. The forms, however, of teeth, to cut in both directions, are sometimes more varied, especially when the material is not of uniform non-fibrous character. When this equality of tension in both directions cannot be had, and the workman is required to cross-cut the timber by a one-handled saw, it is clear that he must consider the action as that of tension or thrust alone—one of these only. The sole reason why both are not adopted seems to be that were it so, very different muscular motions and postures of the body would be introduced, and probably experience has shown that these are more fatiguing than the alternate pressure and relaxation which takes place in the ordinary process of hand-sawing. Now, if the cut is in the thrust only, then the form of the back of the tooth must be the very reverse of that of the front, for it ought to slide past the wood, because not required to separate the fibres. In this case the back of the tooth may be sloped away, or it may be shaped otherwise. The faces of the teeth are no longer bound to be formed in reference to an equality at the back. Indeed, with the liberty thus accorded, there has arisen an amount of fancy in the forms of teeth, which fancy has developed into prejudice and fashion. Names dependent either upon uses or forms are given to these, and they are distinguished by such names in the trade. Peg tooth, M tooth, half-moon tooth, gullet tooth, briar tooth; also "upright pitch," "flat pitch," "slight pitch." Of these varieties, custom has selected for most general use in England the one in which the face of the tooth is at right angles to the line of the teeth. The backs of the teeth are, therefore, sloped according to the distance between the teeth and the coarseness or fineness of the saw. This is called ordinary, or hand-saw pitch.

A consideration of the action of the saw in cross-cutting timber settles the cutting edge, and so suggests the mode of sharpening. Taking our ordinary cross-cutting single-handed saw as the type, the forward thrust is intended to separate the fibres, and this not in the way of driving a wedge, but in the actual removal of a small piece by two parallel cuts. For example, if ◯ ◯, Fig. 300, be a fibre, then the action of the saw must be to cut clean out the piece a, b, so making a space a, b, wider than the steel of which the saw is made. The cleaner the cuts a d, b c are the better.

Now this clean cut is to be made by the teeth advancing toward the fibre. If they come on in axe fashion, then the separation is accomplished by the direct thrust of a sharp edge, in fact, by a direct wedge-like action. Now a wedge-like action may be the best for separating

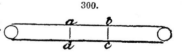

300.

fibre adhering to fibre, but it is an action quite out of place in the cross-cutting of a single fibre, in which cohesion has to be destroyed. There is needed a cutting action, i. e. a drawing of an edge, however sharp, across the mark for separation; this drawing action is very important. Admit for the present that such action is essential, then the saw tooth as constructed does not supply it. Clearly the sharp edge must somehow or other be drawn and pressed as drawn across the fibre. Two ways of accomplishing this present themselves. The effect on the action of the workman is very different in these cases. In the first we must press the saw upon the fibre, and at the same time thrust it lengthwise. Now in soft timber, and with a saw having teeth only moderately sharp, this pressure will tend rather to force the fibres into closer contact, to squeeze them amongst each other, to solidify the timber, and increase the difficulty in cutting. Two actions are here, pressure and thrust. In the second case the pressure must be very light indeed; if otherwise, the point of the tooth will gather up more fibres than the strength of the workman can separate; indeed, as a rule, in the cross-cutting of broad timber, with all the saw teeth in action, pressure is not required, the average weight of the saw-blade sufficing for the picking up of the fibres. It is probably from the delicate and skilful handling which a tooth thus constructed requires, that hand-saws are not more generally constructed with teeth of this form. In addition to these there is the penetrating tooth, as the points of the peg tooth and others. Whatever may be the form of the teeth, the small piece *a b, c d*, Fig. 300, has to be removed so as to leave the ends from which it is taken as smooth and clean cut as possible, therefore the cutting edge must be on the outside of the tooth. This being so, it follows that the act of severing a fibre will be attended with compression whose effect is to shorten it. Thus condensed it is forced up into the space between the teeth. If now this space is not so formed as to allow the condensed piece to drop freely away so soon as the tooth passes from the timber, then the saw will become choked, and its proper action will necessarily cease. In large saws this is provided for in the shape of the "gums" in which the teeth may be said to be set. What in America are called "gums" are frequently in England called "throats." Saws cannot work easily unless as much care is bestowed upon the "throats" or "gums" as is given to the teeth.

Any exhaustive attempt to deal with the considerations which present themselves to one who enters upon the question, what under all the varying conditions of the problems should be the form and set of a saw-tooth, would require more experimental knowledge and patient research than the subject seems to have received. There are more than 100 different forms of teeth. Sheffield and London do not agree upon the shape of the handle. The Eastern hemisphere and the Western do not agree whether sawing should be an act of tension or one of thrust.

The quantity of timber cut down in America must have led to investigations with respect to saws such as the requirements of this country were not likely to call forth. Hence we have very much to learn from the Americans on this point.

As it seems most judicious to investigate the principles by considering a large and heavy tool, perhaps it may be well to examine the largest handicraft saw. This (Fig. 301)

301.

is a "one-man saw" 4 ft. long, by Disston, Philadelphia. Long as the blade is, it is not too long. The travel is near, but still, within the limit of a man's arm. To enter the wood, the teeth at the extreme end are used. These are strong, but of the form generally met with in the largest of our own cross-cut saws. The acting teeth are of an M shape, with a gullet or space between them. The angle at which the teeth are sharpened is very acute; the consequence of this and of their form is, that they cut smoothly as a sharp knife would do; indeed, much as a surgeon's lancet would. Some teeth are formed on the principle of the surgeon's lancet, and these are called "fleam" teeth. The spaces between the M's in the "one-man saw" are "gums" for the reception and removal of the pieces cut out of the separated fibre. In the particular case before us, the M is $\frac{3}{4}$ in broad and $\frac{3}{4}$ in. deep; the upright legs of the M are sharpened from within, the V of the M is sharpened on both sides. The legs are "set" to one side and the V to the other side. Thus arranged, the saw cuts equally in tension and in thrust, and the débris is brought out freely at each end. The M tooth for this double-cutting results from an observation on two carefully-toothed short cross-cut elementary saws, where it will be noticed that the form of tooth to cut both ways, resulting from the combination, is M. The set of this large " one-man saw " is worthy of notice. An inspection of the cutting points will show that each point is diverted from the plane of the saw blades not more than about $\frac{1}{32}$ in. When the object of " set " is considered, it will be allowed that so little is sufficient.

The annexed diagrams (Fig. 302) of teeth of certain cross-cut saws used in America may illustrate the present subject. A single tooth will in some instances be observed between the M teeth: this is a "clearance" tooth, and is generally shorter than the cutting tooth. Sometimes it is hooked, as may be seen in c; in such case it is shorter by $\frac{1}{32}$ in. than the cutting teeth, and acts the part of a plane iron by cutting out the pieces of fibre separated by the other or cutting teeth, which cutting teeth under these circumstances are lancet-like sharpened to very thin edges.

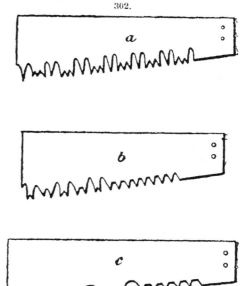

302.

That the " set " of the teeth should be uniform in the length of the saw follows from a moment's reflection upon the object of this set. If one tooth projects beyond the line of the others, that tooth will clearly scratch the wood, and therefore leave a roughness on the plank. As more than its share of work is then allotted to it, the keenness of edge soon leaves it, and thus increases the labour of the sawyer. The American contrivance for securing a uniformity in the set of the teeth is the "side-file." The three set screws determine the elevation of the file above the face, and the travel of the short length of fine cut file reduces all excessive "sets" to a uniform " set " through the entire length of the saw.

The " crotch punch " is also an American contrivance for obtaining a clearance set out of a spreading of the thick steel of the saw by an ingeniously formed angular punch.

It is occasionally required to saw certain cuts to the same depth, as, for instance, in the making of tenons. The saw to which the term " tenon " is applied is more suited for cabinet than for carpenters' work. However, an ordinary saw may be provided with a gauge, which can be adjusted so as to secure a uniform depth in any number of cuts, and in this respect it is even superior to a tenon-saw, and may be suggestive to some whose labours might be facilitated by the adoption of such a contrivance.

The rip-saw considered as a cutting tool, may be likened to a compound chisel, and the form of teeth which would operate with the least application of power would be the same as that of a mortising chisel; but knots and hard wood are conditions which call for rigid teeth, rendering the chisel form impracticable, except for sawing clear lumber, and with a high degree of skill in filing and setting. The limit of endurance of such steel as must be employed for saws, will not admit of pointed teeth; these will break in cutting through knots and hard wood, and no form of saw-teeth which permits their points to crumble and break should be adopted. In actual practice, with the skilled filer, there is a tendency to create pointed saw-teeth, and when there is a want of skill in the filer the tendency is the other way, and teeth unnecessarily blunt are common. " The action of a saw when ripping or cutting with the fibres of the wood is entirely different from that when cross-cutting or severing the fibres of the wood transversely; the shape of the teeth and the method of sharpening should therefore differ. In the case of a rip-saw, the action of the saw is chiefly splitting, the teeth acting like a series of small wedges driven into and separating the longitudinal fibres of the wood; whilst with cross-cutting saws, the fibre of the wood has to be severed across the grain : it is comparatively unyielding, the teeth of the saw meet with much more resistance, and it is found necessary to make the teeth more upright and more acute or lancet-shaped than for cutting with the grain. The faces of the teeth should be sharpened to a keen edge, and for hard wood filed well back, so that in work they may have a direct cutting action, similar to a number of knives. Care should also be taken that the teeth are made of sufficient depth to afford a free clearance for the sawdust. This is an important point too with rip-saws. The teeth should also be equal in length; if not, the longest teeth get the most work, and the cutting power of the saw is much lessened. The length of the teeth should depend on the nature of the wood being sawn : for sawing sappy or fibrous woods, long, sharp, teeth are necessary, arranged with ample throat space for sawdust clearance ; care must be taken, however, that the teeth are not too long, or they will be found to spring and buckle in work. In sawing resinous woods, such as pitch pine, the teeth of the saw should have a considerably coarser set and space than for hard woods. It will also be found advisable—especially with circular saws—to lubricate the blades well, as the resinous matter is thus more easily got rid of. In sawing hard woods, either with reciprocating or circular saws, the feed should be not more than one-half as fast as for soft wood, the saw should contain more teeth, which should be made considerably shorter than those used for soft wood, roughly speaking, about $\frac{1}{4}$; it is impossible, however, to make a fixed rule, owing to the great variety of woods and their different hardnesses; the length of teeth which may be found to suit one wood well may in another case require to be increased or decreased. In cutting woods which are much given to hang and clog the saw-teeth, increment teeth may be used with advantage ; these are arranged with fine teeth at the point of the saw, which gradually get coarser till the heel of the saw is reached ; thus the fine teeth commence the cut and the coarser ones finish it, obviating in a great degree the splintering and tearing of the wood caused by coarse teeth striking the wood at the commencement of the cut. As regards the angles of the teeth best adapted for cutting soft or hard woods no absolute rule can be laid down. The following may be modified according to circumstances. If a line be drawn through the points of the teeth, the angle formed by the face of the tooth with this line should be : For cutting soft woods, about 65°–70° ; for cutting hard wood, about 80°–85°. The angle formed by the face and top of the tooth should be about 45°–50° for soft wood, and 65°–70° for hard. The angle of the tooth found best for cutting soft woods is much more acute than for hard. Terms used in describing the parts of a saw are :—"Space" : the distance from tooth to tooth measured at the points. "Pitch" or "rate" : the angle of the face of the tooth up which the shaving ascends, and not the interval between the teeth, as with the threads of a screw. "Gullet" or "throat" : the depth of the tooth from the point to the root. "Gauge" : the thickness of the saw, generally measured by the wire gauge. "Set" : the amount of inclination given to the saw-teeth in either direction to effect a clearance of the sawdust. "Points" : small teeth are reckoned by the number of teeth points to the inch. The chief facts to be borne in mind in selecting a saw with the teeth best suited to the work in hand are the nature and condition of the wood to be operated on. No fixed rule can, however, be laid down, and the user must be guided by circumstances. All saws should be ground thinner towards the back, as less set is thus necessary, the friction on the blade is reduced, and the clearance for sawdust is improved. Care should also be taken that they are perfectly true and uniform in toothing and temper. The angle of the point of a tooth can be found by subtracting its back angle from its front, and to do the best and cleanest work this angle should be uniform in all the teeth of the saw." (M. Powis Bale, M.I.M.E., A.M.I.C.E.)

The following table includes saws generally used by mechanics who work wood by hand:—

Names.	Length in Inches.	Breadth in Inches.		Thickness in Inches.	Teeth to the Inch.
		At Handle.	At End.		
Without Backs.					
Rip-saw	28–30	7 –9	3 –4	0·05	3½
Fine rip-saw	26–28	6 –8	3 –3½	0·042	4
Hand-saw	22–24	5 –7½	2½–3	0·042	5
Cut-off saw	22–24	5 –7½	2½–3	0·042	6
Panel-saw	20–24	4½–7½	2 –2½	0·042	7
Fine panel-saw	20–24	4 –6	2 –2½	0·035	8
Siding-saw	10–20	2½–3½	1¼–2	0·032	6–12
Table-saw	18–26	1¾–2¼	1 –1½	..	7–8
Compass or lock-saw	8–18	1 –1½	½– ¾	..	8–9
Keyhole or pad-saw	6–12	½– ¾	⅛– ¼	..	9–10
With Backs.					
Tenon-saw	16–20		3¼–4¼	0·032	10
Sash-saw	14–16		2½–3½	0·028	11
Carcass-saw	10–14		2 –3	0·025	12
Dovetail-saw	6–10		1½–2	0·022	14–18

(Holtzapfel.)

Qualities.—Hodgson made a number of experiments on saws to test their qualities and capabilities; and after using them in various ways, fairly and unfairly, he arrived at the following conclusions:—

(1) That a saw with a thick blade is, 9 cases out of 10, of a very inferior quality, and is more apt to break than a thin-bladed saw; it requires more "set," will not stand an edge nearly so long as a thin one, is more difficult to file, and being heavier and cutting a wider kerf, is more tiresome to use.

(2) Saws hung in plain beech handles, with the rivets flush or countersunk, are lighter, easier to handle, less liable to receive injury, occupy less space in the tool chest, and can be placed with other saws without dulling the teeth of the latter by abrasion on the rivets.

(3) Blades that are dark in colour, and that have a clear bell-like ring when struck with the ball of the finger, appear to be made of better stuff than those having a light iron-grey colour; and he noticed, in proof of this, that the thinner the blades were, the darker the colour was, and that saws of this description were less liable to "buckle" or "twist."

(4) American-made saws, as a rule, are better "hung" than English ones. And, where beech is used for handles, and the rivets are flush or countersunk, all other things being equal, the American make is the most desirable.

(5) Polished blades, although mechanics have a strong prejudice against them, cut freer and much easier than blades left in the rough, and they are less liable to rust.

(6) Saws that ring clear and without tremor, when held by the handle in one hand and struck on the point with the other hand and held over at a curve, will be found to be well and securely handled; but saws that tremble or jar in the handle, when struck on the point of the blade, will never give satisfaction.

Selecting.—The following valuable suggestions on the purchasing of saws are given by Disston, the well-known saw-maker of Philadelphia. The first point to be observed in the selection of a hand-saw is to see that it "hangs" right. Grasp it by the handle and hold it in position for working. Then try if the handle fits the hand properly.

These are points of great importance.   A handle ought to be symmetrical, and as handsome as a beautiful picture.   Many handles are made out of green wood; they soon shrink and become loose, the screws standing above the wood.   An unseasoned handle is liable to warp and throw the saw out of truth.   The next thing in order is to try the blade by springing it.   Then see that it bends regular and even from point to butt in proportion as the width of the saw varies.   If the blade be too heavy in comparison to the teeth the saw will never give satisfaction, because it will require twice the labour to use it.   The thinner you can get a stiff saw the better.   It makes less kerf, and takes less muscle to drive it.   A narrow true saw is better than a wide true saw; there is less danger of dragging or creating friction.   You will get a smaller portion of saw-blade, but you will save 100 dollars' worth of muscle and manual labour before the saw is worn out.   Always try a saw before you buy it.   See that it is well set and sharpened, and has a good crowning breast; place it at a distance from you, and get a proper light to strike on it, and you can see if there be any imperfections in grinding or hammering. We set our saws on a stake or small anvil with one blow of a hammer.   This is a severe test, and no tooth ought to break afterwards in setting, nor will it, if the mechanic adopts the proper method.   The saw that is easily filed and set is easily made dull.   We have frequent complaints about hard saws, but they are not as hard as we would make them if we dared; but we shall never be able to introduce a harder saw until the mechanic is educated to a more correct method of setting his saw.   The principal point is that he tries to get part of the set out of the body of the plate when the whole of the set must be got out of the tooth.   As soon as he gets below the root of the tooth to get his set, he distorts and strains the saw-plate.   This will cause a full-tempered cast-steel blade to crack, and the saw will eventually break at this spot.

Grimshaw says that a hand-saw must be springy and elastic, with almost a "Toledo blade" temper.   There is no economy in buying a soft saw; it costs more in a year for files and filing than a hard one does, dulls sooner, drives harder, and does not last so long.   A good hand-saw should spring regularly in proportion to its width and gauge; that is, the point should spring more than the heel, and hence the curve should not be a perfect arc of a circle.   If the blade is too thick for the size of the teeth, the saw will work stiffly.   If the blade is not well, evenly. and smoothly ground, it will drive hard and tend to spring.   The thinner the gauge and narrower the blade, the more need for perfectly uniform and smooth grinding ; the smoother and more uniform the grinding, the thinner and narrower a saw you can use.   The cutting edge is very often made on a convex curve, or with a "crown" or "breast," to adapt it to the natural rocking motion of the hand and arm.   By holding the blade in a good light, and tapping it, you can see if there are imperfections in grinding or hammering.   Before buying a saw. test it on about the same grade of work as it is intended to be put to.   It is a mistake to suppose that a saw which is easily set and filed is the best for use.   Quite the reverse is the case.   A saw that will take a few more minutes and a little harder work to sharpen will keep its edge and set longer than one which can be put in order quickly, and it will work better in knots and hard wood.

Using.—The first thing to be considered is the position of the stuff while being operated upon.   Board or plank should be laid on one or more saw-horses a in either a sloping or flat position, the saw being held more or less nearly vertical, while the workman rests his right knee firmly on the work to secure it.   If the stuff is more than 3 in. thick it should be lined on both sides, and repeatedly turned so that the sawing proceeds from opposite sides alternately; this helps to ensure straight and regular cutting.   The saw is held firmly in the right hand with the forefinger extended against the right side of the handle.   The workman's eyes should look down on both sides of the saw.   As the work progresses, a wooden wedge should be driven into the slit or "saw kerf" b, to allow a free passage for the saw.   Care is needed not to draw the tool too far out of the cut, or the end will be "crippled" by sticking it into the wood when returning it to the

P

cut. Grease should be applied freely to lubricate the teeth. Sometimes the saw-horse is dispensed with and the work is laid on the bench and held down by the hand or by mechanical contrivances, either with the end of the stuff hanging over the end of the bench, or with the edge hanging over the side. The operator can then stand erect at his work and can use one or both hands. Continental workmen often use the rip-saw with the back of the saw towards them; they place the work on saw-horses and commence in the usual way, then turn round and sit on the work and drive the saw before them, using both hands.

For cutting wide tenons, the stuff is first gauged with a mortice gauge (p. 61), and then secured in a bench vice in a more or less vertical position. The saw is first applied in an almost horizontal position, the workman taking care to adhere to the line so that the tenon may have the proper size when done. As soon as the saw has entered the line it is inclined in such a way as to cut down to the bottom of the mark on the side farthest from the operator. When that has been reached, the stuff is reversed, and the saw is worked in an inclined position till the opposite shoulder has been reached. This gives the limit of the cut at each edge, leaving a triangular piece uncut in the middle of the slit, which is finally removed by setting the work and using the saw in an exactly horizontal position. This facilitates working with truth and accuracy to the square. Large work is best done with a rip-saw; small, with a hand- or panel-saw. The left hand seizes the wood to steady the work and the workman. The workman makes a cut with the grain of the wood, which should always be the first half to be performed. When the longitudinal cuts have been made, the cross-cuts or shoulders are made by laying the wood flat on the bench against a stop.

For cross-cutting timber, the hand-saw is commonly used; the teeth are finer than in the rip-saw, and are set a little more to give greater clearance in the kerf, as the tool is more liable to gain when cutting across the fibres of the wood. The saw is held in the right hand, the left hand and left knee being placed on the work to steady it on the saw-horses. The workman must proceed very cautiously towards the end of the cut, and provide some support (generally his left hand) for the piece which is about to be detached, or it will finally break off and perhaps produce long splinters that will render the work useless for its intended purpose. When cross-cutting on the bench, the work rests firmly and flat on the bench, the end to be removed hanging over the side so that it can be held by the left hand. Unless the piece is very heavy, some means must be provided for holding it still during the sawing, or a slight movement may twist and damage the saw.

For sawing work that is slightly curved, a narrow rip-saw must be used, and the kerf must be kept well open by inserting a wedge. In ripping planks or tenons, both hands may be used to advantage in guiding the saw. In all sawing, the tool should be grasped in the right hand, while the left may rest on the material, or may be used to assist in working the saw. In the first few strokes, the length and vigour of the stroke of the saw should be gradually increased, until the blade has made a cut of 2–4 in. in depth, after which the entire force of the arm is employed : the saw is used from point to heel, and in extreme cases the whole force of both arms is used to urge it forward. In most instances, little or no pressure is directed downwards, or on the teeth ; when excessive effort is thus applied, the saw sticks so forcibly into the wood that it refuses to yield to the thrust otherwise than by assuming a curved form, which is apt permanently to distort it. The fingers should never extend beyond the handle, or they may be pinched between it and the work. To acquire a habit of sawing well, the work should, as often as practicable, be placed either exactly horizontal or vertical; the positions of the tool and the movements of the person will then be constant. The top of saw-benches should be level. The edge of the saw should be exactly perpendicular, when seen edgeways, and nearly so when seen sideways : the eye must narrowly watch the path of the saw, to check its first disposition to depart from the line set out for it : look only so far on the right and left of the blade alternately as to be just able to see the line. To correct a small deviation at the commencement, twist the blade as far as the saw kerf will allow; the back being somewhat thinner than the edge, the true line may be thus returned to. Make it a habit to watch the blade so closely as scarcely to require any correction. The saw, if most "set" (having the teeth standing higher) on one side, cuts more freely on that side, and has a tendency to run towards it.

The "table" or "ship-carpenters'" saw has a long narrow blade intended for cutting sweeps of long radius; it is handled similarly to the rip-saw. The "compass" saw with its long (12 in.) and narrow (tapering from $\frac{1}{8}$ in. to $1\frac{1}{4}$ in.) blade generally resembles the hand-saw; in use it is apt to buckle and snap in short curves, unless it is filed so as to cut by a pulling motion instead of with a thrust. The "pad" or "socket" saw is a more diminutive form of the preceding, made to slide into a hollow handle, where it is held by screws, only so much of the blade being drawn out as is required; it should be filed for the pulling stroke. The "web" or "bow" saw is a narrow ribbon-saw fastened in a frame; it has very fine teeth, adapted for cutting both with and across the grain; the chief use is for fretwork, the blades being made to twist round to suit the work. "Back" saws are of several kinds, all characterised by deep thin blades: the "dovetail" is the thinnest, and simple filing usually gives it sufficient set; great care is necessary with it to prevent buckling and kinking, a twist of the hand sufficing to ruin it. "Tenon" and "sash" saws being somewhat thicker require a little set. All back-saws need to be kept well oiled and polished, and are best used in a mitre-box (p. 62) or other guide rest; they should be held firmly when in use, but with the least possible force exerted in controlling their direction; the cut should be commenced by placing the heel (handle end of the blade) of the saw on the farthest edge of the work and drawing it towards the body of the operator (Hodgson).

This tool, it must be remembered, in forming its saw kerf, removes, in the shape of sawdust, a solid bit of the material, which is thereby channelled as much as if the kerf had been formed by a very narrow iron fitted in a grooving plane. This is practically ignored by many amateurs, who carefully saw to line, and remove that line in doing so, and then find that the piece is cut too small. Of course, the wider the saw is set, the broader is the piece removed. A great many apparently unaccountable misfits are due to this error, which accounts also for the absence of squareness in framed work—for *all* the marked lines are seldom thus effaced. Casting the eye along a saw of which the teeth are turned upwards, this tool will be seen to contain an angular groove caused by the alternate bending outwards of its teeth. These, if properly filed, present also, taken together, 2 knife-like edges *d e* (Fig. 303), which are very keen, and form the outside limits of the saw kerf: one of these edges, therefore, right or left, as the case may be, must just touch the ruled line upon the work, but must not encroach upon it. The result will be a clean true cut if the saw be in good order; but one tooth having too much set (projecting beyond the general line) will spoil it. Thus, in Fig. 303, *b c* are the limits of the intended kerf, of which the darker line *b* is the guide line to be left on the work; but the tooth which stands out too far reaches to the line *a* and quite effaces *b*.

Filing and Setting.—These subjects have been so ably discussed in such works as Grimshaw on 'Saw Filing'; Holly on the 'Art of Saw Filing'; and Hodgson on Hand Saws,' that it is difficult to attack them without in some measure traversing the same ground.

A saw tooth consists of 4 parts—face, point, back, and gullet or throat. Teeth vary in spacing, length, angle, rake, set, fleam, and form of gullet. A saw blade may contain several kinds of teeth in succession; but all teeth of a kind must be either quite uniform or arranged in a regular order of change.

The ordinary spacing of saw teeth is as follows : Hand-saws, 5-12 points in an inch; rip, 3-5 at the heel and 6-8 at the point; panel. 8-12 ; tenon, 11-15 ; mitre, 10-11 ; band-saw teeth should have a tooth space equal to ½ the width of the blade for soft wood, and ⅓ for hard, while the depth of the tooth in each case should be ⅕ the width of the blade.

The length of tooth is governed by the hardness of the wood, the longest teeth being best adapted for wet, fibrous, and soft woods, as giving greater clearance ; but more care is needed in having a moderate and regular set.

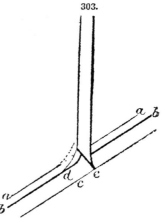

303.

The angle of saw teeth may vary between about 60° and 40°. The fundamental angle is 60°. This may be in the form of an equilateral triangle for hard and knotty wood, but for soft wood it is better that all the pitch should be on the cutting face,—an upright edge with sloping back. For varied work the usual angle is 40°, the pitch being equally divided. Teeth of any angle but 60° are not so readily filed with an ordinary file.

The degree of rake may increase in proportion to the softness of the wood ; in hard woods it causes a tendency to spring in. It may also be greater in a circular saw on account of its greater speed. Fig. 304 (from Grimshaw) shows various degrees of rake, the arrows indicating the direction of the strain.

The set of a tooth may be either " spring " (bent) or " swaged " (spread). The former cut only on one side, have more tendency to spring in, and are more subject to side strains : the latter cut on both sides, unless they are sheared, and they are less liable to spring in and suffer from side strains. The more gummy the wood, the greater set is needed. Circular saws require more set than straight ones.

The fleam or side angle of the teeth varies from 80° or 90° horizontally for hard

304.

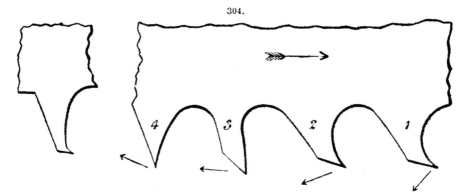

woods, to 60° or 70° horizontally and 30° or 35° vertically for soft. It is most effective in the case of soft woods free from knots ; and should not accompany a bent set, as both tend to aggravate the tendency to spring in.

The gullet or throat should always be rounding and never square, as the latter condition gives a tendency to crack. Fig. 305 (modified from Grimshaw) shows when the gullet requires deepening, by a process known as " gumming." The tooth a is in perfect order ; b is still capable of doing good work ; but c demands gumming. The higher the speed and the faster the feed, the greater the necessity for rounding the gullet, especially in band-saws. Spaulding's rule for finding the amount of gullet in sq. in. per tooth for circular saws is to double the number of cub. in. of wood removed at one revolution, and divide by the number of teeth. Insufficient gullet causes choking, heating, and uneven running.

The depth, fleam, hook, and rake of teeth may increase in direct proportion to the softness of the wood ; the spacing and depth of gullet should be augmented for fibrous and porous wood ; thin blade and slight set are desirable for costly wood ; a thick blade is demanded for hard wood.

The operations entailed in keeping a saw in working order are threefold—filing, setting, and gumming. These will be described in succession.

First of filing. It is a great deal easier to keep a saw sharp by frequent light file-touches, than to let it get so dull as to need a long-continued filing down, after it gets so

305.

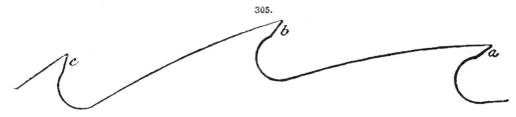

dulled as to refuse to work. The saving in power, by using a sharp saw, is very great. Thinner blades may be used than where the teeth are dull ; because the duller the saw, the more power required to drive it through the wood, and the more strain on each tooth separately, and on the blade as a whole. For the same reason, longer teeth may be used where they are sharp, than where they are dull. The advantage of using sharp teeth is greatest in those saws in which the strain of cutting tends to deform the blade—as in all "push-cut" straight saws and in circulars. (Grimshaw.)

The saw, secured in a proper clamp, should be placed where a strong light will fall on the teeth, so that the filer can have the full advantage of all the light he requires. Should there be a deficiency of light, the filer should provide a good lamp, and place a dark shade between the light and his eyes, so that he can see at a glance when every tooth is filed to a complete point. One careless thrust of the file, when a tooth is filed enough, will do a saw more harm than can be repaired by $\frac{1}{2}$ hour's filing. A beginner should always take a try-square and the sharp point of a small file, and make a hair-mark from the point of every tooth at a right angle with the teeth on the sides of the blade. This should be done when the points of the teeth are all at a uniform distance apart. Such marks will enable the filer to keep the face of every tooth dressed at the most desirable angle. These directions, however, are only applicable to saws intended for cross-cutting. Beginners must always exercise un-usual care when filing the back of each tooth that has been finished. After the teeth are filed to complete points, it is an excellent practice to go over them carefully with a half worn-out file, for the purpose of bringing the points to a more perfect cutting edge. (Hodgson.)

Both hand filing and machine filing have their advocates. The former is generally more convenient, and may be rendered sufficiently regular by means of guides. The latter gives greater speed and regularity at less cost.

For hand filing, reference has already (p. 68) been made to a clamp for holding the saw. A very old and convenient form is shown in Fig. 306, and consists merely of 2 strips of wood (which may be pine, but hard wood is better), about 3 in. wide and $\frac{7}{8}$–$1\frac{1}{4}$ in. thick, joined laterally by a wooden screw passing through both at one end, and having their upper outside edges chamfered off. The toothed edge of the saw stands sufficiently high above the clamp to allow the saw to be used in a slanting direction without coming into contact with the clamp. Another form consists of an A-shaped horse, whose standards are hinged together along the top, where the saw is placed and held fast by putting the foot down firmly on the cross bars supporting the legs of the horse. Other forms have been already described under Holding tools. Much of the noise produced in saw filing may be remedied by having a layer of leather, rubber, or a few folds of paper between the saw blade and the jaws of the clamp. There must be no shake or jar in the saw while under operation, or the teeth of the file will be damaged.

To put a saw in order, the first thing to be done is to joint the tops of the teeth, or render them uniform in length. This is termed "top-jointing" in straight saws and "rounding" in circular saws To carry it out, Hodgson recommends the following cheap and expeditious plan. Procure a block of wood, say 6 in. long, 3 in. wide, 1 in. thick, dressed straight and true, then nail a similar piece on one edge, thus forming a corner in which to place a file. The file can then be held with the fingers, or be secured in various ways. Place the file flatly on the teeth, and press the larger block against the side of the saw blade, then file off the points of the longest teeth until the file just touches the extremities of the

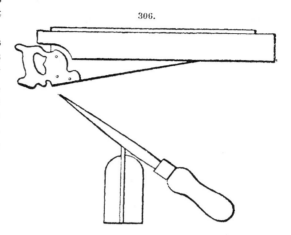

306.

short teeth. It is important that the file be held in such a position that it will take off the points exactly at right angles with the blade, otherwise the teeth will be longer on one side than the other, which will cause the saw to deviate or "run" more or less. Grimshaw remarks that the operation is generally performed with a flat or "mill" file, although it may be done with a plane emery rubber or a whetstone. "Side-jointing" is the term applied to a process for correcting irregularity in the set, or preventing undue side projection of any tooth; each tooth is thus made to do only its fair share of the work, and scratching or ridging of the sawn surface is avoided. It is most effective on swaged eeth, and is performed by a side file set in an adjustable clamp as shown in Fig. 307.

Very useful adjuncts to inexperienced workmen are the so-called filing guides, which determine the angle of contact and degree of force with which the file is applied. Fig. 308 shows a simple form, easily worked, and adapted to both straight and circular

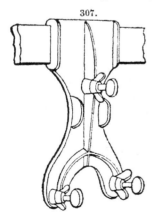

307.

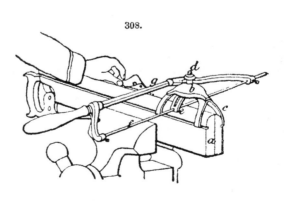

308.

saws. The saw is held in the clamp a. On the guide is a circular plate b graduated to a scale for setting the file to a bevel for either side or square across the saw. Legs c extend from the plate over the clamp into grooves in the sides of the clamp. On the nether side of the plate b are a number of grooves corresponding to the scale on the edge, and into which a raised rib on the arched piece e mashes, and is held in place by the thumb-screw d on the top of the plate. Through the ends of the arched piece e slides a rod f, to which are secured by screws the arms that carry the file g. By loosening the thumb-screw d, the file is readily changed to any desired bevel, and the handle of the tool may be lowered. When the file is set to the required bevel it is secured by tightening the thumb-screw d, and its pitch is regulated by a set-screw in the socket of the arm at the handle. During the operation of filing, the rod f governs the pitch and bevel, so that every tooth is equally filed. The machine is adapted for full, hollow, straight-edged, or circular saws. A table is issued with the machine, giving the correct bevels and pitches for the various kinds of saw to be filed.

Fig. 309 shows the Amesbury band-saw filing machine, fastened to an ordinary bench. The file is in 2 sections, one stationary, the other movable in the direction of the axis; the stationary section carries the feeders and a thin segmental file, which files only the gullets and faces of the teeth; the movable section carries a thick bevelled file with varying grades of teeth, rotating in a higher plane, and destined to file the backs and take the burr from the points. The thumb-screw a varies the height of this section to suit the grade of teeth and to change the pressure. The thin face and throat file is cut only on its face and corner. The filing head runs in an oblong bearing, so that it can move to allow for high teeth. An adjustable pressure spring b holds it to the work, and another spring under the head keeps it to the tooth-face, thus giving the high teeth the most pressure, and bringing them down to the general bevel. The saw is held in a clamping-jaw, with the back resting against the gauge c, which is adjustable to any saw width by the screw d, and can be set at any angle. The clamping-jaw is operated by a cam on the hub of the gear, and opens and closes as the machine is feeding or filing. This jaw acts like a vice upon the saw when the files are in contact with the teeth, and releases it when in contact with the feeder. The filer will work on saws from $\frac{1}{16}$ in. to 2 in. in width, and having 2–20 teeth to the inch.

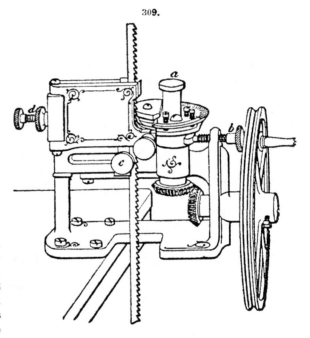

309.

Elkin's patent saw sharpener, Fig. 310, enables any person to accurately and quickly sharpen any straight saw, including rip, cross-cut, buck, band, jig, &c. It is a combination of clamps and adjustable guides, by means of which the saw can be firmly clamped and correctly sharpened. The adjustable guides can be so marked as to give the tooth the same bevel, pitch, and elevation. The machine is simple, strong, and durable in construction, being made from the best iron and steel. It only occupies a space in inches of 16 × 3 × 3. For use, secure it to a bench with 2 screws, place the saw in the clamp, with the teeth just above the face or upper part of the jaws—the handle to the right. The rod, upon which the travelling plate slides as each tooth is filed, can be secured at any desired elevation by means of the thumb-nuts at the ends. Having obtained the elevation, the file is brought across the saw at an angle corresponding with the bevel of the tooth, and there made fast by turning the thumb-screw beneath the travelling plate

In order to get the correct pitch of the tooth, the loose bushing, through which the file carrier passes, must be perfectly free, and by pressing the file down between the teeth, you have the pitch. This bushing is held in its proper position by a set screw. Always file from the handle toward the point of the saw, and never press down upon the file when it is being drawn back. Having filed one side of the saw, it should then be reversed with the handle at the left. Then swing the handle of the file to the left,

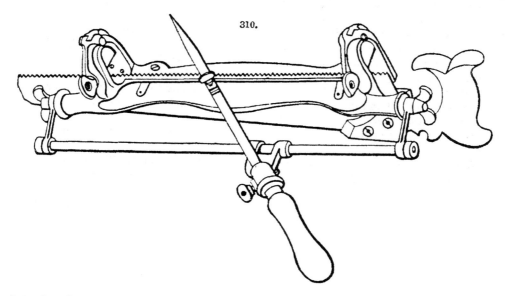

310.

bringing the file across the saw to the correct bevel. The pitch of the tooth is again to be obtained as before. The price, including 1 file, is 20s.

The files employed for sharpening saws include flat ("mill"), triangular, round (for gulleting), and special shapes, varying of course in size and in grade of cut. The width of the file should always be double the width of the surface to be filed. Preference is given to files in which the grade of the cut (distance between the teeth) increases progressively from point to heel; with this exception, hand-cut files are esteemed superior to machine-cut. For small teeth set at 60° it is convenient to use a file which will sharpen the back of one tooth and face of the next at the same time. "Float" or single-cut files are the best. Double-tapered triangular files are not to be recommended; when used, they should have a button at the point end. Files for band-saws are made with rounded angles to suit the gullets of the teeth. Order and regularity in filing are essential. Common rules for filing are: (1) File the faces before the backs; (2) if the teeth are to be square, file in regular succession—1, 2, 3, 4; (3) if they are to have fleam, file 1, 3, 5, 7 to right, and 2, 4, 6, 8 to left; (4) file the fronts of all teeth set from you, and the backs of those set towards you. (Grimshaw.)

In sharpening saws by means of emery wheels, the speed of the wheel has great influence on the cutting action. The coarseness or fineness of the grit composing the wheel must be suited to the nature of the work. The average speed of periphery adapted for most purposes is 4500–6000 ft. per minute, the slower speed being for wheels of 12 in. diam. and less. These wheels are only employed satisfactorily on large circular saws.

Setting, whether of the bent or spread kind, is performed both by simple hand-tools, and by more modern and complicated appliances.

(a) In bent setting by blows, the saw is laid nearly flat with its teeth along the ridge of a round-edged anvil held in a vice, of varying curve to produce an angle suited to the character of the saw, or the saw blade is gripped in a horizontal vice close to the ends of the teeth. Alternate teeth are then struck in a most careful and uniform manner with a peculiar hammer, the object of the blow being to bend every tooth in exactly the same degree sideways. When half the teeth have been so treated, the saw is reversed, and the second half are similarly served, only in the opposite direction. There is a risk of giving either too short or too long set: the former results in bending the tooth too sharply near the point, while the latter requires greater expenditure of force. Over-setting may be corrected by slight blows in the opposite direction. A very simple apparatus for bent setting may be made as shown in Fig. 311. It consists of a wooden framework *a*, carrying at the base a movable steel anvil *b*, each of whose 8 edges may be chamfered to a different bevel. The framework also supports a steel punch *c* free to slide up and down; the end of the punch is bevelled, the angle corresponding (there are 8 punches) to the angle of the side of the anvil to be used, which varies with the kind of saw required to be set. To set the saw, it is laid on the anvil with the teeth overhanging the bevel desired and under the line of fall of the punch, which latter is applied to alternate teeth in succession by striking it with a hammer. The advantage of the apparatus is that the amount of set given to each tooth must agree with the bevel of the punch and anvil.

(*b*) Bent setting is perhaps more commonly effected by leverage. The simplest form is a notch cut in the end of a file, which is applied to each tooth in order, and the requisite set is given by a turn of the wrist. Fig. 312 shows a handsaw-set with 6 different gauges to suit the thickness of the saw blade; and Fig. 313 is an improved set

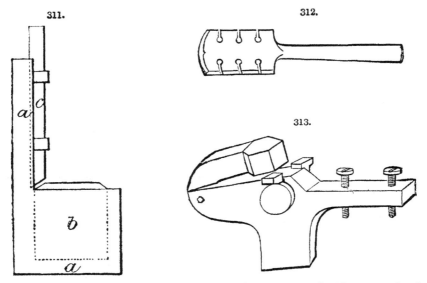

311.   312.

313.

for fastening to a bench. In using these tools, the saw must first be securely clamped. For bent-setting band and circular saws by leverage, special machines are necessary, of which there are several forms in the market. Goodell and Waters, Philadelphia, make a band-saw set suited to saws $\frac{1}{8}$ in. to 2 in. wide, holding the saw in a rigid position and setting the teeth without straining the blade. It works by an easy, uniform crank motion, and when the tooth to be set is fed into position, the blade is firmly locked between the steel jaws of a vice, and remains immovable while the tooth is set to any degree required. As the crank goes forward, the blade is released, when the next tooth is fed up to the dies, the blade again locked in vice, and this tooth set in the opposite direction. All these movements are automatic, and can be carried on at a speed of 300 teeth per minute. The feeder picks up only the tooth that is to be set, consequently each tooth is fed to its proper position, regardless of their irregularity. The band-saw is simply hung up over the machine on a wooden bracket, and the lower part left pendent near the floor.

(c) Spread setting is generally performed by "crotch punches" or "upset dies" having suitable outline and faces, applied to the tooth-point by sharp blows from a hammer. There should be 2 notches, one for spreading the tooth-point and the other for regulating the side play and making the cutting edge concave when necessary. Care should be taken to always leave sufficient metal behind the corners of the saw teeth, or they will break off. The accompanying illustrations, reduced from Grimshaw, represent the edges of teeth when "swaged" or "upset." In Fig. 314, *a* is the best attainable in practice; *b* has extremely weak corners. In forming the swage, the tool should be held so as to deliver the blow in a straight line with the face of the tooth, otherwise cracks may be started in the gullet, especially in frosty weather.

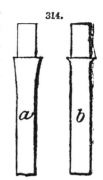

Many appliances for bending and spreading teeth are described in Grimshaw's large work on 'Saws.' The crotch-punch of ordinary form is shown in Fig. 315. It is made of steel and case-hardened in the fork, where it comes into contact with the points of the saw

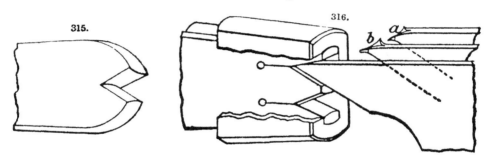

teeth. There is much difficulty in making crotch-punches of a satisfactory character, as the tempering has to be extremely hard just for the jaws, while if it runs back too far they have a tendency to split. They should be fitted with a side guard to prevent the operator's hand being injured by the punch slipping off a tooth. This guide may be made to serve also as a means of keeping the punch central or of giving it an inclination to either side. Crotch-punches have been introduced which are claimed to act on the teeth behind the cutting edge as well as at the edge, spreading the teeth without reducing their length and consequently the diameter of the saw (circular). Fig. 316 is a diagram of the end of the punch with part of the covering sleeve removed to show the form. If a

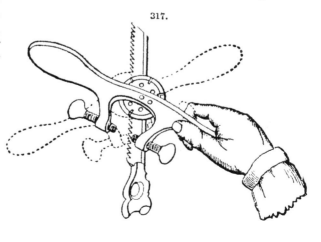

tooth is struck with the convex-sided lower angle, the resulting tooth is as shown at *a*; a second blow with the upper angle produces the flattened and double set tooth *b*.

Disston's revolving saw set is shown in Fig. 317. Its price is 1s. 6d. or 2s., according

to size.   Among the advantages claimed for this useful little tool are the following :—
it is portable, simple, effectual, and cheap ; it can be readily adjusted to any size tooth.
from a 14-point back-saw to a 4-point rip-saw.   The tooth in front of the one being set
forms a guide for the tool, and the operator can readily and with certainty slide the set
from tooth to tooth.   The different bevels on the disc are in accord with the different
slots for the various-sized teeth.   The screws on each side determine the amount of set.
The implement is sold by Churchills.

Trickett's lever saw set, sold by Melhuish, at 2*s.* 6*d.*, is represented in Fig. 318.

318.

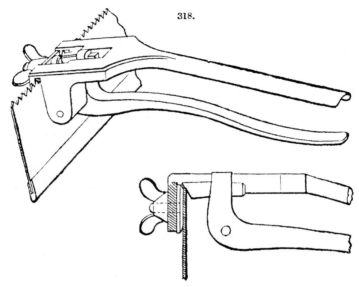

For use, place the set on the saw as indicated, holding it in the right hand ; place the
punch in line to tooth requiring to be set, then grasp the lever and handle together ;
the punch in lever forces the saw tooth over on the bevelled head of the bolt, and the
tooth is set.

Morrill's saw sets for hand, band, scroll, cross-cut, circular, and mill saws, are sold by

319.

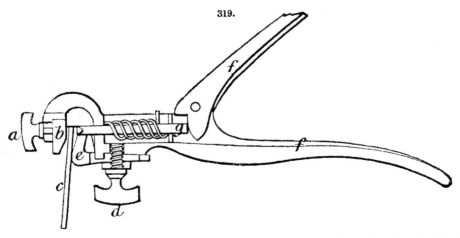

Churchills at prices ranging from 3*s.* 8*d.* to 16*s.*   Fig. 319 illustrates the application
of the implement.   Hold the saw on any level place, teeth upwards.   Place the set on
the saw as shown.   The anvil *b* is movable up and down, and must be regulated to suit

the distance that the operator desires to set his saw teeth down from their points. Care must be taken not to have the angle or the point where the bend is made below the base of the tooth. The nut or screw *a* fastens the anvil in any desired position. The guard *e*, when moved forward, increases the amount of set to be given; when moved back, decreases it. The guard is made fast by the screw *d*. The set is operated by compressing the handles *f*, which carries the plunger *g* forward, and takes effect on the tooth of the saw *c*, as shown. Great care should be taken against setting saws too wide, as, with too much latitude, they will chatter and tear rather than cut, at a great cost of power and waste of lumber. All saws should be set or pressed into line 3 times to 1 filing, as by constant use the teeth wear off on the outside at their points, causing them to heat and spring out of true, thus spoiling the saws, burning the wood, consuming power, and retarding the work, besides rendering it dangerous to the operator.

A spring set with a slightly shearing tooth performs its cutting in the easiest manner, but as only the corners of the teeth operate, twice as many teeth are required to do the same amount of work in a spring set saw as in a fully swaged one; the latter is generally preferred as being more easily kept in order. In bent setting, care must be taken that it is only the tooth and not the plate of the saw that is operated upon, or there is a risk of distorting or cracking the blade.

Gumming consists in deepening the throat or gullet of a saw, and is effected by means of punches, or preferably by rotating steel cutters or emery wheels. Too often the gumming is neglected, more of the face of the tooth being filed away instead, thus reducing the diameter of the saws and causing waste. Grimshaw illustrates several efficient machines for gumming.

According to Duncan Paret, the simplest method by which solid emery wheels can be applied for saw gumming is by placing them on the spindle of the circular saw. The saw to be gummed can then be laid on the saw table, or supported in any convenient way. A simple way is to pass the end of a rope with a small cross stick on it through the eye of the saw, and thus suspend the saw so that it swings evenly balanced just in front of the emery wheel. The weight being thus carried, the operator only has to use his hands to guide the saw against the wheel. Where expensive machinery is scanty, and where people are slow to introduce the latest improvements, there is a steady demand for saw-gumming wheels 14-24 in. in diameter. Where the latest improvements are quickly added, regardless of price, nearly all the emery wheels used for saw gumming are 12-8 in., none of the machines specially designed for saw gumming being intended to carry anything above a 12-in. wheel. Emery wheels are unfavourably contrasted with grindstones as causing a heating of the saw, but this can be obviated by using the wheel under a small constant stream of water. One advantage of a rotating steel-cutter gummer over an emery wheel is that, whereas an inexperienced hand can ruin a saw by case-hardening with an emery wheel, this cannot be done with a steel cutter or "burr gummer." Most of the emery gummers for circulars require that the saw shall be taken off its arbor to be gummed; all burr gummers work with the saw in position. (Grimshaw.)

The order followed in renovating the cutting edge of a saw should be (1) gumming, (2) setting, (3) filing; but as the last named is often the only kind of attention the saw receives, it has been described first.

Having discussed the general principles on which the renovation of saw teeth is based, and detailed the manner in which the operation is conducted, a few illustrated examples may be given of the teeth of the chief kinds of saw in use (see Fig. 320).

(1) Cross-cut saws (hand) vary from 12 to 32 in. in length. Their tooth edge should be straight or a trifle bulged in the middle. The teeth should be fully set and well-jointed. *a* (Fig. 320) shows the best tooth for soft wood; *b* is better adapted for wood of medium hardness and for mitreing soft wood; *c*, for harder wood, has the back of the teeth filed square. For cutting timber, the teeth are made much larger, but resemble

those in *b*, the set being increased with the wetness of the wood. The long cross-cut for 2 men is toothed as at *i* (Fig. 320), the cutting edge of the saw being appreciably highest in the middle and gradually tapering towards each end; the bevel shown is adapted to soft or wet wood, and must be lessened for harder or drier material. *k* represents an American hook tooth, which is based on the principle that the while the fleam teeth or knives cut into the wood, the hook teeth remove the "dust." These saws work easily and cut rapidly. The rake of a cross-cut saw is at the side. It takes less

320.

inclination than the cross-cut. The cross-cut requires finer and more particular filing than the rip or web saw, and cannot be considered well filed unless a needle will travel down the angular groove which is formed by the line of alternating points of teeth seen in all well-filed saws. When the teeth are so regularly formed that a needle will travel from end to end in the angular groove, and the points are sharp and keen, the saw will cut a kerf in the wood that will have a flat bottom. The last teeth of cross-cuts may be rounded at the points, to prevent tearing the wood when entering and leaving the cut.

(2) Back-saws are shown at *d* and *e* (Fig. 320); the former suits soft wood, while

the latter is for harder wood and for mitreing. The thinness of the blade of the back-saw is compensated for by the extra back, which must be kept tightly in place.

(3) The fleam tooth is illustrated at f (Fig. 320). It is only adapted for very clean soft wood, which it cuts rapidly and smoothly. It has no set, and is filed while lying quite flat.

(4) Buck-saws are represented at g and h (Fig. 320), the former being for wet or soft wood, and the latter for dry or hard.

(5) Web, scroll, and compass saws are best provided with teeth as shown at l (Fig. 320), for whilst they have to perform both ripping and cross-cutting, a tooth adapted for the latter will perform the former operation, though more slowly, but the converse rule does not hold good. Finer teeth will be necessary for hard wood. The backs of all saws of this class are made very thin, to avoid the necessity for giving a set to the teeth.

(6) The rip-saw, for cutting wood longitudinally, requires an essentially different tooth from the cross-cut. For a vertical mill-saw, the best form of tooth is that shown at m (Fig. 320), the edge of each tooth being spread out by means of the crotch-punch. An inferior-shaped tooth is seen at n, the setting being on one side of the tooth only, taking opposite sides in succession. o illustrates the best form of tooth for a hand rip-saw, the action being precisely like that of a mortice chisel. The rake of a rip-saw is in front. It takes more inclination than a cross-cut. The points of the teeth should be trued with a straight-edge, as, in general experience, a rip-saw does more work, with greater ease, straight, than when either rounding or hollow on the cutting edge; some good workmen, however, prefer rip-saws slightly hollow, not more than $\frac{1}{4}$ in. in the length of the blade. The hand rip-saw is usually a few inches longer than the cross-cut, but has far fewer teeth. Rip-saws are often given too little rake and gullet. The first 6 or 8 in. at the point of a hand rip-saw may have cross-cut pitch, to allow of cutting through knots without having to change the saw for a cross-cut.

(7) Circular-saw teeth generally have greater space, angle, and set than the teeth of straight saws. They should be filed on the under side; widely spaced, very hooking, and with plenty of gullet to let out the chips. Teeth of circular saws can be gauged to exact shape by having a piece of sheet steel cut out to fit. Absolute likeness in all respects can be controlled by having a piece of sheet metal cut to the required outline and attached to an arm forming a radius of a circle from the shaft carrying the saw. Three light filings are preferable to one heavy. The shape of under-cut teeth is apt to be altered in filing. The flaring sides of M teeth require special files. When a tooth is broken so as to be only slightly short, it can often be brought out to line by using the crotch-swage as a lever while hammering upon it. The saw should always be allowed to run free for a few minutes before removing it from the shaft. Circular saws should always be either hung up in a free perpendicular position, or laid quite flat. Fig. 321 shows a series of circular-saw teeth of varying shape and rake. The softer the wood, the greater rake admissible. In some cases (b, c) the back rake tends to reduce the acuteness. e is recommended for ripping hard wood in winter; c, for hard wood in summer; g, for all kinds of wood in summer; b, c, for harder woods than when no back rake is given; f, with a rounded gullet, 2 in. long for soft wood, $1\frac{3}{4}$ in. for hard; h, i, j, k, n, are forms of ripping teeth little used in soft wood; l is popular in Europe; m is a cross-cutting tooth, very liable to break on a knot in frosty weather. The question of few or many teeth in a circular rip-saw depends almost entirely upon the character of timber being ripped; and the feed per revolution should be made dependent upon the strength of the teeth to resist breaking, and the capacity of the gullet to hold the cuttings. In a cross-cut, the conditions are different. To straighten a circular saw, get a hard-wood block 12 in. by 12 in.; bed it on end on the ground (not floor); round the top off with $\frac{1}{4}$ in. rise; nail up a joist at the back of the block, for the saw to rest on; let its face be an inch below the top of the block. Use a 3 or 4 lb. blacksmiths' hammer for saws over 50 inches, a lighter one for smaller and thinner blades. For large saws, the

straight edge should be about $\frac{1}{16}$ in. thick, 20 in. long, $3\frac{1}{2}$ in. wide in centre, 1 in. at end; the edge of the straight side chamfered or rounded off. Balance the saw on a mandrel, and apply the straight-edge; mark the high places with chalk; have a helper to hold the saw on the block, and hammer on the humps, testing frequently. (Grimshaw.)

When a saw is not round, the defect may be corrected by adopting the following directions: Take a piece of grindstone or a cobblestone and hold it against the points of the teeth while the saw is revolving, and thus reduce or wear down the most prominent

321.

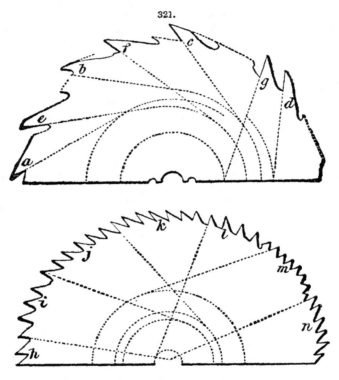

teeth; or a piece of red chalk may be held against the points, which will mark them in proportion as they are long or short, when the long teeth are reduced by filing. Circular saws sometimes burst from what appear as unknown causes. There can be no doubt when a saw does fly in pieces that a thorough investigation would trace the occurrence to one of the following causes: (1) Square corners at bottom of tooth; (2) Out of round, with the backs higher than the points, so that instead of cutting, they scrape the dust off with the back; (3) Undue strain put upon the saw by the plate rubbing against the timber, causing it to heat, which takes the life out of a saw. In a recent report of the French Society for Preventing Accidents from Machines, a recommendation is made for the avoidance of the use of circular saws in workshops where practicable. The following are the reasons for this recommendation: (1) Circular saws are dangerous to workmen; (2) they require more power than other saws; (3) they cut a broader line, and are consequently more wasteful. The speed of circular saws varies with the size, approximately as follows:—8 in. diam., 4500 rev. per minute; 12 in., 3000; 16 in., 2200; 20 in., 1800. The speed for cross-cutting can be increased with advantage 1000 ft. beyond those used for ripping, say to 10,000 ft. per minute. Never cut stuff that measures more than $\frac{1}{3}$ the diameter of the saw. The manner in which a circular saw is hammered has much to do with the speed at which it can be run, and often when a saw becomes limber and "runs," it is the fault of the hammering instead of the speed. When slack on the periphery, it will not stand speed, and becomes weaker and bends more readily when in motion than when it is still; on the contrary, if it is properly hammered, a little tight, as it is termed, on the periphery, it becomes more rigid when in motion up to a certain limit. The theory of this is that the steel is elastic, and is stretched by the centrifugal strain in proportion to the speed, which is greatest on the line of teeth, and diminishes to the centre. If saws evince a tendency to spring and a want of rigidity, have them rehammered at once, before changing the speed in an endeavour to remedy the defect.

(8) The band-saw is never used for cross-cutting, except when cutting scroll-work, and may generally be treated as a rip-saw. It requires special regularity in shape and set of teeth to prevent it from breaking and from running into the work. In order to set it up, or join the 2 ends together, the 2 tongues are introduced simultaneously into the 2 corresponding openings, and the ends of the saw are pressed together laterally in such a manner as to cause the snugs on the tongues to engage with or hook on to the bevelled edges in the openings, and the thin ends of the tongues then lie in the inclined recesses in the sides of the saw. When the parts are in this position, the 2 extremities of the saw cannot be separated either by a considerable strain in the direction of its length or by a diminution of the tension. To disconnect the ends of the saw, separate the hooked and bevelled edges by applying lateral pressure, and at the same time draw the ends apart in opposite directions. The junction of the 2 extremities is effected by means of a hook or interlocking joint. A portion of the saw near each extremity is reduced in thickness in such a manner that, when the ends are laid together, the two combined do not exceed the thickness of the remaining part of the saw. Portions of the back and front of the extreme ends are also cut away, so as to leave narrow tongues at each extremity of the saw, and these tongues are provided on opposite sides relatively to each other with snugs or hooks. In the thin portions at the extremities of the saw there are formed, at equal distances from the tongues, 2 longitudinal slits or openings, presenting bevelled or inclined surfaces at the edges nearest the ends of the saw, corresponding exactly to the snugs on the tongues. The opposite edge of each opening is also bevelled or inclined, but at a much more acute angle, so as to form a recess in the side of the saw for the reception of the extreme end of the corresponding tongue, which is suitably reduced in thickness towards the extremity, in order to enable it to be well within the said recess. Where gas is used for lighting purposes, it is often employed for brazing band-saws, and nearly in every case where this is done, the blade of the saw operated upon deteriorates, and breakages gradually increase. As these breakages do not occur exactly at the joint, no blame is attached to the use of gas, and the cause of continual failures is rarely discovered. A gas flame not only scales steel deeply, but also destroys its nature by burning the carbon out, and this occurs especially at the edge of the flame. Band-saws brazed by gas almost invariably break again at a point some little distance from the previous fracture, at the point where the outer edge of the flame has damaged the metal. The only really satisfactory way of repairing is to make a thick, heavy pair of tongs bright red-hot, and clamp the joint with them. The heat melts the spelter instantly, and makes a good joint without scaling or damaging the steel.

For a joint which has to stand constant heavy strains and bending, it is better to use an alloy of equal parts of coin-silver and copper, melted together and rolled out thin. This alloy never burns, cannot be overheated, and makes first-rate joints, which will stand hammering and bending to almost any extent. The working action of a band-saw is, generally speaking, similar to the working action of a circular saw,—continuous. "Owing chiefly to the thinness of the gauge, the small area of the blade which operates on the wood at one time, and the constant cooling action which is going on, as the saw passes through the air, a comparatively small amount of heat is engendered:

the saw therefore can be run at a considerable speed without detriment. On machines in which the saw-wheels are of small diameter, say below 36 in., and where the arc of contact of the saw on the wheels is necessarily more acute, the speed of the saw-blade should not much exceed 4500 ft. per minute for all ordinary kinds of sawing. With saw-wheels above 36 in. diameter, this speed may safely be increased up to 6000 ft. per minute; this is, however, on the supposition that the top wheel is of the lightest construction, and is mounted elastically, i.e. has a spring or other adjustment to allow for the expansion and contraction of the saw-blade. There is no advantage in running band-saws beyond 6000 ft. per minute, as the risk of breakage is increased without affording any corresponding gain. In sawing hard woods, the speed should be reduced. The band-saw may be said to have a blade of superior thinness, capable of tension in varying degrees, moving in right lines through the material at a speed that is almost unlimited and can exceed that of circular saws, operating by machinery consisting only of rotating parts. and of the most simple construction, the sawdust all carried down through the timber and offering no obstruction in following lines and peculiar adaptation to curved lines.

"The speed of sawing, or the cost of sawing, which is much the same thing as the movement of the teeth, is with the band-saw almost unlimited. Its performance, contrasted with jig-saws for cutting plain sweeps or scroll-work, shows a gain of time or cost of 3 to 1, with the important advantage of being easier to operate, and much more popular with workmen. The greatest objection to a band-saw is that it cannot be used for cutting inside work. Some workmen saw clean through the stuff to get at the inside, when the nature of the work will admit of such treatment without weakening or injuring the design. Strips of the same kind of wood as the design are firmly glued into the saw-kerfs when the work is completed. Of course, this method of reaching inside cutting can only be adopted where the design is not intended to bear any strain. Many devices have been suggested for separating and joining band-saws, but most of them are unavailable or impracticable. One, however, enables the operator to separate the saw, pass it through a hole bored in the wood and join it again, in less time than it takes to disconnect the blade of a jig-saw, pass it through the wood and connect it again to the machinery. This arrangement gives the band-saw an important advantage over the jig-saw in its own special province, as it renders it possible for much thicker material to be sawn than could be done with the jig-saw, and the work will be better done in less time." (M. Powis Bale, M.I.M.E., A.M.I.C.E.)

(9) "The jig-saw or reciprocating saw is a blade arranged to work upright by means of a crank in a table. One is shown in Fig. 322, p. 101. In setting up a jig-saw, choose the most solid part in the building, over a post, pier, or timber; if on a ground floor, it should be set on solid masonry or piles. If obliged to put the saw on an upper floor, use a counter-balance equal to three-fourths the weight of the movable parts; this will throw the vibration on a horizontal plane. When a jig-saw is set on solid masonry, no counter-balance is required, as it is better to let the vibration fall vertically on the masonry. It is not wise to drive jig-saws a too high a speed, as the wear and tear of the machinery will more than balance the gain in speed of sawing: 300 strokes per minute is about the correct pace. The speed of the feed may be varied according to the nature of the wood being sawn. For very hard wood, a feed of 6 in. per minute is suitable, whilst for very soft wood as much as 30 in. may be cut in the same time; it is a great mistake, however, to force the feed, as the sawdust has not time to escape, and the saws become choked and buckled, and run out of line." (M. Powis Bale, M.I.M.E., A.M.I.C.E.)

(10) A sawing table for using either a jig-saw or a circular saw may conclude this section. An example is shown in Fig. 322. The table consists of 1½-in. planed plank a, about 3 ft. by 2 ft., of beech or good deal, supported on 4 legs b, 2 or 3 in. square, tied by a framing c to which the plank is screwed. From the centre of the back of the table rises a wooden pillar d, 2½ ft. high and measuring 3 in. by 2, mortised into the table

and further held and strengthened by screw-bolts and a T-iron brace, or carried to the floor, or to a longitudinal brace (not shown) joining the 2 back legs near the ground. A strong rubber door-spring f attached to a screwed eye in the arm e pulls the saw g up at each stroke. The lower end of the saw g may be attached directly to the crank of the treadle h, giving only 1 stroke of the saw for each revolution of the fly-wheel i; or, to obtain several strokes for each revolution, the saw is attached by a hook and band to a smaller crank and axle worked by a strap from the fly-wheel, and the saw is at the

322.

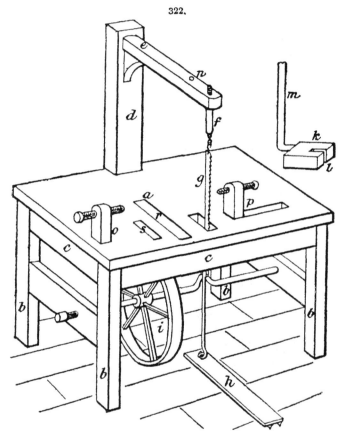

same time made to work vertically by passing the band over a pulley under the table exactly in line with the upper end of the saw, before taking it to the crank. For holding down the work whilst sawing, and simultaneously acting as a bearer to keep the saw engaged in its work, a convenient arrangement is to have a block of hard wood k with a slit in the front edge l carried by an iron rod m fitting into the hole n in the arm e, and adjustable by screw-nuts. The fly-wheel may be 18 in. diam. with a heavy rim, and the main crank $1\frac{1}{2}$–2 in., giving a 3-in. stroke. For working a small circular saw, the wooden poppets $o\,p$ are used, o being tenoned into a square hole in the table, while p is free to slide in a groove. The circular saw and its pulley work in the holes $r\,s$ respectively in the table.

Fig. 323 shows a home-made fret-saw, having a capacity ranging from $\frac{1}{8}$-in. to 6-in. stuff. The 2 uprights a are of spruce, and measure 7 ft. high and 4 in. sq.; they are mortised at foot into stout planks b screwed down to the workshop floor, and at top into a beam c, 6 ft. long, 4 in. wide, and 3 in. thick. The space between the uprights is 5 ft. 6 in. in the clear. The inner frame d is of pine, 3 in. wide and 2 in. thick, the transverse pieces being composed of 2 lengths of 1-in. stuff, glued and screwed together with the grain reversed. The spring *e* at the top of the frame is made of 3 pieces of ash, $\frac{3}{8}$ in. thick, planed down to $\frac{1}{8}$ in. at each extremity; a bolt and nut attaches the spring to the frame, and short lengths of chain or rope connect it with the saw-frame *d*. The treadle *f* is hinged to the floor at the lower end, and suspended by straps *g* from the frame at the upper end. The table *h* for carrying the work, and through which the

323.

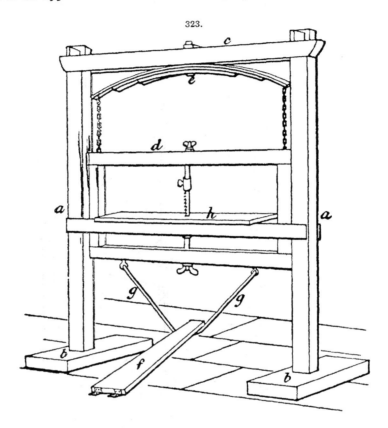

saw passes, is supported by 2 strips of batten screwed to the outer frame, and measures 2 ft. long and 18 in. wide. The saw is set up in the usual manner. Obviously the dimensions may be altered to suit any particular need.

Files. Principles.—A file is a steel instrument having the surface covered with sharp-edged furrows or teeth, used for abrading or smoothing substances, chiefly wood and metals. A file proper differs from a rasp, in having the furrows made by straight cuts (produced by a chisel or a sand blast), either single or crossed, while the rasp has coarse single teeth raised by the pyramidal end of a triangular punch. The effective power of the file resembles that of the saw, represented by a wedge not encumbered by the friction of one of the faces. The angle of the faces of the wedge is formed by the direction of the applied power and a tangent to the teeth. The diagonal position of the furrows of the file gives an additional shearing wedge power.

Forms.—Examples of the cutting faces of files and rasps 12 in. long are shown in the annexed illustrations; the cuts of longer and shorter sizes vary in proportion. Figs. 330–335 are float cut; Figs. 324–329, double cut; and Figs. 336–341, rasp cut. Fig. 324 is rough; 325, middle; 326, bastard; 327, second cut; 328, smooth; 329, dead smooth; 330, rough; 331, middle; 332, bastard; 333, smooth; 334, dead smooth; 335,

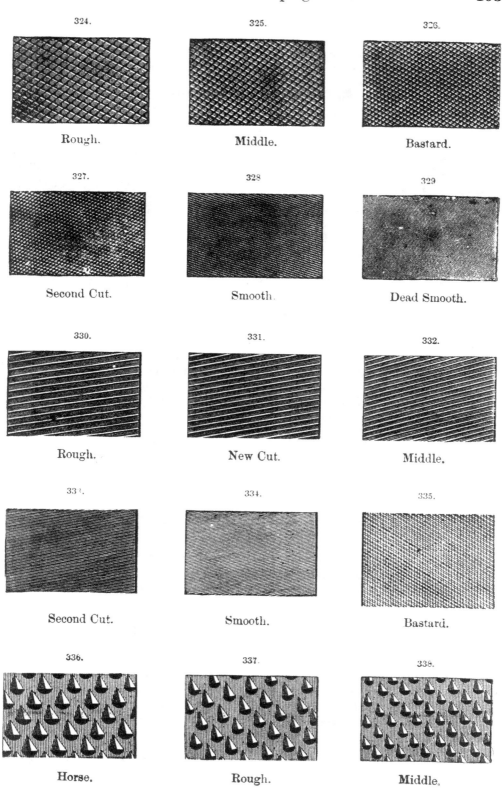

324. Rough.   325. Middle.   326. Bastard.

327. Second Cut.   328 Smooth.   329 Dead Smooth.

330. Rough.   331. New Cut.   332. Middle.

333. Second Cut.   334. Smooth.   335. Bastard.

336. Horse.   337. Rough.   338. Middle.

new cut; 336, horse; 337, rough; 338, middle; 339, bastard; 340, second cut; 341, smooth.

Using.—In using a file care should be taken that it is applied evenly to the work, or there is a danger of wearing it away rapidly in one spot. When a file loses its cutting power it may be resharpened.

Sharpening.—Until recently this was done by recutting the grooves in machines devoted to that class of work, but lately the sand blast has been most successfully

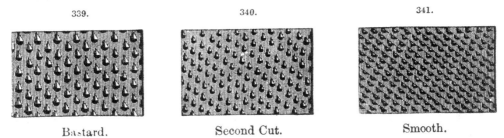

339.	340.	341.
Bastard.	Second Cut.	Smooth.

applied to the purpose. The operator holds the files which have to be sharpened, one at a time, in a long gas-pipe handle, into the end of which has been driven a plug of wood; the file is not held still, but is moved to and fro, resting upon a slip of gun metal, the file being also occasionally turned over. The slip not only forms a rest, but as the operator moves the file backward and forward upon it he learns when the file has reached a good cutting state. As far as the sharpening is concerned, this is the whole operation. It will be easily understood that a little practice is necessary to enable a man to make the best job of a file. In Fig. 342, a b are sections of file teeth. a shows the form of the teeth as they come from the file cutter or machine. From this it will be seen that the upper part of the tooth is turned backward somewhat, and the top is rather weak. The effect of the sand blast is to remove this bent-over or rounded top, and to take off the tops of the extra high teeth. The form then is as shown at b. It might be expected that the sand would cut the point or fine edge of the teeth, but this is not the case, for smooth files are improved as much as those of the coarser descriptions. The sand used is exceedingly fine, and is the waste material resulting from the grinding of plate glass. It is so fine as to be like smooth, clean mud, and it seems remarkable that this will do the work. In the ordinary way, cleaning files after the hardening and tempering processes is a dirty, laborious operation. They have to be scoured with brushes and sand by hand, then put into lime-water, and dried. By one workman, only about 3 doz. per hour can be cleaned. It is an accident of the sand-blast process that it cleans the files as well as sharpens them. As they pass from the sand-blast hand they go to a boy, who passes them under a jet of hot water, which cleans out sand sludge, and, the file being then hot, it dries of itself. Before the use of the hot-water jet, one man used to be employed in brushing the dried sand mud out of the files at the cost of one man for each machine and 6s. per week for brushes. Now a lad does all. With one machine, 14-in. files may be sharpened at the rate of—flat bastard, 5-8 doz. per hour; second cut, 10-12 doz.; smooth, 12-15 doz.; half round bastard, 4-6 doz.; ditto second cut, 8-9 doz., and so on. The apparatus is now being used a good deal to sharpen worn files, which it does at a very low cost. There is another method

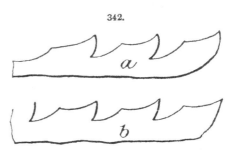

342.

spoken of as being employed in French dockyards, consisting in pickling the files in an acid bath (dilute sulphuric and nitric acids, 1 part of each in 7 of water) for 45 minutes, after a washing with hot alkaline water; but it is not explained how the action of the acid is prevented from exerting the chief degree of erosion upon the exposed angles of the file face, instead of in the hollows where it is wanted to act.

EDGE-TOOLS.—This section comprises chisels and gouges, planes, and miscellaneous smoothing tools (e. g. spokeshaves), as well as the means adopted for keeping up a keen cutting edge (grindstones, oilstones).

Chisels and Gouges. Principles.—The chisel in its simplest form constitutes a slice of an axe, but as the impact is not from the motion of the chisel, but from that of a swung mallet or hammer, the eye of the axe is replaced by a contrivance for receiving the blow. When the element of thrust enters, then the chisel is passing into the " plane iron." For applying the chisel, 2 contrivances are in general use. One is to put a tang on the metal of the chisel, and to let this be driven into a handle so shaped at the extremity as to receive the blow of a mallet. A very few blows would soon drive the handle forward, and so the tang end would then project through the handle and receive the blows. To avert this a shoulder is forged, where the tang is supposed to end, and the chisel proper to begin. When the blows have been repeated, so that the handle rests upon the tang shoulder, then the handle is "home," and the tool completed. In turners' chisels where mallets are not used, the shouldered tang is not required. A suitable handle being selected, a ferule is loosely put on it, and a hole is bored down the handle a little shallower than the length of the tang, and widened at the mouth so as to show a square, the sides of which are just shorter than those of the tang under the ferule—now, enter the chisel-tang, and let it be pressed in by the hand until it is so retained by friction, that by pointing the chisel edge downwards, the metal does not fall out. The operation of fixing the handle may now be said to commence. The line of the handle and blade is then inclined at about an angle of 45° to the horizon. A blow with a mallet is struck at the end of the handle; the inclination remaining the same, the tool is turned round on its longitudinal axis, say, $\frac{1}{4}$ rotation, another blow given; the operation of turning and striking being continued until the feruled end of the handle and tang meet. As to the effects of a blow upon the end of a handle, there being no apparent resistance, this takes place: The velocity of impact is communicated to the handle and chisel. Now the greatest effort is required to cause the first motion, so here a high velocity in the mallet has to be divided between a supported tool and itself. What is sometimes called "inertia" has to be overcome in the act of this transference of velocity through the length of the handle and chisel; that portion which offers the least resistance will be the first to move. No velocity can be communicated to a body at rest without what is usually called resistance. The friction between the tang and the handle is so adjusted by the preliminary formation of the hole, that the resistance from friction is less than the resistance from inertia; hence the gradual approach of the ferule and the flange. Now as to the turning in the hand about the axial line. The wooden handle is held in the left hand, therefore the effect of gravity upon it is neutralized. Not so with the chisel; gravity produces its full effect upon this. Consequently some part or other of the hole becomes a fulcrum, the cutting end of the chisel is drawn downwards by gravity, and therefore the tang end is pointed upwards. Continued impact in this position would place the chisel oblique to the axis of the handle; the turning is to avert this. Again, it was said that the depth of the hole should be less than the length of the tang. The reason is this: the end of the hole is of greater diameter than the end of the tang; if, therefore, the tang does not enter and fix itself in the wood, there may be unsteadiness in the chisel. Assuming the instrument to be under the operation of repeated blows, the effect of these will be first expended upon the end of the wooden handle, and then transmitted to the cutting edge Unless provision be made, the destruction of the end of the wooden handle will be assured. To diminish as much as possible liabilities to such a result, the end of the handle is formed as a portion of a sphere. Further, the impact blow is modified in the mallet, which is of wood, with a curvilinear face; thus these 2 wooden surfaces act and re-act upon each other. The yielding elasticity of the wood also gives to the blow and so transmits to the work a different effect to that which would take place if the handle and chisel were of iron. Another way of fixing the tool in the handle is to have a long tubular top to the tool, into which a wooden handle is driven. This is preferable for heavy work, as the repeated blows only tend to condense the fibre of the wooden handle and increase its firmness in the shank; but as it adds much to the weight of the complete tool, it is not adapted for ordinary cases. (Rigg.) Much annoyance is caused by the tendency of the butt end of the chisel handle to split under the effects of repeated blows from the mallet. A remedy suggested for this is to saw off the round end, leaving it quite flat, and on this to nail 2 round discs of sole-leather to form a pad for receiving the blows. When the leather has expanded inconveniently it can be be trimmed round with a knife.

Forms.—Forms of chisels and gouges are shown in the annexed illustrations. The

343.

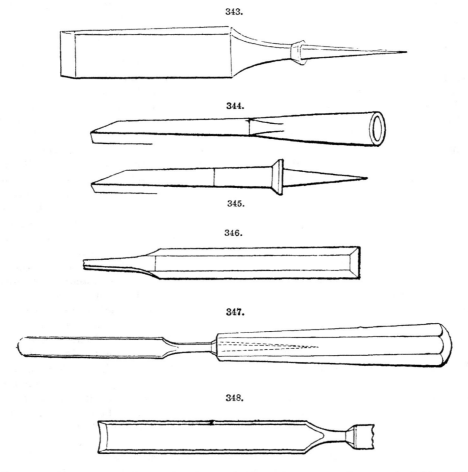

344.

345.

346.

347.

348.

difference between a chisel and a gouge is that the former has a straight cutting edge while the latter is more or less curved. Fig. 343 is a common paring chisel; Fig. 344, a socket mortice chisel; Fig. 345, a common mortice chisel; Fig. 346, a thin paring chisel with bevelled edges; Fig. 347, a common gouge in its handle; Fig. 348, a long thin paring gouge, cannelled inside. Mortice chisels range in width from $\frac{1}{8}$ in. to 1 in., the sizes increasing $\frac{1}{16}$ in. at a time; paring chisels advance $\frac{1}{8}$ in. at a time, from $\frac{1}{8}$ in. to 2 in. wide; gouges have a similar range, in addition to which they are made with 8 different degrees of curve, as shown in Fig. 349, and known respectively as A or very flat, B or flat, C, D or middle, E, F or scribing, G or half fluting, H or fluting. In the figure, all are 1-in. size.

Using.—The chisel cannot be used satisfactorily over a surface wider than itself, and though the gouge was devised to excel it in this respect, there is still a tendency for this tool to follow the leadings of the fibres of the wood rather than cut through them at a very slight obliquity. The only guidance the tool receives is from the hand of the workman, hence everything depends upon the degree of his skill. The impossibility of ensuring the amount and direction of the cut given by the chisel was the main incentive to introducing its modified forms the spokeshave and the plane, which will be discussed presently. In paring, the chisel is held in the right hand and applied with a thrusting motion without the aid of a mallet, the left hand being employed to hold the wood, and always kept well in rear of the tool to avoid accidents in case of the tool slipping. The wood to be operated upon should be held securely and in such a manner that if the tool goes beyond it or misses a cut it will neither damage its own edge nor meet with anything that will be injured by it, such as the surface of the bench. In paring horizontally or lengthwise with the fibres of the wood, the forefinger should be extended along the tang of the tool; but in paring vertically across the grain, all the fingers should firmly grasp the handle. When cutting mortices and tenons, the chisel is tightly held in the left hand while the right wields the mallet for giving effect to the cutting tool. To make a close joint, it is very necessary that the edges cut by the chisel (as well as those cut by the saw) shall be perfectly square and flat. This can only be attained by observing the correct way of applying the chisel-edge to the work. If the flat side of the chisel be held

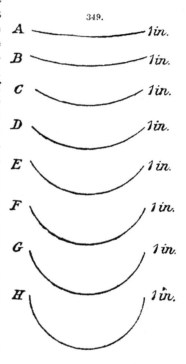

349.

against the shoulder that is to be cut away, the chisel will "draw in"; if the bevelled side is against the shoulder, the contrary effect will be obtained. This is illustrated in Fig. 350. If the chisel is held as at *b* or *d*, just (and barely) allowed to cut, it will act as a paring tool; but its tendency will be found to follow the dotted line *b c*, so that, if not checked, it will "undercut" the shoulder. When held as at *a*, its tendency is in the opposite direction, when the sloping end can be rectified without spoiling the work. The same care is needed in cutting a mortice (Fig. 351). Let the mortice be carefully marked on both sides, but cut right through from one side only; the chances are that it will be found to have been cut too long on the farther side of the stuff from the drawing in of the chisel. The section will be as at *a*, Fig. 351. Of course, therefore, the safe plan when a mortice *must* be cut only from one side is to cut it more like *b*, and to pare it back carefully at the finish. Whenever possible, however, a mortice should be cut from both sides—half through from each; but the same tendency of course prevails, the result being shown in *c*, and here the faulty work will not be visible in the least when the tenon is in its place. The joint will appear quite close-fitting and neat, but it is evident that it will have little strength, as the component parts are only in contact just at the 2 surfaces, the rest being quite hollow. The best way to begin a mortice is shown at *d*. It should be commenced by cutting out wedge-shaped chips from the middle, cutting each side by turns, and it will be found in many cases easier to take out the main part of the chips with the bevel of the chisel downwards. Each chip is thus heaved by pressing on the bevel as the fulcrum, and the mortice is gradually lengthened each way. After the main part of the wood has been removed, the back of the chisel is used next the shoulders, as already stated, care being taken, as the work approaches completion, that the hole is not undercut, but that the mortice

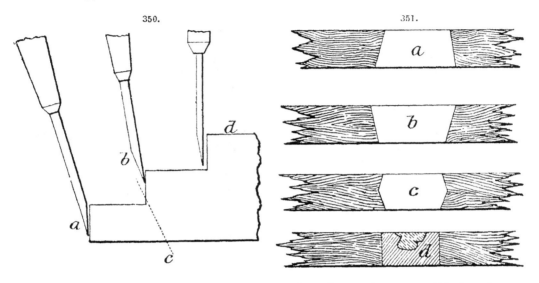

350.   351.

when finished shall have 4 perfectly flat walls, the sides as free as possible from loose fibre.

Another cause of failure in making a clean tight joint is the bruising of the fibres on the surface of the board at the end of the mortice by using a blunt chisel. It is mainly avoided by commencing in the middle, as just explained, and using a keen chisel to finish with. Certainly the work may be passed over again after the mortice is cut, but this is not always allowed for in squaring up the piece originally. In soft wood, especially when the fibres are loosely compacted, they will bruise and start up considerably if struck with a blunt tool, and often come completely away, leaving a depression that cannot be effaced without deeply planing the surface. Stray tacks, chips, and inequalities in the surface of the bench will also produce bad results.

The gouge is used and held in the same way as a paring chisel. When driven by a mallet it should always have a perpendicular position.

Spokeshaves.—The drawing-knife, Fig. 352, is practically a 2-handed chisel, which can only be used by drawing it towards the operator. Beyond its greater effective surface it is no improvement upon the chisel. A desire to govern the depth of

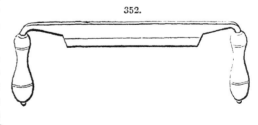

352.

cut performed by the chisel led to the adoption of a tool called a spokeshave, in which the long blade of the drawing knife is retained, the depth of the cut being determined by the nearness of the edge to a parallel wooden handle. This tool may be used in both directions, towards and from the workman. But owing to the position of the application of the power, viz. the hands, and the tendency of resistance by the work to turn the whole tool in the hand, it is not of general utility. When, however, the curvature of surface varies, the parings to be removed are light, and the operator has convenient access, the tool is capable of doing good work, and possesses some advantages over the plane. (Rigg.) Besides the original simple long-bladed spokeshave, this tool is now made with cutters of varying forms, for chamfering, rabbeting, and other purposes, being then often termed a "router," especially by the American makers who have introduced the novelties.

Planes.—Principles.—The plane, in its simplest form, consists of a chisel inserted at an angle into a box, generally of wood, and with the cutting edge projecting through the bottom of the box. If the actions of a workman be noted as he is smoothing wood with a chisel alone, it will be seen that he holds the bevel edge on the wood, and so elevates or lowers the handle as to secure a proper and efficient cut. Then he advances the tool in a line at right angles to its cross section. If now, instead of thus continuing to hold the tool, the chisel was so fixed in a movable piece of wood as to be at the same angle as the workman required, then if the mouth were broad enough, and the instrument were propelled along the wood, a shaving would be removed very nearly the same as that obtained from the chisel alone. In the arrangement thus sketched, the workman would be relieved from the care needed to keep the tool at a constant angle with the surface of the timber. There is, however, a fixity of tool here, and consequently an optional or needful adjustment called for by any varying condition of the problem cannot be had. When operated upon by hand alone, if an obstacle to the progress of the tool is presented, as, for instance, a twist or curl in the fibre or grain of the plank—the presence of a knot—then the workman by hand can adjust the handle, and so vary the inclination of the cutting edge as the circumstances of the case require. Not so if the tool is securely fixed in a box as described. Whilst therefore one has gain has been had, one loss has been encountered. Observe the defects of the primitive plane, as hitherto described, and note what hopeful elements it contains.

The front of the sole of the box will clearly prevent the penetration of the encased chisel into the wood, because it cannot now be drawn to follow the fibre should it lead inwards. Suppose, however, that in the progress of the work such a place has been reached as would have so drawn the chisel inwards : either the strength of the indrawing fibre will be so great that the workman will be unable to propel the tool, or, if not thus impeded, he must by extra effort separate the fibre and so release the tool. This separation, however, may not be by the process of cutting, but by that of tearing, and shavings so torn off will have left their marks in the roughnesses which attend the tearing asunder of fibrous woods. Thus the tool will defeat the very purpose for which it was designed. To obviate the difficulty described has exercised much ingenuity, and led to more than one contrivance in planes as generally used.

The causes which so forcibly draw, or tend to draw, the tool downwards below the surface of the timber are the hand of the workman and the tenacity of the fibre. If the tenacity is greater than the power, the workman must stop. That the tool cannot follow the direction of the fibre is clear, because the front part of the wooden sole forbids the penetration, but that it may be brought to a standstill, or must tear off the fibre, is also very clear. The mechanician has therefore to consider how to defeat these tendencies which, as now sketched, result from a collision between the indrawing strength of the fibre and the power of the man to cross-cut the fibre by the tool, or else to tear it asunder and leave the surface rough. Since the tool, as now contrived, cannot efficiently cross-cut the resisting fibre, and since that fibre has to be removed, the object must be either to prevent such an accumulation of fibres as will stop the progress of the tool, or to destroy the fibre piecemeal as it is operative for hindrance. Both plans have been adopted. A consideration of the former may prove introductory to the latter, which appears in almost all attempts to perfect this tool and its appended contrivances.

As the tool progresses, and the fibres become more and more impeding, it will be clear that a portion of this impediment results from a condensation of the fibre in the mouth of the wooden box. The more numerous the fibres admitted here, the greater will be the condensation. This state of affairs can be partially obviated by a narrowing of the mouth of the plane; such an act of course requires that the introduced chisel should enter less deeply into the timber being operated upon. Although thus abated, the cause is not removed, and even if so far abated as to prove no real impediment to the workman, yet the quantity of material removed on each occasion will be so small that the tool becomes one for finishing work only, and not for those various operations to which its present powers enable artisans to apply it. To be the useful tool it is, the mouth must not be so narrowed, nor the inserted chisel so withdrawn, that the shaving is thus the thinnest possible. This led to a contrivance now almost universal, that of breaking the fibre so soon as it is separated from the piece of timber. The designer seems to have considered that as soon as a short length of shaving had been removed, it would be well to destroy the continuity of the fibre, and so prevent an accumulative resistance from this cause. Hence, instead of allowing the cut-off fibres to slide up the inserted chisel, he bent them forward, in fact, cracked them, and so broke the cumulative indrawing force of them. This he accomplished by the use of what is now called the "back iron," and from henceforth the boxed-in chisel loses its identity, and must be regarded as part of an independent tool.

The tool thus built up is called a plane. Three forms are in general use in English workshops, called the "jack," the "trying," and the "smoothing" plane. These are on the bench of all workers in smooth straight surface wood. Although externally alike except in size, they are yet used for different purposes, and each has a specialty in its construction. These specialties may now be considered.

Forms.—After the wood has passed from the sawyer into the hands of the carpenter, the surface undergoes those operations which render it true and smooth. These 3 planes do this work. The "jack," usually about 15 in. long, and the "trying" plane, ranging from 18 to 24 in. long, but, in exceptional cases, far exceeding these dimensions, are to external appearances alike; indeed, some regard the different handles as the only dis-

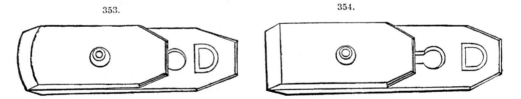

353.   354.

tinction between them, and that these handles show which must be used for rough work and which for smooth (see Fig. 355 as an example of the handle of a "jack-plane," and Fig. 356 as an example of "trying-plane" handle). This is an error. There are other differences, but the main and leading one is the different form given to the edge of the cutting iron.

If the iron of the "jack" plane be looked at from the front end of the plane, the form of the edge will be curved, as in Fig. 353; but the iron of the "trying" plane is straight, as in Fig. 354. Upon the curvature of the edge depends the efficient action of the "jack."

Sufficient has been said of the tendency of the fibre to draw the tool downwards; but it must not be forgotten that the same adhesion of fibre to fibre takes place between the surface fibres as amongst those below the surface. For the purpose of separating the surface connected fibres, the jack iron is convex. Note its action. The convex sharp edge is pushed along a horizontal plank, penetrating to a depth determined by the projection of each vertical section below the sole of the plane. The ends of this convex edge are actually within the box of the plane, consequently (sideways) all the fibres are separated by cutting, and are therefore smooth and not torn The effect of this upon the entire surface is to change the surface from the original section to a section irregularly corrugated. The surface after using the "jack" is ploughed, as it were, with a series of valleys and separating hillocks, the valleys being

355.

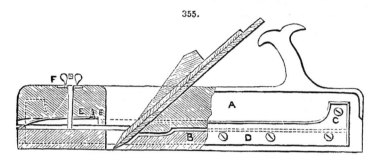

arcs from the convexity of the tool and the separating hillocks being the intersection of these arcs. All traces of the tearing action of the saw have been removed, and from a roughened but level surface a change has been made to a smooth but in cross-section an undulating one.

The mechanician's next object is to remove these lines of separation between the valleys. For this the trying-plane is required. The trying-plane is longer than the

356.

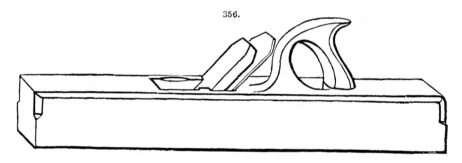

jack, because the sole of the plane which is level is, so far as its size goes, the counterpart of that which the surface of the wood is to be; further, the trying-plane should be broader than the jack, because its object is to remove the hillocks and not to interfere with the wood below the bottoms of the valleys. If its action passes below the bottoms of the furrows, then occasion arises for cutting the side connection of the fibres, and however a workman may sharpen the edge of his trying-plane for this purpose, he in one respect has destroyed one object of the plane, because, so soon as the iron penetrates below the surface, then does the effect of the jack action begin to reappear, and the cutting edge should pass from the shape shown in Fig. 354 to the shape in Fig. 353. The result of the trying-plane following the jack is to remove all the elevations of wood above the valleys the jack left; and, secondly, to compensate by its great length for any want of lineal truth consequent upon the depth of bite of the jack. Again, the mouth of the trying-plane is much narrower than that of the jack; hence the shavings removed are finer, therefore the slope of the iron, or its inclination to the wood may be less than is the iron of the "jack"—hence the line of cut is more nearly accordant with that of the fibre, and by so much the surface is left more smooth from the trying-plane than from the jack, as there is more cutting and less tearing action than in the jack. The reasoning hitherto pursued in reference to the purpose of this sequence of a jack and trying-plane might and does legitimately produce the conclusion that, after the trying-plane has done its duty, the work is as perfectly finished as it can be. Custom, and perhaps other considerations, have established that after the long trying-plane must follow the short and almost single-handed smoothing-plane (Fig. 357). So far as the form of the iron of the smoothing-plane is concerned, there is no difference between it and the one used in the trying-plane; each (as across the plane) is straight, the corners being very slightly curved, but only so much as to ensure that they do not project

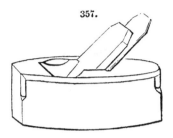

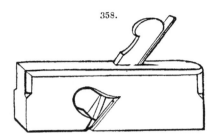

below the line of the cutting edge. It would seem that, whilst the trying-plane levelled down all the elevations left by the jack, and brought the surface of the wood as a counterpart to that of the plane, there might be in the fibre, or grain of the wood, twists, curls, and other irregularities which, whilst levelled, were yet left rough in consequence of the direction in which the cutting edge came upon them. Indeed, this cutting edge, in a long plane, which must advance in the direction of its length, must at times come across a large number of surfaces where the fibre is in opposite directions. The consequence is that there will be various degrees of smoothness; for good work these must be brought to uniformity. This is effected by passing a short-soled plane over the respective parts of the surface in such directions as observation may indicate. Hence the smoothing-plane is of use chiefly to compensate for such changes in the direction of the fibres of the wood as the greater length of the trying-plane could not conveniently deal with.

The plane shown in Fig. 355 is claimed to possess some advantages over the ordinary jack-plane, in that it gives a control over the thickness of the shaving and depth of the cut by the pressure of the hand, and prevents the drag of the bit on the board when the plane is drawn back. The stock of the plane is made in two parts, the upper portion A, which holds the bit, being pivoted to the lower part B at the rear end by a screw C passing through metallic guide plates D on each side the plane. The front end of the upper portion is raised from the lower portion by means of a spring E, which, when the pressure of the hand on the front of the plane is withdrawn, lifts the upper portion together with the bit or plane iron. The amount of this movement is governed by the thumb-screw F.

The "rabbet" or "rebate" plane, Fig. 358, differs from the preceding examples in that the cutter reaches to the edge of the wooden block, so as to enable the smoothing operation to be carried right into the corner of work. It is employed in making window frames and similar articles in which a recess (termed a "rebate" or "rabbet") has to be cut for the insertion of some other material, as, for instance, a pane of glass. The cutter has not of necessity a square edge, but may be shaped like the examples shown in Figs. 359, 360, which are termed "skew," "round," and "hollow" rabbet-irons respectively.

Another form of simple plane is the "plough," intended for cutting a deep groove along the edge of a board for the purpose of inserting in it a corresponding "tongue" along the edge of another board to be joined to it. The tongue may be formed by using the rabbet-plane along each side of the board edge; but it is more convenient to employ "match" planes, which are made in pairs, one cutting the plough and the other the tongue. Their cutters are shown in Fig. 361.

The stop-chamfer plane, sold by Booth, Dublin, for 4*s*., is a very useful tool for cutting any chamfer from $\frac{1}{8}$ in. to $1\frac{1}{2}$ in. with a constant angle and size. It is shown in

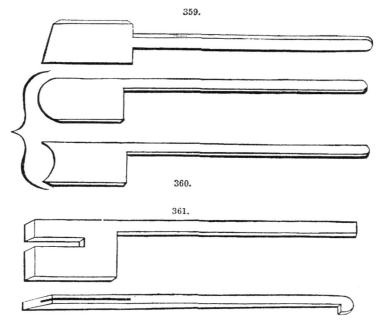

Fig. 362. The box of the plane is made in much the same way as that of ordinary planes, and the iron is inserted and held in place in the same manner. The point of difference is that a ∧-shaped channel is cut along the sole of the plane, the sides of the channel being at right angles to one another, and at an angle of 45° with the sole of the plane; meeting in a point in a line drawn perpendicular to the sole, and exactly up the centre of the end of the plane. Thus the sides *ac bc* of the groove are at right angles to each other, and at an angle of 45° to *de*, the sole of the plane, and they meet in *c*, a point in *fg*, which is perpendicular to *de*, and drawn exactly up the centre of the end of the plane, as shown. The depth of the iron, which is indicated by the shaded part of the figure, is regulated to suit the width of the chamfer that it is proposed to make.

The preceding include all the kinds of plane in most general use; but it is obvious that the same principle may be applied to almost any form of cutter. Hence a great variety of tools, known as "moulding" and "filletstering" or "filister" planes, have been introduced, whose cutters consist of combinations of chisel and gouge edges. These are employed for cutting mouldings and beads of numerous designs, which are familiar to every one who has observed the edge of skirting boards in rooms, the panels of doors, or the sash-frames of windows. The great bulk of this class of work, however, is now performed by rotating cutters worked by steam power, and such beads and mouldings, of any desired pattern, can be procured better at the manufactory than they can be made by hand.

Adjusting.—Reference has already been made (p. 110) to the second iron introduced into the plane for the purpose of curling up and breaking off the shaving produced by the cutter. The arrangement of the 2 irons is shown in Fig. 363, a being the cutter, and b the back or break-iron, the two being united by a screw-nut and bolt c. The united irons are fastened in a hole in the stock of the plane by means of a wooden wedge, and so adjusted that they traverse the stock and project very slightly through a narrow slit in the sole provided for that purpose. The angle ordinarily formed between the sole and the irons is one of 45°, but this is reduced to 35° by the head of the cutter. In adjusting the plane to its work, 2 considerations have to be borne in mind: (1) the degree to which the cutter projects beyond the sole, and (2) the distance between the edges of the cutter a and breaker b. In regulating the position of the double iron, in relation to the sole, it will seldom be necessary to apply a blow of the hammer to either the top or sides of the wedge or irons; by taking the plane in the left hand so that the palm of the hand covers the hole where the shavings come out, a gentle tap with a hammer or mallet can be administered to either end of the stock of the plane: this will effect the purpose. A blow given in this way even suffices to loosen the double iron enough to permit its complete withdrawal, when it is necessary to sharpen its cutting edge. An occasional side tap may be needed to make the iron set square with the sole. The relations of the edges of the cutter and breaker can be altered by unscrewing the nut c that unites the 2 plates, a long slot being provided in b with that object. The distance between the edges of the 2 irons varies from about $\frac{1}{8}$ in. for the coarsest roughing-down work to $\frac{1}{20}$ in. for smoothing, the breaker being placed of course that much above the cutter. The higher the breaker, the easier the plane works; the lower it is, the cleaner the cut. It is necessary to caution the operator against wedging up his planes too tightly, as such a procedure will cause the cutting iron to assume a curved form and prevent smooth work being done. Care must be also taken that the projection of the cutting edge beyond the sole of the plane be perfectly square with the sole, and level in itself; in fact it is better that the corners be rounded off, to prevent the possibility of their catching. Many of the planes of modern pattern are made either self-adjusting or so that their adjustment is very easily and accurately performed.

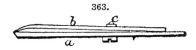

363.

Using.—Wood to be planed should be laid quite flat on the bench, and tight against a "stop" to prevent its moving. The planing must always follow the direction of the grain of the wood, and never meet it or cross it. If a piece of wood should exhibit the grain running in different directions in different portions of its surface, the piece must be turned about accordingly so that the plane may always go with the grain. The sole of the plane is necessarily subjected to a considerable degree of wear, which ultimately renders it useless for all but the roughest work. This effect can be much reduced in the case of a wholly wooden stock, by occasionally oiling the surface. A more enduring but more costly method is to shoe the sole with metal, or to have a metallic stock, as most of the new American planes have. As the sole (wooden) wears, it must be periodically planed up true again.

The method of applying the jack-plane is as follows. The right hand grasps the handle or "toat," the forefinger being extended along the wedge ; the left hand partially encircles the front part of the plane with the thumb turned inwards. The trying-plane is also held similarly for "facing up," but in applying the force of the arms there is this difference, that while with the jack-plane the pressure of the hands should be uniform throughout the stroke, with the trying-plane the chief pressure should come from the left hand for the first half of the stroke and from the right for the last half. For "shooting" work, the trying-plane is held differently, the fingers beneath the sole serving as a sort of gauge for keeping the plane on the narrow edge of the board being worked. The smoothing-plane is held by the right hand clutching it behind the knife (there is no handle) and the left grasping its front end with the left thumb on top and pressing it down. The rabbeting plane is also called a filister or filletster. It is provided with a "screw stop" and a "fence" for the purpose of limiting the range of its cut in both width and depth. The small grooving iron in front of the plane proper should extend a little beyond it, with the object of detaching the wood sideways before the plane has to remove a shaving downwards; thus the angle is cut out perfectly clean. The plough, in many respects closely resembles the filister. Indeed the latter may easily be extemporised out of a plough by adopting the following suggestion put forward by Ellis Davidson. Supposing a (Fig. 364) to represent the plane looking at the fore end, and b a board in the edge of which it is required to cut a rebate $\frac{1}{2}$ in. wide and $\frac{1}{4}$ in. deep; a strip of these dimensions has literally to be planed away, and the plane must therefore not travel horizontally farther on the surface of the board than $\frac{1}{2}$ in., nor vertically sink deeper than $\frac{1}{4}$ in. The plane with which the work is to be done is $1\frac{1}{2}$ in. wide. Plane up a strip of wood c to the width of 1 in. (the thickness will not be any consideration), and screw it at right angles to another piece d, thus forming the letter L. This forms a case which will, when planed and fastened to the side of the plane by a couple of screws, shut off 1 in. of the width of the sole, allowing it to encroach upon the surface of the board to the extent of $\frac{1}{2}$ in. only ; a mere strip e screwed on the other side at $\frac{1}{4}$ in. from the sole, will prevent the plane sinking deeper than is required. On no account should the guide be screwed to the sole of the plane, which should always be kept perfectly smooth, the surface uninjured by screw holes. Nor is it necessary to damage the sides of the plane by more than 2 small screw holes, for the same side-piece d may be permanently used, the width of the strip c being altered according to circumstances; and the width of e can also be regulated, either by planing a portion off below the screws if the rebate is to be deeper, or moving the screws lower down in the strip if it is to be shallower, taking care that the holes correspond with those in the side of the plane, and that the strips do not cover the apertures through which the shavings should escape.

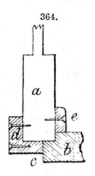

364.

Sharpening.—The sharpening of the cutting edges of planes and chisels is performed primarily on a grindstone or its equivalent an emery grinder, and secondarily on an oil-stone.

Grindstones.—The implement known as a grindstone consists of a wheel of sandstone mounted on a revolving axle in a trough capable of containing water, its ordinary form being sufficiently familiar to dispense with illustration. There is probably no instrument in the machine shop or factory which pays better for the care bestowed upon it than the grindstone; and considering that nearly every tool, and all edge tools, require it, before they can be used to advantage, or in fact at all, it is somewhat surprising that more attention has not been bestowed on the proper selection of the grit for the purposes for which it is intended. As grindstones are almost constantly in use, their first cost is of little consequence if the quality is calculated to do the work in the shortest time and in the most perfect manner, as more time can be lost on a poor grindstone, badly hung, and out of order, than will pay for a good one every 3 months. This state of things should not continue, as with the great improvements made in the manner of hanging them, and the endless variety of grits to select from, every mechanic should have a grindstone which will not only do its work perfectly, but in the shortest time. This can be accomplished by sending a small sample of the grit wanted to the dealer to select by. Grindstones are frequently injured through the carelessness of those having them in charge. The grindstone, from being exposed to the sun's rays, becomes so hard as to be worthless, and the frame goes to pieces from the same cause; it will have a soft place in it, caused by a part of it being allowed to stand in water overnight, and the difficulty arising from this cause increases with every revolution of the stone ; but as this homely implement is in charge of all the men in the shop in general, and no one in particular, and as the workmen are all too busy to raze it down, double the time is consumed in imperfectly grinding a tool than would be required to do it perfectly if the stone were kept in order by some one, whose business it would be to attend to keeping all the grindstones of the establishment in order. The wages of a man for this duty would be saved in the time and perfection with which the numerous tools could be kept in order for work.

Most commonly grindstones are made to turn by hand, and necessitate the services of an assistant. It is much better to have one that may be driven by the foot of the operator, with a handle to attach for a second workman to turn it when necessary. When the needs of the workshop will admit of it, the best plan is to have a large grind-stone (say 2 ft. diam. or more) for heavy work, and a smaller one (say 9 in. diam.) capable of being fixed to the end of the carpenters' bench and driven by foot power for lighter work. The stone should never be used dry, and with this object a trough is provided for containing water ; but the stone must not under any circumstances be allowed to remain immersed in the water when not in use, conse-quently the water must be drawn off through a bung-hole, or a hinge attached to the trough for lowering it away from the stone, or a prop introduced for supporting the stone out of reach of the water. A sponge held against the revolving stone by a small rack is useful for preventing the water travelling round with the stone and wetting the handle of the tool and the hands and clothes of the operator. An absolutely essential quality in a grindstone is a true level face. This may be partially secured by distributing the work over the whole breadth of its surface, so as to wear it away equally all over ; but every care in this respect will not suffice to keep it even enough for some tools, and then it must be refaced by means of a steel tool wider than itself. Fig. 365 illustrates an

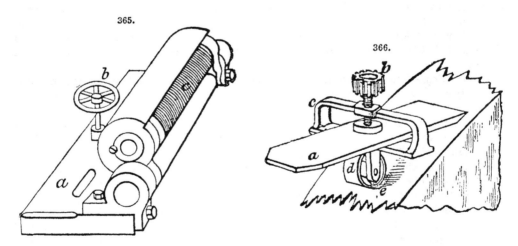

American device (sold by Churchills, Finsbury) for keeping the face of the grind-stone constantly true while at work, without interfering with the use of the stone or raising any dust. The main stand or bottom piece a is securely clamped upon the trough close to the face of the stone ; then by turning the handwheel b, the threaded roll c is brought into contact with the face of the stone, and allowed to remain so long as it is necessary to produce the desired result. The water is left in the trough as usual. When the thread of the rod c is worn it can be recut. The price of one of these implements suited to a 12-in. stone is 3l. 12s. The tool to be ground should be held against the stone in such a way that the bevel or slope of the cutting edge lies flat on the stone, while the handle maintains a horizontal position. The stone should revolve towards the operator, i. e. against the edge. Usually the trough of the grindstone has high ends or similar means of supporting the tool during the grinding. Such means may take the form of a bevelled block to support the blade, or a notched rest to hold the handle, in either case securing that the grinding is done at the correct angle. Fig. 366 shows a contrivance for resting the tool, and ensuring its being ground at the desired angle. The plane iron *a* is held by a clamp screw *b* in the frame *c*, while the wheel *d* revolves on the stone *e*, and steadies the whole. This rest is sold by Churchills, Finsbury, for 1*s*. 6*d*. The amount of angle or bevel given to the edge varies with different tools and with the fancies of different workmen. In the case of a plane iron it must always be more acute than the angle formed by the sole of the plane and its mouth. The bevel produced on the grindstone should not be quite flat nor rounding (bulging) but rather hollowed out, a result naturally following from the circular form of the grinding surface of the stone, and varying of course with the size of the stone. Many workmen object to the use of any form of rest for the tool during grinding, as tending to produce a hollow edge—the very thing desired by another class. Gouges are best held across the stone, as otherwise they are apt to score the surface of the stone. In grinding the jack-plane iron, the cutting edge should be somewhat round, so that the shaving taken off is thicker in the centre than at the edges. The trying iron is also slightly round, but so slight that it is hardly noticeable. The smoothing iron should be a straight line on the cutting edge, with the corners very slightly rounded, but on no account should the edge be curved, though ever so little. These irons are all ground on the back only—that is, the bevel side; the bevel or ground part is about ½ in. across. If too long, the iron when working is apt to jump.

Oilstones.—These are of several kinds, the best known being the Charnley Forest, Turkey, Arkansas, and Washita brands. They are sold in pieces of convenient size at about 1*s*. 6*d*. to 2*s*. a lb., and smaller slips for gouges at 4*s*. a lb. They can be procured ready cased, but if bought without a case, they should not long remain so, as they are then easily broken and exposed to dust and other evils. The casing may be accomplished in the following manner. Supposing the stone to be 9 in. long, 2 in. broad, and 1 in. thick, get 2 pieces of clean, straight, hard wood, 1 in. longer and wider than the stone, and $\frac{7}{8}$ in. thick. Plane one side of each piece flat, so that they will lie closely together. On one of the pieces, place the stone, keeping uppermost the side of it which you mean to use. Draw a line all round the wood close to the stone, when you will have a margin outside the line of ½ in. With the brace and centre bit ($\frac{5}{8}$ in. or ¾ in.) bore all over the portion within the line ½ in. deep, then with a sharp chisel ($\frac{7}{8}$ in. or 1 in.) cut down to the draw-point line all round, clearing out all within to ½ in. deep, and making the bottom of this hollow box level throughout. If it is pared square down at the edges, the stone will slip into it; take care to put it in the same way as when you previously drew it. When the stone is bottomed, ½ in. will project above the wood, and this part is to receive the top or cover. The stone is placed upon the second piece of wood, which is to make the cover, and drawn in the same way; and this piece has to be bored and cleared out in the same way to fully ½ in. deep. It must have a smoother finish inside than the under piece; and must be pared a little without the draw-point line, so that the cover will slip on to the stone easily, but without shaking. The stone being within, the case is planed on the edges and ends, by catching it in the bench vice. The 4 corners may be rounded as well as the edge of the cover, and a ⅓-in. bead may be run round the cover where it joins the under part. (Cabe.) The oilstone will always wear most in the middle, becoming hollow in both length and breadth. This may not matter much for sharpening jack-plane irons, as the roundness thereby communicated to the corners of the cutting edge is rather an advantage. But when the hollow is of such a degree that it is inconvenient, the surface must be levelled. This may be effected by rubbing it on a flat sandstone or grindstone, or by an emery slab, prepared by scattering emery powder on slips of wood previously well glued to hold it, and leaving for 24 hours to dry. The very best oil for use on the stone is either sperm or neat's foot, but this is often replaced by olive (salad) oil or by petroleum. In applying the tool, its bevel edge is rubbed to and fro on the stone, great care being necessary to ensure that the tool is held at exactly the same angle throughout the whole length of its travel backwards and forwards. That is to say, the natural tendency of the tool to lie flatter as it advances farther away from the operator's body must be compensated for by raising the hand slightly as it goes forward and lowering it as it returns. Square the elbows, let hand and arms have freedom, grasp the tool above with the right hand so as to bring the fingers underneath it, and let the fingers of the left lie together, and straight upon the upper side, their ends tolerably near the edge of the tool, the thumb being underneath. The tool will be thus held firmly, and also under control. Holtz-appfel gives a way the reverse of this. He says the first finger only of the right hand should be held above, and the thumb and rest of the fingers below, the left hand grasp-ing the right, with the finger above the tool and the thumb below. It is probably in a great measure a question of habit. Apply the ground side of the iron to the stone, and rub backwards and forwards nearly the whole length of the stone. Hold the iron slightly more upright than at the grindstone, so that the extreme cutting edge only may come in contact with the oilstone. After 5 or 6 rubs on the bevel, turn the iron over and give it 1 or 2 light rubs when lying quite flat on the stone. This double operation is repeated till a keenly sharp edge is obtained. If the irons are newly ground, very little setting is needed, but as they are dulled or blunted when working, a fresh edge has to be brought up on the oilstone; this sharpening may go on for 20 or 30 times before the irons require re-grinding. A blunt iron, looked at on the bevel side, presents a whitish rounded or worn appearance, and the sharpening has to be continued until this white worn edge disappears, which is also ascertained by touching the edge lightly with the thumb. When an iron is sharpened or set, a very fine " wire edge " remains along the edge; this is removed by a dexterous slapping backwards and for-wards on the palm of the hand, and is the same in effect as finishing the setting of a razor by stropping on a piece of leather. Gouges and bead-planes are generally set with a stone slip, several being necessary for the various bead and other moulding planes.

The slips are usually about 6 in. long, 2 in. broad, and $\frac{1}{8}$ in. to $\frac{1}{2}$ in. thick, with the edges rounded to fit the irons to be set. The cutting part of a bead-plane iron is a little smaller than the corresponding curve in the stock of the plane, the difference being the thickness of the shaving taken off. When the iron has been set a number of times with the slip, the curve has a tendency to get wider, and consequently is soon as wide as the curve in the stock. The iron will not then take off a shaving of equal thickness throughout the whole curve, but thickest in the middle, so the iron must be reground and set anew by the plane-maker, who has very thin round-edged grindstones for the purpose. The same thing occurs with most other moulding planes. In setting with the slip, the hollow part is continually getting wider, and the round part which is set on the ordinary oilstone is getting smaller. From these causes, the moulding gets out of proportion, and the iron does not fit the stock with a cutting edge even throughout its whole breadth, and will not turn a good shaving as before. The tool-maker must re-grind the iron when in this condition. (Cabe.)

Miscellaneous Forms. Circular plane.—All the forms of plane hitherto considered have been provided with a guide principle which shall repeat a straight level surface. The guide may, however, be the counterpart of any required surface. The American adjustable circular plane shown in Fig. 367 has an elastic steel sole, which, by means of adjusting screws, enables the workman readily to convert a straight-faced sole into one either concave or convex. It also possesses an advantage in the mode of fixing the iron, viz. by a cam action. Often in ordinary planes the wood splits when the holding wedge binds on the box.

Rounder.—Wheeler's rounder is shown in Fig. 368. It is a very useful tool for producing a smooth and even surface on a cylindrical-shaped article, such as a broom handle; *a* is the cutting edge, and *b* the handles by which it is made to revolve round the wood.

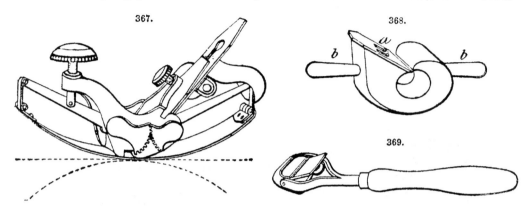

367.   368.   369.

Box scraper.—Fig. 369 illustrates an adjustable box scraper, made of malleable iron, with 2-in. steel cutters, and costing 2s. 6d.

Veneer scraper.—An adjustable veneer scraper is represented in Fig. 370. Its price with a 3-in. cutter is 12s. 6d., extra cutters costing 1s. 3d. each. The two latter tools may be obtained of Churchills, Finsbury, or Melhuish, Fetter Lane.

Mitre-plane.—The Rogers mitre-plane, Fig. 371, is made entirely of iron, and is arranged for planing any desired angle on straight or curved work. The main bed-piece is semicircular in form, with a way or frame at its rear on which the plane runs. The upper or movable bed-plate is in quadrant form, having, at right angles, sides which act as guides for the material to be planed, and revolving on a pivot *a* at the end, enabling the user to form the desired angle for straight work, and place it in its proper position against the face of the plane. When the quadrant or movable bed-plate is in the centre of the main bed-piece, its side elevations form an exact mitre, so that no change is required in planing the ends of parts for frames of 4 sides. In the sides of the quadrant are 2 adjust-

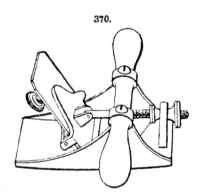

370.

able guides or rests kept in position by set-screws *d*. The special object of these rests is to enable one to finish the ends or angles on curved work with exactness. In preparing pieces for circular or oval work, frames, pulleys, emery wheels, circular patterns, &c., it is necessary to plane the ends of the various segments at varying angles. In planing these, the point of the quadrant near the plane and the adjustable guides form the rests required for accurate work. The quadrant is kept in position at any angle desired by pressing the catch *c* down into the notches prepared for it, or by the thumb-screw *b*, and can be used in connection with the arms or guides as desired. It is sold by Churchills, Finsbury, at prices varying from 90s. for the 2-in. size, to 135s. for the 4-in.

Combination Filisters.—Miller's combination, Fig. 372, embraces the common carpenters' plough, an adjustable filletster, and a perfect matching-plane. The entire assortment can be kept in smaller space, or made more portable, than an ordinary carpenters' plough.   With each plough, 8 bits ($\frac{1}{8}$, $\frac{3}{16}$, $\frac{1}{4}$, $\frac{5}{16}$, $\frac{3}{8}$, $\frac{7}{16}$, $\frac{1}{2}$, and $\frac{5}{8}$ in.) are furnished ; also a tonguing tool ($\frac{1}{4}$-in.), and by the use of the latter, together with a $\frac{1}{4}$-in. plough bit for grooving, a perfect matching-plane is made.   A metallic bed-piece, with $1\frac{1}{2}$-in. cutter in it, can be attached to the stock of the tool by means of 2 screws passing through the slots in the base-piece of the stock.   Over this bed-piece the gauge, or

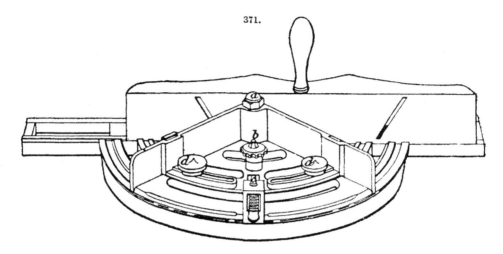

371.

fence, will move backward or forward, and when secured to the bars by the thumb-screw, will constitute an adjustable filletster of any width required.   The upright gauge on the back of the stock is adjusted by a thumbscrew likewise, and regulates the depth for the use of the filletster, as for all the other tools embraced in the combi-nation.   Churchills sell it at 37s. 6d.

Trant's adjustable dado, &c., sold by the same firm at 29s. 6d., is shown in Fig. 373.

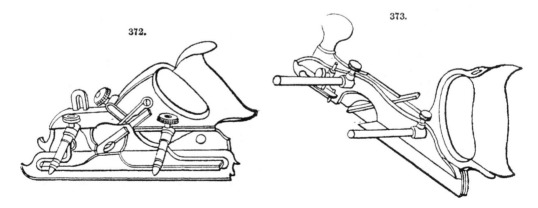

372.

373.

It consists of 2 sections—a main stock with 2 bars or arms; and a sliding section, having its bottom, or face, level with that of the main stock.   It can be used as a dado of any required width, by inserting the bit into the main stock, and bringing the sliding section up to the edge of the bit.   The 2 spurs, one on each section of the plane, will thus be brought exactly in front of the edges of the bit.   The gauge on the sliding section will regulate the depth to which the tool will cut.   By attaching the guard-plate to the sliding section, the tool may be readily converted into a plough, a filletster, or a matching-plane—as explained in the printed instructions which go in every box.

The tool is accompanied by 8 plough bits ($\frac{3}{16}$, $\frac{1}{4}$, $\frac{5}{16}$, $\frac{3}{8}$, $\frac{1}{2}$, $\frac{5}{8}$, $\frac{7}{8}$, and $1\frac{1}{4}$ in.), a filletster cutter, and a tonguing tool. All these bits are secured in the main stock on a skew.

Iron planes.—The Bailey and Stanley iron planes with improved adjustments (Churchills) are largely replacing wooden planes.

BORING TOOLS.—These comprise awls, gimlets, augers, bits and braces, and drills.

Awls.—The simplest form of boring tool is the awl or bradawl as it is more generally called, Fig. 374. It consists of a piece of small steel rod, with one end fastened in a wooden handle, and the other doubly bevelled to a sharp edge, which serves the purpose of compressing and displacing the fibres of the wood so as to form a hole without producing any chips or dust from the wood operated on. Its greatest drawback is the readiness with which the awl proper may be pulled out of its handle in withdrawing the tool from the hole it has made, especially in the case of hard woods. Superior awls are, however, made to overcome this fault, the handle being hollow and containing a selection of awls of different sizes, each fastening into the handle by means of a screw-nut. The use of the awl is to prepare holes for the admission of nails and screws.

Gimlets.—The gimlet is an offspring of the awl, and of more recent origin. The gimlet of the Greeks had the cross-head or handle of the style now prevalent. It also had possibly a hollow pod, as the earliest specimens found are of that type, but no screw-point, and it demanded a large expenditure of muscle, especially in boring hard

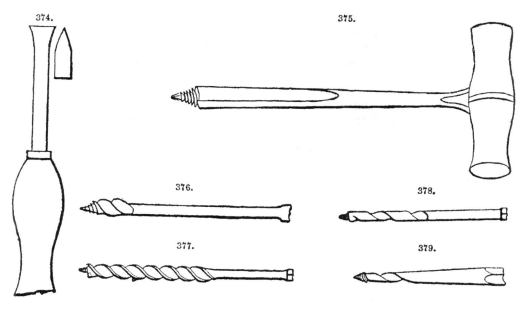

woods, where it was not very effective. Later, a gimlet of square section, having sharp corners and tapering to a sharp point, was introduced, and gave the hint for a form of auger now in use. In course of time, the screw point was added, and the hollow-pod gimlet, with a point of this kind, was the only sort in use for many centuries. In England, this was called a "wimble." This form is still in use to some extent, and is effective where very shallow holes only are to be bored, but as it has to be removed whenever the pod becomes full of chips from boring, it causes a waste of time when deeper holes are desired. The twisted or spiral form of gimlet, which is self-discharging, is an American invention, and only of very recent date. It has, however, superseded all other forms, and is now in common use. The field of the gimlet is becoming greatly narrowed, giving ground to the more rapid and convenient brace and bit. (*Industrial World.*) Some gimlets are made with twisted shanks, which allow the dust and little chips to escape more easily, and some have only a gouge-shaped channel with a pointed screw below. These tools cut away the material as they go, the screw point only serving to give a hold at first, and gradually to draw the tool deeper into the work. The shell or gouge-shaped are generally preferred by carpenters, as being stronger and more suited for rough work in various woods; but they are more likely to split the work, especially if the latter be at all thin or slight. In such case, it is best to use very little pressure, and to give a quick movement to the handle. Fig. 375 shows the commonest form of gimlet, termed a "spike." Fig. 376 is a "treble twist"; Fig. 377, an auger gimlet; Fig. 378, a patent twist; and Fig. 379, a brewers' twist. The prices of awls and gimlets range from 1*d.* to 6*d.* each, according to size. An assortment is needed.

Augers.—These are only magnified gimlets for use with both hands. They are represented in Fig. 380, *a* being the "twisted," and *b* the "shell" form. A wooden bar is thrust through the eye *c*, and the hands exchange ends of this bar at each half revolution given to the tool. Their sizes advance $\frac{1}{8}$ in. at a time from $\frac{3}{8}$ in. to 2 in. in diameter, and prices range from 8*d.* to 6*s.* 6*d.*

Bits and Braces.—The faults inherent in all forms of awl, gimlet, and auger are that the rotation is necessarily interrupted to enable the position of the hand or hands to be changed, and that the pressure exercised on the tool is in most cases limited. These drawbacks are overcome by the brace and its accompanying bits. The ordinary form of brace is shown in Fig. 381. It consists simply of a crank, one end *a* being provided with a round head for receiving pressure from the breast of the workman, the other end *b* recessed for the introduction of the bit, and the centre *c* rendered smooth for the application of the hand that turns the whole. It will be obvious that much greater working efficiency can be got out of the boring tool by the continuous rapid rotation and heavy pressure secured by this implement than by the simpler forms previously described. The tools adapted for use with the brace (Figs. 382–394) are made fast in the end *b* by means of a thumb-screw catching in the notch seen near the end of their stems. This constitutes the weak point in the ordinary form of this compound tool. In the first

380.

c

a

381.

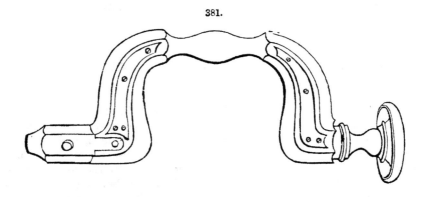

place, the use to which the implement is subjected has a direct tendency to wear the thumb-screw in such a degree as to soon render it loose and incapable of holding the boring tool firmly; and in the second place, the square hole in the end *b* is of fixed size, and will only admit tools which fit it accurately. These defects are remedied in Barber's patent brace, which is provided with an expanding chuck that adapts itself to all shapes and sizes of stems, and holds them tight and true. It is made in several sizes and styles, the most useful being the 8-in., costing 3s. 0d.; the common socket iron brace of the same size may be had for about 1s. 6d. Of the tools employed in the brace, Fig. 382 is a centre-bit, useful for boring large and deep holes; Figs. 383, 384, 385, countersinks for enlarging the entrances of holes when it is desirable to let the screw or other occupant of the hole lie completely beneath the surface of the wood— they are termed respectively "snail-horn," "rose-head," and "flat-head," from their shapes; Fig. 386, a screw-driver; Fig. 395, a bobbin bit; Fig. 387, a taper bit, for boring funnel-shaped holes; Fig. 388, a sash bit; Fig. 389, a shell bit; Fig. 390, a nose bit; Fig. 391, a spoon bit; Fig. 392, a square rinder; Fig. 393,

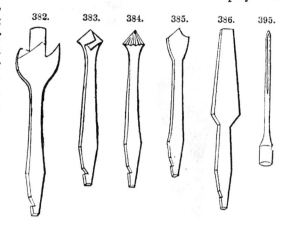

a half-round rinder; Fig. 394, a gimlet bit; Fig. 396, a dowling bit. Many other forms might be mentioned, including those employed in metal working, for which the implement is equally well adapted.

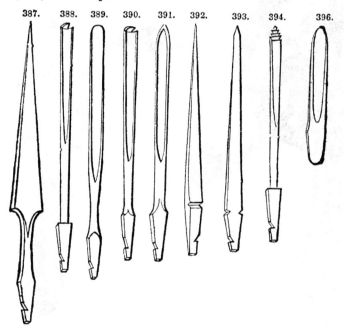

Drills.—No. 396a drill is made of round wrought-iron, $\frac{5}{8}$ in. in diam. The handles are rosewood, the head malleable iron, and the chuck jaws of steel. It has changeable gears, one even and the other speeded three-to-one. The change from one to the other can be made in an instant. The chuck will hold any shape shank—round, square, or flat. The stock is nickel-plated, and finished in a superior style. Price 16s. each.

No. 396b drill has a malleable-iron stock, japanned; rosewood handles, nickel-plated chuck, two speeds, gears, and Barber's improved chuck, holding shanks of all styles. Price 12s. each.

These hand drills have cut gears, the bright parts are heavily nickel-plated, with rosewood head and handle. The head is hollow, and contains six drill-points. The chuck is adjustable, and will hold firmly drills ¼ in. and smaller sizes. No. 1.—11 in. long, holds drills ⅛ in. and smaller; price 5s. 6d. each. No. 2.—13 in. long, holds drills ¼ in. and smaller; price 12s. each.

396a.

396b.

Miscellaneous.—Several improved tools of recent introduction scarcely fall under any of the foregoing classes. They are as follows:—

Angular Bit Stock.—This very useful adjunct to the brace and bits is shown in Fig. 399. Its object is to alter the direction of the pressure in boring (so as to permit boring in a corner), for which purpose it is placed between the brace and bit, forming their connecting link. The angle at which the hole is to be bored is decided beforehand, and the stock is properly set, the ball joint enabling the tool to turn without hindrance. It is sold by Churchills for 8s. 6d.

Wheeler's Countersink.—The bit of this countersink, Fig. 400, is in the shape of a hollow eccentric cone, thus securing a cutting edge of uniform draft from the point to the base of the tool, and obviating the tendency of such a tool to lead off into the wood at its cutting edge, and to leave an angular line where it ceases to cut. It works equally well for every variety of screw, the pitch of the cone being the same as the taper given to the heads of all sizes of screws, thereby rendering only a single tool necessary for every variety of work. It cuts rapidly, and is easily sharpened by drawing a thin file lengthways inside of the cutter. By fastening the gauge at a given point, any number of screws may be driven so as to leave the heads flush with the surface, or at a uniform depth below it. The gauge can be easily moved or detached entirely, by means of the set-screw.

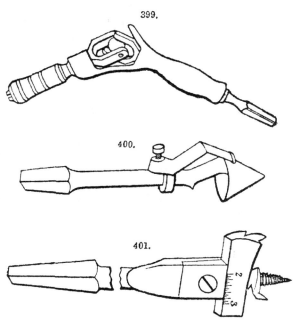

Expansion Bit.—Clark's expansion bit, Fig. 401, is designed to cut holes of varying size by means of a shifting cutter. It is made in 2 sizes, one ranging from $\frac{1}{2}$ in. to $1\frac{1}{2}$ in., and costing 6s. 6d., and the other embracing all diameters between $\frac{7}{8}$ in. and 3 in., and costing 9s. 6d. One of these tools not only replaces a complete set of the ordinary kind, but enables holes to be

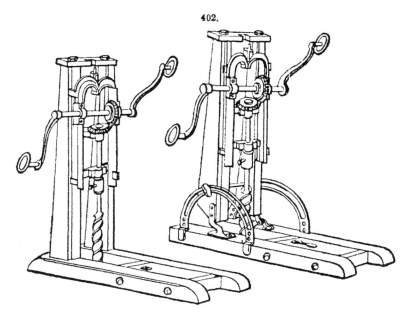

bored of all intermediate sizes. These, however, are seldom required in the general way.

Boring Machine.—Fig. 402 represents a plain and an angular boring machine, adapted for heavy work, costing respectively 22s. and 30s. without augers; a set of augers to match, $\frac{1}{2}$ in., $\frac{5}{8}$ in., $\frac{3}{4}$ in., $\frac{7}{8}$ in., 1 in., $1\frac{1}{4}$ in., $1\frac{1}{2}$ in., $1\frac{3}{4}$ in., and 2 in., costs 42s. 6d.   The diagrams will explain themselves.

STRIKING TOOLS.—The only members of this group are the familiar hammer and mallet.

Hammers.—Hammers, with and without handles, are in use; hammers of various weights from $\frac{1}{2}$ oz. to 10 lb., and from 15 lb. to 56 lb., are now employed as hand-hammers. The angles of attachment of handles to heads are various; the position of the centre of gravity of the head in reference to the line of penetration of the handle is various; the faces have various convexities; the panes have all ranges and forms, from the hemispherical end of the engineer's hammer, and the sharpened end of the pick and tomahawk, to the curved sharpened end of the adze, or the straight convex edge of the hatchet and axe; the panes make all angles with the plane in which the hammer moves. Various as are the uses to which hammers may be directed, yet like many other handi-craft tools certain contrivances are requisite in order either to direct or give full effect to the tool itself. Art has given to the hammer head only the handle as its contribution. Nature supplies other and more essential contrivances. These contrivances are mainly the muscles of the arm, although under certain circumstances other muscles of the body, especially those about the loins, are called into action. The weight of the hammer head, and the balance of the head in the handle, are the most important considerations govern-ing the suitability of the hammer to the nature of the work as well as to the capacity of the workman. The ordinary (" Exeter ") carpenter's hammer is shown in Fig. 403, consist-ing of a wooden handle fastened in an eye in the steel head by means of a wedge. Fig. 404

403.

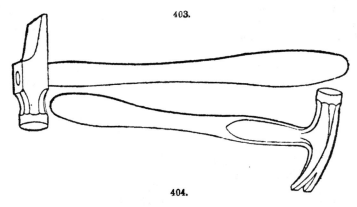

404.

is the next common form, termed a " claw " hammer, and secured head to haft by means of side flanges. This is an inferior plan, as the elasticity of the blow is not only inter-fered with, but the head is liable to be loosened by using the claw for drawing nails. It

405.

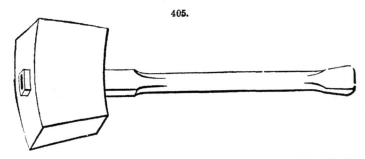

is well to have 2 or 3 sizes for various work, costing 1s. to 3s. each. No hammer should ever be used to strike a wooden surface, especially an article lighter than the hammer itself, as it will certainly do mischief.

Mallets.—In these tools the steel head is replaced by a wooden one. Fig. 405 shows the usual square form; there is also a round form. The former ranges from 6 in. long and $2\frac{1}{2}$ in. by $3\frac{1}{2}$ in. wide, costing 9d., to 7 in. by 3 in. by 4 in., costing $13\frac{1}{2}d$.; the latter, from 5 in. long and 3 in. diam., costing 7d., to 6 in. by 4 in., costing $11\frac{1}{2}d$. These have hickory heads; similar tools made of lignum vitæ cost nearly double. The chief use of the mallet is in conjunction with the chisel.

CHOPPING TOOLS.—These comprise axes, hatchets, and adzes. They consist of a combination of a striking tool with a cutting tool, the cutting edge being of stronger form than those described in a previous section (p. 105), in order to support the strain resulting from their being applied with greater force. The construction of these tools necessitates the addition of a handle or " helve," whose shape, length, and method of attachment to the blade have no small influence on the effectiveness of the tool.

Axes and Hatchets.—Principles. Axes are tools to be used with both hands; they have long handles, and may be swung as sledge hammers. Hatchets are to be used with one hand, have short handles, are much lighter and thinner than axes, and are employed more in the trimming than in the hewing of timber. Both narrow and broad axes are employed in forestry, the woodman's choice being affected by the size of the timber and the character of the fibre. A hatchet is handled with the centre of gravity nearer the cutting edge than the line of the handle; an axe, with the centre of gravity in the line of handle produced. When we pass from the tool and its contrived handle to the mode of using, and the purpose for which it has been constructed, we find, as a rule, a cutting edge formed by 2 inclined surfaces meeting at an angle, the bisecting line of which passes through the middle of the metal. It is very apparent that the more acute this angle is, the greater, under the same impact, will be the penetrative power of the axe into the material against which it is driven. This supposition needs to be qualified, for suppose the material offers a great resistance to the entrance of this edge, then the effect of the blow, upon the principle that action and reaction are equal, will react upon the edge, and the weakest, either edge of axe or object struck, must yield. Here experience would be obliged to qualify the simple tool in which the edge was keen and acute, and would naturally sacrifice the keenness and acuteness to strength. When early uses of the axe are considered, it will be noticed that even in fashioning with an axe or adze the same piece of wood, different conditions of edge are requisite. If the blow be given in the direction of the fibre, resistance to entrance of the edge is much less than in the blow across that fibre. So great, indeed, may this difference become, that whilst the axe seems in all respects a suitable tool, yet as the attention of the workman passes to directions inclined to the fibre at an angle of more than 45°, he will be induced to lay it aside in favour of the saw. These remarks apply only to tools used in dividing materials, and not to tools used in preparing surfaces of materials. This preliminary consideration prepares us for the different circumstances under which these 2 classes of tools may be respectively used. And as the contrast of the effect of the same tool under different circumstances in the same substance is considerable, great also is likely to be the contrast between the edges of the tools and the manner of using them, e. g. the axe, which is the proper tool in the direction of the fibre, is operated upon by impact, whilst a saw, which is the proper tool across the fibre, is operated upon by tension or thrust, but never by impact.

Using.—The mode in which the axe is used will explain why it is unsuited for work across the fibre. The axe is simply a wedge, and therefore arranged to cleave, rather then to cut, the wood. Now a calculation of the pressure necessary to thrust forward a wedge, and the impact necessary to cause the same wedge to enter the same depth, would explain why (regarded as a wedge only) the handle proves an important adjunct to the arm of the workman.

The motions of the hands on the handle of an axe are similar to those of a workman on that of the sledge hammer. The handle of a properly handled axe is curved, that of a sledge hammer is straight. For present consideration this curvature may be overlooked, although it plays an important part in the using of an axe with success and ease. If the almost unconscious motions of a workman skilled in the use of an axe be observed, it will be noticed that whilst the hand farthest from the axe head grasps the handle at the same or nearly the same part, the other hand, or the one nearest to the head, frequently moves. Let us follow these motions and consider the effect of them. The axe has just been brought down with a blow and entered between the fibres of the wood. In this position it may be regarded as wedged in the wood, held in fact by the pressure of the fibres against the sides of the axe; from this fixity it must be released, and this is usually done by action on or near the head. For this purpose the workman slides his hand along the handle, and availing himself (if need be) of the oval form of the handle after it has passed through the eye of the metal, he releases the head. The instrument has now to be raised to an elevation ; for this purpose his hand remains near to the head, so causing the length of the path of his hand and that of the axe head to be nearly the same. The effect of this is to require but a minimum of power to be exerted by the muscles in raising the axe ; whereas if the hand had remained near the end of the handle most distant from the head, then the raising of the axe head would have been done at what is called a mechanical disadvantage. Indeed, if a workman will notice the position of the hand (which does not slide along the handle) before and after the blow has been given, he will find that its travel has been very small indeed. Reverse the problem. Take the axe head as raised to such an elevation as to cause the handle to be vertical (we are dealing with ordinary axes, the handles being in the plane of the axe blade). Now the left hand is at the extremity of the handle, the right hand is very near to the axe head—the blow is about to be given. The requirement in this case is that there should be concentrated at the axe head all the force or power possible ; hence to ease the descent would be as injudicious as to intensify the weight of the lift. Consequently whilst with the hand nearest to the head (as it is when the axe reaches its highest elevation) the workman momentarily forces forward the axe, availing himself of the leverage now formed by regarding the left hand as the fulcrum of motion, he gives an impulse, and this impelling force is continued until an involuntary consciousness assures him that the descending speed of the axe is in excess of any velocity that muscular efforts can maintain. To permit gravity to have free play, the workman withdraws the hand nearest to the head, and sliding it along the handle, brings it close to the left hand, which is at the extremity of the handle ; thus the head comes down upon the work with all the energy which a combination of muscular action and gravity can effect. The process is repeated by the right hand sliding along the handle, and releasing as well as raising the head.

Form of handle.—The form of the axe handle deserves notice, differing as it does from that of the sledge hammer. In the latter, it is round or nearly so ; in the axe, it is oval, the narrow end of the oval being on the side towards the edge of the axe, and, more than this, the longer axis of the oval increases as the handle approaches the head, till at its entrance into the head it may be double what it is at the other extremity. It often has also a projection at the extremity of the handle. The increasing thickness near the head not only gives strength where needed, as the axe is being driven in, but it also supplies that for which our ancestors employed thongs, viz. assistance to the strain necessary to release the blade from the cut. There is, too, this further difference—in a sledge hammer more or less recoil has to be provided for, and the handle does this ; in the axe no recoil ought to take place. The entrance of the axe edge is, or ought to be, sufficient to retain it, and the whole of the energy resulting from muscular action and gravity should be utilized. The curvature, too, of the handle is in marked contrast with the straight line of the sledge hammer handle. The object of this curvature is worthy of note. In the American forester's axe, the handle is very long and curved. If laying the axe handle across the finger where the head and handle balance, the blade of the axe is placed horizontal, the edge does not turn downwards : in fact, the centre of gravity of the axe head is in the horizontal straight line prolongation of the handle through the place where the finger is. Now in sledge hammer work the face is to be brought down

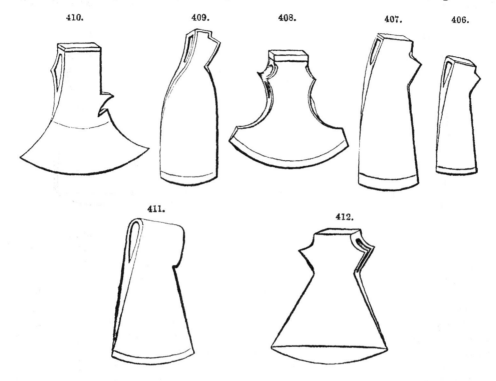

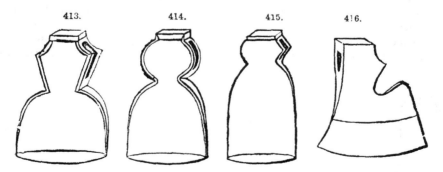

flat, i.e. as a rule, in a horizontal plane. With the foresters' axe, it has to be brought down at varying obliquities. If the hewer's hand had to be counteracting the influence of gravity, there would be added to him very needless labour, hence the care of a skilled forester in the balance of the axe-head and the curvature of the handle.

Form of cutting edge.—The form of the cutting edge as seen in the side of the axe is often convex. The line across the face in Fig. 417 indicates the extent of the steel, and the corresponding line in Fig. 407 the bevel of the cleaving edge. It will be noticed that the cutting edge in each case is curved. The object of this is to prevent not only the jar and damage which might be done by the too sudden stoppage of the rapid motion of the heavy head in separating a group of fibres, but also to facilitate that separation by attacking these fibres in succession. For, assuming the axe falls square on its work in the direction of the fibres, a convex edge will first separate 2 fibres, and in so doing will have released a portion of the bond which held adjoining fibres. An edge thus convex, progressing at each side of the convexity which first

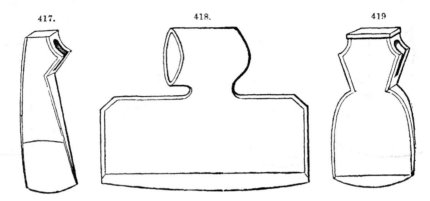

strikes the wood, facilitates the entrance of successive portions from the middle outwards. If the edge had been straight and fallen parallel to itself upon the end of the wood, none of this preliminary preparation would have taken place; on the contrary, in all probability there would have been in some parts a progressive condensation of fibres, and to that extent an increase in the difficulty of the work.

The equally inclined sides of the wedge-form of edge hitherto alone described as belonging to axes, and the equal pressure this form neces-
sarily exerts upon each side if a blow is given in the plane of the axe, suggest what will be the action of an axe if the angle of the wedge is not bisected by the middle line of the metal. Assume that one face only is inclined, and that the plane of the other is continuous to the edge, then let the blow be struck as before. It will be obvious that the plane in the line of the fibres cannot cause any separation of these fibres, but the slope entering the wood will separate the fibres on its own side. Supposing a hatchet sharpened as previously described, and one as now described, are to be applied to the same work, viz. the cutting from a solid block the outside irregularities—say to chop the projecting edges from a square log and to prepare it for the lathe. It may be briefly stated that the hatchet described in the

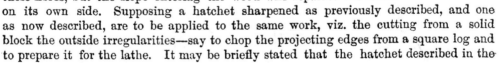

second case would do the work with greater ease to the workman, and with a higher finish than the ordinary equally inclined sides of the edge of the common hatchet. Coach-makers have much of this class of hatchet-paring work to do, and the tool they use is shaped as in Fig. 416. The edge is bevelled on one side only, and under where the handle enters the eye, may be noticed a piece rising towards the handle; on this the finger of the workman rests in order to steady the blade in its entrance into the timber in the plane of the straight part of the blade, and to counteract the tendency of the wedge side pressing the hatchet out of its true plane.

The principal forms of axe and hatchet, illustrated below, are as follows:—Fig. 406, colonial felling axe; Fig. 407, Australian felling axe; Fig. 408, wheelers' axe; Fig. 409, north country ship axe; Fig. 410, Dutch side axe; Fig. 411, Brazil axe; Fig. 412, broad axe; Fig. 413, Kent axe; Fig. 414, Scotch axe; Fig. 415, blocking axe; Fig. 416, coachmakers' axe; Fig. 417, coopers' axe; Fig. 418, long felling axe; Fig. 419, common ship axe; Fig. 420, Kentucky wedge axe; Fig. 421, Canada hatchet; Fig. 422, American shingling hatchet, with claw; Fig. 423, shingling hatchet, with hammer head.

Adzes.—Those whose business requires the forming of lengths of wood into curved shapes, and who rely upon the adze for the preliminary operation, use an Indian form of adze. In India it is held so near the metal that the workman's hand touches the metal. He accomplishes blows chiefly by acting from the elbow. This very general mode of holding gives a pretty uniform length to the radius of the swing, hence the form of the adze in the plane of the swing is nearly that of the circle described. The angle of the handle and the adze is very much the same as that of the handle of the file-makers' hammer and the head. The handling of the adze, as used by English wheelwrights or shipwrights, briefly described, is the following: The workman stands with one foot upon the wood, this foot being in the line of the fibre. He thus assists in steadying (say) the felloe of a wheel. From this felloe much of the wood on which the sole of his shoe rests has to be removed. The long handle of the adze is curved; the object of this is to permit an efficient blow to be given, and the instrument brought to a stop before the handle strikes any part of the workman's body—in fact, caused to stop by the exhaustion of its impact energy in and amongst the fibres of wood to be separated. The edge is often so keen as to cut through a horse hair held at one end and pressed against it. This instrument is raised by both hands until nearly in a horizontal position, and then not simply allowed to fall, but steadily driven downwards until the curved metal, with its broad and sharp edge, enters near to, if not below the sole of the workman's shoe, separating a large flake of wood from the mass; the handle is rapidly raised, and the blows repeated. This is done with frequency, the workman gradually receding his foot until the end flakes of wood are separated. It is fearful to contemplate an error of judgment or an unsteady blow. So skilled do men become in thus using the adze, that some will undertake, with any pre-determined stroke in a series, to split their shoe sole in two.

Curvature.—Clearly the adze must be sharpened from the inside; and when the action of it is considered, it is also clear that the curvature of the adze iron must be circular, or nearly so. The true curvature of the metal may be approximately deduced from considering the radius of the circle described by the workman's arms and the handle of the adze. The edge of the adze is convex (Fig. 425), the projection in the middle being so formed for the same reasons as influenced the curvature of the edge of the axe already alluded to. The curvature in the blade also serves (though partially) as a fulcrum, for, by slightly thrusting the handle from him, the workman may release such flakes of timber as are over the adze, and yet so slightly adherent as not to require another blow. Thus the adze when applied lever-fashion discharges its duty as the curvature in the claw of a hammer does. Fig. 428 is a gouge formed adze; a modification of this is used in making wooden spouts and similar hollow work.

The principal forms of adze are illustrated below. Fig. 424 is an ordinary carpenters' adze; Fig. 425, ship carpenters' adze; Fig. 426, coopers' adze; Fig. 427, improved wheelers' adze; Fig. 428, spout adze; Fig. 429, coopers' adze with sexagon eye; Fig. 430, coopers' nail adze.

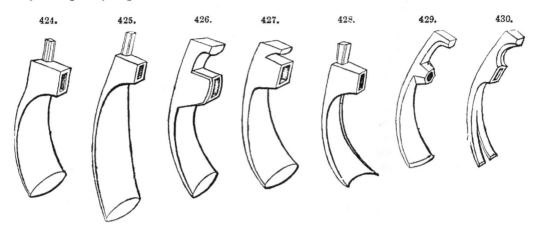

424.　425.　426.　427.　428.　429.　430.

ACCESSORIES.—The principal accessories to a carpenters' workshop are a bench, nails and screws, and a few trifles which could not be conveniently placed in the preceding categories.

Bench.—The essential qualities of a carpenters' bench are that it shall be very strong and firm to resist the sawing, planing, and other operations performed on it; also that the surface shall be level and even. The wood must be good and sound, but not of an

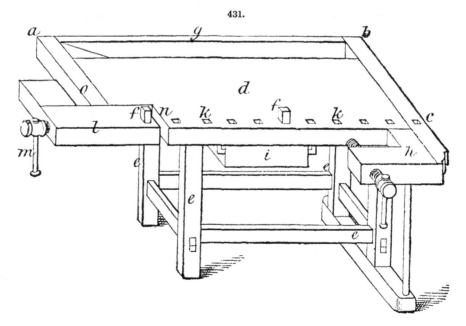

431.

expensive kind (beech is a favourite), nor need it be planed. Excellent benches may be purchased of tool dealers; on the other hand a home-made article may be quite as good and will cost much less. An example will be given on a future page.

Fig. 431 shows a solid bench of the so-called German pattern, sold by Melhuish

Fetter Lane, in 4 different sizes: carpenters', price 80s., length 68 in., breadth 24 in., height, 33 in.; trade, price 45s., length 48 in., breadth 16½ in., height 31 in.; amateurs', price 42s., length 40 in., breadth 16½ in., height 31 in.; boys', price 37s. 6d., length 40 in., breadth 16½ in., height 29 in. The length is measured from a to b, and the width from b to c, thus excluding the projections. A description of the "carpenters'" size will do for all. The top d is movable, and can be taken off the stand e, which also takes to pieces, so that it can be packed. Two pegs in the upper rails of the stand fit into holes made for their reception in the under part of the bench top, and by this simple arrangement, combined with the weight of the top itself, the parts are sufficiently connected and rendered firm. The mortices which receive the tenons of the lower rails, in front and at the back and sides, go through the legs, and the top part of the front and back rail at either end passes over the side rails, so that the mortice is deeper on the inside than on the outside; a tapering wedge is driven into the mortice at each end of both front and back rail, which has the effect of forcing these rails down on the ends of the side rails, and locking the whole together. When the bench is put up for work the ends of the wedges may be sawn off. The massive legs to the right are tenoned into a thick piece of timber, which is further utilized as a support for the end in which the bench-screw works. The top of the bench presents many points in which it differs from the ordinary form in common use. The central part is a solid piece of beech, 4 in. thick, 60½ in. long, and 16⅞ in. wide. To this portion all the surrounding parts are added. It is lengthened by 2 pieces a b clamped on one at each end, also 4 in. thick, and 3¾ in. wide, thus bringing up the length of the bench to 68 in. The 3 parts are bolted together by an iron bar, at the left end of which is a nut whereby they are screwed up as closely as possible. The piece a is 18¾ in. and b 33 in. long. They project beyond the central piece at the back to the distance of 7⅛ in., and by inserting a board g 1⅛ in. thick, and another at the bottom, a trough 6 in. wide and extending the whole length of the bench forms a useful receptacle for tools not in actual use. The shoulder h is formed of a solid piece, 4 in. thick, 8 in. wide at its widest part, and 2¾ in. wide at the narrowest part in which the bench-screw works, leaving an opening of 5¼ in. between the edge of the front of the bench and the inner surface of the narrow part of the shoulder. To plane the edge of a board, the screw is turned out sufficient to admit the board and a check piece supplied with the bench, which is intended to receive the pressure of the end of the screw, and prevent injury to the wood to be planed. To the bottom of the bench is appended a drawer i 18 in. sq., which works by means of cleats in grooved L-shaped timbers, screwed to the under surface of the bench; this drawer pulled out a little acts as a support for timber being planed. Along the front edge of the bench runs a row of 10 holes k, 1½ in. long by ⅞ in. wide, serving as receptacles for bench-stops f. These are used in conjunction with another in the movable vice jaw l, and when planing a board, all that is necessary to fix it is to insert a bench-stop to the left, at a suitable distance from the bench-stop in the movable piece l, lay the board between the 2 stops, and grip it by turning the screw m. The bench-stops can be adjusted to any height likely to be required. The movable bench-vice l has a projecting fillet on its inner face, which works in a groove of corresponding size cut in the central part of the bench. This vice, which is 22 in. long in its longest, and 6¾ in. wide in its narrowest part, presents intervals of different widths between the ends of its 2 parts and the end of the bench at n o. These openings afford the means of gripping pieces of wood in the most convenient manner for cutting tenons, dovetails, &c.

Another excellent bench is that furnished by Syer, Wilson Street, Finsbury, and termed a portable cabinet bench. It is shown in Fig. 432, and is formed of an iron stand a, made in separate pieces bolted together, with a wooden top b of sound white deal, traversed by 3 iron bolts c to prevent warping, and measuring 6 ft. by 1 ft. 10 in. All the parts are joined by screw-bolts, and therefore quite rigid but easily taken apart. The ordinary bench-screw is replaced by an instantaneous grip vice d, and the usual bench-stops are superseded by a screw rising stop *e*. The whole costs 72*s.*, or a smaller size (4½ ft. by 1½ ft.) may be had for 63*s.* The upright piece of wood *f* is perforated with holes to take a peg wherever it may be necessary to support a piece of board, one end of which is held in the grip vice *d*. The space between this and the standard to the left can be partly filled with a nest of 5 drawers—one large at the bottom, and 2 tiers each containing 2 smaller drawers above. These chests are 22 in. long, 18 in. high, and 16 in. deep,

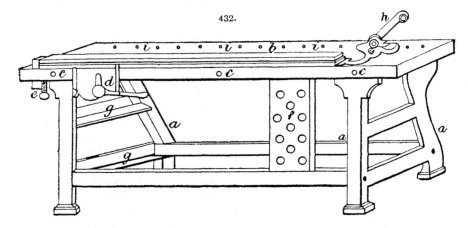

432.

and are supplied with the bench at a cost of 35*s.* extra. If not required, the ledges *y* within the standards can be utilized as supports for boards on which large tools can be laid when not in use. Another useful adjunct to the bench is the bench-knife *h*, supplied at 3*s.* 6*d.*, and consisting of a small bed-plate, having 2 pins on the under side to drop into holes made in the top of the bench to receive them, and an arm or knife for holding the work firmly between itself and the bench-stop, the arm being pushed and held against the work by the action of a small lever handle and cam attached to the upper surface of the bed-plate. This plate is only 9 in. by 3½ in., and the weight of the entire appliance is only 2 lb. The knife works smoothly and easily on the surface of the bench-top, and never injures it by cutting into it as is frequently the case with the ordinary bench-knife. The row of holes *i* near the inner edge of the bench-top shows how provision is made for using the bench-knife with various lengths of wood. The perforated piece *f* slides backwards and forwards between the bench-top and the lower rail of the frame at pleasure. The bench-stop *e* is a rectangular block of wood, cut and fitted to the top of the bench in such a manner that the side nearest any piece of wood that is brought against it slopes a little so as to bring a slightly projecting edge against the wood at the top. The screw has a plate at the upper end, which is let into and held with screws to the lower end of the bench-stop. It works in an internal screw, cut in a projection at the back of a small iron bow, each end of which is screwed to a block of wood attached to the under side of the bench-stop. The price of the iron fitting for bench-stop is 1*s.* 2*d.* A bench-top made of beech instead of white deal adds 12*s.*–15*s.* to the cost of the bench.

In choosing a position for the bench, attention must be paid to the light, the floor, the wall, and the space. The light should fall immediately upon it, hence it is best placed against the wall and under the window. The floor must be level and firm, and is best made of boards. The wall next the bench should also be covered with match boarding. If sufficient firmness cannot otherwise be secured, the bench should be fastened to the floor and wall by strong angle irons.

Bench-stops.—These necessary adjuncts to the bench consist of an arrangement capable of projecting above the surface of the bench to hold pieces of wood against during the operation of planing. One of the simplest contrivances is to have 2 or more stout screws standing up in the table of the bench itself, and easily raised or lowered to suit the thickness of the wood being operated upon; but this of course tends to spoil the surface of the bench. A better plan is shown in Fig. 433; it is easily manipulated, being

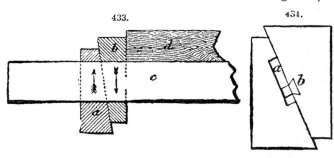

433.   434.

adjusted from the top of the bench, and a very slight tap loosens or tightens it at any height desired. All blows are struck on the top, and no damage results to the bench from its use. It consists simply of 2 wedges $a\,b$ tightening against each other in a mortice cut for their reception in the bench-top c, while d is the piece of wood to be planed. An improvement designed to prevent the wedges falling out when loosened is shown in Fig. 434. It consists of a slip of wood b let into one wedge and a slot a cut in the other, both slot and slip running the whole width of the stop. Fig. 435 is an improved iron stop, which is let in flush with the top of the bench; the top can be raised 2 inches, and is fixed or released by a quarter turn of the screw.

Holdfasts.—These are intended for holding wood down firmly on the top of the bench. For securing wood edge-wise on the table an excellent contrivance is shown in Fig. 436. The strips $a\,b$ are of any hard wood, $1\frac{1}{2}$–2 in. thick, 6–9 in. long, and chamfered underneath. These are screwed firmly to the plank c by 3 ordinary wood screws, with their ends converging somewhat; 2 hard wood wedges d, chamfered, slide in the groove formed by the 2 fixed pieces. Their sides opposite the chamfered part are planed up true and square to the flat sides;

435.

between these the strip to be planed is placed on edge, and the wedges are tapped until they grip the work between them. The pressure of the plane at each stroke has the

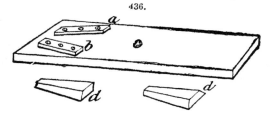

436.

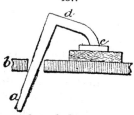

437.

effect of still further tightening the grip of the wedges. The work is held at any part of its length, so that the plane can pass over its whole surface. By a slight pull in the contrary direction, the work is loosened, and can be shifted and refixed.

For holding work in a flat position, use is generally made of the implement illustrated in Fig. 437, and termed a "valet." It is formed of a bar of 1 in. diameter iron, drawn down square, and bent into form. The lower end *a* is inserted in a circular hole through any convenient part of the bench *b*. When it is required to hold work down firmly with it, the work is placed under the end *c*. A sharp blow is then struck with a mallet at *d*, which causes *a* to jamb slightly crosswise in the hole, and so the work is held firmly until by a slight blow at the back of *d* the valet is loosened. Its help is invaluable, as it gives free use of both hands for mortising, carving, or the like; and it is equally an assistant in sawing. To prevent the end *c* leaving ugly marks or dents in soft wood, a small piece of softer wood is placed between it and the work. It is also well to thicken the top of the bench at this spot by screwing a piece of board on beneath But still it is apt to damage the bench, from the nature of the grip of the stem in the hole. A better form is shown in Fig. 438, wherein the necessary pressure on the work under *a* is obtained by means of the screw *b*, which meets the elbow of the rod *c* and transfers the pressure to *a* through the medium of the pivot *d*.

Sawing-rest.—Fig. 439 represents a handy article for holding a piece of wood on the bench while using the tenon-saw. It consists of a strip of hard wood about 9 in. long,

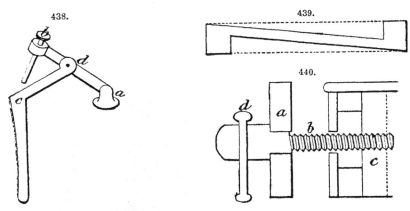

4 in. wide, and 1 in. thick, cut with blocks at the ends as shown. In use, one end hangs over the edge of the bench, and against the other end the work in hand is thrust.

Bench-vices.—Various forms of independent vice have already been described (p. 68). Those now to be mentioned differ in that they are either attached to, or form part of, the bench, and are for the most part of wood. The object of the bench-vice is to hold boards while planing their edges, and pieces of timber while cutting tenons, &c. The simplest substitute for a vice to hold boards for planing is a 1½-in. sq. strip of wood screwed to the front of the bench about 4 in. below the top, and having 2 or 3 thumbscrews or buttons distributed along its length, with wedges to fit between the thumbscrews and the wood to hold it quite tight. The ordinary wooden screw bench-vice, Fig. 440, is a cumbersome arrangement, not particularly effective, and wastes much time in adjusting. It consists of a solid wooden cheek *a* and a wooden screw *b*, the latter working in a female screw cut in a block attached to one leg *c* of the bench in a secure manner. The head of the screw *b* is perforated for the admission of a wooden handle *d* by which it is rotated. The manner of using the vice is sufficiently obvious to need no description. One great fault in the ordinary wooden bench-vice is that there is no means of maintaining parallelism between the cheek of the vice and the leg of the bench against which it grips, so that the screw is sure to be strained sooner or later by the uneven hold it gets of the material placed in the vice. Several plans have been devised to overcome this drawback. That shown in Fig. 441 consists in having a supplementary screw *a* beneath the first; this screw *a* being fixed to the cheek *b*, and working freely through a hole in the leg of the bench *c*, on both sides of which are screw-nuts *d e* that regulate the amount of insertion or withdrawal of the cheek *b*.

The evils of this plan are the trouble and time consumed in the manipulation, and the weakening of the bench-leg *c*, not only by the hole which penetrates, but also by a recess cut in it to receive the screw-nut *e*, in order to permit the jaws of the vice to be completely closed when necessary. A simpler arrangement, which somewhat modifies the undesirable features just noted, is shown in **Fig. 442**, and consists in replacing the

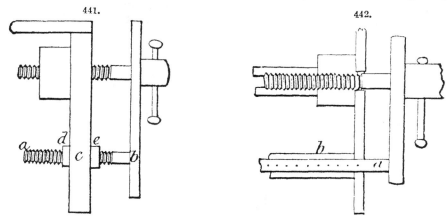

second screw by a sliding bar *a* working in a box *b* fitted to the frame of the bench, and perforated at intervals with holes for the reception of an iron pin to keep it in position. Perhaps the least objectionable plan is the so-called "St. Peter's cross," shown in Fig. 443, consisting of two bars of flat iron placed crosswise, joined by a pin in the centre, and also pinned at the top, one to the cheek and the other to the bench-leg; their lower ends are free to work up and down in the recesses cut for them, and thus maintain the cheek in a perpendicular position, whatever may be its distance from the bench-leg.

A great improvement upon all these forms of vice is the instantaneous grip-vice, represented in Fig. 444. The manner of manipulating it is as follows: Raise the

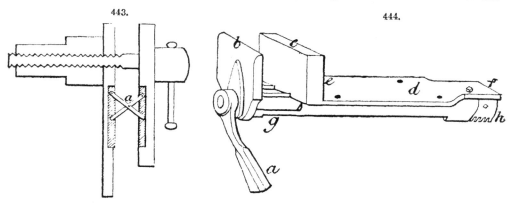

handle *a* to a perpendicular position with the left hand, and draw out or close, as may be necessary, the front jaw *b* the required distance. Place the piece of wood to be operated upon between the jaws *b c*, and press the front jaw *b* nearly close to the wood; then press down the lever, when the wood will be held firm in the vice. To remove the piece of wood, raise the lever. The grip is caused in the following manner: On the under side of the plate *d*, and in the straight line that lies between the letters *e f*, is a plate indented with a row of V-shaped depressions inclined at a slight angle to its sides, in other words, a longitudinal strip cut out of a female screw. At the end *h* of the bar *g h*, which is held in position, and travels in and out between 2 curved flanges projecting from the under side of the plate, is a short cylinder which is grooved along part of its surface with screw-threads, the remainder being left plain, and carrying a stop or stud, which prevents the progress of the screw beyond a certain point, so as not to cause injury to any substance placed within the bite of the jaws. When the piece of wood has been placed within the jaws, and the front jaw pushed nearly close to it, the downward turn of the lever or handle brings the threads of the male screw within the threads of the female screw, and draws the front jaw against the wood tightly, and with

445.

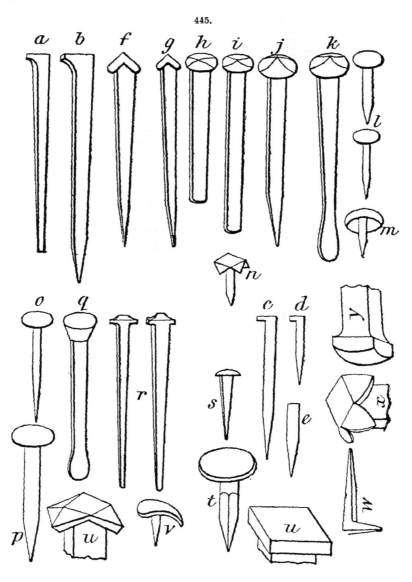

a firm grip, so that it is impossible to remove the material without injuring it, until the ever is raised and the pressure relaxed. The drawing action of the screw causes the pressure of the jaws to be brought gradually, though swiftly, to the point that is required to hold the material immovable within their grasp. The principal advantages of this bench-vice are : (1) it grips and relaxes its hold instantly in any distance up to $13\frac{1}{2}$ in. ; (2) the action and working are so complete that a piece of ordinary writing-paper can be secured and held as firmly as a piece of timber; (3) it effects a saving of about 75 per cent. of the time employed in working the ordinary bench-vice; (4) if wood facings are fitted to the faces of the iron jaws, all possibility of the indentation of the article placed in it is removed; (5) it can be fitted to any description of bench, new or old. The price of the vice is 14s., or if supplied with wood facings fitted to the jaws, 16s. As the jaws are of iron, the vice will serve the purpose of an iron bench-vice for holding pieces of metal, as well as that of an ordinary bench-vice for holding wood; and by placing within the jaws 2 pieces of wood of sufficient length to hold a saw, it may be further utilized as a saw-vice.

Nails.—These are of various shapes and sizes, and are made of wrought, cast, and malleable iron. Fig. 445 illustrates many kinds in general use: *a*, joiners' cut "brad," varying in size from ¼ in. to 2 in. long; *b*, flooring brad, of larger sizes, running 10 lb., 14 lb., 16 lb., and 20 lb. to the 1000, and costing 3s.–5s. per 1000; *c d*, fine cabinet brad, ⅜–2 in.; *e*, sash glaziers' brad; "brads" must be driven so that the head does not cross the grain of the wood, or they will be likely to split it. *f g*, strong and fine "clasp," the former running 7–36 lb. to the 1000, and the latter, 2–6 lb., useful in soft woods; *r*, another form; *h i*, fine and strong "rose," with flat points, the former ranging from 1 to 3½ in. long, and 2½ to 13 lb. per 1000, the latter 5–26 lb., also called "patent wrought"; *j*, "rose" or "gate," with sharp points, 2–3 lb. per 1000, much used in coarse work; *k*, flat point rose, driven across the grain they do not split the wood. *l*, Flemish "tacks"; *m*, round "hob"; *n*, clasp "hob." *o*, fine "clout," 1¾–7 lb. per 1000; *p*, strong "clout"; *q*, countersunk "clout"; *r s*, clog or brush nail; *t*, scupper; *u*, die deck and clasp deck "spikes"; *v*, clinker "tack"; *w*, tenter hook; *x*, diamond deck-spike; *y*, composition spike. Holes should always be prepared for nails by means of a bradawl one size smaller than the nail to be used. Driven across the grain they hold twice as firmly as with it. Wetting the nail before driving causes it to rust slightly and therefore to hold all the more securely.

Nail-punch.—This is simply a piece of tapering steel, used with a hammer for driving the heads of nails below the surface of the wood they are in. Some 3 or 4

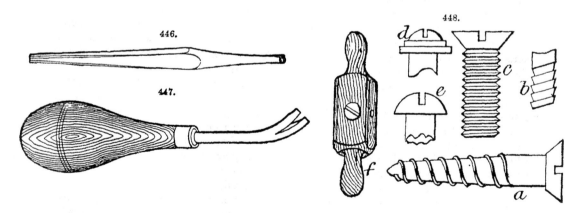

446.

447.

448.

sizes are needed to suit the various nails. The punch is held in the left hand, with the thumb and forefinger grasping the top, and the little finger encircling it below, while the middle and third fingers are placed inside it. Holes in the wood left by the punch must be filled with putty before painting is done. The punch is shown in Fig. 446.

Nail-pullers.—Fig. 447 shows a handy little tack-wrench for drawing small nails out of wood. A more complicated implement is the "Victor" nail-puller, which is said to remove nails without injuring either them or the wood, and which costs 10s.

Screws.—These are made in many sizes and degrees of stoutness, and of both brass and iron. In Fig. 448, *a* is the ordinary "gimlet pointed" wood screw; *b* is the Nettlefold, with a stronger kind of thread; *c*, a stove screw; *d*, head of brass lock screw; *e*, head of japanned lock screw. *f* is a screw box for cutting wooden screws, costing 5s.–15s. Screws are made of the following lengths: $\frac{1}{2}$, $\frac{5}{8}$, $\frac{3}{4}$, $\frac{7}{8}$, 1, $1\frac{1}{4}$, $1\frac{1}{2}$, $1\frac{3}{4}$, 2, $2\frac{1}{4}$, $2\frac{1}{2}$, 3, $3\frac{1}{2}$, 4, 5, and 6 in.; and in each length there are 12–30 different thicknesses, called "numbers."

Screw-driver.—Screws are driven into wood (in holes previously made by a bradawl or gimlet one size smaller) by means of a screw-driver or turnscrew, shown in Fig. 449. This tool consists of a steel blade tapering to a blunt edge at the working end, and fixed by a tang in a wooden handle at the other. The shape and size of both blade and handle depend on the sizes of the screws and the positions in which they are placed, cabinet screw-drivers for

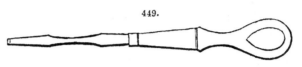

449.

instance being long and light to reach into deep work. Screws hold three times as firmly as nails without risk of splitting the wood, and may be withdrawn without suffering or causing any injury. They are sunk below the surface when necessary by means of a tool called a countersink, described on p. 123. The improved ratchet screw-driver (Churchills) is becoming popular.

Hints on the Care of Tools.—The following hints on the best means of keeping tools in good condition cannot fail to be useful :—

Wooden Parts.—The wooden parts of tools, such as the stocks of planes and handles of chisels, are often made to have a nice appearance by French polishing; but this adds nothing to their durability. A much better plan is to let them soak in linseed oil for a week, and rub them with a cloth for a few minutes every day for a week or two. This produces a beautiful surface, and at the same time exerts a solidifying and preservative action on the wood.

Iron Parts. Rust preventives.—The following recipes are recommended for preventing rust on iron and steel surfaces :—

(1) Caoutchouc-oil is said to have proved efficient in preventing rust, and to have been adopted by the German army. It only requires to be spread with a piece of flannel in a very thin layer over the metallic surface, and allowed to dry up. Such a coating will afford security against all atmospheric influences, and will not show any cracks under the microscope after a year's standing. To remove it, the article has simply to be treated with caoutchouc-oil again, and washed after 12 to 24 hours.

(2) Anti-corrosive oil; an absolutely pure neats-foot oil prepared by Holtzapffel & Co., of Charing Cross, is the best for the lubrication of lathe mandrils and all parts of delicate machinery, it is used by clock and watch makers. A slight coating of this oil wiped over bright steel and iron articles effectively preserves them from rust, it is cleanly in use.

(3) All steel articles can be perfectly preserved from rust by putting a lump of freshly-burnt lime in the drawer or case in which they are kept. If the things are to be moved (as a gun in its case, for instance), put the lime in a muslin bag. This is especially valuable for specimens of iron when fractured, for in a moderately dry place the lime will not want renewing for many years, as it is capable of absorbing a large quantity of moisture. Articles in use should be placed in a box nearly filled with thoroughly pulverized slaked lime. Before using them, rub well with a woollen cloth.

(4) The following mixture forms an excellent brown coating for protecting iron and steel from rust: Dissolve 2 parts crystallized iron chloride, 2 antimony chloride, and 1 tannin, in 4 water, and apply with a sponge or rag, and let dry. Then another coat of the paint is applied, and again another, if necessary, until the colour becomes as dark as desired. When dry, it is washed with water, allowed to dry again, and the surface polished with boiled linseed-oil. The antimony chloride must be as nearly neutral as possible.

(5) To keep tools from rusting, take ½ oz. camphor, dissolve in 1 lb. melted lard; take off the scum and mix in as much fine blacklead (graphite) as will give it an iron colour. Clean the tools, and smear with this mixture. After 24 hours, rub clean with a soft linen cloth. The tools will keep clean for months, under ordinary circumstances.

(6) Put about 1 qt. fresh slaked lime, ½ lb. washing soda, ½ lb. soft soap in a bucket; add sufficient water to cover the articles; put in the tools as soon as possible after use, and wipe them up next morning, or let them remain until wanted.

(7) Soft soap, with about half its weight of pearlash; 1 oz. of the mixture in about 1 gal. boiling water. This is in every-day use in most engineers' shops in the drip-cans used for turning long articles bright in wrought-iron and steel. The work, though constantly moist, does not rust, and bright nuts are immersed in it for days till wanted and retain their polish.

(8) Melt slowly together 6 or 8 oz. lard to 1 oz. rosin, stirring till cool; when it is semi-fluid, it is ready for use. If too thick, it may be further let down by coal-oil or benzine. Rubbed on bright surfaces ever so thinly, it preserves the polish effectually, and may be readily rubbed off.

(9) To protect metals from oxidation—polished iron or steel, for instance—the requisite is to exclude air and moisture from the actual metallic surface; wherefore, polished tools are usually kept in wrappings of oiled cloth and brown paper; and, thus protected, they will preserve a spotless face for an unlimited time. When these metals come to be of necessity exposed, in being converted to use, it is necessary to protect them by means of some permanent dressing; and boiled linseed-oil, which forms a lasting film of covering as it dries on, is one of the best preservatives, if not the best. But in order to give it body, it should be thickened by the addition of some pigment, and the very best—because the most congenial—of pigments is the ground oxide of the same metal—or, in plain words, rusted iron reduced to an impalpable powder, for the dressing of iron or steel—which thus forms the pigment of red oxide paint.

(10) Slake a piece of quick-lime with just water enough to cause it to crumble, in a covered pot, and while hot add tallow to it and work into a paste, and use this to cover over bright work; it can be easily wiped off.

(11) Olmstead's varnish is made by melting 2 oz. rosin in 1 lb. fresh sweet lard, melting the rosin first and then adding the lard and mixing thoroughly. This is applied to the metal, which should be warm if possible, and perfectly cleaned; it is afterwards rubbed off. This has been well proved and tested for many years, and is particularly well suited for planished and Russian iron surfaces, which a slight rust is apt to injure very seriously.

Rust Removers.—(1) Cover the metal with sweet oil well rubbed in, and allow to stand for 48 hours; smear with oil applied freely with a feather or piece of cotton wool, after rubbing the steel. Then rub with unslaked lime reduced to as fine a powder as possible. (2) Immerse the article to be cleaned for a few minutes until all dirt and rust is taken off in a strong solution of potassium cyanide, say about ½ oz. in a wine-glassful of water; take out and clean it with a tooth-brush with some paste composed of potassium cyanide, Castile soap, whiting, and water, mixed into a paste of about the consistence of thick cream.

Construction.—This section of the art of carpentry may be conveniently dealt with in 2 divisions, the first containing a description of the multifarious forms of joint which underlie all kinds of construction in wood, and the second being devoted to some examples illustrating the manner of making various articles of every-day use.

Joints.—The following remarks are principally drawn from an excellent paper on "Joints in Woodwork," read before the Civil and Mechanical Engineers' Society by Henry Adams, and embracing nearly all that need be said when the preceding sections on woods and tools have been duly studied.

Definition of Carpentry and Joinery.—The use of wood may be discussed under the 2 heads of carpentry and joinery : the former consists principally in using large timbers, rough, adzed, or sawn; the latter employs smaller pieces, always sawn, and with the exposed surfaces planed. Carpenters' work is chiefly outdoor, and embraces such objects as building timber bridges and gantries, framing roofs and floors, constructing centreing, and other heavy or rough work. Joiners' work is mostly indoor, and includes laying flooring, making and fixing doors, window sashes, frames, linings, partitions, and internal fittings generally.

Principles of Joints.—In all cases the proper connection of the parts is an essential element, and in designing or executing joints and fastenings in woodwork, the following principles, laid down by Professor Rankine, should be adhered to, viz. :—

(1) To cut the joints and arrange the fastenings so as to weaken the pieces of timber that they connect as little as possible.

(2) To place each abutting surface in a joint as nearly as possible perpendicular to the pressure which it has to transmit.

(3) To proportion the area of each surface to the pressure which it has to bear, so that the timber may be safe against injury under the heaviest load which occurs in practice, and to form and fit every pair of such surfaces accurately in order to distribute the stress uniformly.

(4) To proportion the fastenings so that they may be of equal strength with the pieces which they connect.

(5) To place the fastenings in each piece of timber so that there shall be sufficient resistance to the giving way of the joint by the fastenings shearing or crushing their way through the timber.

(6) To these may be added a 6th principle not less important than the foregoing; viz. to select the simplest forms of joints, and to obtain the smallest possible number of abutments. The reason for this is that the more complicated the joint, or the greater the number of bearing surfaces, the less probability there will be of getting a sound and cheaply-made connection.

Equal Bearing.—To ensure a fair and equal bearing in a joint which is not quite true, it is usual, after the pieces are put together, to run a saw-cut between each bearing surface or abutment; the kerf or width of cut being equal in each case, the bearing is then rendered true. This is often done, for instance, with the shoulders of a tenon or the butting ends of a scarf, when careless workmanship has rendered it necessary.

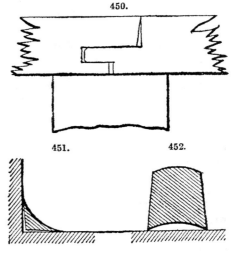

Close Jointing.—When the visible junction of 2 pieces is required to be as close as possible and no great strain has to be met at the joint, it is usual to slightly undercut the parts, and give clearance on the inside, as in Fig. 450, which shows an enlarged view of a tongued and rebated heading joint in flooring. In pattern-making, the fillets which are placed at the internal angle of 2 meeting surfaces are made obtuse angled on the back, in order that when bradded into place the sharp edges may lie close, as shown in Fig. 451. The prints used by pattern-makers for indicating the position of round-cored holes are also undercut by being turned slightly hollow on the bottom, as shown in Fig. 452. This principle is adopted in nearly all cases where a close joint is a desideratum. Clearance must also be left in joints of framing when a settlement is likely to take place, in order that, after the settlement, the abutting surfaces may take a fair bearing to resist the strain.

Strains.—The various strains that can come upon any member of a structure are—(1) Tension: stretching or pulling; (2) Compression: crushing or pushing; (3) Transverse strain: cross strain or bending; (4) Torsion: twisting or wrenching; (5) Shearing: cutting. But in woodwork, when the last-named force acts along the grain, it is generally called "detrusion," the term shearing being limited to the action across the grain. The first 3 varieties are the strains which usually come upon ties, struts, and beams respectively. The transverse strain, it must be observed, is resolvable into tension and compression, the former occurring on the convex side of a loaded beam, and the latter on the concave side, the 2 being separated by the neutral axis or line of no strain. The shearing strain occurs principally in beams, and is greatest at the point of support, the tendency being to cut the timber through at right angles to the grain; but in nearly all cases, if the timber is strong enough to resist the transverse strain, it is amply strong for any possible shearing strain which can occur. Keys and other fastenings are especially subject to shearing strain, and it will be shown in that portion of the subject that there are certain precautions to be adopted to obtain the best results.

Classification of Joints.—(1) Joints for lengthening ties, struts, and beams; lapping, fishing, scarfing, tabling, building-up; (2) Bearing-joints for beams: halving, notching, cogging, dovetailing, tusk-tenoning, housing, chase-mortising; (3) Joints for posts and beams: tenon, joggle, bridle, housing; (4) Joints for struts with ties and posts: oblique tenon, bridle, toe-joint; (5) Miscellaneous: butting, mitreing, rebating.

Classification of Fastenings.—(1) wedges; (2) keys; (3) pins: wood pins, nails, spikes, treenails, screws, bolts; (4) straps; (5) sockets; (6) glue.

Lengthening Joints.—One of the first requirements in the use of timber for constructive purposes is the connection of 2 or more beams to obtain a greater length. Fig. 453 shows the method of lengthening a beam by lapping another to it, the 2 being held

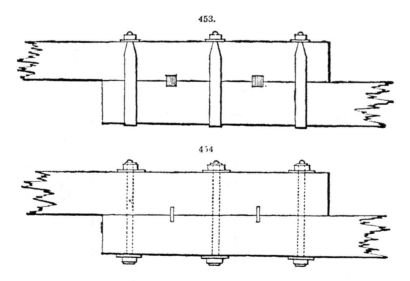

453.

454

together by straps and prevented from sliding by the insertion of keys. Fig. 454 shows a similar joint, through-bolts being used instead of straps, and wrought-iron plates instead of oak keys. This makes a neater joint than the former, but they are both unsightly, and whenever adopted the beams should be arranged in 3 or 5 pieces, in order that the supports at each end may be level, and the beams horizontal. This joint is more suitable for a cross strain than for tension and compression. Fig. 455

shows the common form of a fished beam adapted for compression. If required to resist tensile strain, keys should be inserted in the top and bottom joints between the bolts. Fig. 456 shows a fished joint adapted for a cross strain, the whole sectional area of the original beam taking the compressive portion of the cross strain, and the fishing-piece

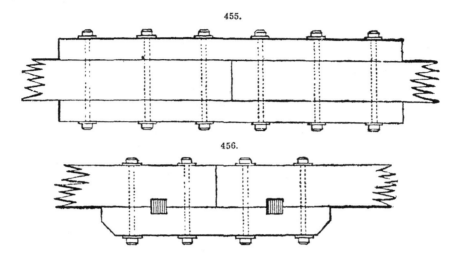

455.

456.

taking the tensile portion. Fig. 457 shows a fished beam for the same purpose, in which a wrought-iron plate turned up at the ends takes the tensile strain. Tabling consists of bedding portions of one beam into the other longitudinally. Occasionally the fishing-pieces are tabled at the ends into the beams to resist the tendency to slip

457.

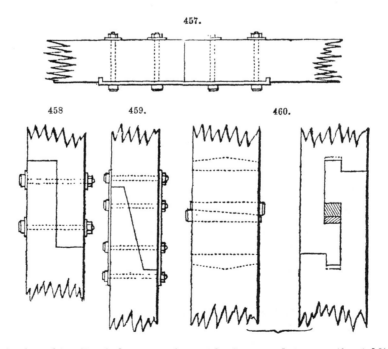

458   459.   460.

under strain, but this office is better performed by keys, and in practice tabling is not much used. The distinction between fished beams and scarfed beams is that in the former the original length is not reduced, the pieces being butted against each other, while in the latter the beams themselves are cut in a special manner and lapped partly over each other; in both cases, additional pieces of wood or iron are attached to strengthen the joint. Fig. 458 shows a form of scarf adapted to short posts. Here the scarf is cut square and parallel to the sides, so that the full sectional area is utilized for resisting the compressive strain. When the post is longer and liable to a bending strain, the scarf should be inclined, as in Fig. 459, to allow of greater thickness being retained at the shoulder of each piece, the shoulder being kept square. In this joint a considerable strain may be thrown on the bolts from the sliding tendency of the scarf, if the shoulders should happen to be badly fitted, as any slipping would virtually increase the thickness of the timber where the bolts pass through. The width of each shoulder should be not less than $\frac{1}{4}$ the total thickness. Joints in posts are mostly required when it is desired to lengthen piles already driven, to support a superstructure in the manner of columns. Another form of scarf for a post put together without bolts is shown in Fig. 460, the parts being tabled and tongued, and held together by wedges. This is not a satisfactory joint, and is, moreover, expensive, because of its requiring extra care in fitting; but it may be a suitable joint in some special cases, in which all the sides are required to be flush. Fig. 461 shows the common form of scarf in a tie-beam. The

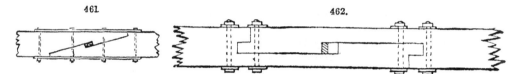

ends of the scarf are birds'-mouthed, and the joint is tightened up by wedges driven from opposite sides. It is further secured by the wrought-iron plates on the top and bottom, which are attached to the timber by bolts and nuts. In all these joints the friction between the surfaces, due to the bolts being tightly screwed up, plays an important part in the strength of the joint; and as all timber is liable to shrink, it is necessary to examine the bolts occasionally, and to keep them well tightened up. Figs. 462 and 463 show

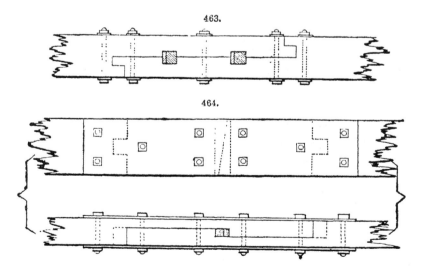

good forms of scarfs, which are stronger but not so common as the preceding. Sometimes the scarf is made vertically instead of horizontally; when this is done, a slight modification is made in the position of the projecting tongue, as will be seen from Fig. 464, which shows the joint in elevation and plan. The only other scarfs to which attention need be called are those shown in Figs. 465 and 466, in which the compression side is made with a square abutment. These are very strong forms, and at the same time easily made. Many other forms have been designed, and old books on carpentry teem with scarfs of every conceivable pattern; but in this, as in many other cases, the simplest thing is the best, as the whole value depends upon the accuracy of the workmanship, and this is rendered excessively difficult with a multiplicity of parts or abutments.

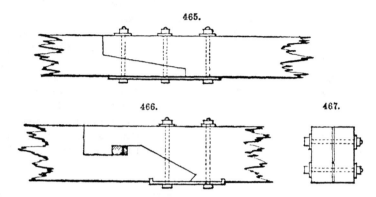

465.

466.   467.

Strengthening.—In building-up beams to obtain increased strength, the most usual method is to lay 2 beams together sideways for short spans, as in the lintels over doors and windows; or to cut one down the middle, and reverse the halves, inserting a wrought-iron plate between, as shown in the flitch girder, Fig. 467. The reversal of the halves gives no additional strength, as many workmen suppose, but it enables one to see if the timber is sound throughout at the heart, and also allows the pieces to season better. A beam uncut may be decayed in the centre, and hence the advantage of cutting and reversing, even if no flitch-plate is to be inserted, defective pieces being then discarded. When very long and strong beams are required, a simple method is to bolt several together so as to break joint with each other, as shown in Fig. 468, taking care that on

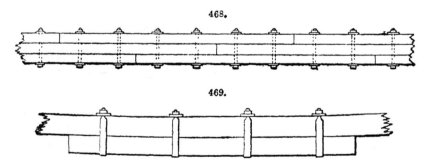

468.

469.

the tension side the middle of one piece comes in the centre of the span with the 2 nearest joints equidistant. It is not necessary in a built beam to carry the full depth as far as the supports; the strain is, of course, greatest in the centre, and provided there is sufficient depth given at that point, the beam may be reduced towards the ends, allowance being made for the loss of strength at the joints on tension side. A single piece of timber secured to the under side of a beam at the centre, as in Fig. 469, is a simple and effective mode of increasing its strength. It will be observed that the straps are bedded into the sides of the beams; they thus form keys to prevent the pieces from slipping on each other. This weakens the timber much less than cutting out the top or bottom, as the strength of a beam varies only in direct proportion to the breadth but as the square of the depth. The addition of a second piece of timber in the middle is a method frequently adopted for strengthening shear legs and derrick poles temporarily for lifting heavy weights.

Bearing Joints.—In a consideration of bearing joints for beams, the term "beam" is taken to include all pieces which carry or receive a load across the grain. The simplest of these is the halving joint, shown at Fig. 470, where 2 pieces of cross bracing are

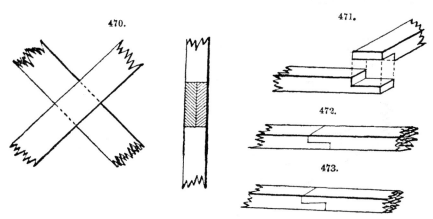

470.
471.
472.
473.

halved together. This joint is also shown at Fig. 471, where the ends of 2 wall plates meet each other. When a joint occurs in the length of a beam, as at Fig. 472, it is generally called a scarf. In each of these examples it will be seen that half the thickness of each piece is cut away so as to make the joint flush top and bottom. Sometimes the outer end of the upper piece is made thicker, forming a bevelled joint and acting as a dovetail when loaded on top. This is shown at Figs. 473 and 474. When a beam crosses another at right angles, and is cut on the lower side to fit upon it, the joint is known as single-notching, shown in Fig. 475. When both are cut, as in Fig. 476, it is known as double-notching. These forms occur in bridging and ceiling joists. When a

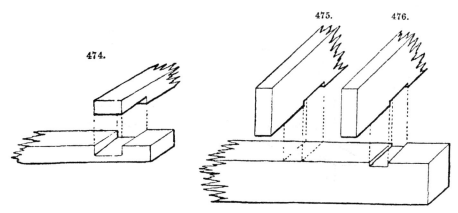

475.
476.
474.

cog or solid projecting portion is cut in the lower piece at the middle of the joint it is known as cogging or caulking, and is shown in Fig. 477. Figs. 478 and 479 show two forms of the joint occurring between a tie-beam and wall plate in roofing. Dovetailing is not much used in carpentry or house joinery, owing to the shrinkage of the wood loosening the joint: 2 wall plates are shown dovetailed together at Figs. 480 and 481; in the latter, a wedge is sometimes inserted on the straight side to enable the joint to be tightened up as the wood shrinks. Tredgold proposed the form shown in Fig. 482, which

is known as the " Tredgold notch ; " but this is never seen in practice.   Tusk-tenoning is
the method adopted for obtaining a bearing for a beam meeting another at right angles
at the same level.   Fig. 483 shows a trimmer supported on a trimming joist in this
manner ; this occurs round fireplaces, hoistways, and other openings through floors.
Fig. 484 shows the same joint between a wood girder and binding joist ; it is also used
in double-framed flooring.   The advantage of this form is that a good bearing is
obtained without weakening the beam to any very great extent, as the principal portion

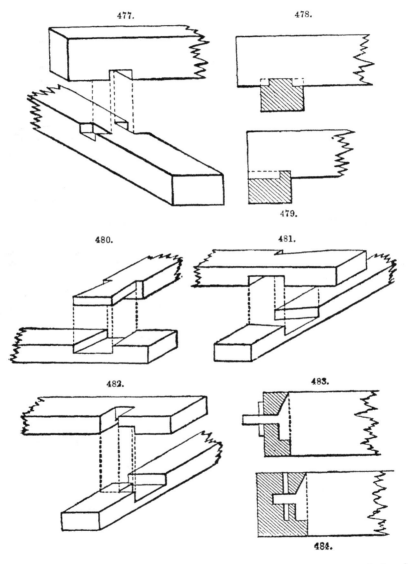

of the material removed is taken from the neutral axis, leaving the remainder disposed
somewhat after the form of a flanged girder.   When a cross-piece of timber has to be
framed in between 2 beams already fixed, a tenon and chase-mortice (Fig. 485) is one of
the methods adopted.   If the space is very confined, the same kind of mortice is made
in both beams, but in opposite directions ; the cross-piece is then held obliquely and slid
into place.   Occasionally it is necessary to make the chase-mortice vertical ; but this is
not to be recommended, as the beam is much weakened by so doing—it is shown in

Fig. 486. In some cases of ceiling joists a square fillet is nailed on the tenon and chase-mortice, to take the weight of the joists without cutting into the beam. While speaking of floors, the process of firring-up may be mentioned; this consists of laying thin pieces, or strips, of wood on the top of joists, or any surfaces, to bring them up to a level. Firring-pieces are also sometimes nailed underneath the large beams in framed floors, so that the under side may be level with the bottom of the ceiling joists, to give a bearing for the laths, and at the same time allow sufficient space for the plaster to form a key.

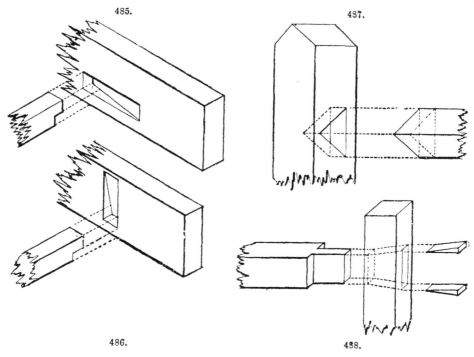

485.

487.

486.

488.

Brandering is formed by strips about 1 in. square, nailed to the under side of the ceiling joists at right angles to them; these strips help to stiffen the ceiling, and, being narrower than the ceiling joists, do not interrupt the key of the plastering so much. Housing consists of letting a piece of wood bodily into another for a short distance, or, as it were, a tenon the full size of the stuff; this is used in staircases, housed into the strings, and held by wedges. Housing is likewise adopted for fixing rails to posts, as in Fig. 487, where an arris rail is shown housed into an oak post for fencing.

Post and Beam Joints.—The most common joint between posts and beams is the tenon and mortice joint, either wedged or fixed by a pin; the former arrangement is shown in Fig. 488, and the latter in Fig. 489. The friction of the wedges, when tightly driven, aided by the adhesion of the glue or white-lead with which they are coated, forms, in effect, a solid dovetail, and the fibres, being compressed, do not yield further by the shrinking of the wood. A framed door is an example of the application of this joint. When it is desired to tenon a beam into a post, without allowing the tenon to show through, or where a mortice has to be made in an existing post fixed against a wall, the dovetail tenon, shown in Fig. 490, is sometimes adopted, a wedge being driven in on the straight side to draw the tenon home and keep it in place. In joining small pieces, the foxtail tenon, shown in Fig. 491, has the same advantage as the dovetail tenon of not showing through, but it is more difficult to fix. The outer wedges are made the longest, and in driving the tenon home, these come into action first, splitting away the sides, and filling up the dovetailed mortice, at the same time compressing the fibres of the tenon. This joint requires no glue, as it cannot draw out; should it work loose at any time, the only way to tighten it up would be to insert a very thin wedge in one end of the mortice. Short tenons, assisted by strap bolts, as shown in Fig. 492, are commonly adopted in connecting large timbers. The post is cut to form a shoulder so that the beam

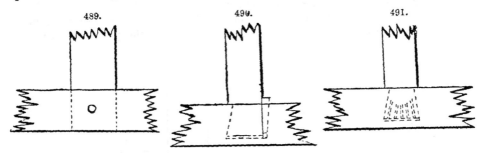

takes a bearing for its full width, the tenon preventing any side movement. When a post rests on a beam or sill piece, its movement is prevented by a "joggle," or stub-tenon, as shown in Fig. 493; but too much reliance should not be placed on this tenon, owing to the impossibility of seeing, after the pieces are fixed, whether it has been properly

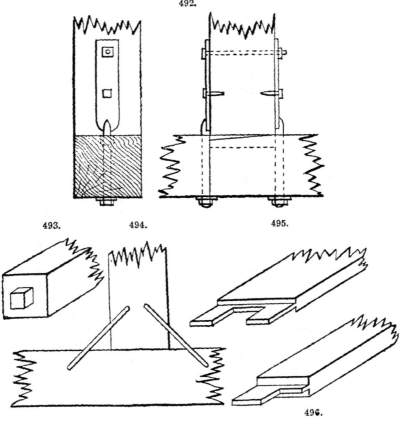

fitted, and it is particularly liable to decay from moisture settling in the joint. For temporary purposes, posts are commonly secured to heads and sills by dog-irons or "dogs," Fig. 494; the pieces in this case simply butt against each other, the object being to avoid cutting the timber, and so depreciating its value, and also for economy of labour

Other forms of tenons are shown in Figs. 495 and 496. The double tenon is used in framing wide pieces, and the haunched tenon when the edge of the piece on which the tenon is formed is required to be flush with the end of the piece containing the mortice. In Figs. 497 and 498 are shown 2 forms of bridle joint between a post and beam.

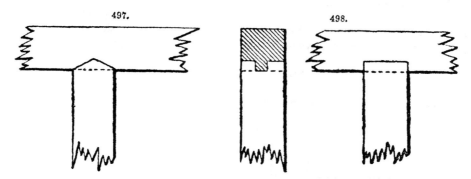

497.   498.

Tredgold recommended a bridle joint with a circular abutment, but this is not a correct form, as the post is then equivalent to a column with rounded ends, which it is well known is unable in that form to bear so great a load before it commences to yield.

Strut Joints.—A strut meeting a tie, as in the case of the foot of a principal rafter in a roof truss, is generally tenoned into the tie by an oblique tenon, as shown in Fig. 499 ; and the joint is further strengthened by a toe on the rafter bearing against a shoulder in the tie   Tredgold strongly advised this joint being made with a bridle instead of a tenon, as shown in Fig. 500, on account of the abutting surfaces being fully open to view.   A strut meeting a post as in Fig. 501, or a strut meeting the principal rafter of a roof truss (Fig. 502), is usually connected by a simple toe-joint.   The shoulder

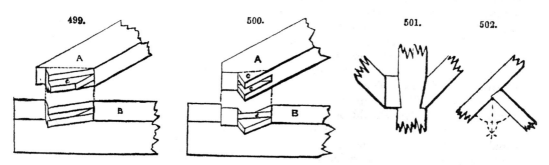

499.   500.   501.   502.

should be cut square with the piece containing it, or it should bisect the angle formed between the two pieces.   It is sometimes made square with the strut, but this is incorrect, as there would in some cases be a possibility of the piece slipping out.   In ledged and braced doors or gates this joint is used, the pieces being so arranged as to form triangles, and so prevent the liability to sag or drop, which is difficult to guard against in square-framed work without struts or braces.   When a structure is triangulated, its shape remains constant so long as the fastenings are not torn away, because, with a given length of sides, a triangle can assume only one position; but this is not the case with four-sided framing, as the sides, while remaining constant in length, may vary in position.   A mansard roof contains various examples of a toe-joint; it shows also the principle of framing king-post and queen-post roof trusses, each portion being triangulated to ensure the utmost stability.

Miscellaneous Joints.—Among the miscellaneous joints in carpentry not previously mentioned, the most common are the butt-joint, Fig. 503, where the pieces meet each other with square ends or sides; the mitre-joint, Fig. 504, where the pieces abut against each other with bevelled ends, bisecting the angle between them, as in the case of struts mitred to a corbel piece supporting the beam of a gantry; and the rabbeted or "rebated" joint, Fig. 505, which is a kind of narrow halving, either transverse or longitudinal. To these must be added in joinery the grooved and tongued joint, Fig. 506; the matched and beaded joint, Fig. 507; the dowelled joint, Fig. 508; the dovetailed joint, Fig. 509; and other modifications of these to suit special purposes. To one of

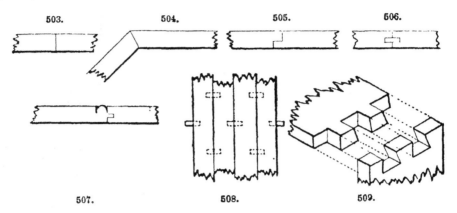

these it may be desirable to call particular attention, viz. the flooring laid folding. This is a method of obtaining close joints without the use of a cramp. It consists of nailing down 2 boards, and leaving a space between them rather less than the width of, say 5 boards; these 5 boards are then put in place, and the two projecting edges are forced down by laying a plank across them, and standing on it. This may generally be detected in old floors by observing that several heading joints come in one line, instead of breaking joint with each other. It is worthy of notice that the tongue, or slip feather, shown in Fig. 506, which in good work is formed generally of hard wood, is made up of short pieces cut diagonally across the grain of the plank, in order that any movement of the joints may not split the tongue, which would inevitably occur if it were cut longitudinally from the plank.

Fastenings.—With regard to fastenings, the figures already given show several applications. Wedges should be split or torn from the log, so that the grain may be continuous; or if sawn out, a straight-grained piece should be selected. Sufficient taper should be put on to give enough compression to the joint, but too much taper would allow the possibility of the wedge working loose. For outside work, wedges should be painted over with white-lead before being driven, this not being affected by moisture, as glue would be. In scarf joints the chief use of wedges is to draw the parts together before the bolt holes are bored. Keys are nearly parallel strips of hard wood or metal; they are usually made with a slight draft, to enable them to fit tightly. If the key is cut lengthways of the grain, a piece with curled or twisted grain should be selected, but if this cannot be done, the key should be cut crossways of the log from which it is taken, and inserted in the joint with the grain at right angles to the direction of the strain, so that the shearing stress to which the key is subject may act upon it across the fibres. In timber bridges and other large structures, cast-iron keys are frequently used, as there is with them an absence of all difficulty from shrinkage. Wooden pins should be selected in the same way as wedges, from straight-grained, hard wood. Square pins are more efficient than round, but are not often used, on account of the difficulty of forming square holes for their reception. Tenons are frequently secured in mortices, as in Fig. 489, by pins, the pins being driven in such a manner as to draw the tenon tightly into the mortice up to its shoulders, and afterwards to hold it there. This is done by boring the hole first through the cheeks of the mortice, then inserting the tenon, marking off the position of the hole, removing the tenon, and boring the pin-hole in it rather nearer the shoulders than the mark, so that when the pin is driven it will draw the tenon as above described. The dowelled floor shown in Fig. 508 gives another example of the use of pins.

Nails, and their uses, are too well known to need description; it may, however, be well to call attention to the two kinds of cut and wrought nails, the former being sheared or stamped out of plates, and the latter forged out of rods. The cut nails are cheaper, but are rather brittle; they are useful in many kinds of work, as they may be driven without previously boring holes to receive them, being rather blunt.pointed and having 2 parallel sides, which are placed in the direction of the grain of the wood. The wrought nails do not easily break, and are used where it is desired to clench them on the back to draw and hold the wood together. Spikes are nearly of the same form as nails, but much larger, and are mostly used for heavy timber work. Treenails are hard wooden pins used in the same way as nails. In particular work, with some woods, such as oak, they are used to prevent the staining of the wood, which would occur if nails were used and any moisture afterwards reached them. Compressed treenails are largely used for fixing railway chairs to sleepers, as they swell on exposure to moisture, and then hold more firmly. Screws are used in situations where the parts may afterwards require to be disconnected. They are more useful than nails, as they not only connect the parts, but draw them closer together, and are more secure. For joiners' work the screws usually have countersunk heads; where it is desired to conceal them, they are let well into the wood, and the holes plugged with dowels of the same kind of wood, with the grain in the same direction. For carpenters' work the screws are larger and have often square heads; these are known as coach screws. The bolts, nuts, and washers used in carpentry may be of the proportions given in the following table:—

Thickness of nut	$= 1$ diam. of bolt.
„ head	$= \frac{3}{4}$ „
Diameter of head or nut over sides	$= 1\frac{3}{4}$ „
Side of square washer for fir	$= 3\frac{1}{2}$ „
„ „ oak	$= 2\frac{1}{2}$ „
Thickness of washer	$= \frac{1}{3}$ „

The square nuts used by carpenters are generally much too thin; unless they are equal in thickness to the diameter of the bolt, the full advantage of that diameter cannot be obtained, the strength of any connection being measured by its weakest part. The best proportion for nuts is that of a Whitworth standard hexagon nut. A large square washer is generally put under the nut to prevent it from sinking into the wood and tearing the fibres while being screwed up; but it is also necessary to put a similar washer under the head to prevent it sinking into the wood. This is, however, often improperly omitted. Straps are bands of wrought iron placed over a joint to strengthen it and tie the parts together. When the strap is carried round a piece, and both ends are secured to a piece joining it at right angles, as in a king-post and tie-beam, it is known as a stirrup, and is tightened by means of a cotter and gib keys, as shown in Fig. 510. When straps connect more than two pieces of timber together, they are made with a branch leading in the direction of each piece; but they are usually not strong enough at the point of junction, and might often be made shorter than they are without impairing their

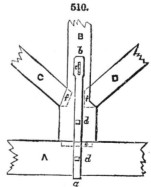

510.

efficiency. Sockets are generally of cast iron, and may be described as hollow boxes formed to receive the ends of timber framing.

With regard to the use of glue for securing joints, it has been found that the tensile strength of solid glue is about 4000 lb. per sq. in., while that of a glued joint in damp weather is 350–360 lb. per sq. in., and in dry weather about 715 lb. The lateral cohesion of fir wood is about 562 lb. per sq. in., and therefore in a good glue joint the solid material will give way before the junction yields.

Keying.—This is a useful joint for uniting pieces of wood at right angles, as in the sides of a box, where much strength is not needed. Each end is mitred off and the bevels are then joined by glue. When the glued joint is quite firm, a few saw cuts are made in the angle, so as to cross both pieces forming the joint, and into the kerfs are driven small slips of wood previously well glued. After all has dried, the projecting ends of the keys are cut off. The direction of the saw cuts should not be horizontal: some may incline upwards and some downwards.

Corner-piecing.—This is another weak joint, only admissible in the lightest work. The bevelled ends of the side pieces (of a box, for instance) are glued together as for keying, and then a triangular piece is glued inside the corner.

Mortising and Tenoning.—This joint is so important and so constantly employed in one modification or another in almost all branches of carpentry and joinery that it deserves special description at some length. The gauge used for marking out the mortice has been spoken of on p. 61 ; and the use of the chisel in cutting it out has been explained on p. 107. In cutting the tenon, a very sharp and accurately set saw should be used, so that the edges left will need no paring or trimming of any kind. The simple mortice and tenon have been shown on p. 108. In sawing the shoulders of a tenon, there should be just a tendency to undercutting them, as a safeguard against rounding them. A few words may be said about wedging and pinning. Suppose that a tenon nicely fitted is to be wedged and glued. Taking it out of the mortice, the latter has a wedge-like portion cut out on each side to be filled in by a pair of wooden wedges of similar form. If these are made short and blunt, they will not be able to be driven home, but will jump back, and have no effect in tightening up the joint by drawing the parts together. The wedges should be long in proportion to their thickness. The object is to convert a straight tenon into a dovetailed shape, which cannot be drawn back out of its mortice. The whole tenon and the wedges are carefully glued with hot glue, about as thick as cream, the wood having also been well warmed. The joint is driven up, wedged, and left to dry. In pinning a tenon and mortice through (which is always the method used in heavy carpentry), having cut and fitted the parts accurately, bore through the mortice carefully at right angles, having just removed the tenon. Use for this a shell or nose bit in a brace. Now insert the tenon, put the nose bit in again, and just begin to bore the tenon sufficiently to mark it. Take it out and bore the hole about $\frac{1}{20}$ in. nearer the shoulder of the tenon than you would have done if it had been left in its mortice and bored while therein. Then make a nice oak pin, and not too tapering, but a tight fit ; as it enters the hole in the tenon, it will draw it in close in the endeavour to bring its hole true with those of the mortice. It must not be so bored that it cannot draw in, and so will be in danger of tearing and splitting : but must almost tally at the outset with the other holes. This forms a perfect joint that can (if need be) be at any time separated by knocking out the pin, which is sometimes left long that it may be more readily driven back

As an example of more difficult fitting, it sometimes happens that the mortice is cut in a piece of hexagonal form, or rather section of that nature, and that a rail has to be fitted in which the shoulders of the tenon must be so made as to embrace the parts about the mortice. Fig. 511, *a* and *b*, represents such. The shoulders *c, d,* are specially difficult to pare, owing to the angular direction of the grain, as the natural way of cutting such a surface smoothly would be to work from *x* to *y* of *e*, and this cannot be done in this case. It may be pared with a chisel more readily when laid down on its side, as at *f*, the chisel cutting perpendicularly ; but the angles frequently prohibit the chisel from cutting into them closely. Still, there is no help for it, and there is no job which requires a sharper tool deftly managed. When the work is small, the finest saw, used carefully, may suffice without any subsequent paring, and is the safer tool to use. When, however, the parts are to be constructed of wood of more than usually curled grain, it may suffice to cut a recess into the standard, to receive the hexagonal rail itself beyond its tenon, Fig. 512, *a*, *b*, and *c*, where the mortice is shown quite black, and the recess is

511.   512.

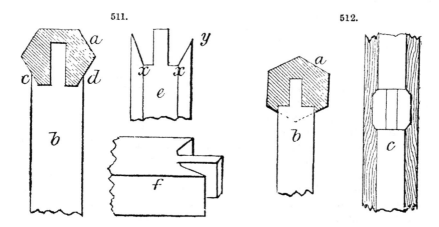

shaded. Neatly done, the effect is the same as when the shoulders are cut, as in the previous case ; but allowance must be made in the length of the rail, or it will, of course, be too short when fitted into its place. The first plan, even if well done, is not so strong as the second, and, in an outdoor job, where exposed, the latter would be far less liable to admit rain to injure the tenon ; but there are many cases in which the same kind of fitting is needed where a plan similar to that first described is essential. It should be borne in mind that a mortice and tenon ought to just slide stiffly into place, without requiring a lot of knocking with the mallet.

513.

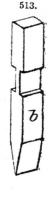

A curious form of mortice and tenon is shown in Fig. 513, and is made in the following manner:—Get 2 pieces of clean, straight-grained yellow pine, recently cut from the log that is not seasoned, 9 in. long, $1\frac{1}{4}$ in. broad, and $\frac{7}{8}$ in. thick. In the middle of one of these make a $\frac{1}{4}$-in. mortice $1\frac{1}{4}$ in. long, as at *a* ; and on the other piece, after it has been dressed to $\frac{3}{4}$ in. thick at 3 in. from one end, make a tenon $\frac{1}{4}$ in. thick and $1\frac{1}{4}$ in. long, as at *b*, and taper the other end as shown, so as to make it easy to introduce into the mortice. Then get both pieces steamed, and while they are heating prepare something to support the sides of *a*, so as to prevent it from splitting when *b* is being driven through, and a strong cramp or vice to compress *b*. When the wood is thoroughly steamed, place *b* in the vice or cramp, with a piece of hard wood on each side, so as to press its whole surface from the tenon to the tapered end equally, and screw up as hard as possible. Withdraw *a* from the

steam, and place it in its prepared position ; try the screw again on *b* ; then take it out, enter its tapered end into the mortice, and drive through until the shoulders that have not been pressed rest on *a* ; put them into warm water for several hours, then take them out and dry ; afterwards cut all the arms to an equal length, and clean off. It will allow of examination better if the tenon on *b* is made 2 in. long, so as to enable *a* to be moved along, as when all is firmly together it will be at once asserted that the cross is made of 3 pieces. Obviously no practical carpenter would use such a joint, as the wood must suffer much in the unequal compression and expansion of its fibres, besides giving no particular strength. It is a sort of puzzle in joinery.

Half-lap Joint.—This is an every-day joint, and apparently one of the simplest, yet it is very often badly made. Each of the pieces has 3 surfaces in contact, viz. the broad face a of Fig. 514, the side d, the front b, corresponding to similar ones on h, to which it is supposed to be necessary to attach it at right angles. As a joint it has no strength however well made; but it is of very frequent use in stuff of all sizes, and is used not only to join a piece at right angles (or at some intermediate angle) to another, but also to join them length wise. The line of the end b must be accurately scribed with the help of a square, and, with the same appliance, the line answering to $c\ e$ of h must be marked round 3 sides of each piece. Then with a marking gauge, $e\ f$ and its counterpart,

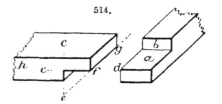

514.

which, together, determine the plane of a, are set off, and this line is carried along the end g. On white wood, a finely-pointed (or finely-edged) pencil will make a better line. It is here that amateurs are apt to be lazy. They mark perhaps b, saw down a shoulder, with no further guide line, and holding a broad chisel at the end, hit it with a mallet, and off goes the whole cheek piece, leaving possibly a fairly true face, and more generally a very *untrue* one—so untrue frequently that no subsequent paring will correct it. But as it will be much concealed from view, it is allowed to pass muster, and a nice botched job it makes. Supposing this intended, as it often is, to be a glued joint, the great object to be aimed at is to make each face as level and true as possible, so as to provide plenty of surface contact. We may, in this way, even make the half-lap joint strong enough. Hence it is essentially necessary to scribe all lines with accuracy, and then to cut precisely up to them. The cutting across the grain will, of course, be done by the tenon saw, which be will carried down to the line gauged to show the line $e\ f$ marking the position of the half-thickness of the stuff. Then the work should be stood end up in the vice, and the cheek piece carefully removed, leaving the surface, if possible, so flat and true as not to need subsequent dressing with the chisel. A small hand saw will do this best, its teeth set out only just so far as to prevent the blade from binding in the cut. A saw known as a panel saw will do nicely; a large hand saw with much set is far more difficult to use.

Dovetailing.—This forms a secure and strong joint, but needs great care in marking out and cutting the work. The dovetails should not have too sharp angles, or they will be liable to be broken off. The fit may be tight, but not so tight as to require considerable force to effect a juncture, or the top and bottom dove-tails may be split off. When a dovetail joint is used at a corner that is to be rounded externally, the joint should be made in the usual way first, and the rounding done afterwards.

Blind Dovetails.—These are so named when the pins or dovetails, or both, are hidden from view in the finished article. One plan, in which the joint is seen at the side only, is shown in Fig. 515. The wood a forming the side should be rather thinner than b on the front. The pins c are cut first, and their outline is marked out on b, in which the sockets are then cut for their reception, noting that these sockets do not extend farther in length than the dotted line d, nor farther in width than the dotted line e.

The plan illustrated in Fig. 516 allows only a line to be seen in the side piece. In this case, each piece has a distance marked off on it equalling the thickness of the piece to be joined to it; at about half this thickness another line is marked to indicate the depth (in the thickness of the wood) to which the pins and dovetails are to be cut. As the pins in *a* have to overlap and hide the ends of the dovetails, half their (the pins') length is cut off after their full dimension has been used in marking out the dovetails. All the cutting must be carefully done with a chisel. When the joint is complete

515.   516.

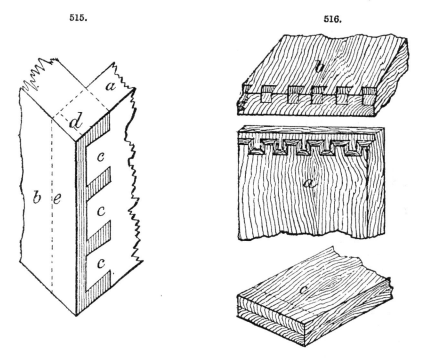

and dry, the edge of the lap on *a* can be rounded. Or again, by making a lap on each piece and cutting the edges of the laps to the same bevel, they will meet so as to exhibit only a single line at the corner.

Mechanical aids in dovetailing.—To an amateur, dovetailing is no easy matter, when beauty and strength of joint are aimed at. The pins are less difficult to make than the dovetails, but they must be truly vertical. The real trouble is with the dovetails, as they are on arbitrary lines. Much assistance may be got from the employment of a fret sawing machine. This should either have a wooden table, or its iron table must be covered with a wooden one $\frac{3}{4}$ in. thick. On this are scribed, $\frac{1}{2}$ in. apart, parallel lines at right angles to the saw front; about $\frac{1}{3}$ in. in front of it is grooved out $\frac{1}{2}$ in. deep between the lines. Fitted to slide in this groove, 2 pieces of hard wood are prepared: one carries, at right angles, a sloping block as a guide for cutting the pins, and the other a similar guide for the dovetails. Screws can be used to hold the guides in place. A slot is cut through the table (or false table, as the case may be) to let the saw work. The guides just described are used to regulate and govern the direction of the saw so that it shall not deviate from the lines marked out.

Dowelling.—The "dowels," which are tapering cylindrical pegs of tough wood, prepared beforehand, and kept dry, should be placed 3–12 in. apart in holes prepared for them by the centre-bit, all of uniform depth (secured by a gauge on the bit), and countersunk. The dowels are cut $\frac{1}{8}$ in. shorter than the united depths of the holes, and rounded at the ends. The dowels are warmed for an hour to shrink them, then the joint is warmed, and thin hot glue is quickly applied to joint, dowels, and dowel-holes. This joint is largely used by chairmakers, and known as "framing." When the work comes shoulder to shoulder, the dowel-hole must be bored square to the shoulder.

Joining thin woods.—For making joints in ¼-in. to ½-in. stuff, the material is cut to size, trimmed clean, and arranged in sets, with the joints numbered. The edges are planed off with a sharp trying-plane on a shooting-board. To make tongued joints, the joints are shot, then grooved and tongued with a pair of piecing-planes, to match the thickness of the stuff, always keeping the fence of the plane to the face of the work. For glueing, the tongue must be slack to allow for swelling when the hot glue is put in. (J. Cowan.) The lighter and smaller the work, the greater is the difficulty of securing accurate joints, because defects in squaring-up are not obvious on very thin wood. In the case of a small box with a deep cover, it is easiest to make box and cover all in one piece, and afterwards saw them apart. A neat and strong joint, allowing the corners to be rounded, is shown in plan in Fig. 517: the end pieces of the box are rebated like *a*, and the front and back pieces are grooved like *b*.

517.

Glueing.—For an account of glue, its qualities, characters, &c., the reader is referred to 'Workshop Receipts,' second series, pp. 78–84, in which full details are given for soaking, boiling, and otherwise preparing the adhesive solution. Glued surfaces need to be forced into the closest possible contact, so that there shall intervene the slightest possible film of the adhesive substance; and there is no point upon which amateurs make greater mistakes. A thick wad of glue does not stick 2 pieces of wood together, but keeps them apart. If we could plane 2 boards perfectly true, so as to exclude even a film of air, they would adhere without glue. But this is not possible. Nevertheless, we make some approach to such condition when, having planed both approximately level, we insert the thinnest possible layer of some adhesive substance—in this case glue—and press them into the very closest contact that we can. The bulk of the glue is squeezed out, and is to be wiped off; but after all is squeezed out that is possible, a sufficient film will remain to give the necessary adhesion; and supposing the glue of good quality and properly applied, the closest union of the parts will be found to take place. The glue should be applied quite hot; and in cold weather it is well to warm the joint before applying the glue, if the character of the work will allow it. With very thin stuff this warming is not advisable, as the fire will warp the wood. A convenient " glue-brush," according to Cowan, may be made from a piece of rattan cane, having the outside crust pared off, and the end dipped in boiling water and hammered out till the fibre is well separated. It is described as the best, cheapest, most durable, and most effective means of applying glue.

Hinging.—Hinging is the art of connecting two pieces of metal, wood, or other material together, such as a door to its frame; the connecting ligaments that allow one or other of the attached substances to revolve are termed hinges. There are many sorts of hinges, among which may be mentioned, butts, chest hinges, coach hinges, rising hinges, casement hinges, garnets, scuttle hinges, desk hinges, screw hinges, back-fold hinges, centrepoint hinges, and so on. To form the hinge of a highly-finished snuff-box requires great mechanical skill; but few of the best jewellers can place a faultless hinge in a snuff-box.

There are many varieties of hinges, and hence there are many modes of applying them, and much dexterity and delicacy are frequently required. In some cases the hinge is visible, in others it is necessary that it should be concealed. Some hinges require not only that the one hinged part should revolve on the other, but that the movable part shall be thrown back to a greater or lesser distance. Figs. 518 to 564 exhibit a great variety of methods of hinging.

Fig. 518 shows the hinging of a door to open to a right angle, as in Fig. 519. Figs. 520, 521, and Figs. 522, 523, show modes of hinging doors to open to an angle of 90°. Figs. 524, 525, show a manner of hinging a door to open at right angles, and to have the hinge concealed. The segments are described from the centre of the hinge A, and light portion requires to be cut out to permit the passage of the leaf of the hinge A B.

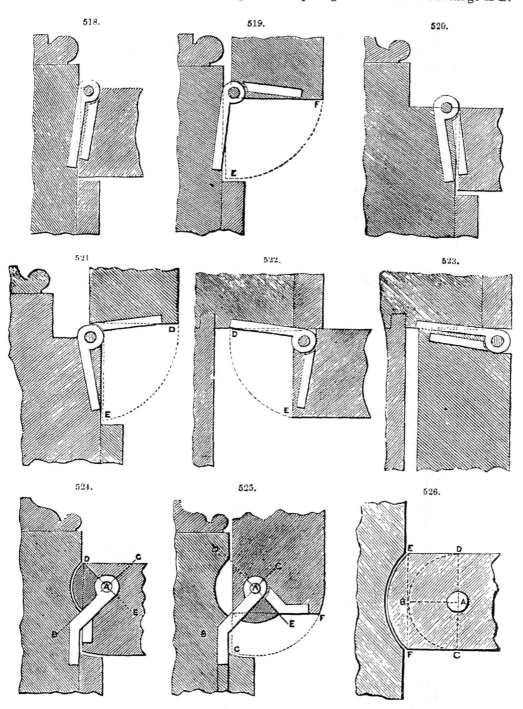

Figs. 526, 527, illustrate an example of a centre-pin hinge, the door opening either way, and folding back against the wall in either direction. Draw E F at right angles to the door, and just clearing the line of the wall, which represents the plane in which the inner face of the door will lie when folded back against the wall in either direction. Bisect E F in B; draw A B perpendicular to E F, which make equal to E B or B F then A is the position of the centre of the hinge.

To find the centre of the hinge, Figs. 528, 529; draw A D, making an angle of 45° with the inner edge of the door, and A B parallel to the jamb, meeting D A in A the centre of the hinge: the door, in this case, will move through a quadrant D C.

Figs. 532, 533, are of another variety of centre-pin hinging, opening through a

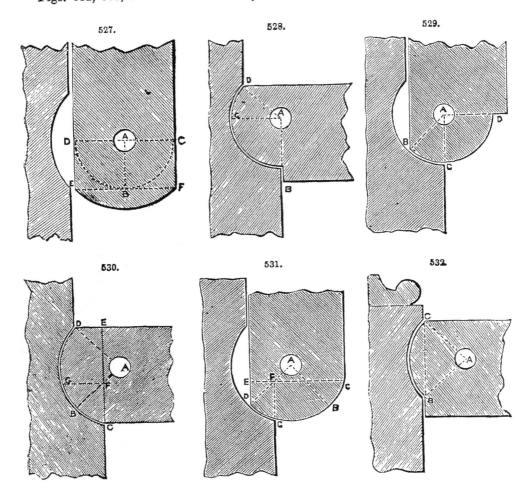

527.   528.   529.

530.   531.   532.

quadrant. The distance of A from B C is equal to half B C. In this, as in a previous case, there is a space between the door and the wall when the door is folded back. In Figs. 528, 529, as well as in Figs. 532, 533, there is no space left between the door and the wall.

Fig. 530; bisect the angle at D by the line D A; draw E C and make $C F = \frac{3}{2} D E$;

draw F G at right angles to C E, and bisect the angle G F C by the line B F, meeting D A in A; then A is the centre of the hinge. Fig. 531 shows, when the door, Fig. 530, is folded back, that the point C falls on the continuation of the line G F.

Figs. 534, 535; Figs. 536, 537; Figs. 538, 539; and Figs. 540, 541, are examples of centre-pin joints, and require no particular or detailed describing.

Figs. 542 to 544 are of a hinge, the flap of which has a bead B closing into a corresponding hollow, so that the joint cannot be seen through.

Figs. 545 to 547 show a hinge *b a* let equally into the styles, the knuckles of which

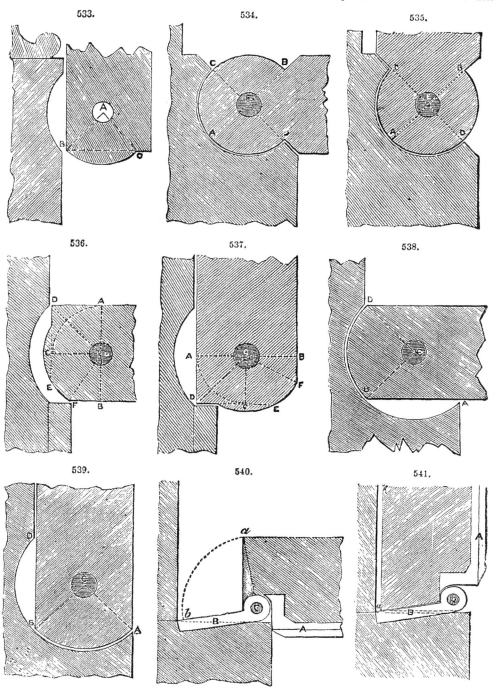

533.   534.   535.

536.   537.   538.

539.   540.   541.

form a part of the bead on the edge of the style B. In this case the beads on each side are equal and opposite to each other, with the joint-pin in the centre.

In the example, Figs. 548 to 550, the knuckle of the hinge forms a portion of the bead on the style C, and is equal and opposite to the bead of the style D. In Figs. 551 to 553, the beads are not directly opposite to one another.

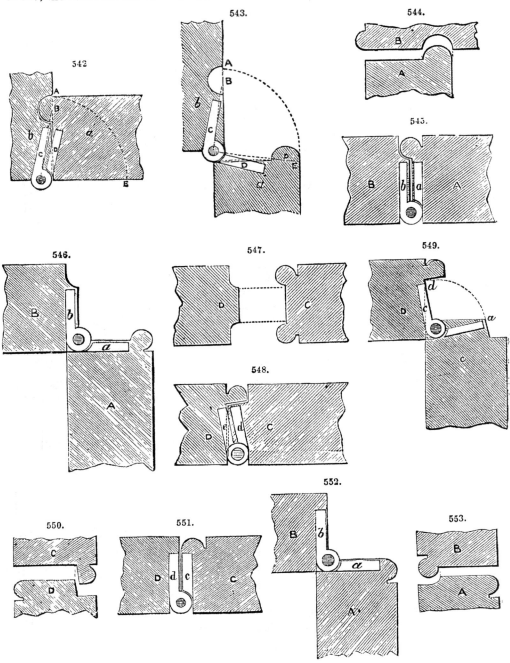

Fig. 554 exhibits the hinging of a back flap when the centre of the hinge is in the middle of the joint.

Figs. 555, 556, relate to the manner of hinging a back flap when it is necessary to throw the flap back from the joint. An example of a rule-joint is given, Figs. 557, 558.

Figs. 559, 560, point out or define the ordinary mode of hinging shutters to sash-frames.

Figs. 561, 562, illustrate a method of hinging employed when the flap on being

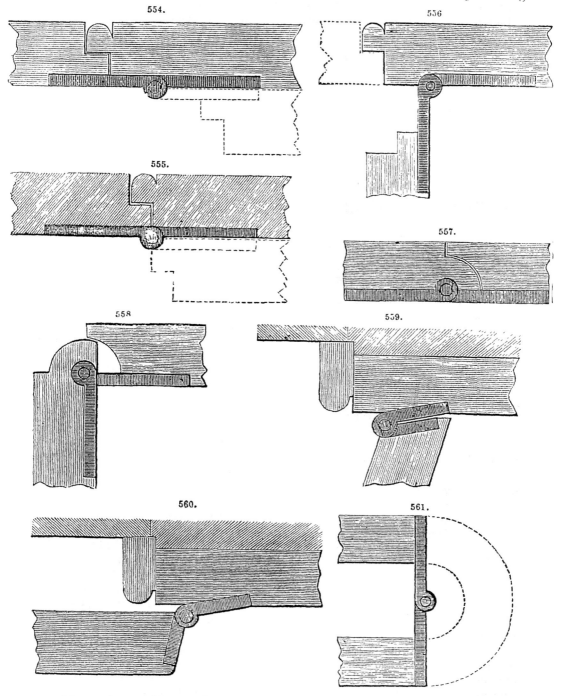

opened has to be at a distance from the style. This method of hinging is used on the doors of pews, to throw the opening flap or door clear of the mouldings.

Figs. 563, 564, show the manner of finding the rebate when the hinge is placed on the contrary side. Let h be the centre of the hinge, $y e$ the line of joint on the same side, $a c$ the line of joint on the opposite side, and $e c$ the total depth of the rebate Bisect $e c$ in d, and join $d h$; on $d h$ describe a semicircle cutting $y e$ in f, and through j and d draw $f b$, cutting $a c$ in b, and join $a b$, $b f$, and $f y$, to complete the joint.

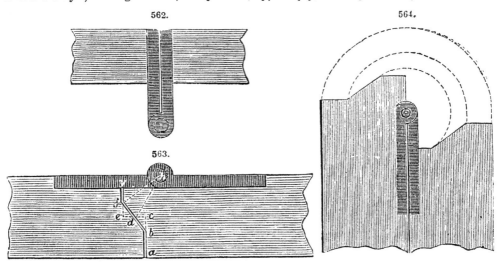

562. 563. 564.

Examples of Construction.—In giving a selection of examples illustrative of the construction of articles in which wood forms the chief if not only material employed, it will be convenient to adopt some sort of classification. The following will be found to have practical advantages :—(1) Workshop Appliances, (2) Rough Furniture, (3) Garden and Yard Erections, (4) House Building.

WORKSHOP APPLIANCES.—The principal workshop appliances which can be made by the mechanic or amateur for his own use are the tool-chest, carpenters' bench, and grindstone mount.

Tool-chest.—The most common way of arranging a tool-chest is in the form of a box, i. e. with the cover opening at top. This has one great disadvantage as compared with what may be called the cupboard arrangement, in that some of the tools must necessarily be below the others and in the dark, giving double trouble to get them out or replace them, and tending not a little to their injury. The chest or cupboard shown in Fig. 565 is based on one described in *Amateur Work* by the designer. It measures 4 ft. high, 3 ft. wide, and 11 in. deep from back to front, the shell being made of $\frac{3}{4}$-in. boards 11 in. wide. These are carefully sawn to size, planed up, and dove-tailed at the joints. The shelves are of $\frac{5}{8}$-in. boards planed down to about $\frac{1}{2}$ in. The back is formed of $\frac{1}{2}$-in. lining boards, which may be bought ready ploughed for putting together. The interior is divided into compartments : a measures about 3 ft. high, and 8 in. wide, and is adapted for hanging saws in, hooks being screwed into h for that purpose ; b is 2 ft. 2 in. wide, and 14 in. deep, so as to admit full-sized bottles containing turpentine, &c., as well as a paint-pot and glue-pot ; c is about 9 in. high and the same width as b ; d, e, f, g equally divide the remaining height of the cupboard, the 2 former being only 2 ft. 2 in. wide, while the 2 latter have the full width of the cup-board. All the boards forming the partitions of the interior are of $\frac{5}{8}$-in. stuff planed down to about $\frac{1}{2}$ in. The ends of the shelves which abut on the sides of the cupboard are rabbeted into grooves $\frac{3}{16}$ in. deep, and those ends which abut on the partition i are supported on triangular strips screwed to i. The shelves may be free to slide to and fro if desired, except h, which receives the upper end of the partition i. The front side of the cupboard is made in the following ingenious manner. A frame of wood 3 in.

broad, and $1\frac{1}{2}$ in. thick, is made to go right round, with an upright bar in the centre, the whole being fixed together with mortice and tenon. Tenons cut on the ends of the centre bar are let into mortices in the end pieces, and tenons on the ends of the end pieces into mortices in the side-pieces. A $\frac{1}{4}$-in. bead-plane is run along the inside edges of the frame before the tenons are cut or the mortices made. If neatly done, this will leave a complete bead round each door. This frame is nailed to the front of the case; and if it has been made slightly large, there will be a little border to clean off with the plane. The doors may be of any desired style. A good appearance, with little cost or trouble, is gained by the following plan. The frame is $1\frac{1}{2}$ in. thick; and the apertures to be closed are about 14 in. wide: take two pieces of board of the necessary length and width, and, when planed, $\frac{5}{8}$ in. thick; fit these into the apertures of the frame as doors; next take some slips of $\frac{3}{8}$-in. wood, $2\frac{1}{2}$ in. broad, dressed and squared; upon one side make a moulding, $\frac{3}{4}$ in. broad, with an O-G moulding-plane, and with the slips thus prepared plant the outside of the doors, of course keeping the square edges along the edges of the doors, and the moulding inwards. There is a little caution needed if the deception is to be complete, as

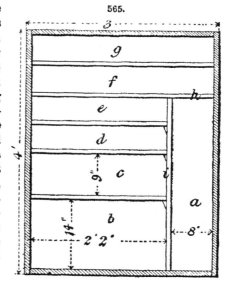

565.

viewed from the outside. Consider that you require to keep the pieces appearing as styles full width from top to bottom of door, but cutting the mouldings at an angle where they meet on the inner edges. For the middle and lower rails, these slips should be considerably broader than the styles and top-rail, but proportionate to the size of the door. While the inside of the doors is plain board, the outside has all the appearance of a proper framed door. Secure the case with a lock on each door, as being most handy and neat. Obviously one or more of the spaces e, f, g may be fitted with a nest of drawers for holding assorted nails, screws, and small tools. These drawers will resemble small shallow boxes, but differing from ordinary boxes, inasmuch as the front side is of thicker stuff than the remainder, because it has to take a blind dovetail (Fig. 515, p.157). The sides, back, and front of the drawers are dovetailed together, and the bottom rests in a rebate or groove. The dovetails need be only 2 or 3 in number, and shallow, as the sides are thin, say, $\frac{1}{4}$-in. stuff. The depth (height) of the drawer should not in general exceed 3 in. The bottom is secured by a few small brads in the rebate or groove cut for it; being supported in this way, it leaves a small portion of the sides of the drawer projecting below it. These form the runners on which the drawer slides in and out, and which may be lubricated by rubbing with a little soap or domestic blacklead (graphite). The drawers, when more than one in depth (height) or width, are separated by a narrow framework running back about $\frac{2}{3}$ of the total distance from front to rear.

Carpenters' bench.—Several forms of bench which can be purchased ready made have been already described (pp. 132-4); but a home-made bench is much less expensive and affords good practice in joinery, accurate work being necessary, while the materials are not too delicate. Good sound deal is a suitable wood to use, and the dimensions must depend on circumstances. Figs. 566, 567, 568 represent a bench described by a contributor to *Amateur Work*; the dimensions refer to the rough unplaned wood, which must all be planed up with the least possible waste. The legs a are $4\frac{1}{2}$ in. by $2\frac{1}{2}$ in.; the side ties b, 1 in. thick, are let into the legs $\frac{3}{4}$ in., and the legs are let into the ties

¼ in., and both are screwed together by stout 2-in. screws placed so as not to interfere with each other. The top *c* is at least 1½–2 in. thick, and made up of two pieces, which are caused to lie close by the following means. When the frame (legs and ties) has been made quite firm and even, the two 11-in. boards to form the top are planed smooth and

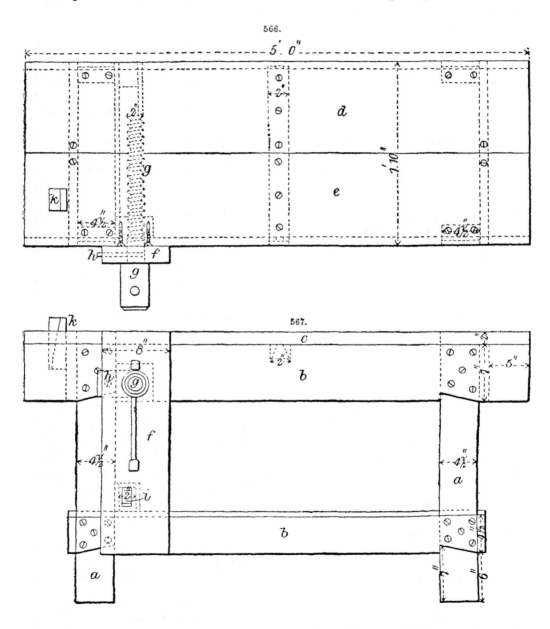

566.

567.

true along the edges that are to meet; the outer edge of the board *d* is screwed securely to the frame, and wedges are put under its inner edge to force it up about ½ in. from the frame; while in this position the other board *e* is thrust as tightly as possible against *d* and has its outer edge screwed down in a similar manner while its inner edge is raised ½ in. The 2 boards thus form a table with a ridge along the centre, whilst an angular trough separates the inner edges of the boards. In this trough hot glue is applied, the wedges are withdrawn, and the boards are gently pressed down quite flat and secured by screws and heavy weights, the latter being removed when the glue has set. This plan avoids the necessity for a powerful clamp. The chop f of the old-fashioned wooden bench-vice is made of beech or oak, 2 in. thick and 8 in. wide, and reaches to the lower edge of the bottom side tie. The screw g passes through the chop f and the top side tie, at the back of which the nut should be screwed. In the neck of the screw is a groove for the reception of a thin slip of hard wood h, to be mortised through the side of the chop, and cut into shape to fit half round the neck of the screw and into the groove, serving to pull the chop outwards. The chop is also furnished with a guide bar i, about 2 in. sq., mortised into it, and sliding in a guide box or channel provided for it; the angles of the guide bar may be planed off to ease its movements. The stop k consists of a couple of wedges let right through the bed of the bench. The bottom ties may support a table of $\frac{1}{2}$-in. boards, convenient for holding tools temporarily. The cost of the complete bench is estimated not to exceed 20s.; say wood 15s., bench-screw

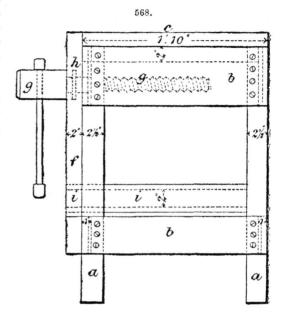

2s., screws, glue, stop, &c., 3s. Obviously the various etceteras of more perfect benches can be added if desired; and there is scarcely any limit to the uses which may be made of the open spaces under the bed of the bench, as situations for drawers, cupboards, tool-racks, or even for a treadle to work a small bench grindstone, circular or band saw, lathe, or other contrivance finding a suitable foundation on the firm frame of the bench.

Grindstone mount.—As already stated (p. 115), grindstones may be bought ready mounted; but while the stone and its iron handle, friction rollers, and other metallic accessories had best be obtained in a complete form from some reputable firm (e. g. Booth Bros., Dublin), the wooden frame can be easily and most cheaply put together (Fig. 569) by the workman himself. A good durable wood for the purpose is pitch pine; of this will be wanted the following pieces :—2 (a) 3 ft. by 4 in. by 3 in., 1 (b) 4 ft. by $4\frac{1}{2}$ in. by 1 in., 1 (c) 2 ft. by 4 in. by 2 in., 1 (d) 3 ft. by 2 in. by 1 in., 4 (e) 3 ft. by 3 in. by 2 in.. the lot costing about 3s. Plane them all true and square. Take the 2 pieces a, forming the long sides of the top, and prepare them to receive, at 4 in. from each end, the ends of the cross-pieces formed by cutting c in half, the joints being made by dove-tailing $1\frac{1}{2}$ in. deep. This should make the inside measurement of the top 20 in. by 7 in. The four pieces e for the legs are mortised into the frame sides a at an angle of about 85°, the mortices and tenons being cut on the bevel to suit; the legs should be $11\frac{3}{4}$ in. apart at the top and 14 in. at the bottom, to give stability to the structure. This is further increased by cutting the piece d into two halves, and letting it into the legs across the ends at 14 in. above the ground. The dovetailed joints of the frame and the tenons of the legs should be put in with white-lead; in addition, a stout 3-in. screw is driven into each dovetail, and the tenon joints are tightened by wedges. The next step is to fix the friction rollers exactly in the centre of each side of the top frame, and accurately parallel; this done, the axle has to be fitted into the stone so that it traverses it precisely at right angles. This has to be done gradually by putting the axle loosely in and plugging it round with red deal wedges just inserted with slight pressure. Then put the stone on the frame with the ends of the axle resting on the friction rollers. Keep the stone slowly turning, holding a rule against the stone, and drive in wedges from both sides of the stone at the 4 sides of the axle, and also at the 4 corners. The stone has to be true 2 ways, so try it on the side as well as the front. When you have it as true as

569.

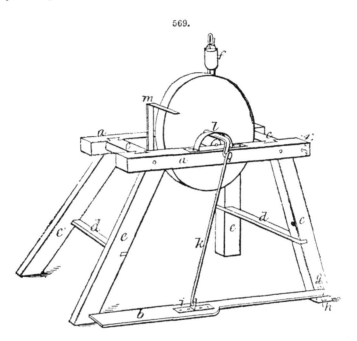

the stone will allow, cut off the wedges, put on the handle, and get some one to turn. Get an old plane iron or a well-tempered piece of steel, and, resting it on the stand, hold it close to the face of the stone. Keep the stone dry, and set it going. Work more on the edges than the centre, so as not to hollow out the stone. Keep at it till you have the stone perfectly true and smooth. Do not put on a trough unless you contrive a plan for raising and lowering it. A can f overhead is better: a meat-tin, with a fine hole drilled in the bottom, will do. A blacksmith can make a set of fittings which will cost about 3s. g is a plate of $\frac{1}{4}$-in. iron, 7 in. by $1\frac{3}{4}$ in., with 4 screw holes in it, and with a spud 3 in. long riveted in the centre, at the end of which a small pin-hole has been drilled. h is a plate of $\frac{1}{4}$-in. iron, 7 in. by $1\frac{3}{4}$ in., with 3 screw holes in it, bent round to an eye, to fit the spud very tightly. i is a plate of $\frac{1}{4}$-in. iron, 5 in. by 1 in., with 4 screw holes and a plate, with an eye in it, riveted in the centre. k is the connecting rod for the treadle, made out of $\frac{3}{8}$-in. round iron, about 36 in. long, bent to a hook at one end, and to an eye (to which i has to be attached) at the other. l is a guard (in duplicate) of $\frac{1}{4}$-in. iron, 17 in. by 1 in., with 4 screw holes, bent as shown, which passes over axle and rollers, and screws to the stand. This must be made carefully, just to shave the axle but well clear of the rollers. m is a rest, made out of $\frac{1}{4}$-in. iron, 15 in. by $1\frac{3}{4}$ in., bent as shown, at 9 in. from the end, with 2 screw holes. Take the piece of wood b, and cut it as shown, half of it the full width, and the other half $2\frac{1}{2}$ in. wide. About $\frac{1}{2}$ in. from the bottom of one of the right side legs, screw g. Underneath the treadle, at the narrow end, screw h. Hang the connecting rod k on to the axle. Fix the treadle on the spud, and raise it about 1 in. from the ground; bring the rod and eye forward till it meets the treadle, mark it and screw it on. The length of the rod, of course, is an essential point and will depend on the height of the top of the stand from the ground; it must be determined by bending a piece of wire to the necessary length. Screw on the guards *l* over the rollers. The hook supplied with the rollers may, if desired, be hung over the axle, on the handle side, and screwed to the wood, and the guards dispensed with, but the guards are preferable. Screw the support for the can *f* into the stand, on the handle side, between the rollers and the stone. Screw on the rest *m*, so that the short arm just shaves the stone. A water guard made out of back board may, if wished for, be tacked on under the rest at one end, and one to match it at the other, but they are not essential unless you have a trough. (W. J. Stanford in *Amateur Work*.)

ROUGH FURNITURE.—Perhaps the term "furniture" is hardly appropriate here in its commonly accepted sense. Furniture proper will come under Cabinet-making and Upholstery; but there are some few articles that admit of being made in a rough and ready style, simply of wood, and these will come under immediate consideration.

Steps.—These are shown in Fig. 570. The sides (2) *a* may be 2½–6 ft. long (high), 5 in. wide, and 1 in. thick; their top and bottom ends are bevelled, so that the finished article shall stand in a slanting attitude. The 4 steps *b* are 6 in. wide, 1 in. thick, and increase about 1 or 1½ in. in length as they descend, i. e. supposing the topmost of the 4 to be 12 in. long internally, the lowermost might be 16½ in.; this gives solidity by spreading the sides. Each of these 4 steps *b* is let about ¼ in. to ⅜ in. into grooves cut in the 2 side pieces *a*, and secured by a few nails or screws. As the side pieces *a* are only 5 in. wide while the steps *b* are 6 in., there remains 1 in. of step projecting beyond the sides; this projection comes in front, where the step is allowed to have the full width so as to come flush with the outside of the side pieces. The top step *c* differs from all the others: it is long enough to have about 1 in. at each end overhanging the sides; it is about 2 in. wider than

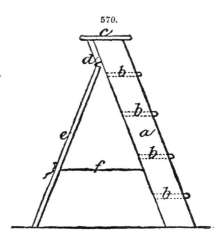

570.

the other steps; and into it the upper ends of the side pieces *a* are mortised, or let into a groove and screwed. When this half of the steps is complete, a piece of board *d*, about 6 in. wide, 1 in. thick, and of a shape to fit flush with the outside of the side pieces *a*, is firmly screwed to the back of the side pieces. To this board *d* is attached, by a couple of stout flap hinges, a light frame *e*, formed by mortising and glueing together 2 upright strips 2½ in. wide by 1 in. thick and 2 cross pieces 3 or 4 in. wide and 1 in. thick, in such a manner that each upright falls at the back of one of the side pieces, while the upper cross piece comes immediately below *d* and receives the lower halves of the 2 hinges, and the bottom cross piece is at the level represented by the cord *f*, which is attached to it at one end and to one of the side pieces *a* at the other. The length of the frame *e* should correspond exactly to that of the side pieces *a*. The front top edges of the steps are rounded off. The distance between the steps is usually 7–9 in.

Ladders.—The simplest form of ladder, and suited only to lengths of 12 ft. and under, consists of 2 pieces of good red deal, about 2 in. by 3 in., placed side by side some 14 in. apart, and joined by cross pieces 2 in. by 1 in., at intervals of 8 in., the cross pieces being generally let into notches about ⅜ in. deep in the side pieces, and securely nailed or screwed. For ladders of greater length recourse is had to a sound fir pole of the requisite length, which is planed smooth all over, and bored through at 9-in. intervals with a series of ¾- or ⅞-in. holes. The pole is then sawn in half down the centre, forming 2 pieces flat on the inside, but rounding on the outside. Spokes cut for the purpose, of ash or oak, are next inserted by one end into all the holes in one side piece, and their free ends are afterwards similarly introduced into the holes of the other side piece. This done, the projecting ends of the "rounds" or spokes are sawn off flush with the outside of the side pieces, a chisel cut is made in each of them (the rounds) in the direction of their length, and these chisel cuts are filled by little wooden wedges driven tight. Extra strength is given in long ladders by inserting an iron rod across under the steps near the top and bottom, and putting a washer and nut on each end to tighten up.

Cask-cradle.—This is simply a stout frame on 4 legs 9–12 in. high, made of quartering which may vary from 2 in. sq. for small casks to 3 in. sq. for larger ones. The proportions given in the annexed illustration (Fig. 571) are suited to a 9-gal. cask. This should be 22 in. long, 15 in. wide, 9 in. high, and made of 2½-in. stuff, of which it

571.

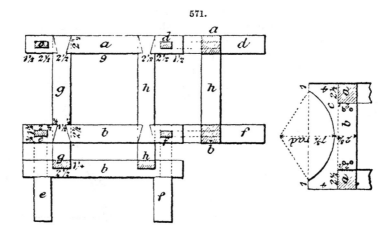

will consume about 9½ ft. run. It will be seen that the sides *a*, *b* are joined to the legs *c*, *d*, *e*, *f* by mortice and tenon joints, while the ends *g*, *h* are dovetailed into the sides *a*, *b*. The joints are secured by pins of oak or red deal driven into holes bored by a gimlet. The stand thus made is only adapted to carry casks stood on end. For holding them steadily on their side, and at the same time giving them a tilt forward to allow all the clear contents lying above the sediment to be drawn out without disturbing the barrel, use is made of 2 pieces of board hollowed out to receive the barrel. For the sized cask mentioned (9-gal.), 15 in. will suffice in length and 1 in. in thickness for each piece. Both are prepared for letting down into the frame by cutting out a piece 2½ in. sq. from each of the 2 bottom corners as at *a*, and can then be screwed to the cross piece *b* of the frame. Previously the cradle is formed by describing on the piece of wood an arc of a circle corresponding to the size of the cask at the point where it is to be supported. Supposing the diameter of the cask to be 15½ in., the radius of the circle to be described will be 7¾ in., as shown. This gives the correct arc, but as the cask will lie sloping and not flat, the foremost edge of the arc must be shaved away till the cask will rest on the entire breadth of the edges of the cradle *c*. For the front cradle the board may be 6½ in. wide, and for the back 8½ in.

Tables.—To begin with a simple example and one where but little finish is necessary, recourse may be had to a kitchen table described by Cabe in *Amateur Mechanics*. The table and its parts are shown in Figs. 572–584; the top measures 3 ft. 6 in. long by 1 ft. 10 in. wide. For the 4 legs get a piece of clean yellow pine, 30 in. long, 8 in. broad, and 2 in. thick; line it out so that each piece has a taper (Fig. 574); this is called cutting one out of the other. The proper method to line out the wood is:—Draw a line down the middle, which will give 2 halves, each 4 in. broad; from the outer edge of each half, mark 2¼ in.

at b, and $1\frac{3}{4}$ in. at c; draw lines to these marks 2 in. thick, and saw up; you thus have 4 pieces each tapering from $2\frac{1}{4}$ in. to $1\frac{3}{4}$ in. Plane up the 2 best adjacent faces of each piece, and square them; when planed, mark their faces with pencil. Set marking gauge to bare 2 in., and gauge from the dressed faces for about 6 in. in length, at the broad end or top of each piece. This is the part of the leg that comes opposite the rails, and has no

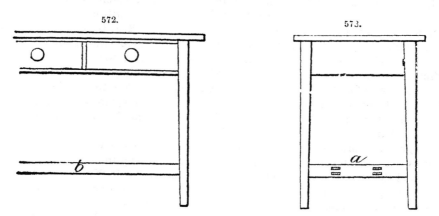

572.   573.

taper. Plane and square the 4 pieces to their gauge marks, and place them together on the bench, even at the bottom. Mark from the bottom 24 in., which will be 6 in. from the top, and square across, continuing the line round the remaining sides; this is the line the tapering commences from. Set the making gauge to $1\frac{1}{2}$ in., and gauge the bottom end of each piece from the dressed side. Taper from the lines mentioned above, stopping at the gauge marks on the end. The legs will be 2 in. square for 6 in. of their length, and the remainder tapered to $1\frac{1}{2}$ in. square at the bottom.

Plane and square the back rail 35 in. long, 5 in. broad, and 1 in. thick; 2 end rails 19 in. long, 5 in. broad, and 1 in. thick; front rail over the drawer, 35 in. by 2 in. by $\frac{3}{4}$ in.; 1 under the drawer, 35 in. by 2 in. by 1 in.; 2 end stretchers, a, Fig. 573, 19 in. by 2 in. by 1 in.; and 2 long ones, 35 in. by 2 in. by 1 in. These pieces prepared, draw in the legs for mortising. Place them on the bench in 2 pairs, each pair having a taper side up, and the remaining taper sides opposite each other, as in Fig. 575, the parallel portions of all 4 lying close, and the bottoms of each pair about 1 in. apart. 2 mortices are made in each leg to receive the 5-in. rail. First draw a line across all 4 at the beginning of the taper a, set a pair of compasses to $1\frac{1}{2}$ in., and mark from a to b; mark 1 in. from b to c, then $1\frac{1}{2}$ in. with the compasses to d. During this operation the legs should be clipped by their ends in a hand screw,

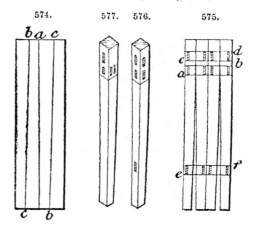

574.   577. 576.   575.

to prevent shifting. Draw in the mortices for stretchers, by making the line e 6 in. from the bottom, and f $1\frac{7}{8}$ in. higher up. Set the mortice gauge to $\frac{3}{8}$ in. mortice line, and set the head $\frac{3}{8}$ in. from the inner spike. Gauge with this all the mortices both for rails and stretchers, from the marked faces of the legs. Square over 1 pair of the legs for the 5-in. long or back rail, which will be on the remaining taper side, as in Fig. 576, and the other pair square across for a rail beneath the drawer, 1 in. thick, the mortice being $\frac{1}{16}$ in. less than the thickness of rail (see Fig. 577). Gauge for mortices as before, from the marked faces, as in the case of Fig. 577 from both faces, as there are 2 mortices in the breadth.

Place the legs for mortising on the bench as in Fig. 575. Mortise for the rails $1\frac{1}{2}$ in. deep, and for the stretchers $1\frac{1}{4}$ in. deep. When mortised clean out, blaze with a $\frac{5}{16}$-in. chisel, taking care not to bruise the edge of the mortices, which should be smoothed a little on the sides with a chisel, but not pared wider, or they will be too wide for tenons.

Draw in the rails and stretchers—first of all for the 2 ends, as they are cramped together first. Draw in the two end rails 16 in. long between the shoulders; this will give 2 tenons $1\frac{1}{2}$ in. long. Draw in the back rail and the 2 front rails over and under the drawers, 32 in. long. This "drawing-in" means marking them across with square and cutting knife for shouldering. Place the 2 end rails edge up on the bench, mark off 16 in., and square both across. Then from these lines square and mark both sides of each rail. The cutting knife is best for this marking, making a good deep cut, which serves as a channel or guide for the dovetail saw.

Though the shoulders of the 5-in. rails are square across, it will be evident that the shoulders of the stretchers a, Fig. 573, are bevelled, arising from the taper on the feet or legs, and the stretcher is also somewhat longer than the rail. Now to find this length, and this bevel, proceed as follows :—To find the length, place a pair of the legs together with a hand screw at top, mortices together; at the stretcher mortice they will be apart about $\frac{3}{4}$ in., and this is the extra length over the rails. To find the bevel, square across any part of the taper of a leg from the outer face with bench-square and pencil, and with a bevel square or bevel stock set the blade to this line. The stock being on the inner or taper side of leg, the bevel thus found is that for stretcher shoulders, the bevel stock being worked from upper edge of stretcher. The shoulders being marked, shift the head of mortice gauge $\frac{1}{8}$ in. nearer the spikes, and gauge rails and stretchers from the outer face. Thus they will be $\frac{1}{8}$ in. within the surface of the legs when cramped together.

The rail under the drawer is flush with the legs, and must be gauged same as the mortices, then shifted to fit the second or inner mortice; see Fig. 577. For this reason the rails and legs should be gauged together, as it saves time and shifting of the gauge. The shoulders are cut in with dovetail saw, and the tenons are ripped with a tenon saw. Then the rails have a piece cut out for the bridge in the mortices, and a rebate of 1 in. at the upper edge, which will leave 2 tenons a little over $1\frac{1}{2}$ in. broad. They should be a little less in length than the depth of mortices. The tenoning being finished, the 2 stretchers a, Fig. 573, are mortised for long stretchers b, Fig. 572. These mortices are shown at a, Fig. 573, where the tenons come through and are wedged. The long stretchers are 6 in. apart, and the mortising is exactly as that for the rail below drawers where let into legs, and also at the division between the drawers. This being done, the insides of the legs are hand-planed and sandpapered, as also the faces of 5-in. rails and stretchers all round.

Now the ends are ready to cramp together. Cut a little off the corner of each tenon, and see that they enter their respective mortices before glueing. The glue should be thin, and while one heats the tenons at a fire another puts glue in the mortices with a bit of lath. A very little glue will do on the tenons. The object of heating is to prevent the glue getting chilled. In cramping up, protect the work with bits of wood under the jaws of the cramps. When cramped, see that it is square by gauging with a rod from corner to corner, diagonally between stretcher and rail; also see that it is out of twist. If the work is well done, the cramp may come off at once, as the shoulders will stay close. If ill performed, no amount of cramping will ever make it a good job. Another important thing in cramping these table ends, and in all kinds of mortised framing, is to see that the legs are not pressed out of the plane of the rails. If the jaws of the cramp are kept too high, then the legs are slanted inwards. If, on the other hand, the cramp be too low, the legs are turned outwards, so that the point of pressure should be opposite the centre of the thickness of the rails. When cramping, place a straight-edge across the 2 legs ; the straight-edge should touch the legs on the whole of their breadth—then they will not be winding.

The 2 ends being framed together, the next operation is to fill them in for drawer guides. These consist of pieces of wood 2 in. broad, and thick enough to flush the table legs, fitted in between the legs, and glued to the rails, being kept flush with the bottom edge of rail. They should be fixed down with hand screws, and laid aside for an hour or so, after which they are planed straight and flush with the legs. The tops of the 2 front legs are cut off flush with the edge of the rails, and planed ; then the ¾-in. rail over the drawers is drawn in same length as that under, and a dovetail made on each end about 1¼ in. long. These dovetails are drawn on the tops of the legs, and then cut out to the depth required—namely, ¾ in. The space from this to the 2 mortices under the drawer is the length to make the short upright division, or fore-edge between the drawers. This has a double tenon each end, same as for the stretchers, the 2 rails being mortised to receive it; see Fig. 578, which is the frame without drawers or top. The rail below the drawers is mortised to receive the cross rail *a* (Fig. 578), which is a rest for both drawers It is 3 in. broad, and same thickness as front rail ; one end is tenoned to enter the front rail, while the opposite or back end has a dovetail, and is let in flush into the under edge of the back rail ; its position is from front to back, and in the centre of the frame. The mortice and tenon being prepared, the proper length of this rail will be found when the frame is cramped up, and stood on its legs.

To find the length of the long stretchers, place the 2 ends together, with the mortices towards each other ; catch them in a hand screw at top, when you can measure the gap between the end stretchers : this is the length that the long stretchers are to be in excess of the rails at back and front. Tenon the long stretchers to fit the mortices in cross ones ; all mortising and tenoning being done, hand plane all the parts that cannot afterwards be reached, before glueing up. Being now ready to glue the frame up, set a cramp to about 3 ft. 2 in., which will allow of 2 pieces of wood to protect the job. The back rail, front rail below drawer, and 2 long stretchers all receive glue, and are fitted in their places at once. Insert them all into one end, first with the hands, then turn them over, and insert them in the other end ; now rap them nearly home with a piece of wood and a hammer ; then apply the cramp. It is almost necessary for 2 persons to be at this part of the job, one heating tenons, and afterwards assisting with the cramp. Cramp all the shoulders close, wedging the long stretchers with the cramp in the centre between them.

Glue and insert the short upright rail between the drawers, then above this the rail with 2 dovetails ; press the short upright home with a small cramp or a hand screw on either side of the projecting tenons, and drive in wedges as explained in glueing the long stretchers. Rap home the dovetailed ends, and drive a 2-in. nail through them into each leg. You will now find the correct length of the rail across the centre, which fit by dovetailing into back rail. Make 2 bearing fillets, 1 in. sq., and nail them inside of each end and level with the front rail, when they will be on the same level with the centre bearing rail, and support the drawers properly on both sides. The 2 drawers are made with fronts ⅞ in. thick, and are fitted closely into the apertures to receive them. Mark the front on the outside thus, ʌ, when you will always know the end to be kept uppermost. Plane the bottom edge first, then make one end square, assuming that the aperture is rectangular. Place the front against the aperture, with the squared end in its place, and draw the other on the inside with drawpoint. Saw off and square this end with the plane on the shooting-board. Having got the ends to the exact length, place the front against the aperture again, letting the lower edge enter a little way. Draw again along the upper edge inside, and plane down to this mark. These fronts should fit tight, and at present it is sufficient if they just enter. Cut out 4 sides of ⅝-in. wood, dress and square the ends on the shooting-board, ½ in. shorter than the width from face of rail to inside of back rail. These 4 sides may be at present a little broader than the finished side. Groove the sides and front with a drawer-bottom plane, and make 2 backs exactly same length as fronts, and 1 in. narrower ; these are also $\frac{5}{8}$ in. thick, and have no grooves like the sides have. Being ready to dovetail, set the cutting gauge to a shaving less than the thickness of sides ; gauge all the pieces with this—the fronts on the inner face and also on the end wood, gauging from the inside ; then the backs and sides on both sides. Mark on the fronts 4 pins, as in Fig. 579, and on the backs 3 pins,

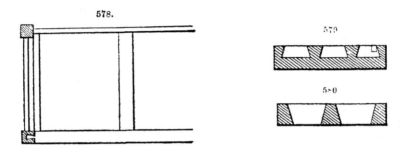

578.

as in Fig. 580, cutting down to the gauge lines. The backs are cut from both sides, as is all " through " dovetailing, while the fronts are only cut to a depth of $\frac{5}{8}$ in.

To draw the sides for dovetailing : Place a pair of sides in position, groove to groove (Fig. 581), and, taking a front, stand on the end of the side flush with gauge line, and flush on grooved edge. Draw close to each pin with the drawpoint, reverse the front, and draw on other side same way. Turn the sides end for end and draw the backs in the same way, having each back marked so that you make no mistake when fitting the drawers together. Observe by Fig. 582 that in drawing the back pins, the back is placed

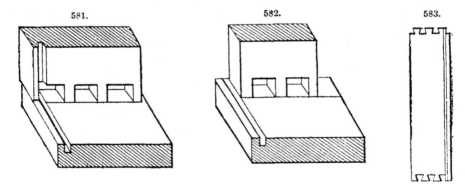

581. 582. 583.

even with the groove in the side, as the bottom slips in under it—in other words, the groove in the sides is clear of the back to receive the bottom. The pieces to be taken out of the sides are ripped with a dovetail saw, and cut out with a $\frac{3}{8}$-in. chisel ; these pieces are 3 at the back end, and 2 at the front, with the 2 corners cut out as in Fig. 583. In dovetailing, it must be observed that the thickness taken by the cut of the saw must come off the piece to be cut out—in other words, the piece cut out is exactly the portion within the drawpoint lines, so that the pins from which they were drawn will fit exactly in the openings thus made. In " through " dovetailing, which is cut from both sides, the chisel is inclined very slightly to cut inwards, which allows the sharp edges to come closely and neatly against the adjoining part when glued up ; this is called making it " lean " in the centre. The same remark applies in dovetails not through, as on the drawer fronts, which are slightly " lean " at the bottom both ways—that is, both from face to end. The dovetails are cleaned neatly out with narrow chisels, and the corners of the sides pared, after sawing off, to the gauge lines.

The drawer stuff, all dovetailed, has to be planed on the inside and sandpapered; then try if the fronts and backs enter their respective sides; after which glue them as follows, and this rule will hold good in all work of a similar kind :—Take a drawer front and the corresponding side, put some glue with a small brush into the recesses in end of front, taking care to allow none to get on to the inner face; put a little on the end wood of the side and on the 2 cut-out corners; stand the front on the bench, glued end up, enter the side, and rap it home with hammer and a bit of wood; turn it over on the bench, the side standing vertically; see that the junction inside is perfectly close; apply a large square inside and press the side to agree with the square. This done, take the back belonging to this drawer, put glue on the pins to enter this same side, enter it and rap home as with the front. Glue the remaining end of front and back, and rap on the remaining side. See that the inside junctions are all close. Lay the drawer flat down on the bench, and square it with a foot rule, applied from corner to corner.

When both drawers are glued, lay them aside, and prepare the bottoms. These are of $\frac{3}{8}$-in. wood, and if not broad enough may be jointed with $\frac{3}{8}$-in. match-ploughs. To do this jointing, mark the best side of each piece, place in the bench-vice lug with marked side next you, plane straight with half-long. It is usual to work the "feather" in the narrower piece, if there is a broad and a narrow; it is also usual to work the feather first. The groove and feather made, rap the joint up dry to see it is close. If it is a perfect joint, use thin glue made by dipping the brush into the boiler of the glue-pot. Apply the glue directly with one stroke of brush, and rap the pieces together very smartly with a mallet; they should need no cramping. When glueing of the bottoms is set, plane up both sides with half-long, one edge and one end squared to each other; hand plane inside of each bottom. Take the drawer bottom—plane, and make a gauge by running a groove in a piece of wood 4 in. or 5 in. long. Lay the bottoms face down on the bench, and bevel the edges now uppermost for about $1\frac{1}{2}$ in. inwards, bringing the thickness down to the size of groove in gauge (Fig. 584), in which g is the gauge and b the bottom. This done on front edge and one end, find the length to cut the bottom, by placing one corner in the groove at back of the drawer; mark at the bottom of opposite groove. From this mark cut the bottom to the square, and bevel the back to fit gauge as before,

584.

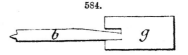

sandpaper the bottoms inside, and before driving them into their places, try that they enter both grooves by inserting the bottom, both back and front edges, because, if wider at the back, they will burst or split the sides. All being correct, drive them down gently with mallet, and see that they enter the groove in the front to the full depth; see also that the sides are perfectly straight and not bulged in the middle.

To block the bottoms, glue on fillets $\frac{3}{4}$ in. broad, and $\frac{1}{2}$ in. thick. These are fitted to the drawers along the bottom and side, and must be bevelled to the required angle. They are well glued, and rubbed in with a motion lengthway, when they will take hold. If they do not lie close along their length, cut them into 2 or more pieces before glueing; 2 or 3 short blockings of this kind are also glued on behind the front; these may be 3 in. or 4 in. apart; whereas those on the sides are continuous, being subject to wear in after use. These blockings should harden for 6 or 7 hours, after which drive 3 nails about $1\frac{1}{4}$ in. long through the bottom into the back.

Fit the drawers to the table frame by planing with jack and half-long. First reduce the breadth of the sides to enter easily, then place a piece of board across the bench, catch the drawer in the bench lug, and let the side rest upon this board. Plane both sides and try into frame: when they push in with an easy motion, but not loose enough to shake, they may be hand planed, the back dressed off, and the front planed to stand even with the face of the frame. They must be stopped at the back by glueing small pieces of wood to the back rail. Push the drawer in $\frac{3}{8}$ in. beyond the face of the frame, and fit the bits of wood in the space left at the back. A guiding fillet is also fitted between the 2 drawers and running from the short upright to the back ; this should not be too tight. The drawers should pull out and in easily, and without sticking or shaking.

The table frame is cleaned off with the hand plane in all parts, the tops of the back legs are cut off, and the upper edges of rails planed, to receive the top. The frame is 3 ft. long by 1 ft. 8 in. broad, and the top 3 ft. 6 in. by 1 ft. 10 in. It is planed both sides with half-long, and squared, then nailed down to frame at back and ends ; the front is fastened by 4 screws passing upwards through the rail over the drawers. The top is planed flat to agree with a straight-edge, hand planed, and sandpapered ; each corner is rounded off and sandpapered. The nail holes in the top are stopped with white putty. The bottoms of the legs are cut all to the same length. Turn the table feet up, take 2 straight-edges, and place one across each pair of feet ; the eye will at once detect whether the legs are all one length or not. Cut a little off the foot that carries the straight-edge too high. Bore a $\frac{5}{8}$-in. hole in the centre of each drawer front for a $2\frac{1}{4}$-in. patent zebra knob.

A modified form of kitchen table is shown in Fig. 585. The slab a is $1\frac{1}{2}$ in. thick ; the legs b are 2 ft. $2\frac{1}{2}$ in. high from floor to slab, 3 in. square, and are slightly bevelled inside ; the rails c are $4\frac{1}{2}$ in. deep, and are attached at each end d by means of a double tenon, let into mortices in the legs to the depth indicated by e, the inner half of the tenon shown by the line f on d entering the leg only so far as the line g on e. The mortice and tenon joints are glued and pinned with wooden pegs. The top is fastened down to the frame by one of the following methods :—(1) It may be screwed to the rail c as at h, by making a small recess in c and driving the screw somewhat diagonally, assuming c to be stout enough for the purpose ; (2) it may be nailed

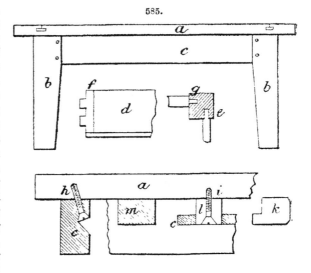

585.

or screwed down from above, the holes in the slab being afterwards stopped with putty ; (3) it may be secured by a number of wooden buttons placed about 1 ft. apart all round it, and each revolving on a screw as at i, the flange on the button k fitting into a groove l cut in the rail c, this plan presenting the advantage that the top may be removed and refixed at will. The rail c is generally " blocked," or strengthened by a series of rectangular wooden blocks m glued into the angle between the top a and rail c.

The construction of a gipsy table is a very simple matter. This form of table consists of a top, usually round, supported on 3 legs, which converge from near the margin of the top to a wooden ball about midway in height from the top to the floor ; from this ball start 3 other legs diverging so as to constitute a tripod stand. The top of the table is built up of boards pinned together, and is usually provided with a fringed cover. Underneath the top is attached a second thickness of wood to receive the upper ends of the 3 top legs. The lower ends of the top legs and the upper ends of the bottom legs fit into holes in the ball, and are secured by glueing.

One more example of the arrangements adopted for supporting table tops must suffice. This consists in having crossed legs (χ-shaped) at each end of an oblong top, see Fig. 586, *a*. The top is formed in the usual manner of ¾-in. boards joined up by tongueing and grooving and by glueing, with 2 or 3 cross ledges *b* screwed on beneath to give additional strength. These cross pieces should come so near the ends of the top *a* (say within 6 in.) as to afford space for the legs *c* (top ends) to abut against them, and be flanked in turn by a rail *d* without the rail coming within say 2 in. of the edge of

586.

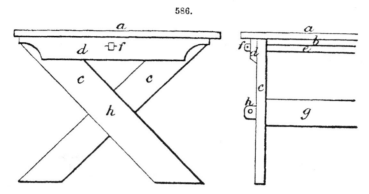

the top. The legs *c* are of red deal, about 3 ft. long, 6 in. wide, and 1½ in. thick, and are halved into one another where they cross. They are held in position by the rail *d* and the bar *e* at top, the latter being run the full length of the table and pinned outside at each end *f*; and by a second stouter rail *g* passing through the legs at the point where they are halved into each other, and held by a pin at *h*. It is obvious that any desired ornamentation by carving, &c., can be given to the legs and rails.

Seats.—Seats are of miscellaneous kinds, ranging from rustic garden chairs to iron benches and the most elegant specimens of artistic furniture. Here attention will be confined to simple forms.

Box stool.—The box stool or ottoman consists of a box without a bottom and with a stuffed lid, supported on knob feet. One is shown in Fig. 587. The box *a* is formed of 4 pieces of wood, 12–15 in. long, and 3 in. wide, dovetailed together. The top *b* is nailed on so as to cover the whole and overlap ½ in. all round; this supports the stuffing *c* covered by a piece of carpet or woolwork. The interior of the box is left empty. There is no complete bottom, but a wide strip of wood *d* is nailed all round the bottom edge of the sides, and into this

587.

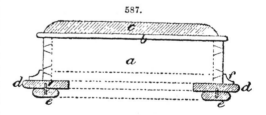

are screwed the 4 knob feet *e*. A bead *f* may be run round in the angle between the strip *d* and the sides of the box. The stuffed top *c* may be made separately and afterwards attached by screws from the inside.

3-legged stool.—This is simplicity itself. The top or seat proper consists of a circular slab of wood 1½ in. thick having 3 1-in. holes bored through it at equidistant intervals about 1½ in. from the edge. Into these holes are driven the stout rods forming the legs, the holes having been bored somewhat sloping so that the legs may diverge outwards to give solidity. When the legs are driven in quite tight, the portion which projects above the seat is sawn off, and a wooden wedge is driven firmly into a slit cut in the top of each leg by means of a chisel. If the legs are less than 1 ft. high, no rails will be needed; but if more, they should be strengthened by joining them together with ½-in. wooden rods let into holes bored in the legs at about ⅓ the height of the seat from the ground, and secured by glue.

Chairs.—A short description may be given here of the general principles underlying the construction of chairs, with some illustrated examples of the commoner and rougher kinds, showing how they are made and repaired. Briefly, a chair consists of a more or less flat "seat" or slab supported at a convenient sitting height above the floor on a wooden framework formed of 4 legs joined by cross rails ; on one side, these legs are prolonged upwards to constitute the "back," and, on each of the sides adjoining the back, they may be similarly heightened to produce " arms." The framework may be plain or ornamented, and the materials of the seat may be wood, cane, rushes, or a "stuffing" (horsehair, flock, &c.), enclosed in a textile or leather covering.

A very cheap and simple kind of chair known as the "cane-bottomed," is shown in Fig. 588. *a* is the back, cut out of 2 pieces of wood to the required shape, and strengthened by 2 flat rails *b* completing the back of the seat, and by a round rail *c*

588.

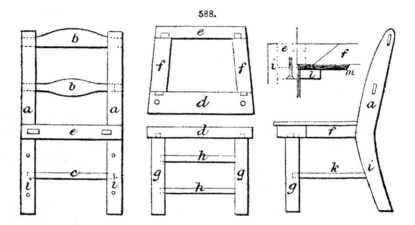

completing the back of the legs. The seat consists of a front rail *d*, back rail *e*, and 2 side rails *f*. The front legs *g* are similarly joined by round rails *h*, and let into the front rail *d* of the seat. The front legs *g* are connected with the back legs *i* by means of round rails *k*. The joints are all made by mortices and tenons, and are well glued, and clamped. There is a tendency in light chairs of this description to suffer injury in the frame, generally in one of the pieces *f* near where they join the back rail *e*. One good plan for repairing such an injury is to introduce a strip of wood *l* from beneath, just long enough to fit tightly between the 2 legs *i*, and to fasten it by screws into the back frame *e* and both sides *f*. Another efficient method is to screw a small angle-iron *m* to the injured frame and to the leg nearest it. As implied by its name, the seat of this chair is formed by stretching strips of rattan cane across it in the manner of a network, attaching them to holes bored for the purpose in the frame of the seat, and securing them by little wooden pegs driven into the holes. It may be mentioned that the front part of the frame of the seat should be wider than the back, and made rounding in shape ; the front legs may be perpendicular, but the back legs should diverge gradually towards the feet.

The Windsor, kitchen, or wooden seated-chair is even simpler than the last, the seat consisting simply of a somewhat dished-out slab of wood, attached to the front legs by having them inserted in holes bored into it, and to the back by mortising. The seat should be of elm and the back and legs of beech. These chairs, though strong, are liable to injury from being used for improper purposes, such as carrying clothes while drying, which causes warping and shrinkage, and consequent looseness of joints. Such evils may be remedied by reglueing and clamping tightly till fixed. A broken rail may be replaced by a new one, but a broken leg is generally beyond anything approaching neat repair. Frequently one corner of the seat will split away at the line where the leg is inserted. This may be put right by temporarily removing the leg, and boring (with a centre-bit) 3 or 4 holes laterally in the wood, from the edge towards the centre of the seat, filling them with wooden pegs dipped in good hot glue, and clamping till quite dry and firm, when the leg may be reintroduced into its place.

Washstand.—A rough handy washstand of simple design is shown in Fig. 589. The legs *a*, of 2-in. or 2½-in. wood, are shown square, but may of course be rounded at the corners by a plane, or completely turned in a lathe, in the intervals between the joints, this being done before the mortices are cut. These latter will be 2 in each inner face of each leg—an upper to take the tenons on the bearers *b* that carry the top *c*, and a lower to receive the supports *d e* of the drawer *f*. The mortices should be cut deeply but not quite through the legs. The bearers *b d* are 3 in. wide and ½-¾ in. thick, placed edge upwards; *e* are only 1½ in. wide and laid flat. All are best situated about the centre of the width of the legs, and therefore flush with neither the back nor the front. The

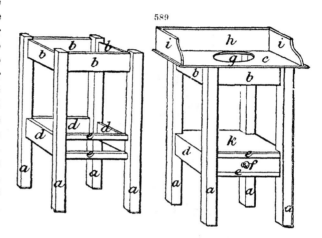

2 side bearers *d* have little strips glued and tacked inside on a level with the top edge of the lower bearer *e*, on which the drawer *f* is supported and can slide to and fro. The drawer *f* is made with half-lap dovetails, as the tool chest, Fig. 565, p. 165. The top should be made complete before it is fixed to the stand. Its table *c* will require to be cut out of 2 pieces to gain sufficient width. These must be pinned and glued securely together, and further strengthened by strips attached beneath while cutting out the circular hole *g*. This latter operation is effected by means of a fret-saw or key-hole saw worked with the face of the table towards the operator. When the table of the top is so far complete, the back *h* and sides *i* are attached, being first dovetailed together at the corners, and then bradded or screwed to the table from the other side. It will be seen that the table *c* is large enough to project about 2 in. beyond the frame on each side and 1 in. in front. It is fixed to the frame by first glueing some triangular blocks on to the sides *b*, inside the frame, and flush with the top of it, one in the centre of each side *b*, in such a way as to offer a flat surface at top, which may take some of the bearing of the table *c*. When these blocks are quite firm, their upper surface, as well as that of the whole frame, receives a coat of glue, and the complete top is laid in place. It may be further secured by driving a screw through it and into the top of the leg at each corner, allowing the heads of the screws to be countersunk and hiding them by putty before painting. The washstand is completed by fastening a board *k*, cut out at the corners so as to fit between the legs, over the drawer *f*, and reaching a little beyond the bearers *d*.

Bedstead. —A simple yet comfortable trestle bedstead is shown in Fig. 590, which *is* an end view looking at the head. The frame consists in the main of 2 lengths of deal *a*, about 3 in. by 2½ in., planed off to the sectional shape indicated in the figure. Into which are mortised 3 sets of cross legs *b*, formed of hard wood 2 in. sq., with the feet cut sloping as at *c*, and joined at the centre by a bolt and nut *d*. To allow for the legs crossing each other, it is obvious that the mortices in the rails *a* for receiving the ends of the legs *b* must not be opposite each other, but exactly the width of the leg apart. The pairs of legs are situated one at each end and one in the middle. Throughout the whole length of the bedstead, coarse sacking *e* is strained tightly across from one rail to the other, and brought round the corner, where it is securely nailed. This sacking prevents the legs opening too wide, and forms the support of the bed and its occupant. An additional solidity and finish is given by attaching a head-board *f*, on

590.

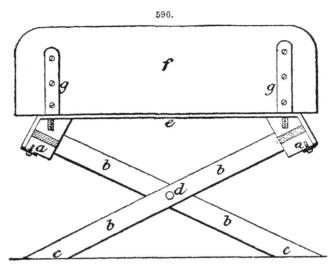

which are screwed 2 strips of iron *g* brought to a pin form at their free ends, and dropping into holes bored for them in the rails *a*. By removing the head-board *f*, the bedstead may be shut up so as to occupy very little space. A foot-board may be added in the same way, and will further strengthen the structure.

Equally simple in constructive detail, only requiring more wood, is the ordinary 4-post bedstead. As to material, almost any wood but deal is suitable, e. g. beech, birch, ash, mahogany. The joints are all simple mortices and tenons, with the addition of a special feature in the shape of a bed-screw. Dimensions vary with requirements; 6 ft. long by 5 ft. wide to 5½ ft. by 4½ ft. forms a "double" size; 5½ to 6 ft. by 3½ ft. is a "single" size; and cots are made smaller for children. The section of the frame timber may run from 4½ in. by 2½ in. to 3½ in. by 2 in., according to the size of the bedstead. These measurements refer to the rough timber, and are reduced considerably by the planing down and perhaps turning. The legs may be 3½ in. sq. in the rough. Their length will depend upon whether there is to be a foot-board, head-board, tester, or other addition to the frame. The height of the frame above the floor varies from 12 to 18 in., and the posts should in any case stand up some 12 or 18 in. above the frame, both to enclose the bedding and to afford sufficient material for the mortices which have to support the frame. When the legs are of minimum length they need only be planed smooth and square, and covered with a piece of chintz or other material, corresponding with that which is hung around the sides and ends to fill up the space between the frame and the floor; but when the legs are prolonged upwards to support head-board and foot-board, it is almost imperative to turn those portions which intervene between the mortices, or the appearance is very mean. The plan of the bedstead having been decided on, the 4 pieces for the legs and the other 4 pieces for the frame are planed up smooth and square. On the sides of the legs are marked where the mortices have to be cut for the reception of the ends of the frame, remembering that in each case there will be 2 contiguous sides of the leg to be mortised. Before proceeding to cut the mortices, which need only be ¾ in. deep, it is essential to mark the spot where a hole is to be bored for the insertion of the bed-screw.

Now, each post contains 2 mortices, as at a, Fig. 591, and a screw has to be inserted through the back (not side) of the mortice and into the end (not side) of the tenon; consequently the hole for the screw must be exactly in the centre of the post so far as its width is concerned, and this is ascertained by drawing diagonal lines, the centre being their point of junction, as at b. But as there are to be 2 screws inserted in the post, one b for the mortice which is hidden in the cut, and another for the mortice a, these holes must not be on the same level, or they would cross each other in the middle of the post—one must be at least 1 in. higher than the other. To ensure these holes being bored quite straight, it is well to mark opposite sides of the post, and bore half-way from each side. The size of the holes should be

591.

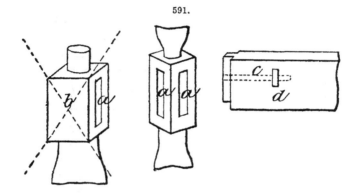

such as just to admit with ease the bed-screws available for the job, several sizes being made. At the outer surface of the hole a recess is cut to allow the head of the bed-screw to drop in out of the way. When the holes are completed, the mortices may be cut; and after this the legs may be turned according to any desired pattern, so long as the portions carrying the mortices are not interfered with. Next the tenons are cut on the ends of the frame-pieces and fitted into their respective mortices. Whilst in this position, each hole which has been bored in the posts is continued into the end of the frame-piece corresponding to it, as seen by the dotted line c, the hole being carried a little deeper than the full length of the bed-screw when its head is recessed. The holes will be alternately a little above and a little below the centre of the tenon, to admit of the screws crossing each other, and not in the exact centre. When a hole is finished, a notch is cut into the side of the frame-piece, as at d, with a sharp chisel, just large enough to receive comfortably the nut of the bed-screw, which must lie so that it is central with regard to the hole for admitting the bed-screw. The nut is made quite tight, so that it shall not revolve when the screw turns in it, by wedging in a little slip of wood, previously glued. When all these preparations have been completed, the bedstead is put together by inserting the tenons on the frame-pieces into the mortices in the legs, and screwing all up tight and firm by the bed-screws. If there is to be a foot-board, it is recessed a little into the legs, and a rail is then generally added above it to connect the tops of the legs. The head legs may also be of a height (5 or 6 ft.) to carry a canopy, the frame of which is mortised into the legs and further supported by angle irons. The recessed ends of the bed-screws are covered by little turned wooden cups made for the purpose.

Chest of Drawers.—This article of furniture may be divided into 3 parts—the case or frame, the cross pieces or partitions, and the drawers. A rough form is illustrated in Fig. 592. The sides a and bottom b of the case are of 1-in. pine about 18 in. wide. The bottom is let into a v-shaped groove in the sides, and further supported by blocks glued on to the sides all round underneath it. The cross pieces $c\ d$ are dovetailed into the top edges of the sides, and serve to hold the sides from spreading out. The cross pieces *e f g* are mortised into the sides of the case, but not so that the tenons come through to the outside of the case. The side ledges *h* running back from the cross pieces on each side of the case are glued and screwed to the sides. A board *i*, 3 in. wide and 1 in. thick, is notched into the cross piece *c* and the bottom *b* and supports by a mortice

592.

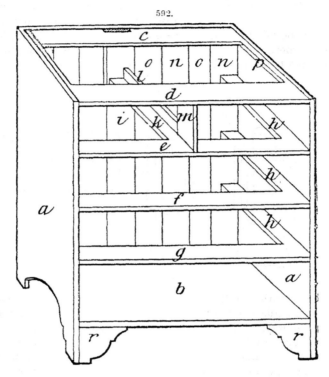

the bearer *k*, whose other end is mortised into the cross piece *e*; this bearer *k* carries the sides of the 2 small top drawers. A strip *l* placed edgewise on it is screwed from beneath on to the bearer *k*, and is replaced in front by a vertical partition *m* mortised into the cross pieces *d e*. The back, which is next put on, consists of alternate pieces of ½-in. and ¾-in. stuff, the outer ones, as *n*, being ¾-in.; these pieces are nailed to the cross piece *c* at top and to the bottom *b*, and the sides *a* are nailed to them. The thicker pieces *n* have their edges rebated so as to cover those of the thinner ones *o*, and thus the surface of the back is flush inside but irregular outside. The top is made of 1-in. pine, screwed on to the cross pieces *c d* and to 2 strips *p* from below, and lying flush with the back but projecting 1 in. over the sides and front. The strips *p* are fastened to the sides *a* by screws. The sides *a* are made in one piece, and are cut out at the bottom; angular pieces *r* glued into the front below the bottom drawer then give the appearance of dwarf legs. The drawers are made of 1-in. wood in the fronts, ⅝-in. in the sides and back, and ½-in. or $\frac{7}{16}$-in. in the bottom. Their construction resembles that described on p. 165. The completed article may be painted, stained, or polished.

The preceding is not a very workmanlike plan. A superior way is as follows:— The case is made like a box turned up on end, all the corners having dovetail joints. The edges of the boards which come at the back of the chest are rebated about ⅓ of their thickness to admit of letting the back in so as to lie flush with the sides, top, and bottom. The partitions for separating the drawers are made so as to completely cover the drawer immediately beneath, and are not merely strips for giving support; they are let into grooves previously cut for them about ⅜ in. deep into the sides of the chest, and, instead of being formed of single boards, which are liable to warp, are built up of frames and panels, after the manner of a door, the joints being made by tongues and grooves, with mortices and tenons at the angles, and wooden pins driven through. The top is formed of an extra slab laid on the top of the case, projecting at the sides and front, secured by screws from below, and having a bead or moulding run round under it. The back is constructed of thin panelling, glued and bradded into the rebate in the sides. The bottom is added in the same way as the top, and may project rather more. A moulding is also run round it. The legs should be turned, and are fastened to the chest by a beech pin screwed into them and into stout beech blocks under the bottom corners of the case.

Dresser.—A useful form of kitchen dresser, removable at pleasure, is shown in Fig. 593. It is constructed out of best clean yellow pine, French polished. The ends are formed by 2 gables *a*, 5 ft. 2 in. high, 20 in. wide in the full body, 10 in. wide at the top drawers *b*, and 1 in. thick. They rest on strips *c*, 2 in. sq., and projecting 2½ in. in front, to which they are mortised. The 3 large drawers *d* are surmounted by a slab *e*, 4 ft. long, 1¼ in. thick, projecting ¾ in. beyond the front of the drawers, and at a height of 3 ft. 2 in. above the floor. Being of the same width as the gables (20 in.), this slab does not reach the back of the dresser by ¾ in., thus leaving a space for the back lining. Boards *f*, 4 ft. long, 9¼ in. wide, and ¾ in. thick, are placed above and below the 5 small drawers *b*, which latter are separated by partitions 7 in. long, 3½ in. wide, and ¾ in. thick. The fronts of the large drawers *d* are 6 in. wide, and of the small ones *b* 2¾ in. There is a clear space *h* 10 in. high between the 2 rows of drawers. As indicated in the

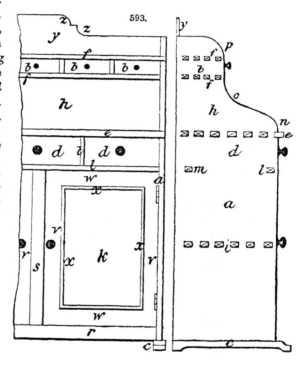

593.

drawing, the joints in the frame are made by mortices and tenons, the latter being of full depth and diagonally wedged. A shelf *i*, 4 ft. long, 18 in. wide, and 1 in. thick, divides the cupboard *k* into an upper and a lower compartment. A fore edge *l* and a back edge *m*, each 3 in. wide, 1 in. thick, and 4 ft. long, are morticed as shown, to support the weight of the large drawers *d*. The curves on the gables are cut as follows. The first one *n* is a quarter circle of 4 in. radius, the next *o* is a reversed quarter circle of 5½ in. radius, the 2 being joined by a straight line; the top curve *p* is a quarter circle of 4 in. radius. The base rail *r* is 4 ft. long, 2½ in. wide, and 1¼ in. thick, and mortised into the 2 gables *a* with its under side resting on the strips *c*. From the centre of the base rail, and mortised into it, rises the mounter *s*, also 2½ in. by 1¼ in., 30 in. long, and mortised into the fore edge *l* at top. The case for the 5 small drawers is made by mortice and tenon joints, carefully fitted, planed, glued, and wedged. The wedging is done in the following way. Diagonal saw-cuts are made in the ends of the tenons before putting together, and for these are prepared little wooden wedges ¾ in. wide, ½ in. long, and $\frac{1}{16}$ in. thick, tapering to a fine edge. When one wedge has been driven into one slit, a second is cut in halves and driven into the other slit at right angles to the first. The frame for the 3 large drawers d consists of the fore and back edges $l\,m$, into which 2 cross rails, 3 in. wide, are mortised exactly under the divisions t between the drawers. These divisions are 6 in. wide, and have tenons at top and bottom, fitting into mortices in the cross rails t and the shelf e. The cross rails may be thinner than l and m, but their upper surfaces must all be made flush. The frame, thus far completed, is glued, wedged, and cramped up till quite firm. The bottom is next fitted in so as to lie close up to the gable at each end, to the base rail r in front, and to the back behind, its ends resting upon the strips c, which project $\frac{1}{2}$ in. inwards for that purpose. The method of fastening the bottom to the base-rail r and strips c by screws presents some peculiarities, and is illustrated at u. At intervals of about 9 in. on the under side of the bottom, recesses are gouged out in triangular form, shallowest at the apex, and deepening to $\frac{1}{2}$ in. at the base, which latter is about $\frac{3}{4}$ in. within the margin. From the edge of the bottom $\frac{1}{4}$-in. holes are bored through into these recesses, for the reception of $1\frac{1}{2}$-in. screws, which are driven from the recess, as shown. The 3 large drawers are made of $\frac{7}{8}$-in. wood for the fronts, $\frac{5}{8}$-in. for the backs and sides, and $\frac{3}{8}$-in. for the bottoms; the 5 small ones take $\frac{3}{4}$-in., $\frac{1}{2}$-in., and $\frac{1}{4}$-in. respectively. The backs of the drawers may be $\frac{1}{4}$ in. lower than the sides, to prevent catching; and the drawers themselves may be $\frac{1}{16}$ in. shorter than their niches in the case, to ensure their shutting in flush with the front. The corners of the drawers are made with dovetail joints, and glued. The bottoms are let into grooves previously cut with a plough, and are further supported by narrow fillets glued beneath along the sides, and two or three blocks of hard wood along the front, the latter making contact with stops in the frame to regulate the degree to which the drawer is pushed in. For the 2 doors k, make 4 stiles v or upright pieces of framing, 3 in. wide, $1\frac{1}{4}$ in. thick, and 2 in. longer than the height of the aperture to be covered; also 4 rails w or horizontal pieces of framing, of the same width and thickness. Draw in the stiles for mortising and rails for tenoning. Find the height and width of the apertures in the dresser front, place the stiles on edge on the bench, and draw at each end with pencil, the breadth of a rail at the outer lines being a little farther apart than the height of the opening. Then mark off $\frac{1}{2}$ in. from the inner lines towards the ends. From this line mark off $1\frac{3}{4}$ in. towards the ends. Between these last 2 lines is the portion to be mortised, leaving $\frac{3}{4}$ in. at the extreme end to give strength to the frame. When drawing in the rails, deduct the breadth of the 2 stiles from the width of opening, allowing $\frac{1}{8}$ in. for fitting; draw in the shoulders at this with cutting knife. Gauge for $\frac{3}{8}$ in. mortice-iron in the centre of the stuff. Mortise about 2 in. deep, taking care to have all mortices in the centre of the stuff for their whole depth, otherwise the framing will be twisted. When the rails are tenoned the thickness way, gauge the inner edge of tenons $\frac{1}{2}$ in. to be ripped off, and $\frac{3}{4}$ in. bare to rip off the outer edge; then the tenon should fill the mortice. Cut it to within $\frac{1}{8}$ in. of the depth of the mortice. All these pieces, being mortised and tenoned, are grooved for the panels. This is done in the centre of the stuff with a slit plough and $\frac{1}{4}$-in. iron, the groove being $\frac{1}{2}$ in. deep; all the grooving is done with the outer face of each piece towards the operator. The panels k are of $\frac{1}{2}$-in. wood, and "fielded" on the front side, i.e. a ribbon about 2 in. wide is sliced off all round, so as to bevel the front face gradually to a thickness of about half at the edge. This fielded edge is let about $\frac{1}{2}$ in. deep into a groove cut for it in the inner edges of the pieces $v\,w$. When the frame and panel have been fitted and glued up, a small moulding x is run round in the angle. When the door is thus completed and has been duly cramped and dried, it may be fitted to the aperture it has to close, and its edges planed away smooth till the adjustment is perfect. The doors are not hung till the back y of the dresser has been put in. The back consists of $\frac{5}{8}$-in. boards arranged to run up and down, or across, or partly both, according as the wood available best suits. The boards are united by groove and feather joints, and any exposed ends are contrived to come where they will not be seen. The curves at z in the top of the back are of

2 in. radius. The boards are secured by 1¼-in. screws, and a bead is run round the edge. The stops for the small drawers may be glued on the back boards, and of such a thickness as to allow the drawer fronts to come $\frac{1}{16}$ in. within the face of the frame. The stops for the large drawers are 2 in. sq. and ¼ in. thick, and are screwed on to the frame under the drawers $\frac{1}{16}$ in. farther in than the point reached by the blocks on the drawers when their fronts are flush with the outside of the frame. The doors are hung on 3-in. brass butt hinges, and great accuracy must be observed in fixing the hinges, so that the doors hang perfectly square and free. Finally the whole work is sandpapered quite smooth, and polished, varnished, or painted.

GARDEN AND YARD ACCESSORIES.—This section is intended to include such articles of every-day use as wheelbarrows, coops, hutches, kennels, hives, flower-stands, and garden frames, as well as such elementary examples of rough building as greenhouses, summer-houses, fences and gates.

Wheelbarrow.—For ordinary work, good sound deal board ¾ in. thick is quite durable enough for the body of the barrow; elm lasts much longer under rough wear, but is much more costly and difficult to work. The dimensions will vary with the size of the person using the barrow, but on the average they may be as follows: Total length, including wheel and handles, 4 ft.; maximum length of body, 2 ft.; width of body, 1¼ ft.; depth of body, 10 in. While the body is 2 ft. long at top, it should slope back to 18 in. at the bottom, to allow for the wheel. The first step is to make a frame of 1½-in. or 2-in. stuff, measuring 18 in. long and 15 in. wide, but with the long sides of the frame projecting about 1 ft. forwards to carry the wheel, and about 15 in. backwards to form the handles. This frame should be dovetailed together at the corners. The body of the barrow is made with the sides perpendicular, while the tail-board may slope a little outwards, and the head-board (next the wheel) much more so. This body is formed with mortice and tenon joints. It is fitted to the frame either by tenons let into mortices in the frame, or by rebating the frame about ½ in. all round on the inside. The legs are attached outside the body, and help to strengthen the whole. They should be cut with a shoulder at such a height as to support the barrow, when at rest, at a convenient distance above the ground. If let in about $\frac{3}{8}$ in. into the frame, so much the better; a ¼-in. iron rod may be carried through the legs and frame from side and side, and 2 or 3 screws secure it to the body. A good wheel can be made by cutting a 10- or 12-in. circle out of a piece of 1-in. elm.; a 2-in. sq. hole is chiselled out in the centre, to receive an axle formed of a piece of oak or ash, having a diameter of 2 in. sq. in the centre, but tapered off to about 1¼ or 1½ in. at the ends. The wheel is strengthened by having a rim of stout hoop-iron " shrunk on," that is to say, the rim is made quite close-fitting, and is then heated ready for putting on; the heating stretches it and facilitates its being put on, when a plunge into cold water causes it to contract and hold firmly. The axle must fit very tightly in the wheel, and this is best secured by making the hole rather large and using wooden wedges for tightening up, driving them from opposite sides alternately. The ends of the axle are each shod with a ferrule, to prevent the wood splitting on driving in the iron pins on which the wheel is to revolve. These pins are square where they enter the wood, and round in the projecting part, which latter passes on each side of the wheel to the front shafts of the frame of the barrow. About the easiest effective way of connecting these pins to the shafts is to drive a staple into the under side of each shaft, of a size large enough to hold the pins without preventing their free revolution. In this way the wheel can be added last of all, and can be removed and repaired, if necessary, without injuring the frame.

Poultry and Pigeon Houses.—A useful size for a hencoop (Fig. 594) to place against a wall is about 4 ft. long, 2 ft. wide, 2½ ft. high in front, and 3¼ ft. at the back. The framework will consist of 6 uprights *a*, a bottom plate *b*, top plates *c d*, and rafters *e*. All the wood but that for the rafters may be 1½ in. sq.; the rafters are 1½ in. wide, 1 in. deep, and 2½ ft. long. The bottom plate is fitted to the uprights, at about 2 in.

above the floor, by halving each into the other. The top plates are fitted on in the same manner, and nailed up. This done, the rafters are cut out to a depth of about half their thickness, and fitted into the top plates. The roof may be formed of 7-in. feather-edge boards, long enough to overhang about 3 in. at each end, fastened by nailing them to the rafters, com-mencing at the bottom edge and lap-ping about 1 in. as they proceed; or it may be flat boarded, covered with felt, and thoroughly tarred. The right end is occupied by a door, the left end is boarded up like the roof, and the 3 front spaces are closed by galvanized iron wire netting. The door frame is made of wood $1\frac{1}{2}$ in. wide and 1 in. thick, and both it and the triangular space above it are filled in with net-ting. The floor is of $\frac{3}{4}$-in. deal boards laid the short way. Perches must be fastened across inside. The wall forms

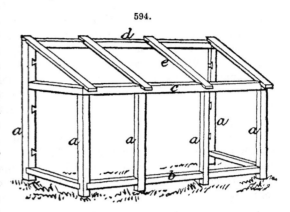

594.

the back of the coop; therefore the coop should be tied to it by means of iron stays driven into the wall and nailed or screwed to the frame of the coop. A strip of sheet zinc having one edge driven into a course in the wall, and the other edge nailed down on the roof, will prevent wet finding its way down into the coop.

Fig. 595 is a plan of a fowl-house of more ambitious dimensions, arranged at the end of garden or yard, so that the back a and sides $b c$ are formed by the walls of the enclosure, thus saving expense. Commencing at one end, the compartment d is a

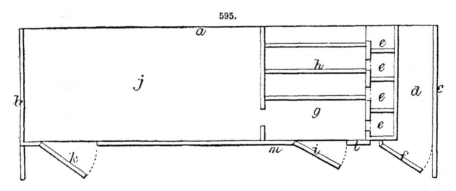

595.

passage giving access to the nests e, and closed by a door f; g is the roosting-place, fitted with perches h, reached by a door i in front, and leading into the run j, also approached through the door k. In arranging the construction, it is best to pursue the following order. First make the front framing, which will consist of a bottom rail 3 in. sq. reaching from b to c at about 6 ft. from the wall a. Into this will be mortised at intervals a series of uprights, about 3 in. by 2 in. and 6 ft. high, these being nowhere more than 3 ft. apart, and in some places less to suit the positions of the doors. A top rail will next be fitted over the tenoned tops of all the uprights. At about 8 ft. from the ground a wall plate 3 in. by 2 in. is nailed to the wall a, and then the rafters are fitted to the wall plate and the front rail. Before proceeding to roof over and close in the framing, it is well to complete the internal fittings. These are better shown in Figs. 596, 597. The 3 perches h are rough poles with the bark on; they are arranged in descending order, and are sufficiently secured at each end by dropping them loosely into wooden blocks nailed to the partitions. The nests e are raised a little above the ground, and closed in on all sides, including the top, a small hole being cut in front just admitting the hen. The fowls enter the nests e from the house g; the nests are provided with doors along the back, opening into d, both for the removal of the eggs and for the occasional cleansing of the nests. The front of the house, as far as the partition separating the run j from the roosting-house g, may be covered with galvanized iron wire

596.

597.

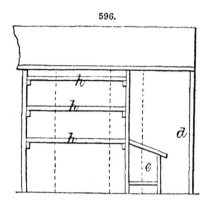
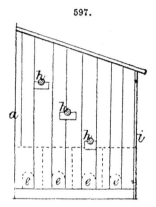

netting, the remainder is boarded. The doors $f\,i$ may be of simple construction, such as 3 or 4 boards placed side by side and fastened together by cross pieces nailed to them. The portions $l\,m$ of the front, coming between the doors, may be "weather boarded," i. e. covered with feather-edged boards overlapping each other and running horizontally. The roof is best boarded flat with $\frac{5}{8}$-in. boards, then covered with felt and well tarred. A zinc gutter along the front adds to the comfort, and a piece of 3-in. zinc pipe inserted in the roof over the middle of the house g forms an efficient ventilator, when surmounted by an overhanging cap to keep out rain. The doors $f\,i$, being heavy, will need T-hinges, while butts will answer for k.

A rough pigeon-coop, only suitable for placing under the shelter of a roof, may be made as shown in Fig. 598, say 3 ft. long, 2 ft. wide, 20 in. high in the sides and 29 in.

598.

599.

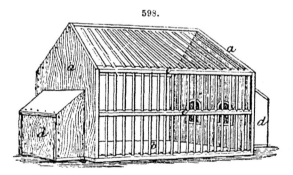

to the top of the roof. For the ends a, 3 strips of 8-in. by 1-in. deal board may be nailed to 2 cross pieces 2 in. by 1 in. The floor b is of $\frac{3}{4}$-in. deal board laid the short way. The back and half the roof may be boarded in, while in the front are fixed 2 strips c 1 in. sq., joining the ends, and perforated at intervals of $1\frac{1}{4}$ in. by galvanized iron wires. At each end is attached a nest box d 18 in. long, 9 in. wide, and 16 in. high, with sloping top; it is made of $\frac{1}{2}$-in. stuff nailed together. The nest box is entered by the holes in the ends *a*. One or more of the front wires may be made movable for the egress and ingress of the birds.

A house for 7 couples of pigeons, adapted for hanging against a wall having a warm aspect, is shown in Fig. 599. The principal part of the house consists of a box of 1-in. deal, measuring 3 ft. long, 2 ft. wide, and 15 in. deep. Lengthwise it is divided into 3 compartments by 2 partitions *a* of ½-in. wood, and these are supported by 3 upright partitions *b* of ¾-in. wood. The bottom of the box forms the back of the house. The front of the house is set back 3 in., so that the sides and floors of all the compartments project that distance beyond their entrances. The object of this is to secure greater privacy for each pair of birds. As the top of the box must be rendered sloping in order to throw off the rain, by the addition of 2 boards *c*, the triangular space thus enclosed forms a convenient compartment for a 7th pair of birds. The 2 boards *c* are best dovetailed together at the top, and protected by a zinc cap; they are secured to the top of the box by the intervention of 2 triangular strips which afford a solid bearing. The entrance holes indicated by the dotted lines measure about 6 in. high and 3 or 4 in. wide, and are cut in the positions shown by means of a keyhole saw.

The following description of a combined poultry and pigeon house is condensed from an interesting communication made to *Amateur Work*. The ground at disposal measures 22 ft. by 8 ft., with walls on 3 sides; it is divided into 3 portions—a central covered-in house 6 ft. sq., and on each side a run 8 ft. sq. The house is divided into 2 unequal parts, one 6 ft. by 4 ft. for a covered shady run during hot or wet weather and another 6 ft. by 2 ft. for a breeding house. The floor is sloped throughout from front to back, and trodden quite hard. The framework (Fig. 600) of the whole rests

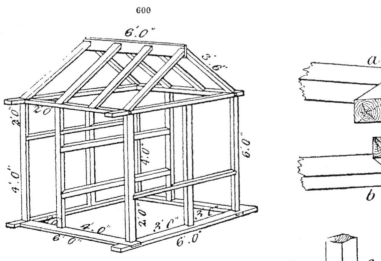

on a course of bricks, protecting it from damp and rendering it portable. The dimensions of the quartering for the construction of the house will be 4 8-ft. lengths of 3-in. by 3-in. for the 6-ft. sq. ground frame, and the upright joists and rafters are 2½ in. sq. The joints employed are illustrated in Fig. 601, *a* being that of a corner of the bottom frame, *b* that of the upper frame with the upright, and *c* that of the cross pieces. In the larger division of the house, the cross pieces are placed 2 ft. from the ground as joists for the loose floor of the compartment reserved for fowls and egg-boxes, this floor forming at the same time a roof to the dry shed beneath. In the smaller division of the house, the joists are 4 ft. from the ground; the lower part is set aside for nesting places, and the upper serves as a pigeon-loft extending to the roof. The object in putting the nests (for sitting) upon the ground is to give the eggs, during incubation, the benefit of the moisture of the earth. Hence the dry run underneath the larger compartment goes no farther than the wooden partition which intervenes. The upright which bisects the front of the house is intended for a stop for 2 large doors, hanging from the outer supports. The 8 rafters, each $3\frac{1}{2}$ ft. long, for the roof are simply nailed in position, the plank placed at the apex acting as a sort of keyboard, and the weight of the roofing material afterwards added being sufficient to make all secure. So far the framework may be made in the workshop, and taken to its place for putting together, temporarily strengthening it by nailing a few diagonal stays to it.

For roofing the building, sheet zinc is perhaps the most suitable material. Felt harbours vermin, requires early renewal, and necessitates a wooden roofing underneath it. Corrugated iron is expensive, and is very hot in the sun and very cold in time of frost; moreover, it wears badly, and soon begins to leak where nails are driven through. Zinc is one-third less expensive, looks as neat, is twice as durable, and can be fixed without trouble. For the roof, 63 sq. ft. of No. 10 zinc will be needed. The weight should be 17 lb. to the sheet, measuring 6 ft. 8 in. wide; 3 such sheets will be sufficient, and if one of them be cut in two, they may be overlapped an inch or so, and, with a few nails, all soldering will be avoided. Out of the same quantity, 3 pieces 12 in. wide and 3 ft. long may be cut. With these, a semicircular ridge, to bend over the key-board of the roof, can be formed; and if care has been taken not to carry the sheets of zinc quite up to the top, a species of ventilator will be the result, the air having free access to the channel running the whole length of the building, whilst direct draught is obviated, and no rain-water can enter. The roof will have eaves extending 4 in. from the sides of the house. In addition to the ventilation provided by the channel on the crown of the roof, it will be found that the zinc plates, resting on the rafters, will not fit closely to the 2 sides of the house, but an aperture will be left underneath the eaves. This aperture should not be wholly closed in as a well-ventilated but not a draughty roosting-house is a necessity. A wooden strip $2\frac{1}{2}$ in. wide should, however, be nailed horizontally under the eaves.

For boarding in the 4 sides, the cheapest, warmest, and most weather-tight material is 6-in. match-lining (it is practically $5\frac{1}{4}$ in. in width). No planing will be wanted, except that which it has received at the mills. The tongue-and-groove method of joining each strip to its fellow, ensures the air-tightness of the interior, and prevents the possibility of the boards themselves warping; in addition, the superadded beading lends an ornamental appearance to the exterior. This match-lining is bought by the "square" of 16 ft., and 3 such squares, at 11s. 6d. each, will give ample material.

The principal distinguishing feature of this poultry-house is the facility with which every part of the interior can be reached without requiring to go inside. Wherever a place is inconvenient to reach the chances are cleansing will be neglected and dirt accumulate, a state of things fatal to success. Therefore, in the whole arrangement of the compartments, every corner is easily accessible; hence the structure consists almost entirely of doors. But the match-lining throughout being used horizontally, the number of doors is not obtrusive, as many of them are hardly noticeable.

Figs. 602 to 605 represent the 4 sides of the house. The rear (Fig. 602) is boarded up from top to bottom with the exception of 2 widths of match-lining 4 ft. from the ground, which are battened together to form a flap a, and are hinged as shown. This flap a is to allow the loose flooring of the pigeon-loft, situated in the uppermost part of the building, to be withdrawn whenever necessary, that the boards may be cleansed. The left side (Fig. 603) of the poultry-house faces north. The small door b is hinged to the outer upright, and does not extend quite to the top. By it the pigeon-lockers are gained. Underneath it is door c, hinged to the same upright, and allowing good height

(4 ft.) to permit of entrance to the breeding-house for fowls, the nests in which, it will be remembered, are placed on the ground. *d* is simply a larger flap than *a*, consisting of match-lining battened together to the width of 2 ft., and hinged from the plank above it. When down, this flap shuts in the dry shed running under the roosting compartment; when open at an angle it enlarges that shed, admitting at the same time fresh air.

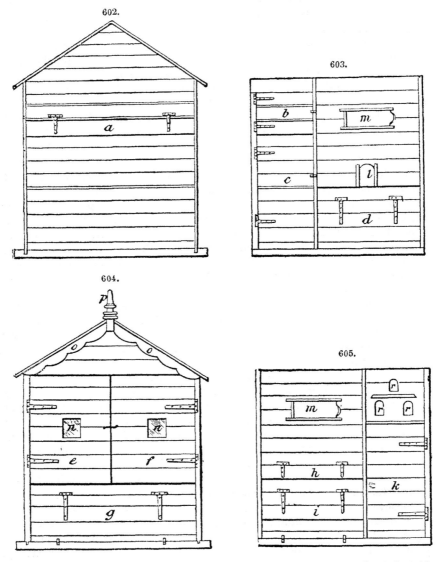

Passing to the front of the house (Fig. 604) doors *e f*, each 4 ft. high by 3 ft. wide, open up the entire roosting compartment. It is important that this pair should be made to fit well. Below is *g*, a flap similar to *d*, but 2 ft. longer. It is intended to allow of the earth of the dry run being removed from the front without the inconvenience of entering the closed yards. The material forming the floor should be changed as often as it becomes polluted. On the right side (Fig. 605) of the house facing south are 2 flaps, viz. a small one *h*, 10 in. deep, which opens on to the egg-boxes, and a larger one *i*, identical in every respect with *d*, on the opposite side. When it is wished that the door run should be at the disposal of one yard exclusively, it will be necessary to keep door *f*

closed, but when there are no chickens and pullets to occupy the other yard, and the whole of the available space is to be given to the adult birds, by lifting flaps d and i at the same time, the dry shed accommodation will be much increased. The last entrance k is 4 ft. high, and leads into the breeding-house. The open space above it is the dormer part of the pigeon-house.

There are 4 windows to be added : one m on either side, the glass of which slips backwards and forwards in a rabbet; and 2 n in the front which are for lighting purposes only, the glass remaining fixed, with strips of wood at the back and a beading in front.

Preliminary to fitting the doors, lengths of 2-in. pine beading are nailed to the uprights as a stop. All the doors are made in the same way, consisting of match-lining nailed to 2 battens formed of the same material, sawn in half. Flat-headed wrought-iron $1\frac{1}{2}$-in. nails should be used, as they drive cleanly into the wood. Some time will be spent in this part of the work, and open-air labour will be saved by nailing together the doors full-large in the workshop, and afterwards fitting each by sawing it to its exact dimensions and planing down the edges when ready. Cross-garnet or T hinges are the best suited to bearing the weight of the doors. For the two largest (e and f), the 16-in. size will be required, as the strain is great from the side. All the other flaps and doors have the 10-in. size. The hinges should be so placed that the $\frac{3}{4}$-in. screws fixing them may be in the centre of the plank. The doors which form integral parts of the divisions of the house, necessary to be weather-tight and warm, should be nicely constructed, and some trouble taken in fitting will be amply repaid. The flaps to the dry shed are not so essential, and less care may be expended upon them. Should the doors warp in the fixing, no great anxiety need be felt, for when they have been hung a short time they will be sure to regain their right shape. They should all be secured with wooden buttons. The window and other apertures should be cut when the match-lining is fixed, a key-saw being first used. They will not lessen the strength of the walls if cut in the centre of the planks.

The exterior of the fowl-house should now receive its first coat of paint, 3 coats being the rule. Priming of the ordinary description may be used for the first. If prepared priming be used, it is the more necessary to paint swiftly, as it dries in almost immediately. About 12 lb. of paint will be needed for the first coat. The main thing to be observed is that the beading shall be properly covered, and therefore the better plan is to paint this first carefully, and afterwards go over the planks, filling in all white places wherever they may be noticed. If beading and planking were treated simultaneously, it would be difficult to discover whether the former had been properly done. For the second coat about the same proportion of lead colour should be laid thinly on, and these 2 coats should suffice to preserve the wood effectually. The third coat may be according to fancy.

On reference to Fig. 603, showing the left side of the house, it will be seen that there is a small opening l, 9 in. high by 6 in. wide, with a circular top. This is the entrance for the fowls, and it is closed with a sliding panel. When desirous of keeping this panel raised, a loop of wire attached to a screw in it may be slipped over a second screw placed a few inches above it on the side of the house. To prevent the sliding glasses of the windows from being withdrawn too far, a screw should be driven in almost flush some few inches beyond the aperture on the side to which each pane is slipped.

To complete the front of the house, 2 planks o, cut to an ornamental pattern, are nailed under the eaves, but not close up to the match-lining, the intention being to allow a current of air to ascend under them, finding its way to the channel on the ridge of the roof. These boards may be mortised into a spike p, which gives a finish to the whole, and nailed at their further extremities to the projecting strip of wood running under the zinc plates at each side of the house. On the right side of the building, 3 pigeon-holes r are provided. These should be cut in a permanent partition, their measurement being

6 in. by 4 in. The partition should be nailed to the inner side of the uprights and 2 shelves, one under each opening, added to serve as an alighting board, which ought not to measure less than 6 in. in width.

The interior remains to be dealt with. As a preliminary, any spare mortar, sand, and lime may be thrown into the dry run, where it will tread down and form an excellent floor. As a means of protection against the burrowing of rats, whilst retaining the advantages of the moisture of the natural soil, a length of 18-in. galvanized wire-work, 1 in. mesh, should be placed on the floor of the breeding compartment. A little mortar will be sufficient to keep it in position.

In the whole interior is but one permanent partition—that is, there is a single part only which is nailed, all the other portions being removable at pleasure. The exception is the boarding which divides the breeding compartment and pigeon-loft above it, from the dry shed and roosting-house. If the first pair of rafters from the back have been placed to correspond with the uprights 2 ft. from the rear, as shown in Fig. 600, the match-lining, nailed vertically, may be secured to them at the top, and to the uppermost joist at the bottom, taking care to nail the planks on the side to allow the top of the joist to remain free to support the flooring of the pigeon-loft. No difficulty will be met with if the match-lining be sawn into 2 lengths, the shorter to reach from the roof to the first pair of joists in the smaller part of the house on the one side, and the longer planks to be nailed to the same pair of joists on the opposite side, and to extend to the ground, in which a piece of quartering 3 in. by 3 in. should be sunk as a stop. If the measurements are a little out, a fillet of wood nailed to the joists will make everything easy. As regards the flooring, all that requires to be done is that broad planks be sawn to the exact length, and fitted to extend from back to front. The boarding need not be of more than ¾-in. stuff, but the broader the planks the better, for they will be easier to remove when it is desired to cleanse them, or for any other purpose, and the quicker to replace when that purpose is accomplished. If the flooring be of a slight nature, however, a plank strong enough to bear a man's weight should be made fast in the centre of the fowl-house, for it will be found convenient to stand upon it, and so obtain command over every corner of the roof. The flooring in the pigeon-loft is best made of planed wood, as it is the most easy to clean. The advantage of having it loose is obvious, for by lifting one or two of the planks the whole of the loft may be easily reached by a person entering the breeding-place underneath.

In the roosting-house, there remain to be fitted the nests and the perches. The former consist of a strip of wood, 4 ft. in length and 4 in. high, which forms the front to a set of 4 egg-boxes, each 12 in. wide, and without bottom, which are simply made by nailing at every foot an upright piece of board 11 in. wide and 18 in. high. Stability may be given to them by a thin length of wood, nailed along the top. As a back to this row of nests, a piece of wood 4 in. high should be dropped into grooves attached to the uprights of the building on the right and left of flap *h*, against which the skeleton boxes should be set so that a person by lifting the flap may take the eggs out of the boxes without entering the house. The reason why the back of the nests should be movable, is that they may be cleaned without inconvenience. The arrangement of the nests and perches is shown by Fig. 606. *a* is the skirting nailed to the front of the boxes; *b*, the movable back running in grooves at each end; *c*, the hinged flap on the outside of the building; *d*, a wide shelf resting upon, but not attached to, brackets, and serving a

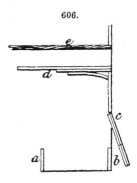

606.

double purpose: first as a roof to the egg-boxes beneath, giving them that privacy in which laying hens delight; and, second, as a tray to catch the droppings of the fowls roosting upon the perch *e*, which is slipped into sockets 4 in. above it. This plan is highly desirable, conducing as it does to the rapid and effectual cleansing of the house daily. The shelf will also serve to prevent the fowls from an upward draught, which may arise from deficiencies in fitting the floor-boards.

The fittings of the pigeon-loft consist of a shelf placed 12 in. above the flooring, on which is an oblong box, without top or bottom, and divided in the centre so as to form a pair of nests, which are reached by an alighting board. A similar contrivance is on the floor below it, and other lockers may be put elsewhere if required. A house of the dimensions stated should accommodate with comfort 6 fancy pigeons and 8 or 9 adult fowls, besides chickens. In regard to the latter, when a hen becomes broody her proper place is in the compartment reached by door c, where a nest may be made up for her with 3 bricks and some moist earth. So soon as the chicks are hatched, they may be allowed the run of the compartment, and as they grow older may be given the use of one yard, from which the grown fowls are excluded by closing flap i. Should great pressure be felt in respect to accommodation for young chickens, an excellent run sheltered from the weather is furnished by the dry shed under the roosting house, the adult fowls being temporarily deprived of it by dropping flaps d and i. Sunshine and air, combined with perfect safety from cats and vermin, may be afforded by wiring in, with 1-in. mesh netting, the front side of the run; and if a piece of small quartering be secured to the bottom of the wirework, whilst the top depends from staples driven into the joist above it, the protecting barrier may be readily raised when food and water are to be given.

The fowls enter the house from the yards by the side doorway already described, which they reach by means of a ladder made of a plank, with half a dozen steps of beading 4 or 5 in. apart. If a staple be driven through the plank and the flap d, a peg will suffice to keep both in position; by withdrawing the peg, the flap falls and the dry shed is closed in, whilst the ladder remains in its proper place. With regard to the yards, the uprights are of 2½-in. by 1½-in. quartering, mortised into a bed of 3-in. by 3-in. stuff. The rafters are 2 in. by 1½ in. The wire below is 1-in. mesh nailed to a plank 1 ft. high. For the remaining portion of the runs, 1½-in. mesh netting is used. A door is at each extremity. Following is a statement of the actual cost of materials required for the combined pigeon and poultry house, exclusive of the yards:—

	£	s.	d.
Quartering ..	0	18	0
Odd planking	0	2	6
Bricks and Lime ..	0	3	6
Wood (beading)	0	2	0
Hinges	0	6	2
Zinc for Roofing	0	14	0
Match-lining	1	14	6
Glass	0	1	9
Paint	0	14	0
Nails and Screws ..	0	3	7
	£5	0	0

The same writer in *Amateur Work* suggests a useful adjunct to the preceding arrangement, for the breeding season, to supply the following demands: (1) secluded spots for sitting hens, the nests placed on the ground, so that the eggs may benefit by the natural moisture of the earth; (2) dry runs for young chickens, in which they may be housed with the mother hen during wet or windy weather; (3) dust bath and ash box for the growing broods, chickens being particularly plagued by insects; (4) coops for fattening cockerels for killing. For pigeons, the most pressing demands are: (1) pairing pens; (2) hospital quarters for lame birds; (3) cages for prize pigeons, or valuable specimens. To supply these requisitions, if the articles be purchased separately from makers, must entail considerable outlay; while for the home construction of a suitable contrivance, the cost for material should not exceed 15s.

Fig. 607 is a sketch of the completed house. Tier a is a portion allotted to pigeons, and as the flooring does not extend for more than $\frac{2}{3}$ of the length the birds can readily obtain access to it from below, where on tier b they are provided with a run, partly roofed, and a compartment in which to nest, reached by holes, and placed within command of the owner by means of a door on the outside. The remaining lower half of the house is apportioned to chickens. On tier c are two boxes—one containing lime and loam, the other cinder-ashes and calcined bones. These boxes are easily lifted, and as they serve to roof over the run underneath, means of reaching the innermost recesses of that part are at once at hand. The sketch represents this lower run shut in by 2 flaps $d e$. Behind the front and larger flap d galvanized wirework is permanently fastened. In the case of the smaller flap e, this wirework is stretched on a frame swinging from above, and so arranged that, fastened back at an ascertained angle, the chickens find room for free ingress and egress under it, whilst the hen is not permitted to have her liberty, the aperture not allowing of her escape. In fine weather, both the outer flaps are opened, thus allowing the light to enter the run, and in themselves providing platforms, of which the chickens avail themselves when basking in the sunlight. Closed, the flaps effectually exclude wind and wet, and render the quarters warm and secure; and again, when both are fastened down, there is ample room for 2 broody hens, which do not appreciate too much light, and require to sit on the soil. The same space may be converted into fattening pens for cockerels whenever occasion arises.

In the construction of the house, the measurements were decided with special reference to the economical use of wood as purchased in small quantities at a timber yard. The framework is formed of quartering $1\frac{1}{2}$ in. sq. obtainable retail in lengths of 12 ft., at 5d. per length. Fig. 608 gives an idea of the skeleton of the whole, and Fig. 609 depicts a frame, of which it is necessary to make 2—one for each end of the house, which is 6 ft. in height and 2 ft. in depth, the length and breadth of the frame. The frames, stood up on end, 4 ft. apart, are braced together on either side by widths of

607.

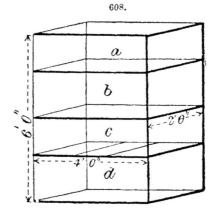

608.

quartering, put 18 in. from top and bottom. As to how the frames are made, Fig. 610 represents the bottom corner, a being the detached pieces of wood before they are screwed together. Fig. 611 in the same way shows the cross-bar mortice. Fig. 612 gives a portion of the left-hand corner of the entire skeleton, a being the cross braces, 4 ft. in length, and b the bar bisecting the frame shown in the smaller sketch in Fig. 608. All the joints are of the simplest mortice; they are quite good enough for the purpose in view, for every board hereafter added to the structure increases its stability. Order 5 lengths of quartering, and these can be cut to the required measurements with a minimum of waste.

In Figs. 607 and 608 on tier *c* in the skeleton sketch, 4 short cross pieces connecting the lower pair of braces are shown. These can be of ¾-in. wood 2 in. wide, and 2 similar pieces can be nailed on the top of the frames from corner to corner, as an additional stay; 2 lengths will afford sufficient stuff. With the framework thus erected, the braces on tier *a* will form joists for the flooring, which is to go ⅔ only, or length of the compartment. This flooring consists of pieces of ¾-in. match-lining, 6 in. wide. The rabbet and groove arrangement locks the several boards into one safe whole, which answers the double purpose—that of a roof to the nests below, and of a platform upon which the pigeons parade in the sunshine. To maintain a rapid disposal of rain-water, give this platform an incline from left to right, which may be done by nailing a tapering fillet of wood upon one end of the joists. The same plan serves for the flooring below, which, in its turn, protects the ash-box and dust-bath beneath; in this case, the floor boards run lengthways instead of across, and the fillet without, being tapered, must be attached to the cross bar of the left-hand frame.

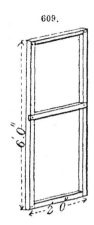

609.

For the sake of economy, it is best to employ match-lining on the other parts of the house, using say 3 lengths of 16 ft. each at 1*d*. per ft. run. Match-lining should be nailed round 3 sides of tier *a*, as shown in Fig. 608. A door 15 in. wide is made by battening the wood together, with the planed surface outwards; it can be hung to the upright by means of 6-in. garnet hinges, at 3*d*. per pair. To divide the breeding place from the run, a few pieces of board nailed together, having

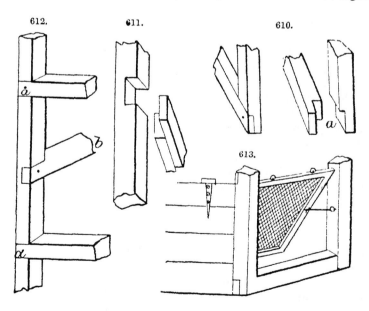

pigeon-holes cut therein, may be kept in position by means of a slide at top and bottom; it will also be necessary to board in that portion of tier *b* at the side and back. Tiers *a b* are under control by the addition of the door at one end; measuring 3 ft. in height and 2 ft. in breadth, it answers for closing in the ends of both tiers, one large door being more convenient and practicable than 2 small ones. This door is a light frame, constructed on the same model as that which is given for the frame in Fig. 609 ; but the quartering used is only 1 in. sq., the price being $2\frac{1}{2}d.$ per length of 12 ft.—of which one will be just enough. It may be attached either by hinges or with latches ; the latter permit of the door being unhooked and carried out of the way. To complete the pigeon part of the house, wirework is wanted to enclose the vacant spaces. A mesh of $1\frac{1}{2}$ in. will do, taking 2 yd., 2 ft. wide, and 4 yd., 1 ft. wide.

On tier c, all that needs attention is the fitting of a skirting to cover in that portion not already roofed, by the 2 boxes shown. Such boxes (old brandy cases) which are thoroughly well made, and measure 20 by 18 in. may be bought of a grocer for say $4d.$ a piece. The skirting consists of the match-lining already obtained.

Tier d is all the better if made draught free, and for the sake of warmth, match-lining may give place to stouter planks, unplaned, with which board in on 2 sides, one end, and the back permanently. The flap, or front is of like material, one board in width, and hung by garnet or T-hinges to the brace, or joist above. The structure is skirted with planks, screwed to the 4 uprights. At one extremity, the smaller flap e, drawn partly open in Fig. 608, is hung in a similar manner, but as it is now and then required to be thrown right up, it is made of match-lining, as less weighty. It has already been explained that under the flaps wirework (1-in. mesh) is stretched in the front as a permanency, and at the end in the form of a swing door. Fig. 613 indicates a mode which answers to confine hen and chickens, or hen alone, at will, according to the angle at which the door is raised and suspended by a stay-hook.

Below is a detailed account of expenditure for materials ; by working with screws instead of nails throughout, every part may be rendered easily detachable and capable of being packed away in small compass, either for removal when changing residence, or storage during the winter months.

Cost of Materials.					*s.*	*d.*
5 12-ft. lengths quartering, $1\frac{1}{2}$ in. square, at $5d.$...	..		..		2	1
2 „ „ $\frac{3}{4}$-in. stuff, by 2 in., at $5d.$	..		..		0	10
3 16-ft. „ $\frac{3}{4}$-in. match-lining, 6 in. wide, at $1d.$ per ft. run					4	0
1 12-ft. „ 1-in. quartering, at $2\frac{1}{2}d.$ ..	..		..	..	0	3
1 „ „ 1-in. planking, 11 in., at $1s.$	..		..	..	1	0
2 old brandy cases, 20 by 18 in., at $4d.$ ..	..		..		0	8
3 pair 6-in. garnet hinges, at $3d.$ ..	..		..		0	9
Nails and screws, catches, say	..	..	..		1	5
2 yd. wirework, $1\frac{1}{2}$-in. mesh, 2 ft. wide, at $4d.$ ..	..		..		0	8
4 „ „ „ „ 1 ft. wide, at $2d.$ ..	..		..		0	8
2 „ „ 1-in. mesh, 1 ft. wide, at $4d.$ ..	..		..		0	8
Paint (3 coats)	..	..	..		1	0
					14	0

Hive.—The construction of a good bar-frame hive at a low cost out of an old tea-chest is thus described by A. Watkins.

Materials.—A full-sized or Indian tea-chest, another packing-case, at least 6 in. longer than the tea-chest, containing some sound $\frac{1}{2}$-in. boards. Have the lids with the boxes. The 2 will cost at the grocer's $1s.$ to $1s. 3d.$ The tea-chest is left whole to make the body of the hive ; the other box is knocked down for the boards in it. In the frames, a piece of best pine is necessary 2 ft. by 11 in. ; have it sawn by the circular into 2 equal boards : they will be $\frac{3}{8}$ in. thick. If at the same time you could get these boards sawn into strips $\frac{7}{8}$ in. wide, it will save a deal of trouble. You will also want a bit of $\frac{1}{4}$-in. board for cutting up into strips for the bottom of the super case ; 17 in. by

Y

6 in. will do. 1 lb. of 1¼-in. wire nails, and a few of the deepest round flat-headed shoe-nails, to be had from the currier's, will also be wanted.

Frames.—These are to be made first. If your pine board is not already cut up into ⅞-in. strips, you must do so by means of a cutting gauge (not a marking-gauge). Set the cutting knife ⅞ in. from the movable block, the knife projecting a full ⅛ in. Make a cut along one edge of the board, keeping the block tightly pressed against it. Do the same on the other side, and a strip of wood ⅞ in. wide will easily break off. The whole of the boards must be cut up into strips, and it will be well to plane the edges. Cut the strips to exact length. You will want 11 for top bars 15½ in. (bare) long, 10 for bottom bars, 14 in. long, 20 for side bars 7¾ in. long. Cut them off exactly square. The frames (as shown in Fig. 614) must now be nailed together in the frame block. They are of the Association size, but with a shorter top bar (15½ in. instead of 17 in.). This makes the hive and super case simpler to make than with a long top bar. The top, sides, and bottom of frame are made of the same thickness of wood for the sake of simplicity; but if the hive-maker possesses a circular saw, he may follow the Association di-

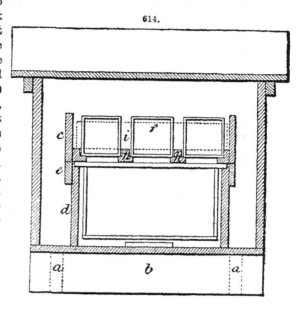

mensions exactly. The frame under consideration has the same outside dimensions as the Association, and will fit into any Association hive.

Frame Block.—A piece of board, thickness not important, is cut off 17 in. long, and 8½ in. deep; 2 strips (a, Fig. 615), 1 in. square, and 8⅛ in. long, are nailed across the ends exactly square, and with a space of 14 in. between. The ends of the strips are level with one edge of the board. Another 1-in. strip b is pivoted in the centre by a screw, the ends are rounded off, and the sides are held firmly while being nailed. Two nails are driven half-way in 15½ in. apart, and serve to keep the top bar in its place while being nailed.

Division Board.—This hangs in the hive in the same manner as the frames d, Fig. 616. A piece of ½-in. board is cut 14½ in. long, and 8½ in. wide; a top bar 15½ in. long nailed to the top edge, and 2 1-in. strips across the ends to keep it from warping.

Distance Guides for Frames.—Advanced bee-keepers often dispense with these, but they are useful to a beginner. The flat-headed shoenails are driven into each side of the top bar (4 to each frame), 1½ in. from each end; the distance between the heads of the nails should be 1⁷⁄₁₆ in., so that the frames will be that distance apart from centre to centre, when hung in the hive; they are indicated in Fig. 614 by small circles on the line above e.

Body of Hive.—The stand and flight board a b, Fig. 616, should be made first; they are fixtures to the hive; 2 pieces of board, 4 in. wide and as thick as convenient (not less than 1 in.), are cut with one end slanting, the shorter side the same length as the outside width of the chest, the longer 6 in. more. They are nailed on edge underneath the bottom of the chest, and the flight board b, 7½ in. by ½ in. and the same length as the chest, is nailed on the sloping ends. The entrance slit, 4 in. long and $\frac{3}{8}$ in. high, can now be cut; it is shown by dotted lines in Fig. 614. In order to fit up the interior of the hive to receive the frames, 2 pieces of $\frac{1}{2}$-in. board $8\frac{1}{2}$ in. wide, and the same length as the interior width of the chest (from back to front), are prepared. One edge of each is bevelled for the frames to rest on, and a strip of $\frac{1}{2}$-in. wood e, Fig. 614, about 2 in. wide and the same length as the board, is nailed to the bevelled side, and $\frac{5}{8}$ in. above the top edges; then a stout strip is nailed across the ends of the boards on the same side as the top strip. The 2 boards thus prepared have now to be nailed across the chest exactly $14\frac{1}{2}$ in. apart; but before doing so, it will be well to clearly understand their use. They form the support for the frames, the projecting ends of which hang on the thin upper edges. It will be seen that the frames do not touch in any other part, but that there is "bee space" between them and the sides and bottom. This space is important, therefore the outside size of the frames and the inside size of that part of the hive

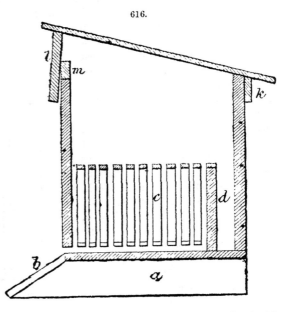

616.

which contains them should always be exact. In nailing the 2 boards across the inside of the chest (as shown in d, Fig. 614) the division board will form a good guide to keep them the requisite $14\frac{1}{2}$ in. apart, and as it is difficult to nail from the outside into the ends, it will be best to nail from the inside, through the strips at the ends of the boards.

Super Case.—Sectional supers are used by most advanced bee-keepers; they can be bought much cheaper and better than they can be made, and as the most used (and probably the best) size is $4\frac{1}{4}$ in. sq. holding when filled 1 lb. of honey, a case will be described to take that size. A bottomless box (c, Fig. 614) is made of $\frac{1}{2}$-in. board, $4\frac{1}{2}$ in. (full) deep, and $16\frac{1}{2}$ in. by $15\frac{1}{2}$ in. outside measurement. Four strips (h, Fig. 614), each $15\frac{1}{2}$ in. by $1\frac{1}{4}$ in. by $\frac{1}{4}$ in., are nailed across the bottom of the box, being let in flush; 2 of them are at the outside, the other 2 at equal distances, forming 3 equal spaces between; 4 strips (i, Fig. 614) $14\frac{1}{2}$ in. by $\frac{1}{2}$ in. by $\frac{1}{2}$ in. are nailed on the top of the wide strips, the 2 outer ones against the sides of the box, the others on the centre of the strips. There must be a space of a little more than $4\frac{1}{4}$ in. between these strips, as they serve to keep the sections the right distance apart. 21 sections, 7 in each row, are placed in the case: they do not quite fill it; but a thin board $15\frac{1}{2}$ in. by $4\frac{1}{4}$ in., with notches cut out of the lower edge to fit over the strips, serves to wedge them up together. "Separators" made of tin, or exceedingly thin wood, not thicker than cardboard, each $15\frac{1}{2}$ in. by $3\frac{1}{4}$ in., are placed between the sections, as shown by dotted lines in Fig. 616. They are necessary to keep the combs from bulging into each other: if they are not used, the sections, when filled, can only be packed in the order in which they come out of the hive. The section case is shown in its place in Fig. 614, but omitted in Fig. 616.

Roof.—This is the most unsatisfactory part of a large hive like this to make. The chief fault is that it is heavy and cumbersome to lift off. A good carpenter, with new boards to work on, would do better to make the roof of a gable shape instead of flat, and it would be worth while to try the waterproof paper roofing, which is not expensive, and very light. To describe the one illustrated : its sides are made sloping like a desk or garden frame, and large enough to slip easily over the hive top like the lid of a box. The front of the roof (*k*, Fig. 616) may be 7 in. deep, and the back 2 in., so that they may both be cut out of one length, and the two sloping sides out of another length of 9-in. board. The flat top is nailed on the top of this frame, projecting $1\frac{1}{2}$ in. to 2 in. all round ; the joints, which must run from back to front, should be as close as possible, and thin strips of board 1 in. wide should be nailed over them. If the boards are smooth, the roof may be well painted; if not, treated to a thick coating of pitch, melted in a pot and applied hot (mind it does not boil over). If the boards which make the roof are very rough and uneven, it may be well to cover them with common roofing felt (cost 1*d*. per sq. ft.). In this case the strips on joints should be omitted. A block of wood (*m*, Fig. 616) must be nailed inside the front, 2 in. from the bottom edge, to keep the roof from slipping down the hive, and a 1-in. ventilation hole, covered with perforated zinc, bored in the back and front. The hive is now complete ; but, before putting a swarm in, the frames must be fitted with wax guides. Most bee-keepers now use full sheets of comb foundation; but if this is not done, a thin line of melted wax must be run along the centre of the under side of top bar. A quilt must be laid on the frames ; a single thickness of China matting (from the outside of tea chests) is best for the first layer, as the bees cannot bite it, and above it 2 or 3 thicknesses of old carpet. The hive is not a mere makeshift one, but can be used to advantage on any system, as there is plenty of room at the rear to add more than the 10 frames, if extracted honey be the object ; or frames of supers can be hung behind the brood frames. It can also be packed with chaff or other warm material during winter if thought necessary. Of course a couple of coats of paint will be an improvement. Frames placed across the entrance are much better than if running from back to front : the first comb acts as a screen, and brood is found in the combs clear down to the bottom bar.

Forcing-frames.—The construction of the wooden portion of forcing-frames is illustrated in Fig. 617, and described below; the fixing of the glass portion will be found under Glazing. A convenient length for the frame is 6 ft., and the width may be

617.

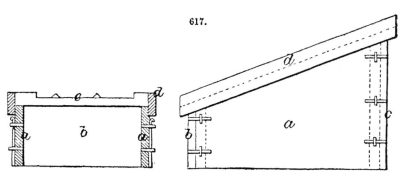

either 4 ft. for single or 8 ft. for double size. It is an advantage to have a frame that will take to pieces, and the one shown is designed with that object. The sides *a*, foot *b*, and head *c* are of $1\frac{1}{4}$-in. deal. The top edge of the sides *a* is cut with a slope so as to allow the glass lid to be at an angle of about 22° 30′ ; therefore if the foot *b* is 1 ft. high, the head *c* on a frame 6 ft. long will be over 3 ft. high. The ends of the foot and head boards *b c* are halved into the ends of the sides *b*, so as to make a good joint. Into the ends of *b c*, staples are driven, and notches are cut out of *a* to admit them ; small bars or wedges are thrust into the projecting loops of these staples in order to secure the sides and ends together in place. Halved into the top edge of the sides *a* are 2 strips *d*, measuring about 2 in. by 1 in. These are firmly screwed to the sides and constitute guards for the sliding sash *e*, to prevent it slipping sideways off the frame. In a double frame there must be a central bar, 3 in. by 2 in., run from the head to the foot of the frame to carry the inner edges of the sashes, and this should have a strip ¾ in. wide placed edgewise down the middle to separate the 2 sashes. On the top edges of the sides *a*, and similarly in the upper surface of the central bar, little channels should be grooved out to carry away any water that may find its way under the edge of the sashes. The sashes themselves are made of 2-in. by 1-in. quartering, dovetailed at the corners, with small bars for carrying the glass, as described on p. 223.

Greenhouses.—Fig. 618 illustrates the construction of a greenhouse with a span roof 20 ft. wide, as recommended by E. Luckhurst in the *Journal of Horticulture.* Following are the details:

The Roof.—This is only 5 ft. high at the eaves, and 10 ft. at the apex. It consists simply of fixed rafters mortised into a ridge-board at top, and an eave-board at bottom.

618.

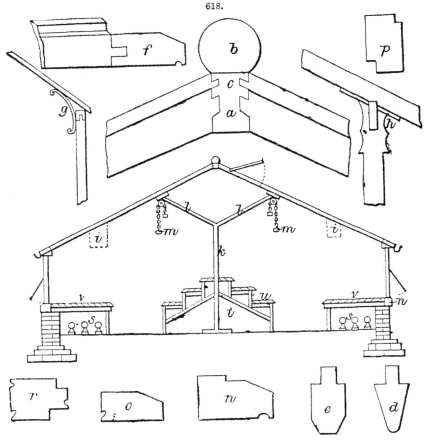

The width of the ridge-board *a* depends upon that of the sashbars; 2 in. will be thick enough for the h use treated of. *b* represents the beading fastened by screws or nails to the top of the ridge-board, to preserve it from the action of the weather, as well as to impart finish to building. *a* also shows how the sashbars are mortised into the ridge-board, and how a groove *c* for the glass is ploughed in the ridge-board above each tenon. In glazing, especial care must be taken to thrust the glass to the top of these grooves, so as to make the ridge weather-proof. The size of the sashbars is determined by their length, and whether it is intended to strengthen the roof with stays, or pillars with supports, as shown in *d*. A bar of the form shown by *d*, 2⅛ in. by ⅞ in. at its widest part, answers very well, with every fifth bar like the section *e*, in size 3¾ in. by 2 in. When interior supports are not used, the bars should be 3 in. by 1¼ in. with every eighth bar 3½ in. by 3 in. The eave-board *f* should be 4 in. by 2 in., bevelled as shown, and with a small semi-circular groove to prevent any moisture creeping into the house, under the eaves, as will happen without the groove. In exposed windy situations, additional strength may readily be imparted by bolting a few iron braces to the angles of the building at any convenient point, as shown by *g*. Pieces of bar iron bent to the required angle, flattened, and holes pierced at the ends by a blacksmith, answer admirably, and are neat enough in appearance when painted. To those who prefer the usual plan of side pillars, *h* will be useful, as showing a longitudinal sectional portion of such a pillar, with a slot cast in the top to admit a flat iron bar on edge, running along under the roof from end to end, and forming a capital support, so light as to make no appreciable shade, and yet very strong; in size it is 3 in. by ½ in. The brackets for hanging shelves *i* are objectionable, as spoiling the appearance of the interior; but such shelves are so useful that they are shown where to be placed, for the guidance of those who are compelled to use them. The roof support shown is considered by Luckhurst preferable to the ordinary style. It consists of central pillars *k*, with arms *l*, the pillars being placed about 9 ft. apart. The hanging baskets *m* are suspended by chains with counterpoise weights, which enables them to be lowered at will for watering and inspection.

The Sides.—Here the sashbars are similar to those in the roof, the only difference being in the large size, which, as they help to support the roof, are 3 in. by 3. They are mortised into the wall-plate *n*, which is about 6 in. by 2½ in. or 3, as may prove most suitable, and into an eave-plate *o* 4 in. by 2¼. The angle pieces *p* for the corners of the building are 4¼ in. by 3, and have rebates for glazing and for ventilators to shut into. When side ventilators are introduced, they consist simply of a frame 2¼ in. by 1½, grooved for the glass, with sashbars mortised into the frame, and are suspended by hinges to a fixed bar, 2½ in. by 1½, into the upper side of which the top side fixed sash-bars are mortised. Although mention is made of side ventilators, it is by no means intended to imply that they are an indispensable necessity, for if the roof ventilation be put through, side ventilation is not wanted, and fixed sides point of course to a considerable saving. Let, therefore, the roof ventilators run from end to end of the roof and consist of a clear space of quite 2 ft. in width, so as to admit so large a volume of air as to ensure a brisk and thorough circulation. Avoid a cheap opening apparatus; let it be strong and yet so easy that a touch may set it in motion. The best principle is that of a spiral shaft and stout-jointed levers by which the ventilators may be regulated to a nicety. The brickwork of the sides and ends consists of 5 courses above ground and 6 courses below, inclusive of the footings. The walls are 9 in. thick, and the footings are respectively 13½, 18, and 22½ in., so that 1 yd. in length of wall and footings will require 112 bricks; and to make enough mortar for 500 bricks it requires 3 bush. new grey lime and 18 bush. sand.

The doors should be 1½ in. in thickness, and the doorsteps 4 in. by 3, with rebates and beading as shown by *t*; one for door, the other for glass. The central stage has upright supports 2 in. by 2, and the braces are 3 in. by 2. The strips *u* forming the shelves are 2 in. by 1, with ½-in. spaces between every 2 strips. The woodwork of the side stages *v* is of the same size.

The glass for the roof is 21-oz. seconds; size of squares, 20 in. by 12; for the sides and ends 16-oz. answers very well. The hot-water pipes are 4-in., and slightly elevated above the floor on pipe stands as shown.

Instead of the pillars *k*, with spreading arms, many will prefer to use simple uprights and tie the main rafters together across the house by iron rods, merely stepping them into the eaves board instead of mortising. The wall, too, may with advantage be made of concrete, where the materials are handy.

Figs. 619 to 621 represent a combined greenhouse and potting shed, designed to be portable. It is span-roofed, situated so as to be exposed on all but the north side, and erected on a bed of earth or masonry 10 or 12 in. above the surrounding ground and 6 or 8 in. wider than the base of the structure. To provide against the building being disturbed by high winds, 4 posts about $2\frac{1}{2}$ ft. long, and 5 in. square, are driven into the ground near the corners, and the ground-plate of the greenhouse is secured to them by $\frac{3}{8}$-in. coach screws. The size of the combined greenhouse and potting shed (the latter being at the north end) is 18 ft. long by 8 ft. wide outside. The ground-plate a, running all round the base, is $1\frac{1}{2}$ in. deep, 5 in. wide, and is formed into a frame 8 ft. 1 in. wide and 18 ft. 1 in. long. Fastened at the corners are 4 upright posts b, 4 in. sq. and kept in a vertical position by 8 struts c, which greatly help to stiffen the framework, until the boards are fastened over it. The space between the end posts is divided

619.

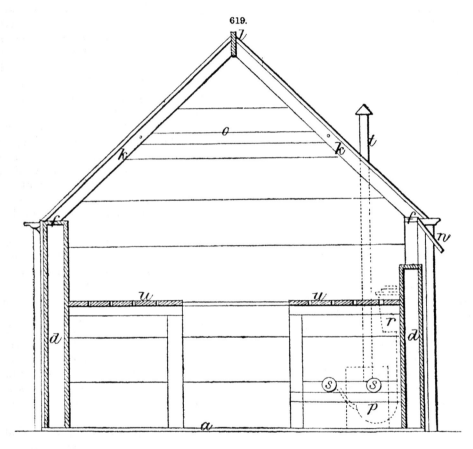

on either side of the house into 5 equal spaces by 4 posts, 3 of them d being 4 in. by 3 in. and the fourth e 4 in. by 4 in. This latter divides the potting shed from the greenhouse. These are all 4 ft. 9 in. long, and as they are mortised into the wall-plate f at the top, and the ground-plate a at the bottom, each of which is $1\frac{1}{2}$ in. thick, the space between the wall-plate and ground-plate is 4 ft. 6 in. The wall-plate f is 4 in. wide; 6 other posts g, 7 ft. 4 in. long, 3 in. thick, and 4 in. wide, are mortised at one end to the ground-plate a, and at the other are nailed to the rafters h. Of these, 2 at either end form the door-posts, of which the doorways i are 6 ft. 3 in. high by 2 ft. 3 in. wide. The rafters h k are nailed at one end on the wall-plate f, and on the other to the ridge-board l, which is 18 ft. 3 in. long, 6 in. deep, and 1 in. thick. Those lettered h are 2 in. by 3 in. and those lettered k of the form shown in section; they are all 4 ft. 9 in. long.

These rafters can be purchased of the section shown, and should be all carefully placed at equal distances, when the width must be measured, and the glass ordered accordingly. To ventilate the house, about 9 in. next to the ridge-board on one side should be unglazed, and the space covered with ½-in. board, hinged in 4 lengths to the ridge-board, and arranged so as to be easily opened from the inside, as shown at *m*, and the same must be adopted at the bottom of the opposite rafters, where 4 lengths of board *n* are hinged to the wall-plate *f*. The outward thrust of the rafters can be counteracted

620.

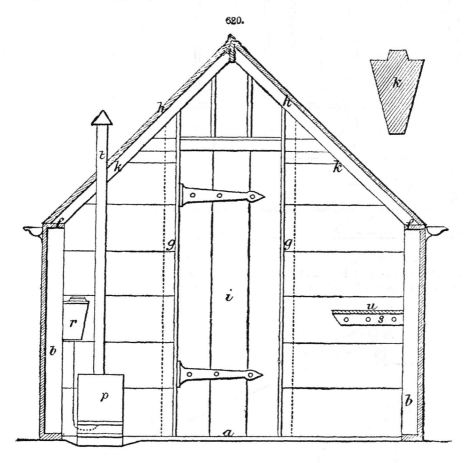

by pieces of wood used as ties, as shown at *o*. The house should be glazed with glass 16 oz. in weight to the sq. ft. With regard to doors, the amateur had better get them made by a carpenter, as, to look well, they require good work, and they are not expensive. The framing of the sides must be covered with ½- or ⅝-in. boarding, tarred or painted on the outside, and the spaces between the inner and outer boards filled with sawdust, which is a slow conductor of heat. The best material for construction will be thoroughly dry, soft deal, as free from knots as possible; and it will save much trouble to obtain the different pieces of the sections shown, only a little larger, from saw-mills, so that he will only have to plane them, and follow the drawings in cutting to required length. When all the woodwork has been put together, and is thoroughly dry, the knots are stopped, and the whole framing is given one coat of white-lead; this will make the putty in the glazing hold well. Then the glass is put on of the required width, the length of each piece being 15 to 18 in., and each overlapping the next to it by about 1¼ in. This completed, the inside and outside wood should receive 2 good coats of pale stone colour or white paint. The heating apparatus employed consists of a small circular boiler p, tank r, and piping s, the fumes of the fuel being carried away by the capped stovepipe t. The pipes s for conveying the hot water, should be 2 in. or $2\frac{1}{2}$ in. in diameter, and lie immediately under the stage u.

621.

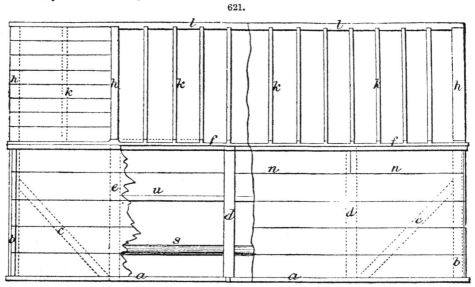

When a suitable wall is available, it is often preferred to make a lean-to greenhouse, in which case the roof is considerably modified. If the greenhouse is to be 6 ft. high in front and about 8 ft. wide, the roof must slope upwards at the back to a height of about

622.

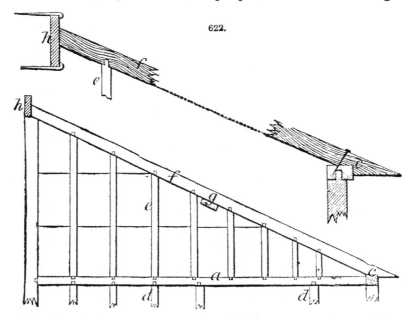

10 ft. If the back wall does not admit of this, the front wall must be made lower, or the floor must be sunk: the latter alternative is very undesirable as conducing to dampness. The construction of the roof and the upper part of the framing is shown in Fig. 622. The bar a is mortised at one end into the tall upright b, which is secured to the wall by

strong hooks; at the other end it is mortised into the front top plate c, and throughout its length it is supported on the ends of the uprights of the lower part of the frame d, all of which are mortised into the bottom plate. From the bar a rise a number of uprights e supporting the outside rafter f. The intermediate rafters are partially supported by a tie bar g running from end to end. They all abut at the upper end against the wall-plate h, to which they are securely nailed, and at the lower end they fit on to the top wall-plate c as shown. The 2 outside rafters are 4 in. by 2 in. in section, but the smaller ones are only 4 in. by $1\frac{1}{2}$ in.

Summer-house.—The following remarks are intended only to describe the materials adapted for building summer-houses and the manner of putting them together. For designs, the reader must exercise his own taste, or he may refer to an interesting series of papers on rustic carpentry written by Arthur Yorke in *Amateur Work*, portions of which have been availed of here.

The wood looks best if left with the bark on, in which case it should be cut down in winter while the sap is out of it; if to be peeled, it is better cut when the sap is rising. The most suitable and durable wood for this purpose is larch, after which come silver fir, common fir, and spruce. Poles should be selected from trees grown in close plantations, these being more regular in form and less branched; smaller wood is got from the branches of trees growing in the open. Oak "bangles" (smaller branches very contorted) look best when peeled, and do well in grotesque work. Elm branches are more durable than oak. Apple branches possess the same advantage, with equal irregularity, and often cost nothing. Hazel rods, and sticks of maple and wych-elm are well adapted for interior work.

Fig. 623 shows the construction of a summer-house 8 ft. long, 4 ft. wide, and 6 ft. high to the eaves. The collar posts a are set 2 ft. deep in the ground, that portion having been first peeled and well tarred. The cross pieces b are joined to the posts in the manner shown at c; when the rafter d is added, a large spike nail is driven through all and into the post, but smaller nails may be used temporarily to hold the cross pieces until the rafter is on. The corner posts a are $4\frac{1}{2}$–5 in. in diameter, and sawn flat at the top. Pieces called "ledgers" are nailed cross-wise at top and bottom, immediately below the wall-plate and above the ground line respectively, on the inside of the house, their juncture with the corner posts being as shown in plan at e. The walls f are formed of split poles, the splitting being best done by a circular saw, if available; they are nailed at top and bottom to the ledgers, with their sawn faces inwards, their upper ends sloping off to fit against the wall-plate, and their lower reaching 2 or 3 in. into the ground. The walls are lined inside, the lining of the lower half being formed of another row of split poles, arranged with their sawn sides towards the first, and so that they cover the spaces between them. The upper half may be lined with smaller half-stuff placed diagonally From the top of the pediment of the roof, a ridge piece extends backwards 18 in.; this keeps the finishing point of the thatch some distance back, and enables the eaves to project over the pediment. The end of the rafters are sawn as at g. When the rafters are fixed, a number of rough rods about $1\frac{1}{2}$ in. thick are nailed across them some 5 in. apart, for carrying the thatch. A 1-in. plank 14 in. wide and fixed at 16 or 17 in. above the floor affords a good seat. The subject of thatching will be found under the section on Roofing. The under side of the thatch is all the better in appearance for being lined. The best material for the purpose is heather (ling), and next to it comes furze. In fixing it, a layer is spread at the bottom of the roof with the brush ends pointing downwards to the wall-plate, and a strip of wood is nailed tightly across the root ends from rafter to rafter; succeeding courses are laid in the same manner, each overlapping the preceding and hiding the wooden strips. Failing heath and furze, recourse may be had to moss, fastened to the thatch by small twig buckles. Another substitute is sheets of elm bark, dried flat on the floor of a shed under pressure, and secured by flat-headed nails, moss serving to fill any interstices. Indeed moss, previously dried, is admirable for stopping all chinks and cracks. For flooring, the best possible plan is to drive short pieces (say 6 in. long) of wooden poles into the ground leaving all their tops level. Intervals may be filled in with sand. Concreting and asphalting are expensive, gravelling is productive of much dust, and flooring has an inappropriate appearance.

623.

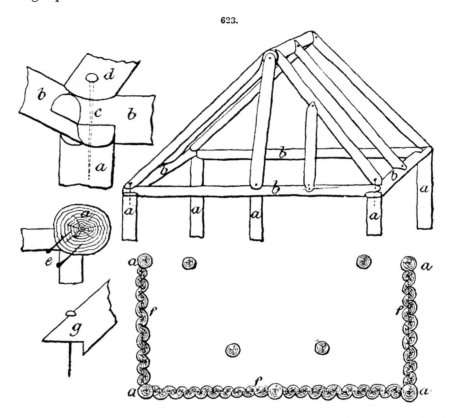

Fences.—This term may be made to include hedges, stone walls, and iron wire, but it will be restricted now to structures formed of wood.

A common fence in America is the "zigzag" or "rail," Fig. 624, in which stout rails *b* are laid about 7 deep with their ends crossed between upright stakes *a* driven into the ground. The rails may be of uneven lengths, instead of even as shown.

Lattice-fencing, Fig. 625, consists of a number of laths *a*, pegged across each other and supported by rails *b* carried on posts *c* fixed at intervals of 8–10 ft. The lattice may be made much more open, and will then consume less material.

Common wood paling is shown in Fig. 626. Stakes *a* are driven by a heavy mallet 12 in. into the ground at 5 or 6 ft. asunder; when the ground is hard, a hole may be made by the foot-pick or the driver; and such stakes will support a paling 3 ft. 3 in. in height. While 2 rails are sufficient to fence cattle, 3 are required for sheep. The rails should be nailed on the face of the stakes next the field, and made to break joint, so that the ends of all the 3 rails shall not be nailed upon the same stake; nor should the broad ends of the rails be nailed together, even though thinned by the adze, but broad and narrow ends together as at *b*, that the weight and strength of the rails may be equalized. To make the paling secure, a stake should be driven as a stay in a sloping direction behind the rails, and nailed to every third stake. The upper rail should be nailed near the top of the stakes, the lowest edge of the lowest one 6 in. from the ground. and the upper edge of the middle one 20 in. above the ground.

Lapped paling of cleft oak is illustrated in Fig. 627. The pales *a* lap over each other, and are nailed to rails *b*, tenoned into posts *c*, while a board *d* is run edgewise along the bottom.

In open paling, Fig. 628, the pales *a* are nailed flat and independently to the rails *b*, of which 2 suffice; these latter are tenoned at their ends into the posts *c*. This is a much cheaper fence than the preceding.

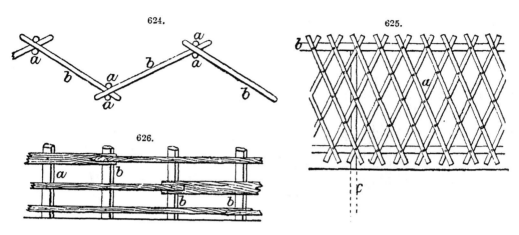

The only important difference presented by the so-called timber-merchant's fence, Fig. 629, is that the posts *a* are provided with "pockets" leading to the mortices into which the ends of the rails *b* are slipped; these pockets meet the mortices in such a way that any section or "bay" of the fence can be bodily removed by lifting it sufficiently to free the mortice and pass forwards by the pockets.

Fields are often temporarily fenced by hurdles, Fig. 630. In setting them up, the first hurdle is raised by its upper rail, and the ends of its stakes are sunk a little into the ground with a spade, to give them firm hold. The next is placed in the same way,

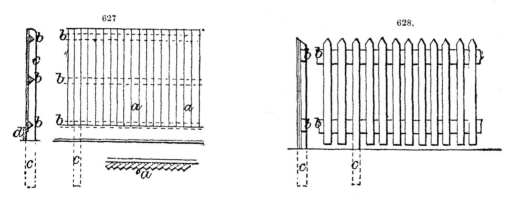

both being held in position by an assistant; one end of a stay *a* is placed between the hurdles, near the tops of their stakes, and the stay and hurdles are fastened together by the peg *b* pressing through holes in both. Another peg *c* is then passed through the stakes lower down, and the hurdles are sloped outwards until the upper rail stands 3 ft. 9 in. above the ground. A short stake *d* is driven by a mallet into the ground at a point where the stay *a* gives the hurdles the right inclination, and a peg fastens the stake and stay together. The remaining hurdles are fastened in a similar manner. It is perhaps more common to pitch these hurdles upright and dispense with the sloping stay *a*, replacing it by a stake driven vertically into the ground between the ends of the hurdles. The construction of the hurdles themselves is obvious from the sketch. The 4 level rails *e* are let into slits in the sides of the stakes *f*, and the 3 cross bars *g* are nailed to the level rails *e*.

A useful form of close fence for temporary purposes is shown in Fig. 631. The boards *a* are simply slipped down one upon another in grooves cut vertically in the uprights *b*, which are let into the ground. By this means the use of nails is avoided, and the boards are but little the worse for being so employed.

629.   630.

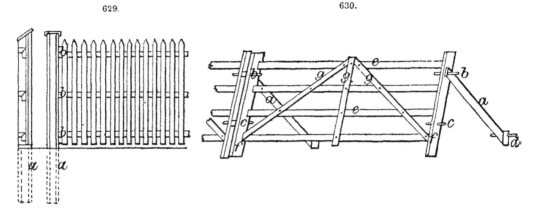

Gates.—A wooden gate, the only kind to be considered here, consists of a frame-work, as *a*, *b*, *c*, *d* in Fig. 632, hinged or hung to a gate-post *e*, which is firmly secured in the ground, and catching on a latch attached to another gate-post at the opposite side of the opening. This framework is generally filled in with 3 horizontal bars *f*. To pre-

631.   632.

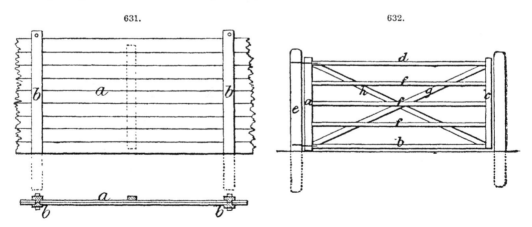

vent the weight of the gate pulling it down at the end *c*, a diagonal brace *g* is added; for uniformity sake this is sometimes supplemented by a second brace *h*. The upright bar *a* of the frame is termed the hanging style, while *c* is the falling style; the bars *b*, *d* and the rails *f* are mortised at each end into the bars *a*, *c*.

Another form of field gate is shown in Fig. 633, where the diagonal stays *a*, *b* meet at the centre *c*. The top and bottom hinges are fixed as shown at *d*, *e*.

Fig. 634 illustrates a much heavier and more substantial form of gate. The hanging post *a* here needs struts *b* placed underground; the falling style *c* is strengthened by iron bands at top and bottom.

A garden wicket is represented in Fig. 635. The frame a, b, c, d and the diagonal stay e are mortised together. Through the top and bottom rails a, c and the stay e bars f of wood or iron are passed. The hingeing is effected by means of iron bands with looped ends secured to the top and bottom rails and resting c̶ somewhat similar iron loops fixed in the post g ; an iron rod dropped through all the loops completes the hinge.

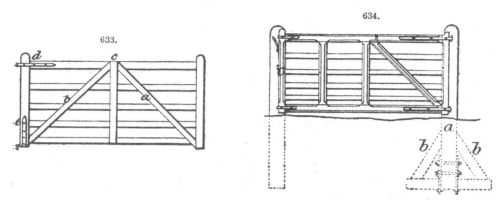

633.

634.

Fig. 636 is a more pretentious garden gate. The usual frame a, b, c, d supports by 4 arms e a central ring f secured by pegged tenons, as shown. The spaces g, h, i, k, l are, best filled up by some lighter work. The 2 bottom ones k, l may have diagonal panelling while g, h, i may have wooden bars ; or the whole may be fitted with ornamental iron castings.

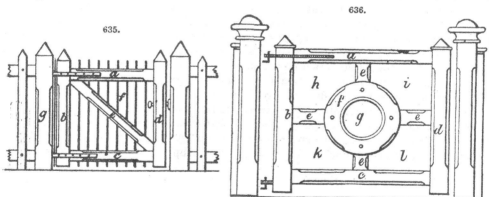

635.

636.

HOUSE BUILDING.—There are 4 important matters connected with house building which come within the range of the carpenter and joiner; these are the laying of floors, the construction of the wooden framework of roofs, and the making and fixing of doors and window frames.

Floors.—The chief considerations to be borne in mind in choosing the material for a floor are: (1) wearing resistance, (2) comfort to the feet, (3) retention of warmth, (4) capability of being laid evenly and repaired conveniently. When the first condition is most essential and the second is unimportant, as in public places where there is great traffic, some form of masonry is best adapted; but for comfort, on the score of elasticity under foot and a generally heat-conserving quality, wood is unsurpassed, especially the ordinary boarded floor. In situations subject to much wear, wood-block flooring is better adapted. The blocks are generally laid to the "herring-bone" pattern upon a concrete bed, and can be equally employed for upper floors on rolled joists filled in with concrete, making a remarkably firm, durable, and comfortable floor, not too resonant or noisy for large rooms, and in every respect more sanitary than the ordinary boarded floor. The blocks, being of a brick proportion, can be laid as parquetry, or in squares placed diagonally, the blocks alternating in direction. The shrinkage is reduced to a minimum, and when the blocks are well bedded and secured to the bed, as in Lowe's patent composition, no more durable flooring can be employed. This composition is said to prevent dry-rot. A more decorative sort of wood flooring is parquetry. The solid Swiss *parqueterie* consisted of pieces about 1 in. thick, grooved and tongued together, and secured by marine glue. Wood veneers, backed by kamptulicon and other substances, have been similarly used for effect. Thin parquet laid on a patent composition or glue (Eberhard's) is a kind of flooring that has been used with much success even on stone foundations; and stone paved floors and staircases worn hollow have been treated by this process, the unevenness of the surface being made up by the glue, which becomes a hard yet slightly elastic backing. Some parquet, as that of Turpin's, is only $\frac{5}{16}$ in. thick, and is prepared on a deal back, and the floor is said to be equal in wear to 1-in. solid parquetry. The plan of fixing thin plates of hard ornamental woods in geometrical patterns upon existing hard floors is one that will commend itself. Of all floorings there is perhaps hardly any so appropriate, so comfortable, or so artistic as parquetry, and even the plain hard woods like teak admit of being used decoratively. The custom of carpeting over the centre of the room only, allowing a border of the real floor to be seen, lends itself to parquetry borders. Smaller carpets and of better quality or design would be selected, while cleanliness and sanitary conditions would be the result of the change. There are many manufacturers who can supply borders at the low price of 6d. per sq. ft. A solidly-backed parquetry floor, supported upon joists partially filled up with concrete, forms an almost impassable barrier to fire. Even wooden joists, well protected by a fire-resisting plaster ceiling, or the interspaces filled up, has been found to stay the ravages of fire, while a closely-jointed block or parquet floor, laid on a good backing, is impervious to air, and would retard the progress of flames above or below it. For the floors of hospital wards no floor can be more suitable or so comfortable.

Passing now to a consideration of the most usual form of flooring, that by parallel boarding, the first feature to be explained is the arrangement of the beams and joists which are to support the boards. It may, however, be well to premise, that, as wood is found to be much more durable when exposed to the air than when built in brickwork at the ends, an effort is always made to secure that condition, and the other ends of the beams or joists are most commonly supported on wall-plates fitting into the space occupied by a course of bricks. Fig. 637 shows a simple method of securing the tie

637.

638.

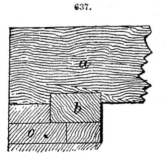
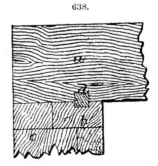

beam *a* to the wall-plate *b* lying on the brickwork *c*, the beam *a* being notched out on the under side to admit *b*. In Fig. 638 this joint is strengthened by the addition of a key or cog *d* fitting closely into grooves in *a* and *b*. Figs. 639, 640 illustrate the junction of the poleplate *a* to the tie beam *b*, both with and without the intervention of a key or cog *c*. Other methods of securing the joist *a* to the wall-plate *b* are shown in

Figs. 641, 642, 643. In Fig. 644 the joist a, instead of lying flat on the upper surface of the wall-plate b, is connected by a mortice and tenon joint, the under side of the joist being mortised as at c, while a tenon d is cut into the wall-plate.

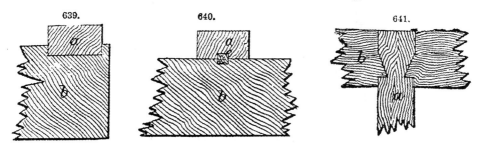

639.   640.   641.

The special uses of the several kinds of joist will be best described when speaking of the sort of floor in which they are employed; but it may be well here to state their respective scantlings, i.e. their sectional dimensions. They vary of course with the

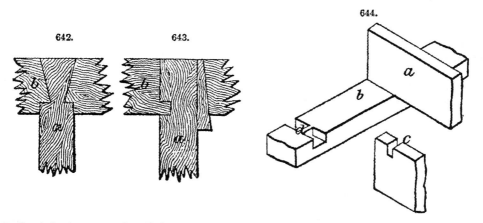

642.   643.   644.

length of the bearing (the distance between the supports that hold them), as given in the first column of figures:—

Flooring joists, 1 ft. apart.

ft.		in. × in.	in. × in.	in. × in.
5	.. ..	$4 \times 2\frac{1}{2}$	$4\frac{1}{2} \times 2$	$3\frac{1}{2} \times 3$
10	.. ..	$9 \times 1\frac{1}{2}$	$7 \times 2\frac{1}{2}$	
15	.. ..	$11 \times 1\frac{1}{2}$	10×2	$9 \times 2\frac{1}{2}$
20	.. ..	11×3	10×4	
25	.. ..	12×3	11×4	

Binding joists, 6 ft. apart.

ft.		in. × in.	in. × in.
5	.. ..	7×3	9×2
7 ft. 6 in.	.. .. ..	9×3	
10	.. ..	9×4	11×3
12 ft. 6 in.	.. .. ..	11×4	
15	.. ..	12×4	
20	.. ..	$13 \times 6\frac{1}{2}$	
25	.. ..	$15 .. 7\frac{1}{2}$	

Ceiling joists, 1 ft. apart.

ft.	in. in.	in. in.
4	2½ × 1½	2 × 2
5	2½ × 2	
6	3 × 2	
7	3½ × 2	3 × 2¼
8	4 × 2	3 × 2½
9	4½ × 2	4 × 2½
10	4½ × 2½	4 × 3
12	5 × 3	
14	6 × 3	

Girders, 10 ft. apart.

ft.	in. in.	in. in.
10	11 × 5½	12 × 4
15	13 × 6½	11 × 11
20	15 × 7½	13 × 13
25	17 × 8½	14 × 14
30	20 × 10	

Flooring boards are generally cut 6⅞ in. (7 in. planed up) wide, but can also be had 4¼ in. and 5¼ in. wide; in thickness they run ¾ in., 1 in., 1¼ in. and 1½ in., at least they are called after these measurements, but are really somewhat less owing to planing.

The simplest kind of floor is that termed "single-joisted," in which the joists are 12 in. apart, resting on the wall-plates, and carrying the boards above, while, if there be

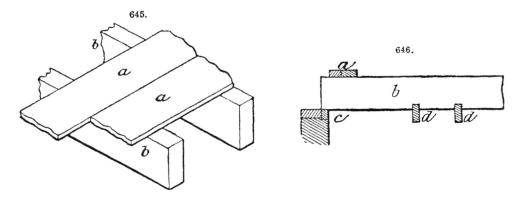

645.

646.

a ceiling, the ceiling laths are nailed on below. Fig. 645 shows the boards *a* as they rest on the joists *b*. When ceiling joists are used, the arrangement is as shown in Fig. 646: *a*, flooring boards; *b*, joist; *c*, wall-plate; *d*, ceiling joists. The scantling of the wall-plate will vary with the length of the bearing of the joists, as follows :—

Up to 10 ft.	3 in. × 3 in.
10 to 20 ft.	4½ in. × 3 in.
20 to 30 ft.	7 in. × 3 in.

The joists should have at least 4 in. of their length resting on the wall-plate and wall, and this may be increased up to 9 in.

When the joists are unusually deep (for greater strength), or far apart (for economy sake), there is a danger that an extra weight on them may cause them to turn over on one side. To obviate this danger, "strutting" is resorted to. In its simpler form this consists of sections of flat thin wood placed edgewise between the joists, as seen in Fig. 647, where the joists *a* are kept vertical by the struts *b*. Great force would be required to crush these struts, but there is a risk of their ends slipping. This is sometimes remedied by attaching them at one end to triangular fillets *c* nailed to the

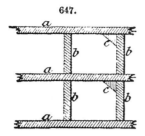
647.

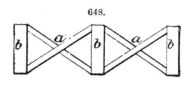
648.

joist. The struts should all be placed in the same line, and the lines may be 2 or 3 ft. apart. A more secure way of strutting is that known as the "herring-bone," illustrated in Fig. 648. It consists of strips of wood *a* of small scantling (say 2½ in. by 1 in., or 3 in. by 1½ in.), crossing each other, and nailed at the top of one joist *b* and bottom of the next, maintaining regular lines at a distance of about 4 ft.

Whenever a space has to be left in a floor, to provide for the insertion of a staircase or a flue, the construction has to be modified by the introduction of a "trimmer" for the support of one end of those joists which are prevented from reaching to the wall-plate as before. Fig. 649 shows the arrangement where the hole is required next the wall: *a* is

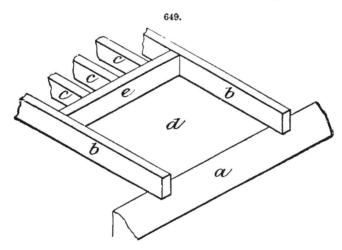
649.

a wall, supporting the 2 joists *b*, while the 3 joists *c* are cut off to leave the space *d*. The trimmer *e* is mortised at both ends into the joists *b*, and carries the free ends of the joists *c*, which are mortised into it. As the extra strain from the 3 joists *c* is thus supported by the 2 joists *b*, it is necessary that these latter be stronger than the others. They are called the "trimming" joists, and it is usual in ordinary flooring to add ⅛ in. to their thickness (not depth) for every joist trimmed. Fig. 650 illustrates the system adopted when the hole is at a distance from the wall, requiring the intervention of 2 trimmers: *a* is the wall, *b*, ordinary joists; *c*, trimmed joists; *d*, trimmers; *e*, trimming joists; *f*, hole.

The preceding paragraphs refer to "single" floors; but when the strain to be borne is great, as in warehouses and similar structures, "double" floors are adopted, as well as "double framed" floors. In the double floor, Fig. 651, a "binder" or "binding joist" is introduced, having a thickness usually half as great again as that of the joists it supports, bearing about 6 in. on the wall, and situated at intervals of 5–6 ft. apart, centre to centre. In Fig. 651, *a* are the ordinary joists resting on the binders *b*, and supporting the flooring boards *c* above, while the ceiling joists *d* are attached to the under side of the binders.

The "double framed" floor differs in having "girders" to carry the binders at intervals of about 10 ft. centre to centre. Fig. 652 represents this plan : *a*, the ordinary

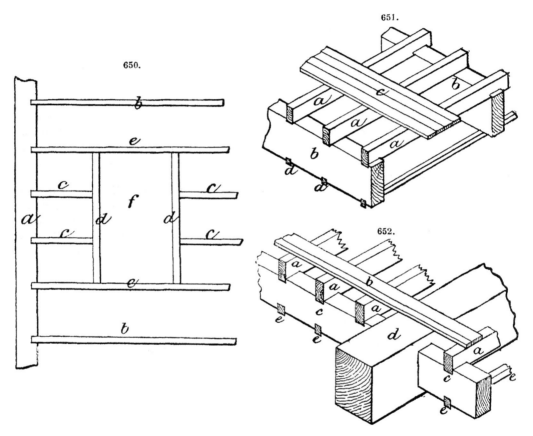

joists, carrying the floor-boards *b*, and resting on the binder *c*, supported by the girder *d* ; *e*, ceiling joists. Girders should always be placed so that their ends rest on solid walls, where no window or door below weakens the structure. The weight of the girder is distributed as much as possible by resting its ends on templates of stone or iron. These templates often assume a box-like form, enclosing the sides and end of the girder but not so as to exclude all air.

Floor-boards may be laid "folding," in "straight joint," or "dowelled," the first being the commonest method. In laying boards folding, 4 or 5 boards are put in place without nailing, and the outside ones are then nailed so as to have slightly less space between them than was occupied by the others lying loosely; the others are then forced into position by putting their edges together and thrusting them down. Thus in Fig. 653, of the 5 boards *a, b, c, d, e*, the 2 outside ones *a, e* would be first nailed and then the intervening *b, c, d* would be forced into the space left for them. In this case, the ends of the boards are made to meet where they will fall on a rafter, and as nearly as possible in the centre of its width, as at *f* on the rafters *g*. When the floor is laid with straight joints, as in Fig. 654, each board is put down and nailed separately, being thrust up close to the one preceding it by means of the flooring clamp. Thus the joints *a* of the ends of the boards *b* fall on the rafters *c* in straight lines with intervals between. When the flooring is "dowelled," the boards are laid separately and straight as in Fig. 654, the only difference being that their edges are united by dowels (small pegs of oak or beech) driven into holes bored for their reception, either between or over the joists. Most commonly, flooring boards simply have their edges planed smooth, and are forced into the closest possible contact, when they are held by the nails that fasten them to the joists. But there are cases when a more perfect tight-fitting joint is needed.

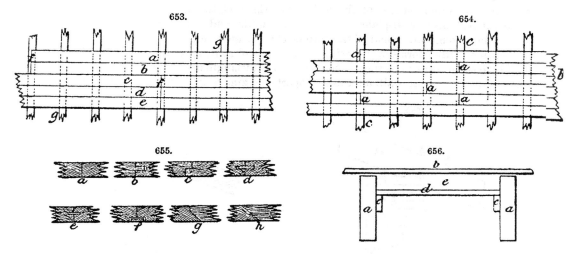

653. 654.

655. 656.

Fig. 655 shows the various ways of joining floor-boards: *a*, plain joint; *b*, ploughed and tongued; *c*, rebated; *d, e*, with a tongue of wood or iron inserted; *f*, with the tongue resting on the joist; *g, h*, splayed.

When a floor is finished, it is usual to hide the ends of the boards where they meet the wall by nailing a skirting board round. This may be plain or ornamental. It rests on the floor and rises close against the wall, to which it is fastened by occasional nails passing into wooden bricks, called "grounds," inserted in the wall to take the nails. In superior work, floors are "deadened" or "deafened" by placing a bed of non-conducting material beneath them. To support this bed, strips of wood are nailed to the flooring joists to carry thin "sounding" boards, on which is spread a thick layer of old mortar or plaster, known as "pugging." This is shown in Fig. 656: *a*, joists; *b*, flooring boards; *c*, strips called "firring pieces," bearing the sounding boards *d* loaded with pugging *e*.

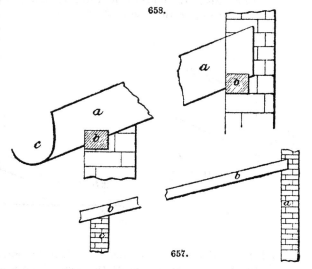

658.

657.

Roofs.—In discussing roofs, attention will here be confined to the timber part of the structure, leaving the covering to be dealt with under the section on Roofing; and the descriptions will stop short at those kinds of roof where architectural and engineering

skill and appliances are called into requisition.   Roofs of an every-day character
may be divided into 2 classes—"lean-to" roofs including those which have only one
slope, a gradual fall from one side to the other; while "span" roofs have 2 slopes
descending from an apex at or near the centre.

The simplest kind of lean-to roof, adapted only for covering a shed of short span, and
with a very light roofing material, is shown in Fig. 657. Here the back wall *a* has the
upper ends of the rafters *b* simply built into it, at distances of 14–18 in. apart centre
to centre, while the lower ends rest upon the front wall *c* and overhang it sufficiently to
cast the rain-water off free of the wall.   In Fig. 658, the top and bottom ends of the
rafters *a* rest upon wall-plates *b* let into the walls, and running their whole length,
while the extreme lower end of the rafters carry a guttering *c* for conveying away the
rain-water.   Other forms of guttering for the ends of rafters are shown in Figs. 659, 660.
In Fig. 659, the rafter *a* resting on the wall *b*, has a triangular block of wood *c* nailed to it
outside the line of the wall, affording support to a zinc or iron gutter *e*, having one edge

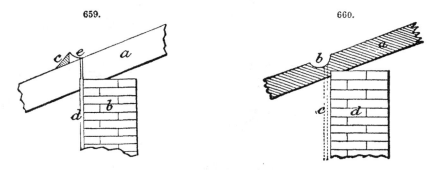

659.   660.

lying under the roofing material. At any point in the length of the gutter a hole is made
for the insertion of a vertical pipe *d* for conveying the water away down the outside of the
wall.   In Fig. 660, the rafter *a* is recessed at *b* for the reception of the gutter, a pipe *c*
from which passes down the front of the wall *d*.   Fig. 661 illustrates a wooden gutter *a*
attached by nails to the ends of the rafters *b*, and provided with a pipe *c*, bent underneath
so that it may run down close to the wall *d*.

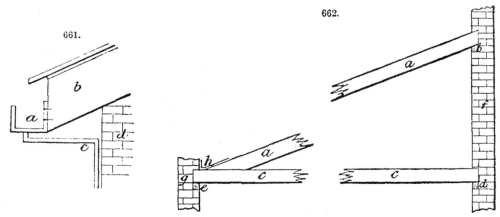

661.   662.

When a wider span is needed in a lean-to roof, a tie-beam has to be introduced, to
counteract the outward thrust of the roof which would tend to force the walls asunder.
Fig. 662 shows the arrangement adopted.   The rafter *a* rests at its upper end on the
wall-plate *b* and at its lower end on the tie-beam *c*, which in its turn is supported in a
horizontal position on the wall-plates *d*, *e* in the back and front walls *f*, *g*.   As the front

wall *g* is carried up above the bottom edge of the roof, forming a parapet surmounted by a coping, instead of lying underneath it as before, another form of gutter is demanded. This as seen at *h*, consists of sheet metal running up underneath the roofing material far enough to form a trough. Another contrivance for guttering along a parapet wall is shown in Fig. 663, and is termed a "bridged" gutter. The rafters *a*, butting against the wall-plate *b* carried by the wall *c*, support a "bridging-piece" *d* of small scantling, on which lies a board flooring *e* bearing the sheet metal (zinc or lead) gutter *f*.

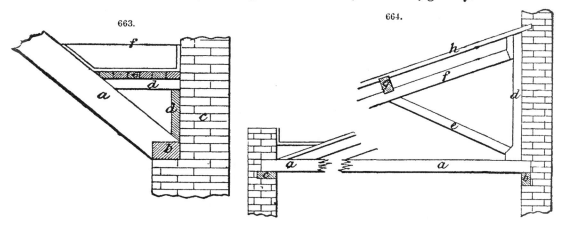

663.   664.

When the roof is required to possess greater strength than can be obtained with the use of a simple tie-beam, the construction assumes a more complicated character, as seen in Fig. 664. Here the tie-beam *a* rests as before on the wall-plates *b*, *c*, but at the back end it supports a king-post *d*, from which the strut *e* passes to sustain the "principal" rafter *f*, whose upper end butts against a fillet on the king-post *d* while its lower end is borne by the tie-beam *a*. Running parallel with the walls, and carried by the "principal" rafters *f*, is the "purlin" *g*, whose duty is to hold up the "common" rafters *h* on which the roofing material is laid. The common rafters lie at intervals of 14 in. centre to centre, while the principal rafters are generally about 10 ft. apart. The upper end of the strut *e* (Fig. 664) is joined to the under side of the principal rafter *f* by a tenon, which may be either simple (*a*) or angular (*b*), Fig. 665. In

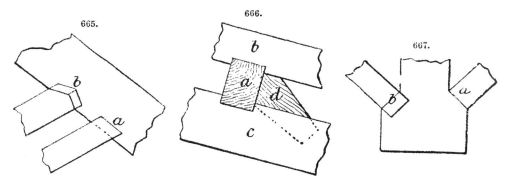

665.   666.   667.

Fig. 666 is seen a way of joining the purlin to the rafters : the purlin *a* is led into grooves in the faces of the common and principal rafters *b*, *c* respectively and butts against the block *d* wedged into the upper face of the principal rafter *c*. The feet of the struts may either butt against the sloping shoulders of the king-post as at *a* (Fig. 667) or be tenoned in as at *b*.

Ordinary span roofs with various modifications are illustrated in Fig. 668. In **A** which is the simplest form, the rafters *a* rest at foot on the wall-plates *b*, to which they are only nailed, while at their upper ends they either butt against each other as at *c*, or are crossed and nailed as at *d*. Obviously this is a very slender structure, and quite

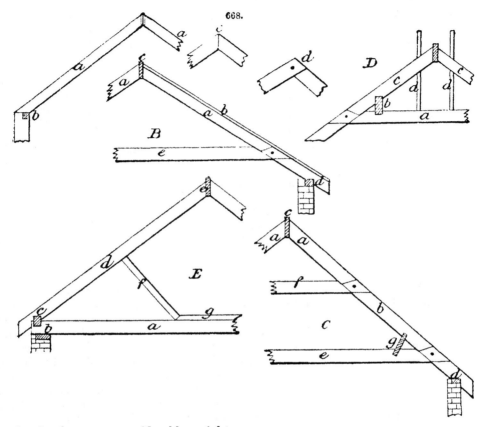

668.

unfitted to bear any considerable weight of roofing material. B, C represent progressive steps in strengthening this form of roof, by the introduction of one or more "collar beams," which prevent the collapse of the sloping rafters, and give their name to this modification of the span roof. In B, the rafters *a*, measuring usually about 6½ in. by 1¼ in. and carrying a covering of 1-in. boarding *b*, butt against the ridge-pole *c* at top, and are cut out for the reception of the wall-plates *d* at bottom. At rather more than ⅓ of the height from the wall-plate to the ridge-pole, the rafters are tied by the collar-beams *e*, having the same dimensions as the rafters, and which may be simply

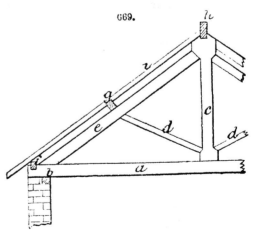

669.

nailed to them at the ends, or halved in, as here shown. C differs from B only in having a second collar-beam *f*, and the extra support of a purlin *g* let into the rafters and the lower collar-beam *e*. D is a modification of B, necessitated by the introduction of a ventilator in the roof: *a* is the collar-beam supporting the purlin *b* and rafters *c* as well as the uprights *d* of the ventilator. In E a new feature occurs in the shape of a "strut" or "brace" supported by a "tie-beam." Here the tie-beam *a* resting on the wall-plates *b* carries at its ends "pole-plates" *c* let in, and which in their turn bear the lower ends of the rafters *d*, butting at the apex against the ridge-pole *e*. To reduce the strain in the middle of the rafters, the struts *f* are employed, receiving their support from the ends of the straining sill *g* against which they abut.

When a strong roof of say 20 ft. span is required, the truss principle is fully carried out, as in the "king-post" roof, Fig. 669. Here tie-beams *a* measuring 9 in. by 4 in. are placed at intervals of about 10 ft. resting on the walls and wall-plates *b*. From the

670.

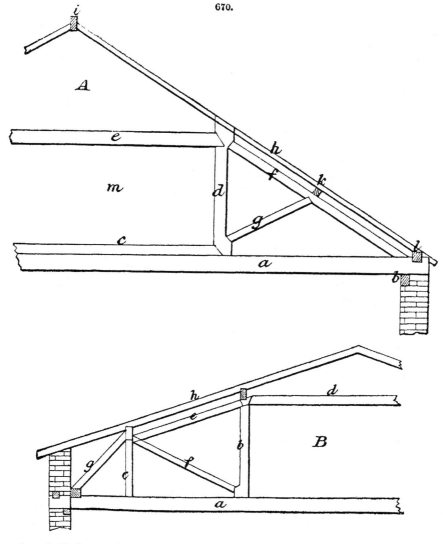

centre of each tie-beam rises the king-post *c*, measuring 5 in. by 3 in.; abutting against its lower shoulders on each side are struts *d*, 3½ in. by 2½ in., reaching to the middle of the principal rafters *e*, 6 in. by 3 in., whose feet rest on the tie-beam *a*, while their heads fit under the upper shoulders of the king-post *c*. Just outside the line of the wall-plate and that of the feet of the principal rafters, the tie-beams *a* have pole-plates *f*, 4 in. sq., let into their upper faces; and running midway along the principal rafters, just over the point where they are sustained by the struts d, are purlins g, 8 in. by 3 in. The pole-plates f, purlins g, and ridge-pole h (8 in. by $1\frac{1}{2}$ in.), between them carry the common rafters i, $3\frac{1}{2}$ in. by 2 in.

The king-post roof, from the manner of arranging the timbers, precludes any use being made of the roof space. When this space is a desideratum, the queen-post roof is better suited, two examples of which are seen in Fig. 670, the form A being adapted to a high-pitched roof, while B is accommodated to a low pitch. In A, the tie-beam a, 9 in. by 4 in., resting on the wall-plates b, 5 in. by 3 in., carries a straining sill c, 4 in. sq., separating the feet of the queen-posts d, $4\frac{1}{2}$ in. by 4 in., which stand on the tie-beam a, and support at top the straining beam e, 7 in. by 4 in., and the upper ends of the principal rafters f, $5\frac{1}{2}$ in. by 4 in. Struts g, 4 in. by 3 in., run from the lower shoulders of the queen-posts to the middle of the principal rafters, whose lower ends rest on the tie-beam a. The common rafters h, 4 in. by 2 in., abut against the ridge-pole i, at top, and are borne by the tops of the queen-posts d, the purlin k, $7\frac{1}{2}$ in. by 4 in., and the pole-plate l, 4 in. sq. These measurements are suited to a roof of 30 ft. span. The space m is available for a room. In the form B, the timbers are differently arranged to suit the low roof. The tie-beam a is 11 in. by 6 in., the queen-posts b, c are 6 in. sq. and 6 in. by 4 in. respectively, the straining beam d is 8 in. by 6 in., the principal rafter e is 6 in. sq., the struts f, g are 6 in. by 4 in., and the common rafters h are $4\frac{1}{2}$ in. by 2 in.

Fig. 671 illustrates two ways of constructing a "curb" or "mansard" roof, which enables a capacious and well-lit apartment to be formed in the roof. In A, the tie-beam a measures 12 in. by 4 in., the struts b are 6 in. by 4 in., the upper tie-beam c is 8 in. by 4 in., the king-post d is 4 in. sq., the principal rafters e are 6 in. by 4 in., the purlin f is

671.

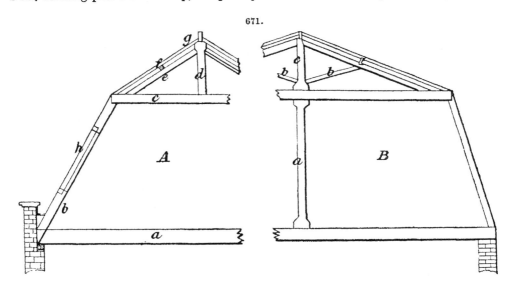

5 in. by 4 in., and the common rafters g are 4 in. by 2 in. The apartment may be lit by the window h or by a "dormer" window. The arrangement B is suited to a roof of wider span, and is strengthened by the stout king-post a and by 2 struts b from the upper king-post c.

The manner of joining the upper ends of the struts to the upper shoulders of the king-post is shown in Fig. 672: the ridge-pole drops into the recess a in the top of the king-post b, and the struts c are let into the shoulders of b either by a simple tenon d or an angular tenon e.

The form of gutter for the bottom between 2 span roofs is shown in Fig. 673. The tie-beam *a* carries a strip of quartering *b*, against which abut the lower ends of the rafters *c*; a bridging-piece *d* supports the floor of the gutter *e*.

Doors.—Ordinary room doors are of 2 kinds, distinguished as "ledged" and "panelled." The former are easier to make, heavier, and stronger, but have a commonplace appearance. Every kind of door requires a wooden frame occupying the margin

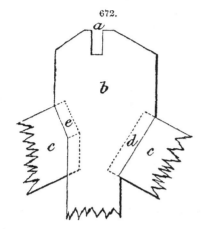

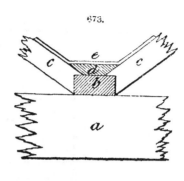

of the space to be closed, and into which the door may shut as closely as possible. If the doorway be situated in a wooden structure, the timbers of this structure will be arranged to form the door-frame; in other case, the frame must be made and secured in place ready for receiving the door. The essential parts of the frame are, as seen in Fig. 674, a lintel *a*, 2 jambs *b*, and a sill *c*; the bottom ends of the jambs are mortised into the sill. When the doorway is in a wooden structure the top ends of the jambs may also be mortised into the lintel; but when the frame has to be built into a brick wall, the lintel and jambs are usually housed or halved into each other and made to project somewhat, as shown. The door represented in the figure is a kind of ledge door, fitting closely into the space enclosed by the frame *a, b, c*; the inner side is shown, in which the latch and hinges should be fastened. On opposite faces of the jambs and on the under side of the lintel a fillet of wood is nailed in such a position as to serve as a stop against which the door may shut, leaving its outside face flush with the frame; and when hanging the door, care should be taken to support it off the sill by a thin strip of wood, so as to ensure

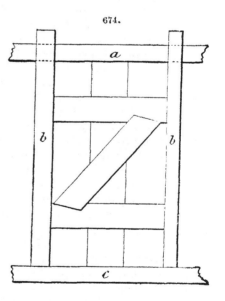

its moving free of the sill when opened and closed. Hinges and latches are chosen according to the weight and finish of the door.

Ledged doors of several kinds are shown in Fig. 675. The simplest and most easily made is A, consisting only of the requisite number of 1-in. to 2-in. boards *a*, placed quite close together (tongued and grooved in better work) and held by the ledges *b*, to which they are fastened by clasp nails. In B, the vertical boards *a* are secured to ledges *b* as before, but these ledges are strengthened by the diagonal braces *c*, the whole forming a ledged and braced door. C is a framed and ledged door, in which the upright boards *a*, of the same thickness as the frame, are tongued and grooved into the lintel *b*, sill *c*, and ledges *d*, while the lintel and sill are mortised and tenoned into the jambs *e* at the corners. D differs from C mainly in the introduction of the braces *f*.

675.

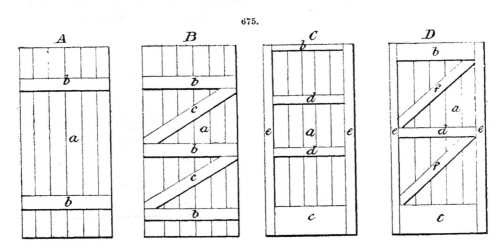

The construction of a panelled door is illustrated in Fig. 676. *a*, *b* are termed long styles, *c*, *d* are short styles, *e*, *f*, *g* are the rails, and *h*, *i*, *k*, *l* are the panels. The pieces *a*, *b*, *c*, *d*, *e*, *f*, *g* constitute the framing, and are joined together by mortices and tenons cut right through in the case of the outside long styles, and not fitting too tightly. When

676.

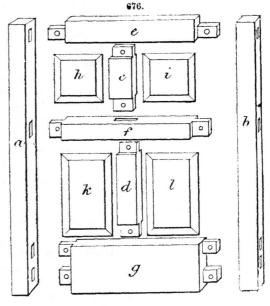

the parts of the framing have been made and fitted, their inner faces are grooved by a plough plane about $\frac{1}{2}$ in. deep and $\frac{3}{8}$ in. wide, to receive the correspondingly bevelled edges of the panels. In better class doors, a beading is run round the edges of the panels to hide the joint and improve the appearance; when this is to be done, it is well not to fit the panels at all tightly into the framing, on account of the risk of splitting the latter. When no beading or moulding is going to be added, more accurate fitting is necessary in the panels. When the panels have been fitted to the grooves in the framing, and everything is properly adjusted, the pieces *c*, *d*, *e*, *f*, *g* are put together, glued and pegged securely; next the panels are slid in sideways, and finally the styles *a*, *b* are driven on to the projecting tenons, previously glued, and wedged from the outside edges. When all is dry, the wedges are cut off, and the edges are planed smooth to fit the frame. The panels may be of very much thinner wood than the frame, thus securing lightness with solidity of appearance, and sufficient strength. Panelled doors are always hung with butt hinges let into little recesses on the frame side of the "hanging" style, as that is called which carries the hinges.

A sash door differs from an ordinary door in the frame being occupied wholly or in part by a window instead of wood.   Light doors for cupboards, &c., may be made in a simple manner by mortising and tenoning the styles and rails together, and cutting a rebate in their inner edge all round, into which thin boards can be dropped to serve as panels, and secured by small brads, with a bead or moulding run round to hide the edges.

Windows.—Windows may be divided into 3 classes—(1) casement windows (opening on hinges or pivots), (2) sash windows (opening by sliding up and down), and (3) skylights.   The construction and arrangement of the woodwork of windows—their frames—will only be dealt with here, leaving the various methods of fixing the glass for discussion under Glazing.

When a window is to be inserted in a wooden structure, provision is made for fitting it to a portion of the framing of the building; but when the walls are of brick, a special frame must be made for the reception of the window.   Fig. 677 shows a plan of the

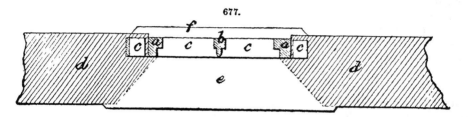

677.

framing for a casement window 4 ft. high and 3 ft. wide.   The side posts *a*, 4 in. by 3 in., are tenoned into the lintels, of the same dimensions, at top and bottom, and midway between them is the centre rail *b*, 4 in. by 2 in.   The ends of the bottom lintel *c* are shown projecting into the walls *d*, and those of the upper lintel are extended in like manner; *e* is the interior window sill, a piece of 1-in. planed board, overhanging about ¾ in.; *f* is the exterior sill, consisting of a piece of quartering 3 in. sq. sloped on the upper side and grooved on the under side, and nailed on beneath the lower lintel *c*.

Fig. 678 shows the construction of the glass frame in its simplest form.   The uprights *a, b* and crossbars *c, d* are bevelled around their outer edge, and rebated for the reception of the glass on their inner edge; the crossbars are mortised into the uprights at the corners, and secured by pegs.   Obviously the frame here shown is intended to carry only one pane of glass.   In larger frames, where it would be inconvenient to have the glass in one piece, the frame space must be divided by partitions, tenoned in as the original parts of the frame, and of the sectional shape indicated at *e, f* being the glass occupying the rebate.   The glazed frame is hinged or pivoted to the main frame, and provided with a hook or rack for holding it open.   The frames shut against stops on the main frame, which exclude wet.

678.

In sash windows, the glazed frames (called " sashes ") are made as before, but they are fixed in pairs, each occupying half the depth of the window.   The construction of the outer frame admits of the sashes passing each other, by which the opening and shutting of the window are performed.   When only one of the two sashes is movable, the window is called " single hung "; when both, " double hung."   Each sash is hung independently, and, if movable, supported by counterweights or ends running over small pulleys.   The top sash occupies the outer position and the bottom sash the inner.   The outer frame, in which the sash-frames work, must always be made specially and fitted into the space in the wall. The construction of the outer frame is shown in Fig. 679. The sashes work on the face of the pulley-piece a, separated by the parting-piece b, so that they may pass each other without touching. The counterweights c are similarly separated by the strip d; e is the front lining and f the back, joined by the end piece g; h is the top sash and i the bottom. The manner of cutting the bottom bar of the upper frame, and the top bar of the lower one, so as to make a close joint, is shown in Fig. 680: a, top sash; b, bottom sash. The bars of sash-frames are generally more or less ornamentally moulded, and a bead is run round the outer frame.

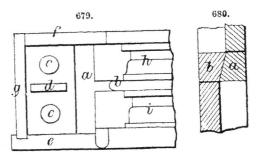

A skylight is a sloping window fixed in a roof, part of which it replaces; that is to say, a portion of the ordinary roofing material, of any desired length, and of a width corresponding to the space between 2 or more rafters, is replaced by a glazed sash. In adjusting the sash to the space, the frame may be recessed to admit the rafters, or the rafters cut off to admit the frame. As both the roof and the skylight present a slanting position, most of the cutting is on the bevel. The space to be occupied by the skylight frame is enclosed by joining the rafters which are interfered with by cross-pieces of stout quartering. The whole structure is well illustrated in Fig. 681, taken

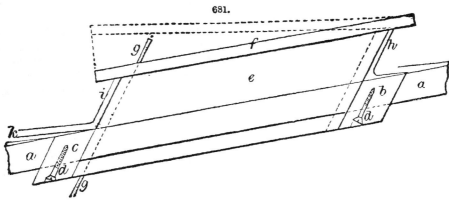

681.

from a practical article on the subject in *Amateur Work*: a is one of the rafters forming a side of the hole in the roof; b, c, pieces of quartering constituting the top and bottom, and secured to the rafters by the screws d whose heads are countersunk; e is one side of a rectangular box made of 1-in. planed deal, about 9 in. deep, dovetailed at the corners, and sloping as shown. This box should fit tightly into the rectangular space made for it, and be secured by nails or screws to the rafters at the sides and the crossbars b, c at top and bottom. The top edge of this box should have a groove ploughed in it to carry off rain-water, and it may have a fillet $\frac{1}{2}$ in. high nailed all round the outside, to form an enclosure for the sash that is to lie on the top. This sash f is made in the usual way, and, if not to be opened, is screwed down securely on the top of the box, which it fits exactly, dropping inside the fillet; but if it is intended to be opened the top edge only must be secured, and that by hinges joining it to the box. The sash is raised and lowered by the rod g, which may be of any reasonable length. When the sash is fixed and completed, the roofing material must be adjusted to it, to exclude the weather. But before laying the roofing (slates, tiles, felt, &c.) up to the skylight, pieces of sheet lead are spread all round it, one at the head h being turned up the woodwork of the skylight and slipped up under the slates *k*, another *i* at the foot lying over the slates *k*, and one on each side, similarly arranged for keeping out the wet. These strips of lead are nailed down in place before the roofing is secured over them. They should extend about 6 to 9 in. in each direction on the roof, besides the turn-up on all sides of the skylight. The lead must be bent and fitted by the aid of a piece of planed hard wood, on which a hammer can be used. The joints may be soldered if desired, as described under Soldering. Angular fillets nailed all round at the base of the skylight reduce the sharpness of the bend in the sheet lead, and hence help to preserve it.

CABINET-MAKING.—The art of "cabinet-making" is usually divided into two classes—"carcase work," embracing the production of articles of chest-like form, such as book-cases, &c., and "chair work," comprising not only chairs and their substitutes but also tables. In point of fact, it is merely joinery of a superior description, working with finer tools on more costly woods, and producing more sightly effects. The subject may be conveniently discussed under the several heads of woods, tools, and veneering, concluding with a few examples in both carcase and chair work.

Woods.—Most woods have already been described more or less fully under Carpentry, especially concerning their sources and qualities; repetition will be avoided by making cross-references to particular pages, and only points specially interesting to the cabinet-maker will be noted here. The woods in ordinary use are named below in alphabetic order.

Amboyna : the beautifully mottled wood of *Pterospermum indicum*, a native of India.

Apple : inferior in all respects to pear.

Ash : see p. 2.

Beech : see p. 3. Takes a walnut stain well.

Beefwood : a common name for the woods of the Casuarinas, described on p. 16.

Birch : see p. 3. The black or cherry kind is most esteemed, and is largely used for plain furniture. It is harder than mahogany, and often occurs beautifully figured (then called "mahogany birch"; such figured pieces are cut into veneers, but only adapted for the caul and hand-screw process, on account of the tendency to swell and shrink on wetting.

Box : see p. 4. Twists and splits in working, if not well seasoned.

Camphor : has an excellent effect when worked into small articles.

Canary : the wood of an Indian tree, *Persea indica*

Cedar : see p. 5.

Cherry : much used by cabinet-makers and musical instrument makers, especially in France.

Ebony : see p. 7. Has a tendency to split and exfoliate. Very expensive.

Holly : a light, close-grained wood, of small size, useful in small articles and for inlaying.

Kingwood : a scarce wood imported in sticks 5 ft. long from Brazil; apparently related to rosewood.

Lime : has a butter-like hue, and is easy to work.

Locust-wood : see p. 11.

Mahogany : see p. 11. Cabinet-makers distinguish 3 kinds—Spanish, Cuban, and Honduras, esteemed in the order quoted. Spanish is known by its hard, close grain, and variously mottled figure. The rarest mottle is "peacock," something like birds'-eye maple. Of ordinary kinds, "stop" mottle is most admired, a light and dark figure being produced by waves of grain breaking up and running into each other. In "fiddle" mottle, the waves run across in nearly regular lines. In the figure called "breck," "curl," or "curb," the light and dark shades slope away from the centre; veneers of this are liable to contract a number of little cracks in time. The Cuban wood is less handsome in figure, lustre, and colour, and therefore employed in large veneers as a cheaper substitute for Spanish, also in solid work.   Honduras (called Bay) wood has little artistic value, but is esteemed for the solid parts of work intended to carry veneer, being straight-grained and free from warping and shrinking.   These qualities render mahogany a favourite wood in cabinet-making, another great advantage being its immunity from decay and worms.

Maple : see p. 13.   The best figured birds'-eye maple is cut into veneers.

Oak : see p. 15.   Oak has little beauty for furniture-making unless it is judiciously cut so as to exhibit the "champ" or silver grain to the best advantage (see p. 53). This champ is better marked in Riga than in English oak, and the former is also a more easily worked wood, consequently it is preferred for this particular purpose, though some-what less strong and durable.

Partridgewood : a name applied to the wood of several South American trees.

Pear : see p. 16.   Takes a black stain well, and often replaces ebony.

Pine : see p. 19.   The American pine, commonly called Weymouth or white pine in this country, is best suited for cabinet-making purposes, and forms the ground for nearly all veneered and hidden work.

Plane : see p. 20.

Rose : see p. 22.   The best comes from Rio de Janeiro, and emits an agreeable odour.   It is hard, heavy, and dark-coloured.

Sandal : chiefly esteemed for its fragrance.

Satin : see p. 22.   Used in fancy articles.   Has a peculiar lustre and fragrant odour.

Teak : see p. 24.

Tulip : see p. 25.   Used for inlaying and marqueterie work.

Walnut : see p. 25.   This wood is very popular both for solid work and veneering. The species common to Europe and Asia affords the best wood; that native of America gives a "black" kind used as a cheaper substitute.   Walnut contrasts well with lighter woods, as birds'-eye maple, ash, and satinwood, and lends itself to most delicate orna-mental work.

Zebrawood : a name given to a beautiful furniture wood obtained in British Guiana from the hyawabolly (*Omphalobium Lamberti*).

In addition there are many excellent cabinet-making woods produced in our tropical colonies about which little or nothing is known in this country.

Tools.—These are mainly the same as employed in Carpentry, but some special forms are added.   These will be de-scribed here, including chest and bench.

Tool-chest. A convenient chest for holding cabinet-making tools is shown in Fig. 682, as described by Cabe in *Design and Work.*   It is 3 ft. 1 in., by 1 ft. 8 in., by 1 ft. 8 in. inside measure-ment, with a till the full length of the inside, 9 in. broad and $10\frac{1}{2}$ in. deep. The body of the chest is made of $\frac{7}{8}$-in. best yellow pine, with a skirting of oak round the lid.   The till and the inside of the lid are veneered with rosewood and walnut.   The 2 sides are squared up 3 ft. 3 in. long and 1 ft. 8 in. broad, and the 2 ends 1 ft. 10 in. long and 1 ft. 8 in. broad.   They are previously slipped on the upper edge —that is, a thin slip of plain walnut, say $\frac{3}{8}$ in. thick, is glued on what is to be the upper edge of each piece.   These 4 pieces are dovetailed together, the dovetails $1\frac{1}{2}$ in. apart

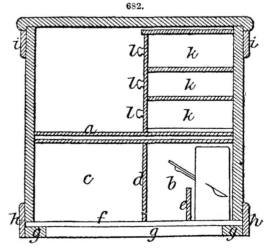

682.

and all going quite through the thickness of the wood. Before glueing the pieces together, 2 fillets *a* of mahogany, 1 in. broad and $\frac{5}{8}$ in. thick, with a groove in the centre, are glued and screwed to the inside of the ends at a distance of $10\frac{3}{4}$ in. from the upper edge; these are to receive a sliding board 11 in. broad, which slides underneath the till, which, when pushed back, covers the planes and tools in the space *b*, and, when pulled forward, covers the tools in the space *c*. This board may well be left out. A partition board *d* between *b* and *c* comes nearly up to the sliding board, and is grooved into the 2 ends. A second partition *e* in the middle of the space *b* is 4 in. broad, and is also let into the ends. These 2 partitions are made of $\frac{1}{2}$-in. wood, and these grooves must be made in the ends to receive them before the body is knocked together. A stain of Venetian red and ochre, with a little glue size, is made somewhat thin, and applied hot to the wood with a piece of cotton rag; then, after standing for a few minutes, as much as will come off is rubbed with another piece of rag, stroking always with the grain. In a short time this stain will dry, when it is sandpapered, using the finest. The body is next put together with thin glue, using a small brush for the dovetails, and taking care that no glue gets on to the inner surface, as taking it off afterwards leaves an unsightly mark. It must be borne in mind that in dovetailing a box such as this, the "pins" are always on the end pieces; consequently they are cut first. In "rapping" the body together, a somewhat heavy hammer is used, and always with a piece of wood to protect the work from injury. The 4 corners are glued and rapped up close. The box has to be "squared." A rod of wood, made like a wedge at one end, and applied from corner to corner diagonally inside, is the readiest method of squaring, a pencil mark being made on the side of the rod just where the side and end meet; then the rod being placed diagonally from the other 2 corners, the pencil mark will show at once whether the box is squared or not; and, if not, the *long* corner must be pressed or pushed to bring it to the square. A bottom *f* is nailed on of $\frac{5}{8}$-in. wood, with the grain running across—i. e. from back to front. Then a band *g* of wood, $2\frac{1}{2}$ in. broad and 1 in. thick, is nailed over the bottom, and flush with the outside of the box all round. The 2 long pieces are nailed on first, and the end ones are fitted between them. To secure these bars or bands properly, a few $1\frac{1}{4}$-in. screws should be passed through the bottom from the inside into them. The box is then planed truly on the outside all round, finishing with a hand-plane and sandpaper. A band *h* is made to go round the sides at the bottom, and another *i* at the top or upper edge; that at the bottom is $3\frac{1}{2}$ in. broad and $\frac{5}{8}$ in. thick, and that at the top $2\frac{1}{2}$ in. broad and $\frac{5}{8}$ in. thick. It makes the best job to dovetail these bands at the corners, making them of a size to slip exactly on to the body of the chest. The upper edge of the bottom band, and the lower edge of the upper, are moulded either with an "ogee" or "quarter round." When the bottom band is in a position for nailing, it covers the bottom bars and the edge of the bottom, coming up the sides of the box about 2 in. The upper band is fixed $\frac{3}{8}$ in. below the edge of the body; this forms a check for the lid, the bottling for the lid being made to check down on this band. The lid is made of pine, $\frac{7}{8}$ in. or 1 in. thick; it has cross ends, $2\frac{1}{2}$ in. broad, mortised on. These prevent the lid splitting or warping. After they are glued and cramped on, the lid is evenly planed and squared to the proper size, which is $\frac{1}{16}$ in. larger than the body of the box on front and ends, and $\frac{1}{4}$ in. over the back. The lid is fitted with 3 brass butt hinges 3 in. long. The lid, being temporarily fitted, is taken off, and a skirting put round it—that is, on front and ends. This skirting is $1\frac{1}{4}$ in. broad, and $\frac{7}{8}$ in. thick, of hard wood—oak or black birch. To make a first-rate job of this skirting it should be grooved, as also the chest-lid and slip feathers inserted. It should also be nailed with fine wrought brads. After it is firmly fixed and dry, it is rounded on the outer edge. The extent of the rounding is found by shutting down the lid and drawing all round at the edge of the band, over which the skirting projects about $\frac{5}{16}$ in. The inside of the lid may be panelled. This panelling is simply a flat veneered surface, the 2 panels being root walnut, and the borders rosewood; the veneering must be done before the skirting is put on. The 2 panels are laid first; when dry, the cutting gauge is set to $2\frac{1}{4}$ in., and cuts away the over veneer all round, which, of course, gives a border of $2\frac{1}{2}$ in. to be veneered with the rosewood; $2\frac{1}{4}$ in. also divides the 2 panels in the centre, and the 8 corners are marked off with compasses set to $1\frac{1}{2}$ in., and cut clean out with a gouge. All the edges are planed with the iron plane, and the rosewood border is planed and jutted all round in the form of "banding"—that is, with the grain running across and not the lengthway of the borders. The round corners are fitted in in 2 pieces mitred in the centre. A till has now to be made. The body or carcase of this is entirely of $\frac{1}{2}$-in. wood. It has 2 drawers in the length at the bottom, 3 in. deep on the face; 3 in the centre in the length, $2\frac{1}{2}$ in. deep on the face; and over these is a tray, covered by a lid. The face of this tray is in the form of 4 drawers, which are shams. The drawers are 9 in. broad from front to back, and run on shelves $\frac{1}{2}$ in. thick, with divisions between of the same thickness. The shelves and divisions, as also the edge of the lifting lid, are slipped with rosewood on the fore edges, and the drawers being veneered with root walnut, the whole has a good effect. The lifting lid is panelled with veneer, similar to the lid of the chest, the rosewood border being $1\frac{1}{2}$ in. broad. It is hinged with 3 brass butts, $1\frac{1}{2}$ in. long, to the back of the till, which projects upwards the thickness of the lid, and is veneered also with rosewood. This lid may be made of bay mahogany or good pine; and if of the latter, it must be veneered on the under side with plain walnut or mahogany, to counteract that on the top and prevent warping. The carcase (case) of this till is constructed as follows:—The 2 ends are cross-headed on the upper edge; these are $1\frac{1}{4}$ in. broad, and may be put on with the ploughs. Then the bottom and 2 shelves are squared up to the length of inside of the chest, having been previously slipped on the fore edges with rosewood $\frac{1}{8}$ in. thick. The bottom is dovetailed into the 2 ends, while the 2 shelves are mortised or let into the ends with square tenons, which pass quite through, and are wedged. The divisions between the drawers are let through, and wedged in the same manner. The front of the tray, which has the appearance of 4 drawers, is of $\frac{1}{2}$-in. mahogany, veneered with root walnut, like the drawer fronts, and an imitation of the fore edges made on it by glueing slips of rosewood, $\frac{1}{2}$ in. broad, to represent the fore edges. The walnut front must, of course, be sandpapered before these are put on. The 5 drawers k are made entirely of straight, plain, bay mahogany, $\frac{1}{4}$ in. thick, excepting the fronts, which are $\frac{1}{2}$ in. The knobs l are of rosewood, $\frac{3}{4}$ in. diameter. The tray, covered by the hinged lid, is so deep as to hold the brace or tools of the like bulk. The left end may be occupied with 3 shallow trays, one over the other, for holding the several bits belonging to the brace, and are very handy, as the bits can be arranged in order, and the trays may be lifted out to the bench, when a number of the bits is wanted. The remainder of the tray is lined with green frieze. and holds the brace, spirit-level, gauges, squares, and other of the finer tools. The 2 long drawers at the bottom are used for chisels, gouges, spoke-shaves, mitre-squares, &c., while the 3 upper ones are for gimlets, bradawls, compasses, pliers, and sundry small tools. In the space b, in the body of the chest and under the till, the planes are arranged as shown. In front of them is a space 4 in. broad and the full length of the chest. In it long tools, such as the trammels, are kept, and any planes that the back space will not admit, such as raglets or grooving planes, which have 2 wedges. It is also useful for holding drawings of large dimensions, rolled up, where they are safe from damage, and in cases of removal it is the receptacle for the hand-saws and other tools which usually hang upon the wall.

Bench.—A full-sized cabinet-makers' bench is generally 7 ft. long and $2\frac{1}{2}$ ft. wide, but a very convenient size is 6 ft. by 2 ft. Such a bench is illustrated in Fig. 683. The top is in 2 parts, the front portion a being 15 in. wide and of $2\frac{1}{2}$-in. red or yellow pine, sound and straight; the back portion b is only 9 in. wide and $1\frac{1}{2}$ in. thick. Both are supported by the cross rails c; and the back part has a fillet d, 1 in. thick, screwed to it in such a position that its top edge is flush with a. The rails c, 5 in. by 2 in., are screwed to the top ends of the 4 legs of good red pine, the 2 back ones e and right front one f

measuring 4 in. by 2 in., while the left front one *g* is 6 in. by 2 in. The back legs *e* diverge at foot to give greater steadiness to the bench. The top is secured to the rails *c* by screws put up from beneath. At bottom, the legs are joined by rails *h*, 3 in. by 2 in., dovetailed into them and held by screws; boards *i* are nailed to their under side, to form a capacious tray for holding tools. The bench stops *k* are let into holes which come

683.

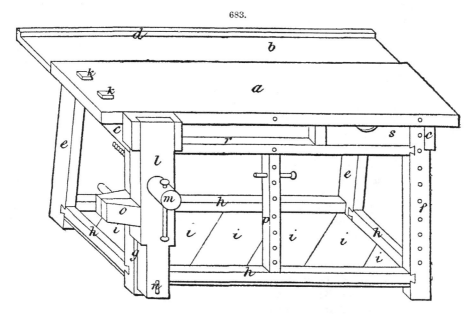

clear outside the rail *c*. The bench vice *l* has its outer cheek working against the leg *g* by means of the screw *m* passing through both. At the bottom is a "runner" or "sword" *n*, consisting of a strip of wood, 2 in. by $\frac{1}{2}$ in., mortised into the foot of *l* and sliding in a corresponding groove in *g*, where it is pegged by an iron pin at suitable distances for keeping the jaws of the vice parallel. This is further aided by the supplementary side screw *o*. The holes in the leg *f* and central bar *p* hold strong pegs for support-ing the ends of work while it is being manipulated in the vice. The space between the top *a* and the rail *r* may be made into a shelf only, or partially occupied by a drawer as at *s*.

Planes.—Besides the ordinary planes, the cabinet-maker uses a "toothing" plane. This has a stock similar to the hard wood hand-plane, but the iron, instead of having a cutting edge, presents a series of sharp teeth to the wood. This serrated edge is formed by long narrow grooves on the face of the iron next the wedge, and when the iron is ground in the usual manner these ridges terminate in sharp points. In setting-up this iron on the oil-stone, only the ground back is applied to the stone. The position of the iron in the stock is nearly perpendicular, so that it is simply a scratch plane, and needs no cover like the others. Its use is to roughen the surfaces of pieces to be glued to-gether, for while it takes off the ridges left by the half-long or panel plane, it roughens the surface by scratching, thereby adapting it better to hold the glue. All surfaces to be veneered upon, as well as the veneer itself, are scratched with this plane.

Dowel plate.—The dowel plate is a steel plate about $\frac{1}{2}$ in. thick, with holes from $\frac{3}{16}$ in. to $\frac{1}{2}$ in., and centre-bits are fitted and marked so that dowel pins made in the holes will fit holes made by the corresponding bits.

Smoothing implements.—The "scraper" is a bit of steel plate about the thickness of a hand-saw blade, 5 in. by 3 in.; its use is to take off any ridges left by the smoothing plane in planing hard wood, producing a surface perfectly free from lumpiness; it is used before the sandpaper. Sandpapering is done with the paper wrapped round a piece of cork. The usual size for large flat surfaces is 5 in. by 4 in., and about 1 in. thick. One side is made quite flat, and on this the paper is placed. Pieces of cork are used for all kinds of sandpapering,—hollows, rounds, mouldings, &c.,—the cork being shaped with the rasp, to fit the part to be prepared.

Sawing rest.—The sawing rest or " bench boy " used by cabinet-makers differs from that employed by carpenters (p.136) in being shorter and broader, say 10 in. by 6 in., of $\frac{7}{8}$-in. pine, the fillets being of mahogany, $1\frac{1}{8}$ in. sq., let into grooves, glued, and screwed.

Moulding board.—This contrivance for holding strips of wood while under the moulding plane somewhat resembles the shooting board (Fig. 268, p. 66). It consists of a plank a of $1\frac{1}{4}$-in. Bay mahogany, 6 ft. long and 6 in. wide, having attached on its upper surface another board b of the same length but only 3 in. wide, thus forming a step (see Fig. 684). The upper board b is free to move laterally on the lower one by

means of slots c 2 in. long, through which screws d pass into the lower board a. Thus the width of the step is regulated. To suit mouldings of various sizes it is well to have 3 guide boards b, $\frac{1}{4}$ in., $\frac{1}{2}$ in., and $\frac{3}{4}$ in. thick, all slotted to fit the same screws. At each end is fixed a bench stop e, exactly like that shown in Fig. 683.

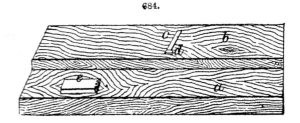

684.

Mitring and Shooting board.—Here again the article used by carpenters (Fig. 260, p. 63) is replaced by a shorter form more suited to light work. It is made by screwing together 2 pieces of Bay mahogany 30 in. long, 6 in. wide, and 1 in. thick, one overlapping the other 2 in. sideways, so as to form a step 4 in. wide. This constitutes the shooting board. The mitring is effected by a triangular piece screwed to the top board, about the centre, with its apex touching the margin of the step, so that its sides form exactly angles of 45° with the step.

Vice.—A wooden vice with jaws 6 in. wide is very useful for holding small work, either on the bench or in the bench vice.

Veneering.—This name is applied to the practice of laying very thin sheets (called veneers) of a more valuable wood upon the surface of a less valuable one, in order to gain superior effects at reduced cost.

The method of cutting veneers, as conducted by the Grand Rapids Veneer Co., is thus described. In the first place the log is drawn up an inclined plane by means of tackle, and brought under a drag saw on a platform at the top, where it is cut to the length required in order to fit the cutting machine. On one side of this platform, which is outside the factory building, is a row of steam boxes, in one of which the log is placed, and allowed to remain about 12 hours, emerging in a very soft and pliable state. This is necessary to prevent chipping and breaking while going through the cutting process, and also to render it more easy to cut. It is lifted from this place by a powerful crane, and after the bark has been peeled off, placed upon the cutter. A veneer cutter resembles a gigantic turning lathe, with a knife ground to a razor-like edge running the whole length of the log to be cut. It is very massive, the knife being backed with an enormous iron beam, and the other portions are fixed in an equally solid manner; for the slightest tremor or yielding in any part would tear the veneer and render it useless. The machine used by this company weighs 10 tons. The chuck consists of a large iron shaft, which is hammered into place by a heavy swinging maul. The log having been placed in position, the cutter is set in motion. The log revolves against the knife, and the veneer is pared off in a continuous sheet. So smoothly and easily does the machine work that it is almost impossible to conceive of the enormous power that is exerted. The feed is supplied by means of a revolving screw, which may be gauged to produce a veneer of any thickness from that of a sheet of tissue paper to $\frac{3}{8}$ in.

Of course there is a limit to the diameter which the machine can cut; and after it has done its work, a piece 7 in. in diameter is left. In plain native woods this can be easily put to other uses; but in French walnut burls it is too valuable to be lost. In such cases, therefore, the knot is fastened to a stay log on whose centre it revolves, and thus very little, and that the least valuable part, of the costly material is wasted. The ash burls, which the company are now cutting, are brought in from the surrounding country, and they avoid the necessity of a stay log by having a sufficient part of the trunk on which the burl grew left to serve for this purpose. As the sheets of veneer come off the cutter, they are taken to a saw which divides them into the required widths, and are then put through the drying machine to remove the moisture with which the steam bath that they have received has saturated them. The subject of drying has been one of the most serious problems with which those in the veneer business have had to deal. A dryer is used by this company, who claim that it is both thorough and rapid in its operation. It consists of 2 series of steam-heated rollers, enclosed in an iron box, between which the sheets of veneer pass as through a planer, emerging in a thoroughly dry state and pressed perfectly flat. The drying is still further expedited by a blast of hot air forced into the iron box referred to by a fan blower. After going through this process, the veneers are taken to the second floor, and such of them as are intended to be sold in this state are packed away, while the remainder is made into 3-ply panels to be used in the manufacture of bedsteads, for looking-glass backs, &c. These 3-ply panels are made by passing the veneers through a glue machine, and then placing them in a press. Great strength is secured in these panels by having the grain of the middle layer of veneer run at right angles with that of the 2 outer layers.

Generally speaking, straight-grained and moderately soft woods are sliced off a log by a weighted knife with a drawing cut, the log, or burl, being 10 ft. long, and the veneers varying from $\frac{1}{8}$ in. to $\frac{1}{40}$ in. in thickness, the width corresponding, of course, to the diameter of the log. A knife machine which gives a half rotary movement to a semi-cylindrical turned log, allowing a veneer to be cut following the log's diameter, produces wide veneers from logs of small diameters. But such woods as ebony and lignum vitæ cannot be cut with a knife, while finely figured and consequently close-grained mahogany, and some rosewood, are difficult to cut. The saw, therefore, has its place. Such saws must be very thin, and so finely adjusted that hardly the slightest variation will occur in the thickness of the veneers turned out. While a nicely arranged circular saw will turn out boards varying $\frac{1}{20}$ in., which would be imperceptible, such a lack of uniformity in thin sheets would prove a damaging imperfection. Before being cut, the veneer material must be carefully steamed, the same as in bending. A tight box 12 ft. long, and 4 ft. deep and wide is used, and exhaust steam is utilized. An ordinary wood like black walnut, which has an open grain, will steam sufficiently in 6 hours, but the close-grained South American woods require 36 hours. Mahogany will steam sufficiently in 24 hours. Mahogany, tulip, and rosewood, being hard to cut, require more and careful steaming, and a knife in the best condition. The veneers wrinkle when laid together, but straighten out readily when glued properly to a body. Veneers will dry in the air in about 12 hours, but are not kiln dried, although the latter method is used for lumber out of which veneers are to be made.

The softest woods should be chosen for veneering upon. Perhaps the best for the purpose are 12 ft. in length, of perfectly straight grain, and without a knot; of course no one ever veneers over a knot. Hard wood can be veneered—boxwood with ivory, for instance; but wood that will warp and twist, such as cross-grained mahogany, must be avoided. The veneer, and the wood on which it is to be laid, must both be carefully prepared, the former by taking out all marks of the saw on both sides with a fine toothing plane, the latter with a coarser toothing plane. If the veneer happens to be broken in doing this, it may be repaired at once with a bit of stiff paper glued upon it on the upper side. The veneer should be cut rather larger than the surface to be covered; if much twisted, it may be damped and placed under a board and weight over-night. This saves much trouble; but with veneers that are cheap it is not worth while taking much trouble about refractory pieces. When French walnut burr is buckled or cockled, as not unfrequently happens, it is treated on both sides with very thin hot size, and, when quite dry, placed between hot plates of zinc, or hot wooden cauls. This is done with the whole veneer, and it is cut afterwards. The cutting is not easy, owing to the tendency of the veneer to split. It should be placed on a flat board, and marked to a size a little larger than necessary; the veneer is then cut lengthwise by a steel point or marker against a straight-edge, cuts across the grain being done with a fine dovetail saw. Very plain wood can be cut with a chisel or shoemakers' knife. Walnut burrs are best cut with scissors.

There are 2 ways of fixing the veneer, known as "hammering" and "cauling," alike in that they are both methods of applying pressure, but differing in that the former is accompanied by damp heat, the latter by dry.

In either case, the wood to be veneered must now be sized with thin glue; the ordinary glue-pot will supply this by dipping the brush first into the glue, then into the boiling water in the outer vessel. This size must be allowed to dry before the veneer is laid. Suppose now that veneering by the hammer process is about to commence. The glue is in good condition and boiling hot; the bench is cleared; a basin of hot water with the veneering hammer and a sponge in it is at hand, together with a cloth or two, and everything in such position that one will not interfere with or be in the way of another. Then :—

(1) Damp with hot water that side of the veneer which is not to be glued, and glue the other side; (2) go over as quickly as possible the wood itself, previously toothed and sized; (3) bring the veneer rapidly to it, pressing it down with the outspread hands, and taking care that the edges of the veneer overlap a little all round; (4) grasp the veneering hammer close to the pane (shaking off the hot water from it) and the handle pointing away from you; wriggle it about, pressing it down stoutly, and squeezing the glue from the centre out at the edges. If it is a large piece of stuff which is to be veneered, the assistance of a hot iron will be wanted to make the glue liquid again after it has set; but do not let it dry the wood underneath it, or it will burn the glue and scorch the veneer, and ruin the work. (5) Having got out all the glue possible, search the surface for blisters, which will at once be betrayed by the sound they give when tapped with the handle of the hammer; the hot iron (or the inner vessel of the glue-pot itself, which often answers the purpose) must be applied, and the process with the hammer repeated. When the hammer is not in the hand, it should be in the hot water. The whole may now be sponged over with hot water, and wiped as dry as can be. And observe, throughout the above process never have any slop and wet about the work that you can avoid. Whenever you use the sponge, squeeze it well first. Damp and heat are wanted, not wet and heat. It is a good thing to have the sponge in the left hand nearly all the time, ready to take up any moisture or squeezed-out glue from the front of the hammer.

The veneering "hammer" resembles an ordinary hammer in little but its shape, the manner of using it being altogether different. The form of the "hammer" too presents some variety. In Fig. 685, A is what may be termed the "shop" style of veneering hammer-head, while B, C are such as may be made by the operator himself. The form A can be purchased at a dealer's and fitted with a wooden shaft. The form B is made in the following manner: a handle a, 12 in. long and 1 in. thick, is inserted in a hole bored in the centre of a piece of hard wood b, 6 in. sq. and 1 in. thick, in the bottom edge of which a slit about 1 in. deep is cut with a thick saw, and into this slit is fitted a piece of iron or steel plate c, 6 in. long and 2 in. wide, secured by a couple of rivets.

This done, the corners of the top and bottom edges of the wood *b*, and the edge of the plate *c* are nicely rounded and smoothed. The construction of C is evident from the illustration; *a* is the handle; *b*, the head. The hammer, of whichever shape, is employed as a squeezer for pressing out superfluous glue; it is therefore held by one hand grasping the handle and the other pressing on the head, and is moved forward with a zigzag motion, each end of the head advancing alternately in short sliding steps.

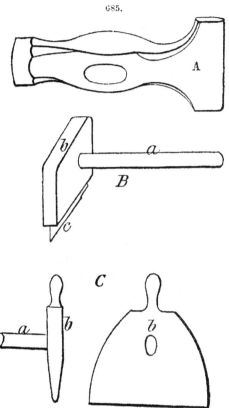

685.

It may sometimes happen that when the veneer is laid a fault may be noticed which renders it necessary to remove and relay the veneer. This is difficult to do without damaging the veneer. The best plan is to first thoroughly clean the surface by hot damp sponging; then dry and warm it by a fire, and while hot rub in linseed oil; hold to the fire again till the oil has disappeared, and repeat the oiling and warming till the glue beneath is so weakened that the veneer can be gently stripped off. Both old glued surfaces are thoroughly cleansed and roughed by the toothing plane before relaying is attempted. The projecting edges of the veneer can be taken off by a sharp chisel or plane when the whole is quite dry and firm, which end is attained by placing the work under weights supported on an even surface, and leaving it in a warm room. The difficulty with hammer veneering is that the glue is not kept always sufficiently hot and that therefore it does not get properly squeezed out at the edges, and sometimes so much hot water has to be used in the operation that the veneer swells and shrinks to a degree that spoils the look of the work. Still, with care, it is quite feasible to lay flat veneers up to 5 ft. long and 18 in. wide with the hammer in a satisfactory manner. The working of the hammer should always be from the centre outwards. The sponge and hot water, or the heated flat-iron, is applied when the glue sets, or an air bubble gets entrapped so as to form a "blister." To veneer a convex surface, it is only necessary to wet the veneer on one side, when it will curl up so as to fit a convex object; it should be held in place by binding round with some soft string.

In veneering with a caul, the process is identical with that already described as far as the glueing; the difference commences in the mode of applying pressure to ensure adhesion between the body and the veneer. Cauls are made either of well-seasoned pine or of rolled zinc plate, with a surface exactly the converse of the veneer to be pressed. Hence cauling, while superior to hammering, and in some cases indispensable, is much more expensive, as, except in the case of small flat work, a new caul is required for every new outline presented by the various veneered articles. The substance of the caul, especially in the case of wood, should be thin enough to bend slightly under great pressure; and it should fit somewhat more closely at the centre than at the edges, so that, when pressure is applied, it will pass progressively from the centre outwards. The object of the caul is to remelt the glue which has been spread on the body and the veneer, for which purpose it is strongly heated before application; pressure is then applied in various ways to expel the superfluous glue and increase the intimacy of contact. Small cauls of 1-in. pine for flat work may be pressed by means of wooden hand-screws, applied at short intervals, commencing always in the centre. The caul should be planed true and smooth on both sides, toothed, and saturated with linseed oil, which last not only augments the heat, but prevents escaping glue from adhering to the caul. This adhesion of the glue to the caul, which would damage the work, is also avoided by soaping the caul, and by covering the veneer with a sheet of clean paper.

When the veneered surface is so large that it cannot conveniently be pressed by means of hand-screws, the work is placed in a veneering frame, as shown in Fig. 686.   It consists of 2 upright bars a, 3½ in. sq., with 2 rails b, 3½ in. by 3 in., let into them, and having between the 2 rails b a clear space of about 10 in., in which works the movable bar c, 3 in. by 2½ in., its position being regulated by the 3 iron screws d, ¾–1 in. in diameter.   The bar c is made with a slight curve on the under side, so that its pressure may be exerted first on the centre of the work.   The middle screw is tightened up first, and followed by the others.   This middle screw has a nut under a collar let into the upper side of c, so as to lift it when necessary, while the side screws simply press on little iron plates e. The frame will admit work about 2 ft. wide; a number are used

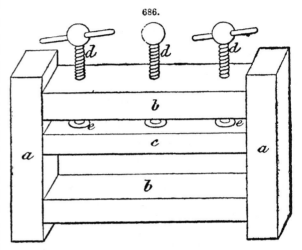

686.

together in a row according to the length of the work. Where steam is available, advantage is taken of it to heat a couple of iron plates arranged together so as to form a shallow tray, and with their opposing faces quite true; the work is placed between them and pressure is applied by iron screws.

Wooden cauls are far inferior to those made of smooth sheet zinc ¼–⅜ in. thick; these are more easily and quickly heated, and never adhere to the glue which comes into contact with their surfaces. For work of large size it is most convenient to use the sheet zinc in several pieces placed closely edge to edge.

So far, the veneering of flat surfaces only has been dealt with. For small corners and places where no clamp will hold, it will be found very advantageous to employ needle points such as are used by upholsterers for securing gilt mountings; these can be drawn out when the work is dry, and the small punctures remaining in the veneer will be effectually hidden by the polish subsequently applied. For simple rounded (convex) work, an effective and easy plan is to encircle the work with pieces of string or wire tied at intervals, commencing in the middle, and placing slips of wood between the string and the veneer to prevent the latter being cut into. A useful contrivance as an accessory to the hammer process for round work (Fig. 687) is made by attaching the 2 ends of a piece of stout canvas a by means of tacks b to the sides of a hard board c, rather narrower and longer than the work, and provided with screws d. The work is put into the receptacle with the veneered side towards the canvas, which latter is brought to bear tightly against it by turning the screws d till they hold firmly against the back of the work. When the work is thus fixed, the canvas is soaked with hot water, and warmed, the screws being meanwhile tightened a little. As the glue commences to exude, the veneering hammer is passed over the canvas covering the veneer, and the pressure is carried to a maximum degree, when the whole is put aside for 24 hours to set. For the various forms of moulding and complicated outlines, it is necessary to make a wooden caul having exactly the converse form of the surface to be veneered; this is saturated with linseed oil, soaped, or covered with No. 12 sheet zinc shaped to it and held by tacks at the edges. The veneer may be made to assume an ogee form by wetting one half its width on one side, and the remaining half on the other. When the work admits of it, 2 pieces may be veneered at once by heating the caul on both sides. An effort should always be made to utilize the figure of the veneer to the best advantage, as will be ascertained by trying the effect of different positions. When a surface is too large to be veneered at one operation in a convenient manner, it must be done piecemeal, taking care that the consecutive pieces match well in figure. In doing work piecemeal, the uncovered surface becomes coated with the glue squeezed out of the covered portion; this escaping glue should be cleared away as fast as it appears, and even then there is a risk of its forming a thin glaze on the wood, so that it is the safest plan to scrape it and pass the toothing plane over it again before veneering.

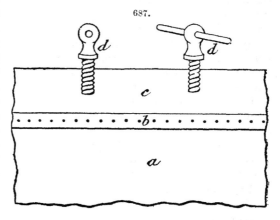

In veneering on a highly resinous wood, such as pitch pine, there is a risk of the heat employed in laying the veneer drawing some of the resin through and spoiling the work. To prevent this, the surface may be superficially charred previous to laying the veneer, by spreading over it a compound of beeswax and turpentine, in such proportions as to produce a thin and not pasty mass, and igniting it at one end. By blowing gently, the flame may be encouraged all over the surface, charring it slightly and especially attacking the resinous veins. The loose charcoal is brushed away as soon as formed, leaving a firm yet charred surface. This is gone over with the toothing plane in a transverse direction, and then well worked over with thin glue before laying the veneers.

The veneering of a bed panel whose length requires 2 veneers is thus described by Edgar. Take the 2 veneers, pair them, cut them to the sizes required, and gently dry them between 2 boards until they are perfectly flat. Then proceed to carefully tooth them on the side to be glued, and if they are roughly sawn, tooth the ridges of the outside; by so doing you will get a thoroughly flat surface when judiciously cleaned off. Should you have a caul press at your convenience, gently rub some glue over that part of the broad end of the feather that contains most end grain, placing a piece of old copybook or other paper over the same; this will prevent it from adhering to anything by which it is laid, and also aid in strengthening the end grain parts together. When thoroughly dry, joint it to make your full length, and be careful that your joint is slightly hollow. Those end-grain parts that you recently papered, are sure to expand by the steam driven out with the glue by the heated appliances necessary to lay them. When the same class of panel is to be laid by hand with the veneering hammer, carefully dry and tooth your veneer as before mentioned, fix your panel firmly to the bench, and proceed to lay one half; have the glue well boiled, thin, and flowing clear and free from strings, and unrendered bits; glue the feather on the side to be laid, place it on your panel, and with a tack or two to keep it in position, glue all over the outside of the veneer. Now move a warm flat iron, not so hot as to scorch the glue, over the amount of surface you consider capable of laying in the one half. On no account use water.

Study to work from the centre to either end of the piece you are laying. Having got all down, clean all glue off, putting the same in your pot for further use. Now with a hot sponge, rinsed out of water in glue kettle, thoroughly clean your tools for the next operation. After a few hours, proceed to make your joint with the other half, carefully observing your joint is slightly hollow. As heretofore, with the panel firmly fixed to the bench, the glue and iron hot, proceed to lay 6 or 8 in. near the joint, working your veneer hammer as much as possible across your veneer linable with the joint. Having got your joint good, glue a piece of paper over the same to keep all air out, and proceed to lay the remainder, in no case using water till all is laid; scrape all glue off into glue-pot, and with hot sponge clean tools as before. Should the end grain blister, wait till all is laid, then with a fine needle point make 2 or 3 punctures for air to escape. Now with a small piece of hot wood, a bit of paper between, and a little pressure, you will easily master the blistered part. In making a star panel, or so many feathers graduating from a centre, it answers well to lay every alternate veneer, such as 1, 3, 5, and 7, in an 8-section panel.

To lay veneers on panel of foot end of bedstead, shoot the joints and lay alternate pieces, leaving them till quite dry. When dry, shoot the remaining pieces in. This will make good joints, and the curls will not shrink when dry. The curls can only be laid by hammer, and must not be jointed dry.

The difficult process of butt-jointing curls of Spanish or Cuban mahogany is thus described by Cowan :—

There are 3 or 4 ways of butt-jointing curls; but the only sure and certain way is by crossing the joint with a piece of inch deal. First flatten about 7 in. of the veneer from the butt with hot wood cauls or zinc plates; when gripped, dry the rest of the veneer carefully, it is so liable to crack and buckle with the fire; when set and cool, joint both on shooting board, keeping them in their natural position if you wish them well matched, but before shooting damp 1 in. of the wood from the end on both sides, and give them 10 minutes to swell, else your joint, when made, will be close in the middle and off at the ends. When shot to a joint, try, as directed in straight jointing, then take down on flat board, take a piece of soft wood 2 in. wide, warm (not hot), and glue on to the joint with pressure, in half an hour you can loose it and turn it over and see if your joint is perfection, if so you may proceed with the laying. This time you must warm your ground, and in the middle only, and glue sharp a belt 2 in. wide corresponding to the piece of deal glued on the veneer, fix quick with 2 hand-screws previously set to the size, so that there be no bungling at the critical moment. Now you may more leisurely proceed to lay the tail ends. Have 2 cauls in readiness, the size (all cauls ought to be larger than the veneer, as the heat leaves the edges first, and if the glue gets set at the edges, it will not move freely from the centre; the result is lumpy, bad work), and hot as fire can make them—as before, have your hand-screws set to the size; get help, and the quicker you get them on (one at a time) the better the work. Begin at the centre, and work out to the ends; before cauling, raise the veneer and glue the ground well; see that the glue-brush reaches the central glueing. Now all being screwed up, see there is no slackness in any one of the hand-screws, for much depends on the uniformity of the pressure. Leave to cool for 2 hours. When the screws are taken off, leave the work face down, on a wood floor for 2 days. At the expiration of that time you may remove the piece of deal from off the joint by planing, and not by heat or water; when the planing gets near to the veneer, use the toothed plane. As curls frequently pull hollow on the face, it is desirable to damp the ground on both sides, and before quite dry, size the face side, and this ought to be done so that the damping and the sizing are not quite dry at the time of laying. To ensure good work, veneering should be 2 or 3 weeks in a dry warm place previous to cleaning off. The neglect of this mars all previous painstaking. (*Amateur Work.*)

Cleaning off consists in planing, scraping, and sandpapering the veneers ready for varnishing or polishing. When the veneer is not excessively thin, it is planed with a hardwood hand-plane set very fine. If too thin to admit of this, it is gone over with a steel scraper, having a blade about $4\frac{1}{2}$ in. long by 3 in. wide, and as thick as a saw. The 4 edges of the scraper are ground and set in the following manner. First they are treated on a grindstone, to make the edge quite square in its width, but a little bevelled (convex) in its length. The burr produced by this operation is removed by rubbing the edges and sides on an oilstone. This done, a slight barb is given to each edge by means of a sharpener consisting of a hard polished steel rod, 4 in. long and $\frac{1}{4}$ in. thick, set in an awl handle, and applied at an angle to the edge of the scraper with heavy outward strokes, the scraper being meanwhile held against a bench by the other hand. Each edge is sharpened in the same way, and will bear 5 or 6 repetitions of the process before regrinding becomes necessary. The scraper is applied to the work with drawing strokes, being held by the fingers and thumbs of both hands. When the planing and scraping are complete, the work is finished by using Nos. $1\frac{1}{2}$, 1, and 0 sandpaper successively.

Inlaying.—Inlaying is a term applied to work in which certain figures which have been cut out of one kind of material are filled up with another. Such work is known as marquetry, Boule work, or Reisner work. The simplest method of producing inlaid work in wood, is to take 2 thin boards, of wood, or veneers, and glue them together with paper between, so that they may be easily separated again. Then, having drawn the required figures on them, cut along the lines with a very fine, hair-like saw. This process is known as counterpart sawing, and by it the pieces removed from one piece of wood, so exactly correspond with the perforations in the other piece, that when the two are separated and interchanged, the one material forms the ground and the other the inlay or pattern. If the saw be fine and the wood very dry when cut, but afterwards slightly damped when glued in its place, the joint is visible only on very close inspection, and then merely as a fine line. After being cut, the boards or veneers are separated (which is easily done by splitting the paper between them), and then glued in their places on the work which they are to ornament.

A new method of inlaying is as follows:—A veneer of the same wood as that of which the design to be inlaid consists—say sycamore—is glued entirely over the surface of any hard wood, such as American walnut, and allowed to dry thoroughly. The design is then cut out of a zinc plate about $\frac{1}{20}$ in. in thickness, and placed upon the veneer. The whole is now subjected to the action of steam, and made to travel between 2 powerful cast-iron rollers 8 in. in diameter by 2 ft. long, 2 above and 2 below, which may be brought within any distance of each other by screws. The enormous pressure to which the zinc plate is subjected forces it completely into the veneer, and the veneer into the solid wood beneath it, while the zinc curls up out of the matrix it has thus formed and comes away easily. All that now remains to be done is to plane down the veneer left untouched by the zinc until a thin shaving is taken off the portion forced into the walnut, when the surface being perfectly smooth, the operation will be completed. It might be supposed that the result of this forcible compression of the woods would leave a ragged edge, but this is not the case, the joint being so singularly perfect as to be inappreciable to the touch ; indeed, the inlaid wood fits more accurately than by the process of fitting, matching, and filling up with glue, as is practised in the ordinary mode of inlaying.

Imitation Inlaying.—Suppose an oak panel with a design inlaid with walnut is wanted. Grain the panel wholly in oil. This is not a bad ground for walnut. When the oak is dry, grain the whole of the panel in distemper. Have a paper with the design drawn thereon, the back of which has been rubbed with whiting, place it on the panel, and with a pointed stick trace the design. Then with a brush and quick varnish trace the whole of the design. When the varnish is dry, with a sponge and water remove the distemper, where the varnish has not touched. This, if well executed, presents a most beautiful imitation of inlaid wood.

Examples.—It will be useful to conclude this section with diagrams and descriptions of a few representative articles in cabinet-making.

Couch.—The style of frame illustrated in Fig. 688 is known as German. The main points to be observed in constructing a couch are (1) let the height of the scroll be a convenient one to give the head repose, (2) let the "roll over" be so arranged that a "break

688.

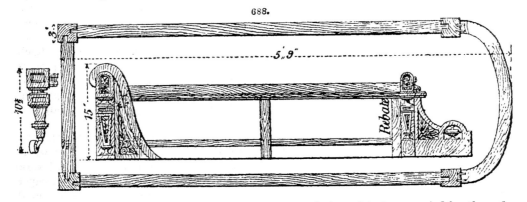

back" result is avoided, and (3) have the vacuum, that used to be occupied by the sofa pillow, filled up. As the head or shoulders frequently seek rest in the corner of the couch, let no obtrusive "show wood" work come in contact with them. Stuffing along the top of the back is the easiest way to secure comfort, but a moulded back may with care be equally successful. In the annexed illustrations the attempt is made to preserve the fashionable squareness without sacrificing the comfort of the "German cabriole" style. The manner of executing this design may be thus epitomized. Having selected suitable wood, and carefully made the moulds from the scale given, get out the long side rails, mortise the feet, and tenon the long rails; after laying moulding slips on same, glue and frame the feet on to the end of the long rails; then lay slips on end rails, cut off to length, and cross frame to 2 end rails. The slip for the elliptic end must next be laid, after which dowel the end to the 2 end feet. This will complete the groundwork of the structure and pave the way for building up the scrolls and back. Use 2-in. stuff for the front and 1½-in. for the back scroll, and after laying glueing on the front scroll, place the scroll on the end of the seat, and fix them with loose dowels, then mark off for the cross rails of the scroll (the position of which is indicated in drawing), glue the scrolls on the cross rails, and then dowel and glue them on to the seat of the couch. The next portion is the back; the "stump," demanding first attention, can be dowelled or mortised into position at once; the length of top rail is thus definitely arrived at, and it simply remains to get out and fix it, as also the stuffing rail below. Iron or wooden battens should be fixed across the seat, and the couch frame is complete.

Chairs.—To make a comfortable chair some respect must be paid to the measurements of the human body in a sitting posture. Thus in a man 5 ft. 9 in. high, the distance from heel to beneath knee-joint will be 18 in.; from knee-joint to bottom of back, 21 in.; from bottom of back to shoulder-blades, 22-23 in.; thence to back of poll 6-7 in. These indicate the dimensions desirable in the legs, seat, and back of the chair, the legs being somewhat shortened in the case of easy chairs.

Fig. 689 well illustrates the construction of a strong comfortable dining-room chair. The requisite suitable wood having been procured it is dealt with as follows:—Having first of all got out the back and 2 back feet, mortise and tenon them, putting them together loose. This will give the pitch or angle of the complete back, and allow of "fits" being made for the top and splat; then mortise and tenon both the latter again, fit up the whole of the back loose, and if the joints are close and satisfactory, nothing now prevents the glueing up of this part of the chair. The next portion to proceed with is the front; either mark off the front rail with a square and straight-edge, or make a fit, which is more convenient. The square end or templet shown can then be used for mortising and tenoning the front, and the front end of side rails. It will be noticed that the back tenons are not square; they "spring in" slightly towards the chair. This is necessary in such a shaped seat for ease in cramping, because if made square, when the chair was cramped up the tenons would break up. It is only in marking these tenons that the angle end of the templet proves useful, the square end being used for all the other joints in the chair. The close braces shown in the drawing are merely fitted and screwed into position. They are introduced more for the sake of appearance than for utility, for a well-made chair should not need such aids to strength. In this shape of chair, mortising and tenoning are secured throughout, whilst a comfortable line adapted to the body is also obtained. This is one advantage of having the back feet to "run out," or go to the top of the chair, because it makes the mortising of the top possible, whereas in put-on tops recourse must be had to dowels, which are always more or less unreliable. The importance of well-seasoned wood need scarcely be urged; more especially let the wood be dry upon which the tenons are made, for this reason, if the mortised wood should be a little fresh it will shrink to the former, and thus make the tenons hold the tighter.

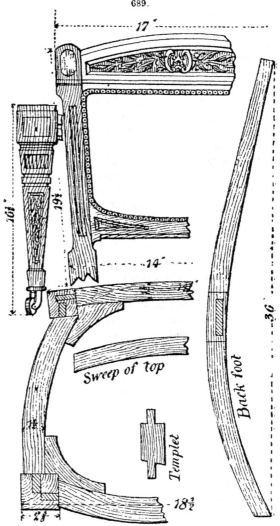

Fig. 690 represents a show-wood gentlemen's easy chair, whose construction may be summarized as follows:—Having cut all the wood to the required dimensions, proceed to mortise and tenon the back feet, top, and splat to the back, putting them together loose to test the fitting. When the back is built up, get out the beech rails and lay the moulding slips; make the mortices and tenons and put in the side rails, front and cross-frame seat to the back. Shape the arms to sleeve-board pattern, wider in front than at back. Glue and screw the moulding piece underneath them; and then loosely mortise and tenon the small end of the arm into the back, doing the same with the turned stump, which latter should be lapped over the side rail of the seat to give perfect strength, as if only dowelled or mortised on the top it is apt to get loose. The under bracket may next be marked off and shaped, then secured to both back and arm, and all glued up completely. Rebate pieces are screwed in at the sides of the back, but are not needed at the top and splat, as sufficient wood remains for the upholsterer to tack to. In this class of chair it is difficult to secure perfect head rest without carrying the back so high as to let the stuffing come under the poll; but a stuff over back may be made by putting beech rails into the back and having the rise flat on top.

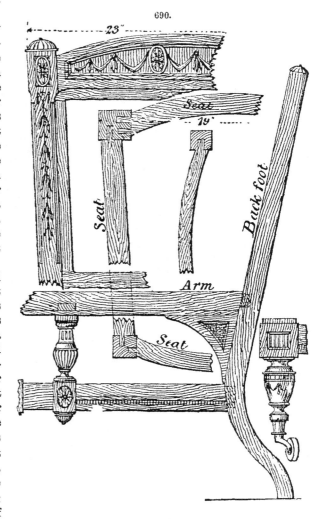

Fig. 691 shows a ladies' easy chair to match the last mentioned, and made in the same way, the dimensions and design only differing. Some makers are in favour of dowelling rather than mortising and tenoning, as taking away less wood; but unless the dowels are dry, the fitting is perfect, and the glue is good, "rickets" will soon follow. A simple protection for a dowel joint is to plaster a piece of strong canvas over. Still dowels may give way, while a tenon with a pin through it cannot.

In the divan chair illustrated in Fig. 692, the frame is set out to allow for what is known as double stuffing, or spring edges to seat. The making of such a frame is a simple matter, and may be briefly described as follows:—First make a mould for the back, taking care that it is a nice graceful line; no other mould will be required for the job, as the rest of the pieces are perfectly straight. Get out stuff to the thickness indicated, and then fit up the back, square the top and bottom, as shown; leave 4½ in. between the top of the seat and the stuffing rail to allow for the double stuffing mentioned above. If the chair is to be upholstered in the ordinary way, with the usual thickness of rolls, only 2 in. need be allowed between these rails. Having thus got the back up, glue and frame up the front, and then cross-frame the chair together from back to front. In fitting the spindle stump which supports the arm, the best plan is to first fit the arm on the stump, a pin having been left on the latter, which may be allowed to come right through the arm, and can thus be wedged in the top when finally fixed. Before fixing, however, mortise and lap over the square lower portion of the stump on to the side rails; when properly adjusted, the arms can be glued up, and the chair frame is complete. It is as well to place an iron batten under the seat to give extra strength. An excellent plan to finish off a frame of this kind is to glue over the joints a strong piece of canvas; thus protected, the "rickets' are almost impossible, even if the stuff is a little "fresh." Either dowels, or mortising and tenoning, may be employed in the manufacture. The sizes given will answer equally well for a similar chair with "stuffed-in" arms. If, however, the latter are required to be full in the stuffing, an extra 2 in. should be allowed in width of seat. For a ladies' chair to go with this, the same moulds and proportions will do, if made 2 in. less all ways (except in height of legs, which may be about the same). As a rule, ladies' chairs are better without arms, in consequence of the extensive character of the dresses sometimes adopted. Arms are possible and comforting, if made 12 or 14 in. long, to catch the elbows. If an extra amount of ease is required in any of the foregoing chairs, they should be made with a seat sloping from front to back; 1 in. longer in the front legs, and ½ in. shorter in the back, will give a desirable angle of comfort. It must be remembered that the joints in the side rails will require adjusting in order to suit this angle.

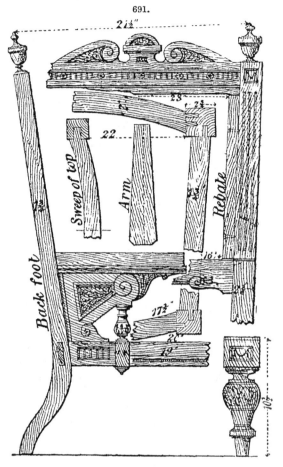

691.

The gossip chair represented in Fig. 693 is measured for single stuffing. The seat has an oval form, and the arms and back are adapted to almost closely encircle the sitter. No support is provided for the head. First make the moulds, then get out the beech rails and frame the seat up. In this shape of seat it is difficult to mortise and tenon, in consequence of the cross grain that would be involved; recourse must there-

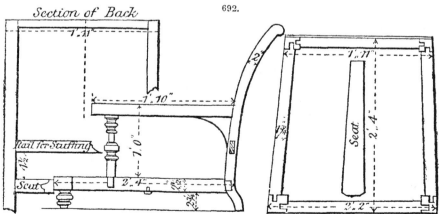

692.

fore be had to dowels, and if they are judiciously placed, great strength will be secured. Having squared the legs and fitted the 4 parts to them with dowels, the seat can be glued up in the following way :—First glue up and knock together a short and long rail with 2 legs, and then the other 2 rails can be similarly treated ; the 2 corners will then more easily come together to the remaining legs. After glueing and knocking up, the seat must be cramped in order to perfectly close the joints. Two methods are adopted in the trade, the first of which is a long cramp from side to side, with another from end

693.

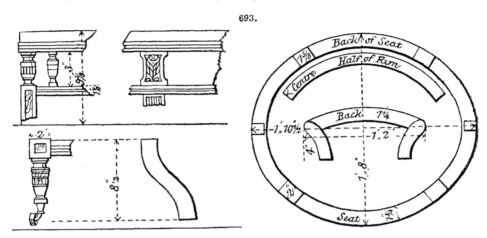

to end of seat; this is a simple way and answers very well for a single article. But if a number of such chairs have to be made, the " collar method " is more convenient. A collar is a piece of beech arranged so as to lap over seat rail, top and bottom, with an iron pin through the overlapping parts and seat rail. The swivel action thus allows the collar to be brought round so as to find a bearing on the seat rail ; and when another collar is fixed to the adjoining rail in the same way, and the ends of the 2 collars are cramped up, the joints are brought together most effectively without any straining of the dowels. One pin-hole in the middle of each rail will give the needful angle for the leverage of the collars. The next stage in the work is to get out rims, viz. the 2 show-wood mouldings and the beech capping for the top. After placing stumps on the seat, lapped through as indicated, the rims must be fitted up to the stump and the banister underneath fitted loose. The spindles, rims, and centre bracket, having been carefully adjusted, can now be glued up together ; and after placing the small supporting bracket on, the seat may be glued and cramped up to the stumps already in position. The foundation of the chair being perfectly sound, the joints clean, and the work free from rickets, the 2 scroll pieces can be dowelled on to the top of beech rim, and the adjustment of the top stuffing rail between the scrolls is then a simple task. Two or three dowels running through the upper beech rim and show-wood moulding will permanently bind them together. This style of chair will come out effectively without the addition of the upper scroll pieces and stuffing rail, leaving merely a stuffed pad all round ; or, instead of spindles and show-wood stumps and mouldings, it may be made entirely of beech and "stuffed in " all over.

Fig. 694 is a combination of an all stuff over and a show-wood gossip chair. The arms can be made just plain "sweeps," without the turning as shown ; but the latter gives an ornamental and novel appearance not otherwise obtainable. A piece left on these side arms when the stuff is cut out makes it a simpler matter for the turner to find his centre. Get out moulds, then the rails, legs, &c., and lay the slips ; then let a carver do the mouldings ; after this frame the back feet on to the back rail, and the front legs on to the front rail : the 2 latter, as may be observed, being square joints. Now find the angle of the side. This may be done in the following manner. The line of the outside of the side rail will be found to be $2\frac{1}{4}$ in. out of square; this gives a $2\frac{1}{4}$ -in.

angle, to which "the bevel" may be set, by simply measuring 2¼ in. from a straight line 17 in. long (length of side rail), and setting the "bevel" to angle-line thus obtained. Having adjusted the angle, the seat may be cross-framed together. This pattern of seat can be readily mortised and tenoned together, as shown, if desired, although dowels are usually applied in making such chairs in the trade. Dowelling being the quicker

694.

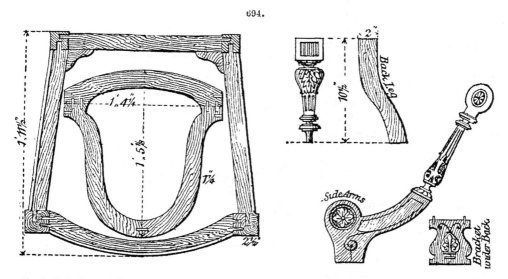

method, it is invariably adopted where price is an object. The back is made of beech, no show-wood being required in it. It can be got out and framed up independently of the other portions, there being the 3 joints in the back indicated. Before fitting the back to the arms and seat, get out the support or banister shown under the back; place it on the seat; then dowel and glue the back and banister on to the seat. The angle or pitch of the back would be determined by applying the mould of the arm and the slope desired for ease. The arms having been already got out, turned, and carved, the fitting of the seat to the back is a simple matter. Some care is necessary in placing the dowels, fixing the side arms to the back; the position shown in the sketch is, perhaps, the most reliable.

Fig. 695 illustrates the wooden frame necessary for an adult easy chair in needle-work. The construction is extremely simple. The first step is to strike out a good set of moulds, taking care to secure a nice easy line; then get out wood for the sides, allowing for the rebate as shown by the dotted line.

695.

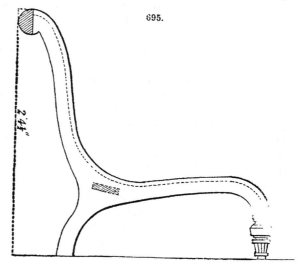

It is then wise to let the carver do as much of his work to the sides as he can. After obtaining the pieces from him, dowel, glue, and cramp up the back, feet, and sides. The cross rails can now be got out to the size indicated, let into the sides at the points shown, and the chair framed up. The front feet of these chairs are usually dowelled on, and, if well done, they are fairly durable. A strong pin left on the leg, square or round, as the case may be, is another method. Having added the front legs, let the carver finish the incising; clean off, and the chair is made.

Bookcase (Folding).—Fig. 696 illustrates the construction of a folding portable book-case, which may be carved and ornamented to any degree. The 2 ends *a* are 4 ft. long over all and 1 ft. wide, either of plain board, or panelled as shown; uprights *b*, 3½ in. wide and 1 in. thick, are fastened to the front, and similar ones *c*, 2¼ in. by ¾ in. to the back. Cross pieces are dovetailed into the bottoms, of the same width as the uprights, and similar ones are mortised into the tops, thus forming shallow boxes. The top board of the bookcase is hinged at one end underneath one cross piece, and folds down parallel to that end piece, allowing suffi-cient space behind it to contain

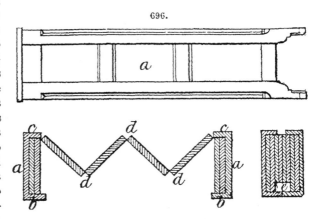

696.

one of the shelves. The bottom board forming the lowest shelf is hinged to the cross piece at the bottom of the other end piece, with sufficient space to admit the second shelf behind it. As the bookcase is 3 ft. 6 in. wide, the back may consist of 4 boards hinged together as at *d*, and folding neatly up. The space *e* will hold the ornamental baluster railing fitted to the top, and which is held in place when the bookcase is up by shallow tenons mortised into the uprights *b*. The shelves are held up by shallow tenons. The back is made of $\frac{5}{8}$-in. wood; the ends and shelves are ¾ in.

Chest of Drawers.—The following detailed and illustrated description of the con-struction of a chest of drawers has been modified from one which appeared some time since in *Amateur Mechanics*. The example here given consists of a base, surbase, and top carcase or body. In the usual method of structure, a large part of the work is veneered, the whole front included. The gables and top are solid, usually bay mahogany, $\frac{5}{8}$ in. thick, the top being clamped on the under side with pine to 1½ in. thick, and veneered round the edges to cover the whole. The breadth across the front is 4 ft. 1 in., and the depth from front to back, 20 in. at the body or upper carcase. The base, which may be called the foundation course, is 5 in. high, having 4 ball feet under it; these raise it 3 in. from the floor. Over this base is the surbase, made to contain a large drawer, 12 in. deep on the face, and having the mouldings mitred on the face of it. The fronts of these bases have semicircular blocks on the ends, that on the base being 6 in. broad, and that on the surbase 5 in. broad; the ends of the drawer are fitted exactly between these 2 latter. The surbase is screwed to the base, and the latter pro-jects beyond the former ½ in. all round. The surbase is surmounted by a "thumb" moulding, $\frac{7}{8}$ in. thick, and over this is placed the body or top carcase. This contains 5 drawers; their depths on the face, starting from the bottom, being 9½ in., 8½ in., 7½ in., 6½ in., and the uppermost, that with the carving, 5 in. The top over this last drawer is 1½ in. thick, the total height being 5 ft. 4 in. The base is made of $\frac{7}{8}$-in. pine, and is veneered all round. The surbase has solid gables $\frac{3}{4}$ in. thick, and the semicircular front blocks veneered. The top carcase has a "ground" up each side at the ends of the drawers. This, including the thickness of the gables, is 3½ in. broad and 2 in. thick. The faces of these grounds are veneered. At the top of the grounds are semicircular blocks, 6 in. long, at the end of the top drawer, and the top over all projects all round

1 in. It is fixed on by mortice and tenon, the tenons being cut on the ends of the gables. It has also circular blocks in front. The fore edges of the shelves between the drawers are $\frac{7}{8}$ in. thick finished. The shelves are dovetailed into the thick grounds in front, raggled into the gables, and made fast by blockings glued in underneath. The various moving drawers have fronts made of 1-in. pine, sides and backs $\frac{5}{8}$ in., and bottoms $\frac{3}{8}$ in. The fronts are covered with showy veneer; the most showy, but not the most durable, being those known as curls. These are short cuts of the log, having a strong feathery-like appearance diverging from the centre. They are usually about 2 ft. long, and the practice is to take 2, cut from each other, to make a drawer front, they being marked, when sawing, for this purpose. The drawer front has consequently a butt joint in the centre, the spreading ends of the pieces being carefully jointed, so that the same figure or marks in the veneer will appear going both ways from this centre joint. These veneers are very showy, but they are very apt, after a time, to get full of cracks, and with age they become very dark in colour. The drawer fronts are surrounded by a "cope" bead, $\frac{1}{8}$ in. thick, and projecting from the face of the veneer half that thickness.

In the construction of the chest of drawers, Fig. 697, the first work is making the base. This is 4 ft. 3$\frac{1}{2}$ in. long, 1 ft. 10$\frac{1}{2}$ in. broad, and 5 in. deep, made of $\frac{7}{8}$-in. pine. The method of procedure is as follows:—Make a front *a* 5 in. broad, a back *b* 4 in. broad; plane both sides, and to an equal thickness throughout; square both ends to a length of 4 ft. 3 in.; plane and square up 2 end pieces *c* in the same way, 5 in. broad, 22$\frac{1}{2}$ in. long when squared up. The front and back are dovetailed into the ends, keeping the back flush on the upper side. The ends have a lip $\frac{1}{4}$ in. thick, or, in other words, they are not dovetailed through, but made exactly as is done with a drawer front; consequently, when the base is put together, it is 4 ft. 3$\frac{1}{2}$ in. long. This dovetailing is shown at *d*, where one of the circular blocks *e* is removed. It is, of course, covered up when these blocks are glued in their places. The object of not dovetailing through is to avoid having end wood on the surface at any part to be covered with veneer. This rule holds good in all veneered surfaces—namely, avoid having end wood and side wood in the same veneering surface, as they do not shrink alike: in fact, end wood does not shrink at all; consequently in a short time any such portion covered by veneer is detected, as it stands above the surrounding surface. There are cases in which this cannot be avoided, but in most cases it can be guarded against.

The base being dovetailed and glued together is to be "filled in." This filling in consists of pieces *f* of $\frac{7}{8}$-in. wood fitted inside the base at the front and ends, and flush with the upper edges. The front piece is 2$\frac{1}{4}$ in. broad, and is fitted in neatly between the ends. The end pieces, which are broad enough if 1$\frac{1}{2}$ in., are fitted in between the back of the base and the edge of the front piece, glued in and pressed close with hand-screws. Then the base is turned over, and the angle formed by the base and the filling in is filled at intervals of 5 in. or 6 in. with blockings 3 in. long. A portion of the base blocked in this way is shown at *g*. The glueing surfaces of these blockings are about 1$\frac{1}{2}$ in. broad. In planing them, these 2 sides must be at right angles, and roughened with the toothing plane. When the glue has set quite hard, the base is planed straight and level with a half-long plane, the ends being made square with the front, and these toothed ready for veneering.

The surbase, which rests upon the base just described, is 12 in. high, and consists of 2 gables, either of solid mahogany or pine veneered. In either case, the grain of the wood runs vertically. These gables should be $\frac{7}{8}$ in. thick, but, if of solid mahogany, they are seldom made more than $\frac{5}{8}$ in., in which case they are clamped on the inside with pine to make up the thickness. The breadth of the gables is 1$\frac{1}{2}$ in. less than the base below, not including the blocks, and in the back edges a check is made to receive a $\frac{5}{8}$-in. back lining.

The next operation is to make 2 frames of $\frac{7}{8}$-in. pine, to form a top and bottom to

697.

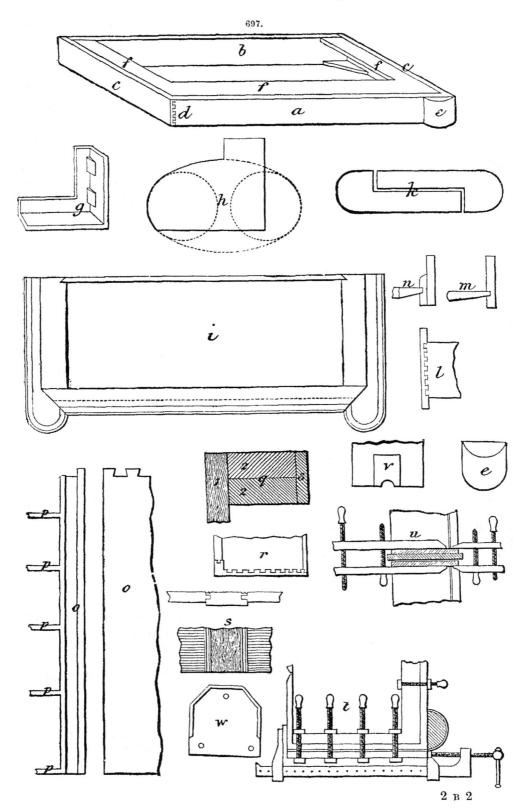

these gables; they are of a length to make the surbase 1 in. shorter than the base beneath, so that the base projects all round ½ in. beyond the surbase—that is, when the drawer front is in its place. The breadth of the frames is the distance from the front of the gables to the check for the back lining. Each frame consists of a front and back rail, 3 in. broad, and 2 cross rails 5 in. broad, let into the former by mortice and tenon. The ends of the front and back rails being dovetailed into the gables, the cross rails fit inside these, and are then made more secure by having blockings of wood glued in the angles.

Two semicircular blocks are made of several layers of pine glued together as described for the base blocks. They are 5 in. broad on the back, the semicircle being drawn with compasses set to 2½ in. The block is 3½ in. thick, however, the additional inch being to allow for the thickness of drawer front, so that when this front is in its place the blocks show but 2½ in. projecting. These blocks are veneered, dried, planed and scraped, then carefully fitted to the face of the surbase and glued down. The veneer on the block where it joins the edge of the gable must be a good joint and both flush, as the veneer, being thin, it will not allow of much reducing when cleaning off.

When this surbase is made, it should fit on to the lower base and show a margin of ½ in. along the ends and round the blocks, and 1½ in. along the central portion or drawer space. The upper side of the surbase is capped with a moulding, usually a "thumb." This moulding h is a section of an ellipse. For the chest of drawers it is made of ⅞-in. mahogany, and in order to economize that wood the necessary breadth is made up with pine, the two being glued together previously to running the thumb. The breadth of mahogany required is 1½ in. backed by 2 in. of pine. i shows the upper side of the surbase with the line of junction of pine and mahogany, also the manner of mitring at the inner corner of the circular blocks. In ordinary chests of drawers the portions of thumb moulding covering the blocks are composed of a piece of ⅞-in. mahogany turned in the lathe, and afterwards cut in halves, which do for both blocks. The portion of moulding along the front is mitred at the corners to these semicircular pieces, and the end pieces are butt-jointed behind them.

In a first-class chest of drawers, however, they are done differently. A piece of mahogany is cut large enough to make both pieces for the end mouldings and the circular portion over the blocks in one. k shows the method of cutting the one out of the other usually pursued. The thumb in this case is worked by hand, and the pieces do not require backing with pine. These mouldings are toothed on the under side, and glued on to the base, a few screws being put in after the hand-screws are removed. This base receives a ⅝-in. back lining, but it is not put on until a drawer is made and fitted in. The drawer front is of pine, "slipped" with a piece of Bay mahogany on the upper edge. This slipping is a process that has to be noticed. A piece of mahogany is cut about 1 in. broad and ½ in. or ¾ in. thick, as free from warping and bending as possible. It is truly planed on one side, and toothed. The edge of the drawer front is also planed perfectly straight with half-long plane, and toothed. Then, with the drawer front in the bench lug, the slip of mahogany is wetted with a sponge, and turning its toothed side up, and on a level with the edge of the pine front, both receive a coating of glue quickly applied. The slip is turned over on the edge of the front and rubbed firmly backwards and forwards lengthways, 2 persons being necessary for the operation. The sliding motion is gradually lessened till it stops with the slip in its proper place, when a few smart rubs with a veneering hammer complete the operation. In most cases a slip thus laid will be found to adhere perfectly in its whole length. When the front is dry, it is planed up and fitted exactly in its place; care must be taken to have the heart side of the plank turned to the front for veneering upon. This drawer front is 12 in. broad, and when in its place rests upon the 2 ½-in. fore edges forming the frame of the surbase. The drawer sides pass between these fore edges, and are consequently only 10¼ in. broad, the extra breadth of front projecting ⅞ in. downwards, and the same upwards of the sides, as in *l*, which shows the drawer side as dovetailed into the front. The drawer sides are ⅝ in. thick, often made of pine, sometimes of American ash, but the best wood of all is cedar, as the strong but not unpleasant odour emitted is a sure preventive of moth. A groove run in ⅝-in. wood *m* for a drawer bottom makes the side very weak. A very great improvement is the fillet clamped to the inside of the drawer side *n*, and the groove run in it.

The carcase consists of 2 gables *o* of solid mahogany, usually ⅝ in., but they ought to be at least ¾ in. thick. The breadth to make these gables is ¼ in. less than the breadth of the upper side of the surbase—that is, ¼ in. within the thumb moulding. The length of the gables is sufficient to admit 5 drawers of the following breadths—namely, 9½, 8½, 7½, 6½, and 5 in., with ⅞-in. fore edges or shelves *p* between, and 1 in. additional to cut into pins or tenons to enter the top, which should show straight pins not dovetailed.

The 2 gables are planed up on both sides, "thicknessed," made to the breadth, squared on the bottom ends, and marked off on the insides for grooves to receive the shelves. The rabbet plane used is 1⅜ in., and the depth of groove is ¼ in. A guide for the plane is made by "stitching" with tacks a thin lath of wood to the gable alongside the groove to be run. These grooves being run, the bottom ends are dovetailed—not through—to receive a ⅞-in. carcase bottom, and the top ends are squared and cut into pins as already mentioned. Two grounds have now to be built to clamp on the inside of the gables. These are of pine, faced on the inner edges with mahogany, as indicated by the lines shown vertically in *q*. The method of building these grounds is to clamp 2 pieces of ⅞-in. or 1-in. wood together for the thickness, as this stands better than one piece. Next a piece of ⅞-in. Bay mahogany is planed up and toothed on both sides. The edges of the ground pieces are also planed straight and toothed. The mahogany is heated on both sides, and, glue being applied to both pieces of pine, the mahogany is placed between them and several hand-screws are applied. When this is hard, it is planed up and sawn through the centre of the mahogany, making a pair of grounds with mahogany slips about ⅜ in. thick when finished.

The grounds are planed to such a breadth that when glued to the gables the total breadth of face is 3½ in. *q* is a cross section of this arrangement of pieces; 1 is a portion of the gable, say ¾ in. thick; 2, the two thicknesses of pine, 2⅜ in. broad and 2 in. thick; and 3, the clamp or slip of mahogany, ⅜ in. thick. After these grounds are fixed to the gables they are squared with the gables on the face, and the inner edge is squared with the face. Then they are drawn for dovetails to receive the shelves in a line with the grooves in the gables. The dovetail is all on the under side of the shelves, and enters into the ground about ⅝ in. As these shelves must be quite level in their whole breadth to allow the drawers to run smoothly, great care must be taken to cut the dovetails in the grounds with exactitude. Otherwise the shelf when entering the dovetail will be bent up or down, as the case may be, and it is hardly possible to make a good fit of the drawers in such a carcase.

The shelves are not of one thickness, or one board throughout their breadth, but are known as "clamped" shelves. About 3 in. of the front portion is ⅞-in. wood, the remainder being ⅜-in. wood clamped at the ends with pieces of ½-in. wood, which makes them up to ⅞ in. The two are joined with matched ploughs glued, and clamped; they are carefully made of a thickness to fit the grooves in the gables; but, previously to this, the front edge has to receive a facing of mahogany. The general practice is to "band" them—that is, to put on scrap pieces of rich veneer, with the grain running across the thickness of the fore edge. This has a showy effect, but it is false and ridiculous, as a shelf of solid wood put in in this way would be an impossibility. The result of such work is also bad, as pieces of this "banding" get easily chipped off with the pulling out of the drawers. The proper way is to "slip" them with good mahogany, at least $\frac{1}{4}$ in. thick, with the grain of the mahogany running in the same direction as the shelf. This will last for an age without chipping. When the shelves are slipped and got to the proper thickness, the corners are cut out to admit the grounds, and the dovetails worked to fit the latter. The shelves should be fitted pretty tight into the grounds, and when driven home the mahogany slip should project beyond the face of the ground the thickness of a veneer ($\frac{1}{32}$ in.), so that when the grounds are veneered the whole will be flush. The carcase bottom—that is, the lowest shelf that rests upon the surbase—has 1 dovetail into the end of the ground. This will be readily understood by reference to r, which shows a portion of the under side of the carcase. The back edges of gables are checked to receive a back lining, which is nailed to the back edge of the carcase, as shown on the right in r.

The gables, carcase bottom, and shelves being ready, the carcase is put together by glueing and rapping up the carcase bottom first, then the top shelf, and after this the intermediate ones. A cramp is necessary to draw these shelves home, care being taken that they all project beyond the face of grounds only the thickness of veneer as above mentioned. All the shelves have now to be "blocked" on the inside—that is, 3-cornered blockings of wood, with their glueing faces at right angles, are glued in against the shelves and gables. Before these are glued in, the carcase must be tested to see that it is square, and that all the shelves are quite at the bottom of the grooves in the gables. After this is made sure, the blockings, 4 in. long, 3 to each shelf, are rubbed in with hot glue, the first one going forward pretty near the back of the ground. When these are hard the carcase will be perfectly rigid and strong.

It is usual to fit the drawer fronts and make the drawers before making a top. The upper blocks are of the same breadth as the grounds, semicircular on the face, but 1 in. thicker than the half circle, to allow for the drawer front between them, as this front projects 1 in. over those beneath it. These blocks are veneered in one length in a canvas bag, as described for the base blocks. When glued on the grounds, their lower ends are on a level with the upper side of the top shelf. The upper ends are faced with mahogany.

The top of the carcase is $1\frac{1}{2}$ in. thick, being a board of $\frac{5}{8}$-in. mahogany, made up or clamped on the under side with pine 1 in. thick. A piece of pine 5 in. broad is glued along the front; the ends are made up with end cuts of pine 6 in. or 7 in. long. As the grain of all the clamping must run in the direction of the grain of the mahogany, a narrow clamp is fitted between the end ones at the back to nail the back lining to. These clamps are put on with large hand-screws; when hard, the top is planed to thickness and squared at the ends. The front edge of the top is veneered before the 2 semicircular blocks are rubbed on. This veneering of the edge of the top is usually "banding," but it should be done by slipping, as described when treating the base.

The carcase has now to be fitted with drawers. The drawer fronts are of pine $\frac{7}{8}$ in. thick, fitted into the various openings in the carcase perfectly close all round, and with the heart side of each front outward for veneering upon.

The top drawer, that between the 2 semicircular blocks immediately under the top, is slipped on its upper edge with a piece of $\frac{3}{8}$-in. Bay mahogany previously to fitting it in, the same as already mentioned for the 12-in. drawer in the surbase.

The other drawers are not slipped in this way; after they are veneered and cleaned off they receive a $\frac{1}{8}$-in. mahogany beading all round. This is called a "cope bead," and the manner of putting it on will be described. When all the drawer fronts are fitted in, they should be each marked on the face in pencil with a ∧ or similar figure pointing upwards, so that there be no mistakes afterwards in the fitting.

The drawer sides for a first-class job are of cedar $\frac{3}{8}$-in. thick. The grooves for the bottoms should not be run in this $\frac{3}{8}$-in. side for a good job, but in a clamp glued to the side, as shown in n. The drawer backs may be of $\frac{5}{8}$-in. pine, and the bottoms of $\frac{3}{8}$-in. pine, but this thickness would be too weak without a centre mounter.

This mounter is a bar of wood 3 in. broad and $\frac{5}{8}$ in. thick, passing across the centre of the drawer from front to back, and dividing the bottom into halves. It has grooves in its edges to receive the bottom, a pair of $\frac{1}{2}$-in. match ploughs being used—one to make a groove in the mounter, and the other a feather on the edge of the bottom, the whole being flush on the upper or inside. A $\frac{1}{8}$-in. bead is run on the mounter on this inside to abut against the drawer bottoms. This is called breaking the joint, and makes a neat finish inside the drawer. *s* shows this mounter and bottoms, the manner of grooving in, and the upper or inner side with the beaded joint.

The drawer fronts have a groove, corresponding to those in the sides, to receive the bottoms. The backs are so much narrower, and the bottoms nailed to them by $1\frac{1}{2}$-in. brads. The direction of the grain of these bottoms runs lengthway of the drawers; consequently the end wood of the bottoms enters the grooves in sides and mounters.

The drawers are dovetailed, and put together in the usual manner. The bottoms are put in and filleted—that is, fillets are rubbed in with glue in the junction of the sides and bottoms, and afterwards planed off flush with the edges and sides, a few short ones being glued along the front in the same way. Of these latter, one at each and is of mahogany, or other hard wood, these being to act against "stops" nailed to the shelves in the carcase, to stop the drawers at their proper places.

It may be mentioned that fillets for drawer bottoms are in many cases omitted, and in good jobs, too, particularly when the bottoms are of American ash, which wood is very liable to shrink or expand with dry or damp situations, and the bottoms are left unfilleted to allow of this movement. But if the wood is as well seasoned as it should be, little or no change in the breadth of the bottoms will take place, and a drawer is infinitely better filleted.

When fitting the drawers in the carcase, no more should be taken off the breadth of the drawer sides than will just admit them between the shelves, as when too much is planed off at first they can never be a satisfactory job. The proper method is to plane the under side of the drawers—which is the edges of the sides and fillets, and also the short fillets along the front—all even and flush, using a straight-edge to get these 2 edges in relation to each other to be out of winding. Then set a gauge to the breadth of the drawer front, and gauge the breadth of the sides from the bottom. When the sides are planed down to this mark, they should enter the opening between the shelves, though somewhat tightly. Next the 2 sides or ends of the drawers are planed down till the end wood of the front and back are touched at the dovetails. The drawers should enter the carcase lengthway as well as breadthway. They are all pushed in in this way, till the fronts are nearly flush with the face of the carcase; the fronts are drawn all round with a draw-point, and planed down on the bench to this mark. The method is to place 2 pieces of board across the bench, letting them project over the front 7 or 8 in., and fastening them at the back with hand-screws. The drawer is hung on the ends of the boards, with its fore end fixed in the bench lug, and in this position is planed and toothed. When planing, the front must be perfectly level across the ends. It will do no harm if a little round at the centre; the veneer has a tendency to draw the face hollow after a time.

As a rule, the base is veneered on what is termed the "banding" system—that is, the grain of the veneer runs up and down, not the lengthway of the base. This is a false principle in construction, because a base made of solid wood, with the grain upright, would be simply ridiculous. The method is resorted to for 2 reasons: It is easier done; and it is a means of using up small pieces of broken veneer, as any may be used if long enough to cover the breadth of the base.

Two blocks have now to be made for this base, similar to the one shown detached at *e*. They are 6 in. broad, 3 in. thick, semicircular on the ends, and are better built of several layers of wood, as shown in the figure, as they do not split or change their shape so readily as when made in one piece; 3 pieces, long enough to make both blocks, are glued together, drawn on the ends with compasses, and carefully planed down to a semicircle, after which they are toothed for veneering. Before veneering, these blocks should be sized with a coat of very thin hot glue applied all over the surface to be veneered upon. When this is quite dry it is again lightly toothed. The best method to veneer these blocks is with a canvas bag and screws (see Fig. 687, p. 235). This method is only suitable when the rest of the base is veneered on the banding principle; for the grain of the veneer runs up and down on the block, so it must run in the same direction on the rest of the base. To veneer the base with banding, strip the edges of each piece with the plane on the shooting board; then lay one piece at a time with the veneering hammer. The first piece being laid, the second is fitted against it and rubbed down, pressing against the piece previously laid, to ensure a close joint.

When the veneer is dry, which will be in about 24 hours, the front only is to be planed, scraped, and sandpapered, the over wood at the edges being previously pared off with a sharp chisel. When the veneered piece for blocks is cut in two, a portion of the veneer at the inner edge is planed and papered. The veneer on the front of the base is cut to exactly the breadth of the back of the block, so that the veneer on the block and that on the end of the base will coincide, forming one surface, and, at the same time, a close joint. The blocks thus fitted are glued on, using hand-screws to ensure close contact. When the glue is hard, the upper edges of the base and blocks are planed quite level, and the end wood of the blocks receives a coat of glue size before veneering. A piece of veneer 3 in. broad is laid along the front, and 2 additional pieces over the ends of blocks. The strips of veneer along the ends of the base are 2 in. broad. When the glueing of these is hard, the whole base is cleaned off, scraped, and sandpapered. After which, provision is made for attaching 4 turned feet by fitting 2 3-cornered pieces in the back corners or under side of base, and clamping 2 pieces inside the front, immediately behind the circular blocks. The ball feet have tenons turned on them, which fit into holes bored in the base.

Following is the method of veneering the base of drawers by having the grain of the veneer running in the same direction as the grain of the groundwork. The body or groundwork of the base is made exactly as described, and the 2 blocks are made and sized for veneering. The face of the base is covered with veneer, except at the 2 ends where the blocks are to be stuck on. This veneer should be laid with a caul. When properly hard, it is planed and finished up with sandpaper; then the 2 blocks are fitted exactly in their places against the ends of the front veneer, and glued down without being previously veneered, as in last example.

The task of veneering the blocks and base ends with 1 piece of veneer is shown in *t*. A yellow pine caul is made the length of the base end, not including the semi-circular blocks; then a piece of No. 12 zinc is procured, long enough to reach from the small block of wood at the inner edge of the circular block, round the block itself, along the base end, and round the ends of the caul, as indicated by the double line in the cut. The caul should be 6 in. broad, and the zinc fixed on with tacks along the edges.

A piece of veneer has now to be cut long enough to go round the block and along the base end, with a little margin both in length and breadth. The portion that goes round the block must be well toothed, and scraped on the outside, before putting on. This is to thin it somewhat, as it has to be bent round the block. The next step is to glue a thin piece of cotton cloth on the scraped side of the veneer. This is to prevent it splitting across the grain of the wood while bending. A cut is made with a dovetail saw, close to the inner edge of the block, about $\frac{1}{4}$ in. deep in the face of the base. The end of the veneer is squared and fitted into this cut.

It will be seen, by reference to *t*, that a cramp and hand-screws are brought into use. There are really 10 hand-screws, another 5 being placed exactly opposite those shown in the drawing. All being in readiness, the zinc caul is well heated, and a copious supply of glue applied to the groundwork to be veneered, and a thin coat to the veneer. The end of the latter is fitted into the saw cut above mentioned.

The hot caul is applied by placing the end with the block close to the circular block, and applying 2 hand-screws. Then the zinc with the veneer is bent gently round the block, and when laid along the base end several hand-screws are applied, and lastly the cramp, using a small block of wood at the back to keep the paw clear of the caul end. The exposed portion of the zinc round the block, which cools very quickly, must be heated with a smoothing iron and more pressure applied to the cramp, when the glue should run out at the edges. The hand-screws are then tightened up, when, if the whole thing has been managed properly, the veneer will be lying perfectly close. This caul should stay on for at least 10 or 12 hours, when the same operation may be performed with the other end of the base.

This method of veneering is much more difficult than the slip-shod method of banding with scraps of veneer, but it is a much more tradesmanlike manner of doing it. In short, it is the method of making a first-class piece of furniture, if veneering of any sort can be called first-class work. When the glueing of the base is properly hard, the over-wood at the edges is cleaned off, the upper side is planed level, and veneered as before described.

The veneers for the drawer fronts are bought in sets of 5 or 6. They are cut from each other, and are all of one figure, being numbered by the sawyers; care being taken to place them on the fronts all in the same way, the various markings will appear almost alike in the whole fronts.

The sets of veneers may be so narrow that they will not entirely cover the 12-in. drawer in the surbase, in which case a piece has to be added to the breadth; the joint thus made is easily concealed beneath one of the mouldings to be planted on the face.

If the veneers are of the feathery curl sort, 2 pieces to each front, the butt joint must be exactly in the centre of each, passing through the centre of the keyhole. In order to make this joint properly, the whole of the veneers are placed together exactly as they were when cut at the mill, and held together by 2 pieces of board and 2 hand-screws. The ends to be jointed are squared across, and cut with a dovetail saw all together, and afterwards planed with the iron plane. Then, being taken separately, each pair is carefully fitted to each other. This done, they are laid on a flat board with the joint placed close, and a few tacks driven in at the edges. A piece of thin calico, about 2 in. broad, is now glued along the joint. When this is dry, the veneers may be laid as one piece. Cauls of zinc, $\frac{1}{4}$ in. thick, are best for this job, but very good work may be done with well-oiled pine cauls.

If wooden cauls are used to these fronts, they should remain in the screws not over 2 hours, as any glue adhering to the caul makes it difficult to remove, and some of the veneer is apt to peel off in the removal.

It is usual to veneer 2 of these drawers at a time, the caul being heated on both sides. The hand-screws require to be pretty large, with long jaws. They should be free from hard glue on the jaws, as it makes an unsightly mark on the inside of drawer fronts.

Help must be obtained to heat the caul while glue is applied copiously to the drawer fronts. The veneers must be previously toothed on the glueing side, and marked as they are to be laid. When laid upon the glued front, they are rubbed all over with the hands, and should project over the front $\frac{1}{4}$ in. or so all round. At the places to be afterwards bored for the knobs, 2 tacks are driven through the veneer into the front to prevent them slipping under the hot caul while the hand-screws are being applied. These latter should be set to about the size before glueing, so that no time may be lost afterwards; 6 large hand-screws for the front or inside, and 6 smaller for the back, are necessary to lay veneers on 2 fronts. Those inside the drawers should go quite to the bottom, so that the jaws require to be at least 8 in. long. u gives a clear idea of this part of the work. It shows the 2 fronts with the caul and veneers between, and the hand-screws as applied. In applying the hand-screws to work of this kind, it is to be observed that the whole length of the jaws must bear equally on the breadth of surface pressed between them, as if they press only at the points, or at the heel, they are comparatively ineffective.

When the veneers have dried for about 24 hours they may be cleaned off. They are always planed first with a high-pitched hand-plane, set very close, then scraped and sandpapered. The drawer in the surbase and that at the top are neatly fitted into their places. They should pull easily backwards and forwards and yet appear quite close both in length and breadth. The accuracy with which they are fitted when finished is a mark of excellence in the workmanship.

The 4 intermediate drawers receive cope beads. After the fronts are planed and sandpapered they are pushed in about $\frac{1}{8}$ in. beyond the face of the carcase, when a small gauge is made to gauge the thickness to check for the beads. This gauge is a small block of hard wood with a steel point in it fully $\frac{1}{8}$ in. from the edge. This gauge is passed all round each aperture in the carcase, the steel point making a mark on the drawer front the depth of the check to receive the beads. The checks are worked out with fillester and guillaume planes. That on the upper edge is made the whole thickness of the front, so that all the pine may be covered with the bead which now serves as a slip. The under edge and the 2 ends are not checked more than $\frac{3}{8}$ in. from the face. The ends are sawn down with a dovetail saw, and worked to the gauge marks with an iron guillaume. The cope bead is bought in boards $\frac{3}{16}$ in. thick; the strips are cut off with a cutting gauge, and must be broad enough to project about $\frac{1}{4}$ in. over the veneered front. When putting them on they are wetted on the upper side with a sponge, then the glue is applied to the dry side, and also to the check, when the slip is placed in position and rubbed backwards and forwards, 2 persons being necessary in the operation. When set in its place it should have a few rubs with a veneering hammer. To ascertain if it is "lying," the glue is scraped gently off along the drawer front with a chisel. When some parts are found not close it is usual to drive in fine brads, but this is a sign of defective workmanship, as no brads are allowed except in putting on the end beads. When a drawer front is slipped top and bottom in this way the glue must be very carefully washed off with a sponge and hot water, a chisel being used to scrape it along the junction of the front with the slip. When these slips are quite dry, the ends are cut off and planed flush with the drawer sides. Then the slips are stripped with the half-long plane on the sides, so that a thickness of fully $\frac{1}{8}$ in. is left, the drawer lying on the bench during the operation. The drawer is then tried in its place in the carcase. It should fit perfectly close against the shelves above and below, at the same time not tightly, the drawer front being in flush with the face of the carcase. When the 4 drawers are fitted in this way, the next thing is to run the beads. This is done with the cope-bead plane. This is a small plane (v) with a hollow along the centre of the sole the size of the bead to be run. The central portion is filled in with boxwood, in which the hollow is run. The drawer is now hung upon 2 boards on the bench, front up as before. The projecting edges of the slips are planed with a half-long till they stand above the front $\frac{1}{8}$ in.; then they are rounded with the cope-bead plane, which is run till the sole of the plane touches the drawer front. This, of course, leaves the bead all of one height in its whole length. When the 2 beads are thus run, the drawer front is carefully papered, the beads included, using for the latter a small hollow cork, something like the sole of the plane shown. After all the drawers are thus treated, the end beads are put on. A piece of the cope-bead stuff is thinned to fully $\frac{1}{8}$ in., the edge made straight, and rounded with the cope-bead plane; then a strip is cut off with a cutting gauge of the required breadth, which should be $\frac{5}{8}$ in. This is cut into lengths to fit in between the long beads by mitring the one to the other and stripping to the exact breadth, so that the same height above the veneered front is obtained. When it lies close in the check, and also close at the mitres, it receives a little glue, and is nailed on with $\frac{3}{4}$-in. fine brads, 3 or 4 to each. These are punched below the flush, and the end beads are carefully stripped; again the drawer is fitted into the carcase, and should fit quite close at the ends also. When in flush, it will look like a plain panel with a bead all round.

Now the whole 6 drawers are in their places. If they feel too tight they should be gently stripped where tightest. This will be readily ascertained by going to the back of the carcase and looking through between the drawers and shelves or grounds. The fitting of these drawers, done as they ought to be, is considered a very nice job in the trade, but it is seldom that this is accomplished. The drawers, while they show perfectly close all round the fronts, ought at the same time to pull out and push in with the utmost ease and freedom. This will only be the case when the carcase is perfect in construction, in which case the various shelves dividing the drawers are truly parallel with each other, and of the same width of aperture from front to back. The shelves must also be truly at right angles with the upright grounds—in other words, the carcase must be truly squared. Without these conditions the moving drawers, however well they in themselves may be made, can never be satisfactorily fitted into an ill-made carcase. When the drawers have received their final stripping, they are carefully sandpapered on all parts that come in contact with the carcase when moving; the cope beads also receive a final finish with sandpaper.

Now they are ready for the guides and stops. The guides are fillets of pine running from the back to the grounds at the ends of the drawers to guide them; they are 18 in. by $1\frac{1}{2}$ in. by 1 in. The stops are pieces of hard wood, such as ash or oak, 2 in. square and $\frac{1}{4}$ in. thick, and shaped like *w*, having 3 holes for $\frac{3}{4}$-in. wrought brads; 12 guides and 10 stops are required for the job, as the large drawer in the surbase requires no stop, the front stopping itself against the fore edges. The stops are put on before the guides. To do this a gauge is used with a groove in the head, close to the shank or stalk, to admit the projecting bead on the drawer front. The drawer is turned bottom up, and with this gauge a line is drawn from the front over the mahogany blocking glued to the bottom behind the front, the gauge being set a little bit less than the width of the front and blocking. The piece thus marked off is carefully pared to the gauge line. This being done with all 4 drawers, the shelves are also gauged from the front edge with the same setting of gauge, and the stops glued and nailed on at the gauge lines. They will thus stop the drawers exactly flush with the face of the carcase, the beads only projecting. The top drawer (that between the circular blocks) stands out 1 in. beyond the face of the carcase—consequently for this drawer the stops are 1 in. nearer the front of the shelf.

All the drawers being now in their places, provide mouldings and carvings. When mouldings or other projections are stuck on flat surfaces, the surfaces are French-polished before " planting " the moulding; the mouldings are also well coated with polish. This method is adopted because the fewer obstructions to the polishing-rubber the better the result. Another advantage is, the glue will not stick to a polished surface, so any superfluous glue, smeared about in putting on the mouldings, is easily cleaned off. In the present job, the exact place of the mouldings is marked lightly with a drawpoint both outside and inside; the space between the markings is cleaned of polish, and toothed. The mouldings are carefully mitred to length on a mitre board, and before glueing they are heated at the fire, the glue being applied to the drawer front. If the mouldings are straight on the glueing side they will only require to be held firmly down with the hands for a minute or two. If inclined to warp, pieces of pine, 12 in. long, are placed across them, and hand-screws applied to the ends. The drawer in the surbase receives a moulding $1\frac{3}{8}$ in. broad and $\frac{5}{8}$ in. thick. There are various forms of mouldings used. The moulding is mitred on the drawer front, the double mitres towards the centre having a break of $\frac{5}{8}$ in. The 2 end portions form a square of 8 in.—consequently a margin of 2 in. is left outside of this portion of the moulding, and $2\frac{5}{8}$ in. along the centre. The 2 knobs are placed exactly in the centre of these squares. These mouldings are fixed on the face of the drawer with glue alone, the surface for nearly the breadth of the moulding being scraped and toothed, as also the back of the moulding. When the mouldings are "planted" and hard, all the mitres are carefully dressed off and papered. Next put on the guides. All the drawers being stopped in their proper places, as above described, the guides, 18 in. long, are bored for 3 or 4 nails. A little glue is applied to each guide, care being taken that no glue is allowed to spread and come in contact with the drawer sides; the guides are rubbed in from the back, pressing against the drawer sides; they are pushed forward to touch the back of the ground. After they stand for $\frac{1}{2}$ hour or so all the drawers are taken out, and the guides nailed with $1\frac{1}{2}$-in. wrought nails. Screws are better, but are hardly ever put in. After this the surbase and body or upper carcase receive the back lining. This may consist of $5\frac{1}{2}$-in. narrow yellow pine boards. A first-class back would be framed and panelled. The surbase back consists of 1 board only, running horizontally, while the carcase back in narrow wood runs vertically. A fillet is glued to the under side of the top to receive the upper ends of the back lining. They are nailed with $1\frac{1}{2}$-in. cut nails. The cedar ends of drawers being of reddish-brown colour, the pine wood, that is the inside of front, back and bottom, is stained the same hue. This stain consists of Venetian red and yellow ochre, equal parts, with a little thin glue and water. It is made to boil, and is applied hot to the wood with a rag; after standing a few minutes, the residue is rubbed off with more rag, and is stroked in the direction of the grain; when quite dry, it is papered with flour paper. All wood that is to be stained must be particularly well planed and sandpapered, as the stains at once show up defects. The same rule holds with all work to be painted or varnished.

Wardrobe.—The description of the making of a $6\frac{1}{2}$-ft. break-front wardrobe in solid wood, as shown in Fig. 698, by W. Parnell, received a prize from the *Cabinet-maker*. It is as follows.

When you have your job set out, get and cut out the whole of the material necessary to make it, choosing (if the choice is left to you) dry and well-seasoned wood for every part. Next shoot and glue all joints, glue on all facings on inside ends and tops and bottoms; on the 2 ends of the centre carcase it will be necessary to joint a piece of solid wood to the front edge to allow for the extra width of that carcase; this piece must be

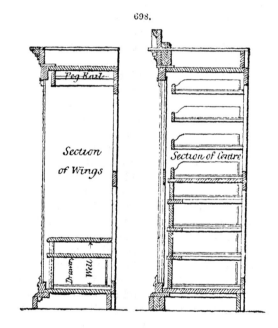

698.

Section of Wings

Section of centre

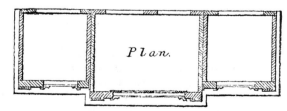

Plan.

$3\frac{1}{2}$ in. wide, and of the same wood as the exterior of the job, whatever it may be. Your joints and glueings being all done, plane up to the proper thickness the whole of the wood, shooting the front edge of each piece straight and square. Do not bring your carcase stuff to the exact width until after it is squared off ; but you may bring the stuff for the plinth and cornice frames to the right width, also the door stuff, allowing the stiles $\frac{1}{16}$ in. wider than the finished size, for fitting.

When you have all your wood planed, proceed to make the plinth and cornice frames : these are in pine, therefore make them $\frac{1}{2}$ in. shorter than the finished size ; let the front rail of the plinth and cornice frames run the whole length less the $\frac{1}{2}$ in. Exactly as if you were going to make a straight-front wardrobe, dovetail the front and ends together, dovetail the back rail down at such a distance from the back ends of the end rail as will admit of a block being glued behind it; allow the cross dovetails to go just " hand tight," for when they are too tight they are apt to force the end of the rail out and make it crooked; dovetail down 2 cross rails to come between the carcases, allow the plinth, back, and cross rails to be 1 in. wider than the front and end rails to allow them to stand level with the plinth mouldings, and the back and cross rails of the cornice frame to stand down $\frac{1}{2}$ in. to be level with the moulding under the cornice. Prepare your break pieces for the cornice and plinth, lining them up at each end to 3 in. thick; let the linings go the same way of the grain as the fronts, and be 5–7 in. long; square the breaks up $\frac{1}{2}$ in. shorter than finished length, and fit them in their exact positions, with 2 dowels, one at each end, but do not glue them yet. Glue your plinth and cornice frames together ; set them square, glue a block in each corner, and put them on one side whilst you proceed with your doors; set out the stiles and rails from your board, gauge for the mortices and tenons, so that the outside of the tenon comes in a line with the inside of the door moulding, which will bring the tenon almost in the centre of the thickness of the stuff. The top rail of the centre door will be as much thinner as the moulding is rebated so as to allow for the arched head, which will be a piece of thin wood grooved into the stiles with a shoulder on the front side only, and after the door is glued together, to be slid down from the top and glued to the face of the top rail ; this will allow the glass panel to be square. Before glueing your doors together, put them up dry and see that they are true ; otherwise, when they are glued you may perhaps have a good bit of trouble with them. The small corners in the wing doors should be the same thickness as the head in the centre door, and should be tongued into the stiles, but need not be to the rail, as it is the same way of the grain, and if well jointed and glued will hold as well. When you have glued your doors together, and seen that they are true and square, and that the stiles are straight with the rails, proceed to mitre a piece of wood $\frac{1}{4}$ in. thick, of the same sort as the exterior of the job, round your plinth and cornice frames ; next make the frames for the carcase, backs, and blind frame for the centre door ; make your mortices and cut your tenons before ploughing the grooves in the edges to receive the panels. In putting the centre upright and cross rails together for the centre carcase, back and blind frame, allow the cross rail to cut through the upright, if halved together, so that it may appear as though the upright was in 2 pieces and mortised into the cross rail, which is done in some shops, but preferably halved together. When you have your frames ready, knock them together, dry, and hang them up out of the way.

Now work your mouldings ; and in working the mouldings for the doors plough a groove on the reverse side, so that when the moulding is cut off the board it will form a rebate to rest on the doorstile. When you have worked and cleaned up all the mouldings necessary for the job, proceed to mitre and glue on those for the plinth and cornice, taking care that for the internal mitres you use parts of the same length of moulding, so that they may intersect without requiring any easing ; do not at present glue the internal mitres, but when the mouldings are all on the frames take off the break pieces, easing the moulding at the mitres if necessary, and now glue the breaks on, and when dry level off any odding, and put the plinth and cornice on one side.

Next clean up the doors on the front sides, merely levelling the backs, and put in the mouldings. Square up all the stuff for the carcases and fittings with the exception of drawers, tray and peg-rail fronts and backs, and one end of drawers and tray bottoms. In squaring the top, shelf and bottom of the centre carcase, allow them to be a trifle large at the back so that the drawers and trays may run freely, but it must be very little, not more than the thickness of veneer ($\frac{1}{32}$ in.), otherwise it will have the contrary effect of giving them too much play. Make the carcase tops and bottoms $\frac{5}{8}$ in. shorter than the extreme length of the carcase, to allow $\frac{5}{16}$-in. lap on each carcase end; and the shelves and partition edges $\frac{3}{4}$ in. longer than the length of the carcase *between* the ends, to allow $\frac{3}{8}$ in. at each end for a dovetail.

Gauge for the dovetails, and cut first those in the ends and chop them out; next place the top and bottom of a carcase on the bench inside uppermost, stand the corresponding carcase end in position, and mark the dovetails on the top and bottom with a marking-awl, repeating the process till you have marked all; then cut the dovetails, taking care to cut to the lines and allowing them to be tight on the outsides so that they may glue up clean and fit well. It is preferable not to cut the shoulders at the front and back now, as unless great care is taken you may, before you are ready to glue up, find the corners knocked off the outside dovetails; chop out your dovetails in the tops and bottoms.

Now take your carcase ends in pairs and set out for the drawers, trays and peg-rails, squaring them across the front edges with a marking-awl lightly, to mark where the grooves come; then square across the width of the end inside and run the grooves; those for the trays and peg-rails $\frac{3}{16}$ in. deep, and right through from front to back; for the runners between the drawers, the same depth, but commencing 4 in. from the front edge; and those for the shelves $\frac{3}{8}$ in. deep, and also commencing 4 in. from the front edge. Chop down from 4 to $7\frac{1}{2}$ in. from the front edge, in the grooves for the runners between the drawers, to $\frac{3}{8}$ in. deep, to receive partition edges. Cut a dovetail on the under side, to 1 in. from the front edge, but cut the top side straight in a line with the groove, so you will have a dovetail on the under side of the partition edge only; having cut the dovetails in the ends, put the partition edges in their respective places, and mark the dovetail on them. Cut them so that they fit, but not too tight, for if they are too tight they will force the partition edge out of square when driven home, and that would interfere with the proper working of the drawers. Plough grooves on the back edges and also on edges of runners for dust-boards. Cut a shoulder on the front edges to fit between the carcase end $\frac{3}{8}$ in. back, that it will allow the edge to come within $\frac{5}{8}$ in. of the front edge of the carcase ends, the shelves to be kept back in the same manner, having a dovetail of the same sort on their ends. The division between the drawers may be dovetailed both sides into the edge and shelf.

Rebate the back edges of the outside carcase ends, bringing them to their proper width; bring also the other ends, tops, bottoms and shelves to their proper widths, and clean up all the deal that requires to be coloured (make your colour or have it made so that it may be ready by the time you have cleaned the wood, and in sufficient quantity to do the whole, so that you may have the inside of the job one colour); before using the colour, try it on a piece of wood to see if it is right, and also if there is sufficient glue in it to prevent its being rubbed off when dry. When you have cleaned up all the parts that require colouring, commence to colour, wiping it off with soft shavings, and smoothing it nicely with the palm of your hand. When the whole is coloured, clean up your outside ends inside and out, also your drawer stuff if not already done; by the time you have done that the colour will be dry. Take the panels for the backs, lightly pass a piece of very fine glasspaper over the insides, and, if customary in the shop, wax them; then glue up your carcase backs. Serve the remainder of your coloured work the same as you did the panels, also waxing the inside of the solid ends where seen, and cutting shoulders of tops and bottoms. Level the frames outside and in, clean up and colour the insides.

Commence to glue your carcases together. A very handy way of doing so is to lay one end on the bench (of course if it is the outside one you must have either a cloth or bench sticks under it), hand-screw it tightly to the bench, and glue the dovetails at one end; drive in the corresponding top or bottom and then the other end. Take off the hand-screws, place the other end of the carcase under the one you now have on the bench, and then turn over the end with the top and bottom glued in, and glue them into the other. Put in your shelf (if there is one), glueing the dovetail only in the groove; place the carcase on its face on the floor, square it with a rod from corner to corner, fit the back, and having waxed the frame inside, screw it in its place and level it off.

When glueing the centre carcase together, commence as with the others, but when you have turned it over to glue the top and bottom into the second end, put your partition edges into the places cut behind the dovetails to receive them; then glue and drive home your top and bottom, glue the dovetails and drive up the partition edges, put in your shelf, glueing the dovetail only; place and glue the division between the drawers in its position. Stand the carcase on the floor on 2 pieces of wood, set it square, and proceed to put the runners in their places, cutting a tenon $\frac{3}{8}$ in. long on the front ends of them to fit in the plough-groove at the back of the partition edge; plane the runner a shaving or so thinner at the back than the front, and fix it in its place; glue the tenon only, and nail the back end to the end of the carcase. Put the centre runner in with a tenon at the front, and suspend it at the back with a thin lath dovetailed into the back edge of the shelf and end of runner; allow this lath to be just a trifle longer between the shoulders than the front division; it may be $1\frac{1}{2}$ in. wide. Now fit and put the dust-boards in, putting a touch of glue to the front edge to prevent their slipping back should they shrink. Care must be taken that the runners are at least $\frac{3}{8}$ in. shorter than the width of the ends; when in their places, lay your carcase on its face, see that it still remains square, fit the back, wax the frame where necessary, and screw it in and level it. Now level the fronts, tops and bottoms of each carcase, cleaning as you go; place your plinth on the floor where your wardrobe is to stand, and put the centre carcase on it, arrange it in position and fix it there; next place and fix the 2 wings to the plinth, put the cornice on the top, place it in its proper position, and fix the carcases to it, and to each other, putting screws where necessary, but not more than are necessary. Now block the carcases to the plinth and cornice, with 4 blocks about $2\frac{1}{2}$ in. sq. on the top and bottom of each carcase, so that when the job is removed each carcase will immediately go into its proper position. When that is done, wedge the wardrobe up so that it stands true on the front and perpendicular, glue a lath $\frac{1}{4}$ in. thick by $1\frac{1}{2}$ in. wide, with bead or edge to the ends of the centre carcase in the angle formed by the wing, and proceed to fit your drawers, trays and peg-rails, and finish them right off, but if possible, when you are ready to glue your drawers together, let in the handles in the fronts before doing so, as it is easier and quicker, for you can lay the front on the bench to do it; when your drawers, &c., are finished, not forgetting the stops, which should allow them to stand in $\frac{1}{8}$ in. beyond the front of partition edges and shelves. The peg-rails standing back about $\frac{5}{8}$ in. from the edge of carcase, proceed to make the clothes-well: first the top should be clamped at each end, with a frame outside it consisting of a back and 2 end pieces tenoned together exactly like the lid of a w.c.; glue 2 runners 1 ft. 3 in. long to the carcase ends, $\frac{1}{4}$ in. from the front edge and $\frac{1}{2}$ in. wider than the side rails of the top frame, having a plough-groove on the edge $\frac{3}{8}$ in. deep to receive a sliding front $\frac{3}{8}$ in. thick; fit in the front and cut a hand-hole at the top to draw it up by; fit the top into top frame and hinge it at the back; place the top frame in its position, resting on the runners at the front, screw through the carcase back into the back rail, and glue blocks under the side rails to fasten them to the carcase ends. Care must be taken not to glue the rails across the ends. Next fit your doors, in doing which allow them to be a full thickness of a veneer ($\frac{1}{32}$ in.) short, so that they may not drag on the plinth, and allow them to be a trifle wide, so that they just project beyond the carcase end. When hinging them, keep them up tight under the cornice; but previous to doing that, when your doors are fitted, glue on the pilasters, fit in the panels, fit blind frame, and clean them up, and when your doors are up with hinges and locks all in working order, place them in their respective positions. Make the beads for fixing them there, and then if you have to satisfy any one but yourself, ask the foreman or employer (as the case may be) to examine it, and afterwards take the job to pieces, colour the outside, and you have finished the task. The choice of wood for the structure and designs of the mouldings do not affect the mode of construction.

Sideboard.—Fig. 699 illustrates the construction of a 7-ft. pedestal sideboard with 3-panel back. The description gained for W. Robinson a prize in the *Cabinet-maker*. Having set out the work full size, first proceed to get out the top, which is a piece of 1-in. stuff, 7 ft. long, and shot to 2 ft. 2 in. broad. This, when finished, has a 2-in. ovolo on the top edge, and a $\frac{1}{8}$-in. bead sunk on the face edge. Get out some $\frac{1}{2}$-in. stuff, $4\frac{1}{2}$ in. wide, and line it up on the under side of the top, letting the end lining run the same way of the grain as the top. Cross line the top also over the inside end of the pedestals; this and the back lining may be pine. Next proceed to get out the drawer frame. It will be made of 1-in. pine, and its extreme length, with its end facings out, will be 6 ft. 5 in., and its extreme breadth from the outside of back to the front edge of the top blade will be 1 ft. $10\frac{1}{2}$ in.; the lower blade sets back 2 in. In getting out the cross rails of the frame, frame a piece of 2-in. stuff, 5 in. wide on one end, cross-ways of the grain, and in putting the frame together let the flush sides of the cross rails go next the centre drawer and the outside ends respectively. When all is fitted, place the 4 cross rails side by side, and shape all together, and leave them with the carver to run 3 flutes $\frac{5}{16}$ in. wide on each. Next proceed to get out the pedestals. These are simply a frame, with the stiles of 2-in. scantling, with $1\frac{1}{4}$-in. cross framing, precisely the same as the door, the panels being $\frac{5}{8}$ in. thick, and bevelled in $1\frac{1}{4}$ in. from their edges. Clean off the face of the panels, and finish off the mouldings, and let the polisher body them in.

In the meantime the framing can be got on with. The top and bottom rails run across, and are framed into the pilasters or angle pieces, and the stiles are checked or sunk into the pilaster $\frac{1}{4}$ in. (see section of pedestal). The inner frame is connected with the outer frame by 4 short rails. Note: the end panels are framed in grooves, but the door panels are framed or fastened in with beads. Having got the panels from the polisher, frame the $1\frac{1}{4}$-in. framing together, and mitre the mouldings offered to the top, give all to the polisher, and when done screw the side panels to the centre panel, place on its face, and block in the silvered glass; put on the blind frames, then screw the job all together. Screw the brackets, pediment, &c., on, and see that the doors work easily, and the locks are oiled. The doors may be hung with centre hinges, or with strong brass butts, 3 in. long, letting the knuckle stand out $\frac{1}{8}$ in. past its centre of motion, and an ornamental hinge plate screwed in, &c., first having cleaned off the face, and got it bodied in. Now proceed to frame the pilasters to the frames, and having dovetailed the top and bottom to the ends, clean all off, and let the carver flute them, and cut the elliptic pateras in the centres.

The doors may now be got out, of course letting the stiles run through.

As the moulding forms the rebate for the panels, it will be seen that the panels will be narrower by $\frac{5}{16}$ in. on each edge than the pedestal panels were, in consequence of no groove being in the stiles, &c.

The frame may now be taken in hand, the drawer fronts fitted on the rake, and the drawer sides fitted and shot to their proper shape, the front dovetails being on the rake in order to take the front.

Get out 4 blocks the same shape as the blocks between the drawers, and glue them on to the ends of the frame over the pilasters. Now get out 2 mock drawer fronts, and fix them between them, and face the frame to represent the blades over and under the drawer. (Note that the blades have a sunk bead on the centre of their faces.) The plinth rails may now be got out and fixed, as also the bases of the pilasters.

To make the bases, get out a piece of cross-grain stuff, $4\frac{1}{2}$ in. wide by 1 in. thick,

699.

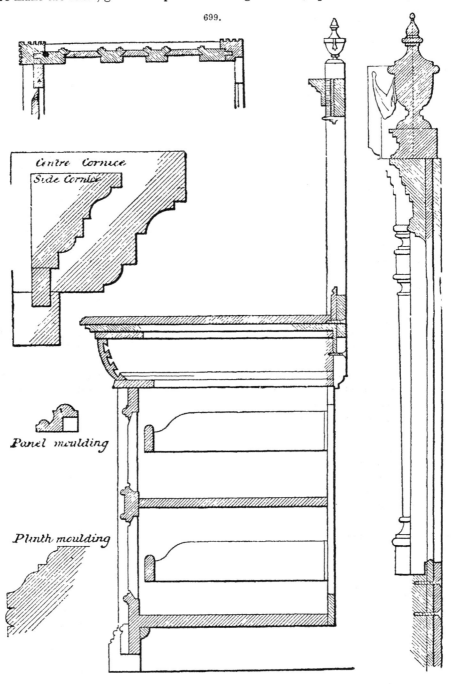

Centre Cornice

Side Cornice

Panel moulding

Plinth moulding

and about 2 ft 2 in. wide, and run the moulding along the edge, and then cut it in lengths, and fix them, leaving their sides flush with the pilasters. The trays and cellarette drawer may now be made, the frame cleaned off, and pieces fitted on

2 o

the fronts &c., and carved as drapery. The flutes on the fronts of the drawers can then be carved, and the ram's head and angle brackets, and centre ornament under drawer, finished.

The door mouldings may now be mitred in, and the panels bevelled $\frac{7}{8}$ in. from the edge. Place the frame on the bench, and put on the runners for the drawers, and afterwards place it on the pedestals and block it in its place. Now fit and hang the doors, &c., and let the carver have them to cut the circular pateras at the angles.

After this take the top, shoot the back edge, joint 2 pieces of stuff $3\frac{1}{2}$ in. long by $1\frac{1}{2}$ in. wide at each end, and run the mouldings through. These are to finish the top off level with the plate glass back. The top and frame may now be finally screwed together, the drawers run and stopped, and their fittings put on. The carcase backs of the pedestals may be put in, levelled, and coloured, and all given to the polisher.

The back is composed of 3 frames, the groundwork of which is $1\frac{1}{8}$-in. stuff; the 2 outside frames have their outside stiles faced on the outer edge by a pilaster, 2 in. sq., and which projects 2 in. above the top of the frame to receive the carved urn. The breadth of the outside frames, including the pilaster, is 1 ft. 8 in., and the extreme height is 2 ft. 2 in., exclusive of the pilaster. These 2 frames are faced with $\frac{3}{8}$-in. stuff, and the bevelled glass is surrounded by a moulding. The pilaster is carved and fluted, and the dentilled cornice then mitred round the top, showing a $\frac{1}{2}$-in. break. A small console is placed at the bottom as a suitable finish.

The centre frame is got out of the same stuff as the side frames, viz. $1\frac{1}{8}$-in., and faced with $\frac{3}{8}$-in. stuff. In getting out this frame, the breadth must be $\frac{3}{4}$ in. narrower than the finished size, in order to allow a side facing to hide the joint of the groundwork and its front facing. The extreme height of this frame will be 3 ft. 9 in., and the extreme breadth 3 ft. 1 in. Now glue 2 pilasters 3 ft. 7 in. long by 2 in. sq. on the face, keeping them flush on the top ends, also on the outsides ; and on the faces of these two, glue 2 shaped pilasters of same length, but only 2 in. by $1\frac{1}{2}$ in. Mitre the cornice round, and also the necking, and leave a break of 2 in. at the centre. This tablet is to be $3\frac{1}{2}$ in. wide.

The edge of the facing on the centre frame is a $\frac{1}{2}$-in. hollow. Get out the ogee pediment, and fit the looping of drapery to the urn, and give all other carvings, &c., to the carver. Note that it is always better to have the glass before finishing the sight measurements, as the bevels can be matched to mitre with the mouldings, and a more even margin secured.

CARVING AND FRETWORK.—These artistic operations may be described under one general head, as they deal mainly with the same material—elegant woods, and can be carried on together.

Carving.—This is an industry which essentially depends upon the native talent of the operator, and in which no progress can be made by simply following directions. It will be found an excellent plan to make a model in clay of the proposed design, and then carve the wood according to the clay model, which latter can be modified till it gives satisfaction. The subject of carving may be divided into Woods, Tools, and Operations.

Woods.—The choice of the woods to be operated upon is a point of considerable importance, and the workman would do well to study the various woods and their peculiarities.

Camphor.—A very fine wood, with a close clean-cutting grain. It produces an excellent effect when worked into small articles of furniture of the Elizabethan and neo-Grecian style. Unfortunately, it is difficult to obtain in Europe.

Ebony.—Of this wood there are several varieties in the market, the only one serviceable to the carver being that with a close and even grain, so close indeed, that under the gouge it appears to have no fibre whatever. The hardness renders it extremely difficult to work, and for this reason ebony carvings are of great value. The great defect which this wood has, is its tendency to exfoliate, and to split. An imitation ebony is sometimes offered, which is made by soaking pear-wood in an iron and tannin dye-beck for a week or more. The colour penetrates to the very heart of the wood, so that the cut is as black as ebony. Ebony is above all woods the most suitable for small carvings of every description, whether for use or ornament, the deep black colour and the hardness and fine texture of grain giving it, when polished, the appearance of black marble. This wood is also somewhat difficult to procure in large blocks—not, however, on account of the growth of the tree, which is very large, but, either from the careless- ness of those who are employed in felling it, or the extreme heat to which it is exposed, it rarely arrives here in logs of any size that are not more or less riven and spoilt by cracks and flaws—" shakes," as they are termed in timber merchants' *parlance*. There are two kinds of ebony—the green and black; of these the former is for some reason the more highly prized, and consequently is the more expensive; but for carving purposes there is little or nothing to choose between them; they are both equally pleasant to use, but the blacker, being the harder of the two, is capable of taking a higher polish, its only drawback being an occasional white or red streak, but these are rare, and can be obliterated by applying a little ink to the spot after the carving is done. Black, or iron wood, as it is sometimes called, is a species of ebony, but has little to recommend it but its extreme hardness and weight; indeed, on the former account it should rather be shunned by the carver, as it will turn the edge of the tools.

Lime.—The easiest of all woods to work, being soft and equal under the tool. But it is of little use for delicate work, as it does not " hold " to fine details; for that reason it is only used for frames, or at most for coarse undercut work, which has neither to bear heavy weights nor sustain much wear. The tint of this wood is something like that of fresh butter. It is less liable to split and splinter than almost any other wood, which qualities render it of great utility to carvers for carrying out designs when lightness and boldness are equally required. It takes a stain well, and a fair polish, or it may be varnished without greatly altering the colour of the wood, but giving to it a very agreeable boxwood appearance. It is suitable, as well as for large festoons, for smaller works, such as book-stands, miniature and portrait frames.

Mahogany, owing to its tendency to chip, when reduced to thin edges or angles, is only used for carvings having a bold outline, in which fine projecting lines are not requisite. There are two very distinct kinds. That suited for carving must not be confounded with the common soft wood known as cedar mahogany, used for ordinary furniture, but is hard and dark, and known as Spanish. This wood is well suited for basso relievo, as is also the Spanish chestnut, the two woods, when polished, being much alike, though the mahogany is of a somewhat richer colouring.

Oak is so well known as not to require description. Its strong fibres and coarse texture render it unfit for the finer kinds of sculpture. The most adapted to the pur- poses of the carver is perhaps the variety found in the Vosges. Those trees which grow in the heart of the forests produce a softer, more brittle wood, more exempt from knots and other irregularities than those which grow on the borders. Foreign oak is much to be preferred to home-grown wood, which is of a hard, tough nature, and liable to knots, which are a great impediment to the carver, and from which the American and Nor- wegian forest-grown oak is comparatively free. These oaks may be known by the close and smooth grain, and somewhat grey tinge, the English wood being closer grained and of a yellower colour. Oak is especially useful for decorative work in library or large hall, and, above all, for ecclesiastical purposes.

Pear.—This wood, owing to the fineness of its grain, its cohesiveness, its durability, and its equable cut, is perhaps the best for all delicate work, such as vegetation, flowers, &c. It takes a beautiful black by staining. Much pear is sold as ebony. Pear-tree is a pleasant wood for working, and a good piece resembles lime in its pliability. It is extensively used in France for the purposes for which we employ lime.

Sandal-wood, from the texture, beautiful colour (a rich yellow brown), and the delicious scent, is especially suited to small carvings. The superabundance of oil, which emits so delightful a fragrance, causes it also to take a beautiful polish merely by rubbing it slightly with the hand. The best sandal-wood is brought from India and Ceylon. It also, like ebony, is difficult to procure in sound pieces. It is sold, as are the most valuable woods, by weight, the price varying from 6d. to 1s. per lb., according to the size and soundness of the logs. Small pieces are cheaper than large ones in proportion, unless they are prepared and squared to any even size, and then they are far more expensive, as in the course of preparation 2 or 3 logs may perhaps be cut up and spoiled before one can be found without flaw, and of course this waste is taken into account and charged for by the wood merchant.

Sycamore, holly, and chestnut are amongst the lightest of our woods. The first is greatly, and, in fact, principally used for bread-plates, potato-bowls, and other articles, when a light tint is a consideration.

Walnut.—The wood of this tree is usually of a brown colour, and on being cut shows a brilliant grain. It is soft, binding, and easy to work. Of all woods, it is the one whose colour varies most. Although its colour is generally brown, samples are to be found in which the veins are almost black on a white ground. This freak of nature is sometimes found in the same tree which at other parts is equably coloured. The best walnut for the carver is that of a brown uniform tint, slightly bronzy ; its veins should be regular and offer an equal grain under the gouge. The white varieties are softer than the above named, and would be preferable, were it not for the black veins before described, which entirely disfigure the work, and necessitate the greatest attention in staining to equalize the tone. The veiny brown wood is generally too fibrous and too knotty, and is often traversed by sap-wood, which in some places becomes decomposed, forming a mass resembling a tough gritty leather, which blunts the tool without being cut. Before beginning to work, the absence of such defects should be carefully ascertained. Trees which grow near marshy lands, or near manure tanks, absorb a sap of a peculiar nature, which has a disagreeable odour of rotten eggs, plainly perceptible when the wood is heated by rubbing, either with the hand or with a tool. The walnut is rather liable to the attacks of worms, especially in the sap-wood. This may be to a great extent prevented by washing the wood with a strong decoction of walnut " shucks " and alum, applied cold. The best walnut comes from abroad, and is much in use amongst Continental carvers, especially the Austrian ; but though it is pleasant and easy to work, it has a dull and dingy appearance, so that a carving would have looked better and been more effective had it been done in any of the other woods mentioned, though the labour would have been far greater. Italian walnut is a rich and beautiful wood for a variety of purposes, such as cabinets, panels, bookcases, and frames. It is hard, but the effect produced by its use amply repays the extra labour caused by the close texture of the material. American walnut is a very good wood for amateurs, and is much in favour with them for its dark colour. It has, however, a more open grain than lime, and therefore requires more care to avoid accidents. It is used for many small works where much projection is unnecessary, as book-racks, letter-boxes, and watch-stands.

Wild Cherry.—Easy to work, and of a vivid red tint, which, however, loses brilliancy with age. It is very liable to be worm-eaten, and is only used in sculpture in making little boxes.

Yew.—This extremely hard wood is well adapted to the carver, although it has almost gone out of use. The sap-wood is white, the heart-wood of a bright orange, the grain is fine and close, the cut being particularly " clean."

To procure good wood for carving, the trees should be felled at a proper time and age, and the wood thoroughly seasoned. The proper time to fell oaks and most other trees is when they fail to increase in size more than 2 ft. per annum. If cut down before that period of their existence, the heart will not be fully developed, and will not be as hard as the other part. When oaks are about 30 years old their growth is most rapid. Autumn is generally considered the best time to fell.

If wood be used in an unseasoned state it is sure to warp and twist; and when it is so used for panels fitted into loose grooves, it shrinks away from the edge which happens to be the most slightly held; but when restrained by nails, mortices, or other unyielding attachments, which do not allow them the power of contraction, they split with irresistible force, and the material and the workmanship are thus brought to no useful service. It is therefore very necessary that the natural juices of the tree be got rid of by seasoning it before use. After a tree is lopped, barked, and roughly squared, it is left some time exposed to the weather, and may be soaked in fresh running water with advantage, and boiled or steamed. Any of these processes tends to dilute and wash out the juices, and the water readily evaporates from the wood at a subsequent period. Thin planks, if properly exposed to the air, will be seasoned in about a year, but the thicker the wood the longer the time it will take.

All woods, to carve properly, should be perfectly dry—but not too old—in this latter case they become brittle and nerveless. If possible, the wood should come from the upper portions of the trunk, as these are less subject to knots. As a rule, the branches should be rejected, as their wood has not sufficient body. The sap-wood should always be refused, as it is too soft, blackens easily, and is sure to suffer from the attacks of worms.

It is often useful to be able to stain the wood after the carving is complete. This is done, either to give an appearance of age, or to imitate some other wood. The ageing is generally performed as follows, though the ready-made oak-stains may be used with equal success. Boil 5 oz. of dry powdered walnut "shucks" in 1 qt. of water. Filter off the clear liquor, and apply cold to the work with a brush. Or, take 2 oz. Cassel earth and 2 oz. American red potash, boil in 1 qt. of water, and apply as above. This latter colour imitates well the tints of old oak, and if applied to oak itself darkens it considerably. With pear-wood, it is usual to use a decoction of gamboge and saffron, to bring up the yellow tone. Lime may be stained of various colours in the following modes. Solutions of tin salts and turmeric applied consecutively give a good orange. Brush over with madder, allowing to dry, and then applying acetate of lead, gives brown with darker veins. Walnut takes a fine mahogany tint if washed with a strong decoction of Brazil or Campeachy wood. All sculptured woods may be dyed of a full black, by being washed over with a solution composed of $1\frac{1}{8}$ oz. powdered extract of logwood, 2 qt. of water, to which is added after boiling $\frac{1}{8}$ oz. potash chromate.

In general terms, oak is the best wood for large surfaces, and ebony or boxwood for small, minute work; but walnut, lime, chestnut (both horse and Spanish), mahogany and plane, are all suited to the purpose, while sandal-wood, apple, pear, holly, cypress, fig, and lemon tree, being hard and fine-grained, may all be used with good effect, according to the style and size of the carving, and other circumstances. Sycamore, lime, holly, and woods of a like nature, being white or cream-coloured, are only suited to that special style of carving whose beauty depends on great purity of colouring—such, for instance, as the minute basso relievo after a picture, models of figures in imitation of ivory, groups of birds or delicate foliage; but all these woods, unless protected by glass, soon lose their extreme whiteness, and with it their chief beauty. Therefore, they are little used, excepting for the trifling purposes just mentioned. The woods of the apple and pear tree are, from the hard texture and fine grain, exceedingly pleasant to work, but the fruiting value of the trees renders the wood rare, and occasional deep-coloured veinings sometimes interfere with the design. Boxwood is equally hard and fine-grained, and is far superior in uniformity of colour, which is a rich yellow. Fig-tree wood is also much prized for small carvings, being of a very beautiful warm red colour; but even in Italy it is rare, owing to the value of the living tree, and extremely difficult to procure in England. The great bar to the free use of all these hard woods is the difficulty of procuring them in pieces of any sizes, for, as their texture indicates, they are mostly bushes of slow growth, rarely attaining to more than 10 in. to 12 in. in diameter, added to which, as regards boxwood especially, it is largely used for other purposes besides carving, which necessarily increases the demand, and makes it more expensive.

When any very delicate designs have to be executed, and the most minute finish is required, boxwood, ebony, or any other equally hard and close-grained woods are decidedly the best to choose.

Woods with ornamental grain, as bird's-eye maple, satinwood, yew, and laburnum, are not desirable for carving purposes; the grain and colour often interfere with the effect which it is an object to produce.

Tools.—The work of the carver rarely needs a special bench, any short deal table answering every practical purpose. This should be of a convenient height to suit the operator, and be placed under a north window for the benefit of the light. The workman should stand rather than sit at his work, and will find a revolving music-stool the least inconvenient seat. The work-table should admit of holes being made in it for the reception of a screw for holding down the work. The cutting tools used are of special forms, representative examples of which are illustrated herewith. Fig. 700 is a straight

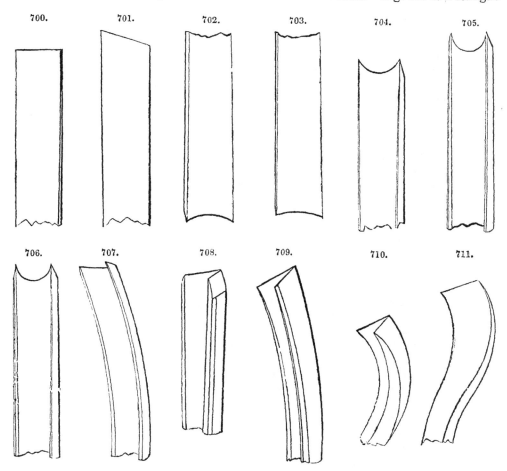

700. 701. 702. 703. 704. 705.

706. 707. 708. 709. 710. 711.

carving chisel; Fig. 701, a skew carving chisel; Fig. 702, a flat carving gouge; Fig. 703, a medium carving gouge; Fig. 704, a carving gouge for scribing; Fig. 705, a deep carving gouge; Fig. 706, a straight fluting gouge; Fig. 707, a front-bent fluting gouge

Fig. 708, a straight parting tool; Fig. 709, a bent parting tool; Fig. 710, a spoonbit parting tool; Fig. 711, a spoonbit chisel; Fig. 712, a skew spoonbit chisel; Fig. 713, a medium front-bent carving gouge; Fig. 714, a spoonbit gouge for scribing; Fig. 715, a deep spoonbit gouge; Fig. 716, a back-bent spoonbit gouge; Fig. 717, a veining tool; Fig. 718, an unshouldered print-cutters' chisel; Fig. 719, a bolt chisel; Fig. 720, a

712.   713.   714.   715.   716.   717.   718.

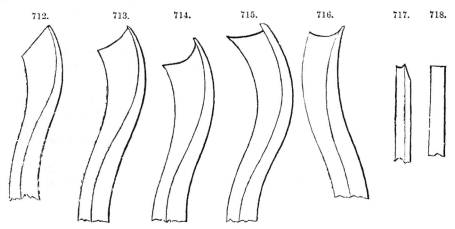

dog-leg chisel; Fig. 721, an improved print-cutters' gouge. Of each kind of cutting tool there are some half-dozen forms, varying in the acuteness of the angle or sharpness of the curve of the cutting edge, so as to be more readily adapted to the sweep or corner of the line being cut. In bent chisels, there is one for the right corner and one for the left. Tools of unusual form can be readily extemporized from old knitting-needles or small files, by heating to whiteness, hammering to shape, and tempering in oil or sealing-wax. Usually the palm of the hand suffices for giving a blow to the cutting tool, but a small round mallet is handy for heavy work. The ordinary marking and gouging tools, and a small brush for removing chips, are necessary adjuncts.

721.   719.   720.

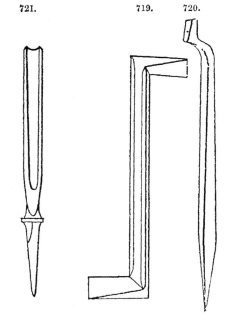

Some order should be observed in arranging the tools on the bench, both for facility in selecting any particular one required and for preserving their cutting edges. A good plan is to lay them with the handles towards the back of the bench, and along the back margin, taking care to drop the handle first in putting them down. As regards quality, the tools should be of the best. A few words may suffice to indicate the points to be considered in selecting good tools. First, as regards substance, for general use, especially if likely to be used much with the mallet, care must be taken that they are not so thin as to make them liable to break in half when in use. The stoutest to be obtained now are hardly likely to be too stout. Especially should they be stout near the handle. Attention must be given also to what may be termed the "lines" of a tool. They should be easy and true. There is an uncertainty about the shape or lines of some tools which give the impression that the maker could scarcely have known what sort of thing he wished to produce. About many that are in the market, there is something more than uncertainty, for their deficiency in this respect is of the most glaring kind. It is not that this is merely a matter of taste or fancy, which has no real effect upon the practical value of a tool. If, for example, a tool is only slightly "twisted" or slightly bent, it is very likely to break when malleted, and can never be used with pleasure. It will be useful to the learner to study, if he has opportunity, the "make" of good old tools or new ones of acknowledged merit, in order that he may be able to make a mental comparison when making purchases. One other point of importance to consider is the "temper." The proof of the "temper" is in the using. It is true that an experienced eye is not likely to be deceived in this matter; it is also true that the temper of a tool may in a measure be tested by a file, but the file must be in the hands of an experienced person. In any case, the final test is in the using. If the tool is so "soft" that the edge turns when brought into contact with hard wood—not the hardest —and that end way of the grain; or if, on the other hand, it is so "hard" or brittle that used in the same way the edge breaks, it had better be discarded.

The "parting tool" is of all tools the most easily broken, and the difficulty and trouble of sharpening it makes this mishap anything but a trivial affair. But it is a most useful and, moreover, a necessary tool, and a carver might well possess a variety— say 6 or 8—of them. Any one having the smallest acquaintance with carvers' tools will have noticed that the sides or blades of some parting tools spread considerably more than others. The carver must make choice of one or more for rough work, and there can be no question that—other things being equal—those with the most spread are the strongest, and therefore the safest for rough work. Small parting tools, with their sides brought nearer together, i.e. having little spread, are invaluable for incised work; and may, in the hands of a skilful workman, be made to do work which could only be accomplished by the help of other tools with far greater difficulty and labour, and even, at times, with a less satisfactory result. Parting tools, which are intended for such light work, must be suitably sharpened and kept for that purpose alone. If they are fit for light work, they are as certainly unfit for heavy work, as a broken tool would soon remind the incautious workman. As already stated, for heavy work, substance, as a quality in a tool, is very important. But this is especially the case with the tool under notice. There must be substance in the blades, and especially where they meet, towards which they should become somewhat stouter. In purchasing, see that the inside is truthfully cut out—i. e. that the "lines" are good—and beware of flaws.

The "voluter" is second only to the parting tool in importance and value to the carver, even if it be not equal to it. And this, again, is a tool which must receive special attention when the subject of sharpening is reached. Of this, too, it will be necessary that the carver should have a variety. Like the parting tool, it is one which affords the manufacturer an excellent opportunity of distinguishing himself, if he has any desire to do so. The sides of a voluter—if in speaking of this tool such a term is admissible—should very slightly, but only very slightly, spread. This is necessary, if it is to free itself when in use. For some purposes, the voluter makes an excellent parting tool. In cutting round leafwork, previous to setting-in, instead of always using a parting tool, try the voluter. It will even answer such a purpose better at times, and has this additional recommendation—that it is less liable to break.

A combination of circumstances and conditions in tool and workman go to make a tool that is termed "handy," i. e. eminently adapted to the work in view. Some of the points necessary to earn this denomination for a tool may be considered. For instance, one purpose for which every carver uses his scroll tools is that known as "setting-in." For this purpose, other things being equal, the tools which are the handiest are the shortest. The long tool is objectionable for one or two reasons. If it is struck hard with the mallet, as it must often be when used for this purpose, there is a certain "spring" in it, unless it is a very thick tool, which creates an uneasy feeling in the mind of the carver, for such a tool is liable to break in half. A short tool is almost sure to be a strong tool. A long tool is objectionable, too, because the carver has to raise his mallet to an inconvenient height in order to strike it. But the main reason for giving preference to short tools when used for this purpose is, that the carver can grasp the handle and at the same time rest his hand upon the work to keep the tool in the desired position. It is obvious that with a long tool this cannot be done. The sharpening of these tools must be done equally from inside and outside. When a tool is grasped in the right hand, and used as in moulding, then it may be full length. A short tool would cramp the hand in using it. We may almost reverse the statement made in connection with tools used for setting-in, and say the handiest are the longest. Not that an inordinate length is desirable. There must be room for the right hand, which pushes, and the left hand, which guides, and more than enough for these if the tool is to have "play," and the carver is to see what he is doing. To produce a long, easy curve is almost out of the question with a short tool. The mode of sharpening tools used in this manner if employed entirely (as in the case of the voluter) or mostly for this purpose is a point of importance. Attention must be directed to the back of the tool, that is the round side, which, when it is used in the manner under notice, is generally downwards—that is, next the wood. There must be no "ridge" running from one side of the tool to the other within $\frac{1}{4}$ or $\frac{3}{8}$ in. of the edge, otherwise the surface, line, or hollow which is being worked will be one series of "dips" or hollows, which would have anything but a " beautifully undulating " effect. The sharpening on the back must be with a nicely graduated angle right up to the edge, that the tool may work in a smooth, easy, sweeping style. The necessary strength may be given to the edge by sharpening on the inside at a much shorter angle, that is by what is called "dubbing it up." These remarks apply in an especial manner to the "voluter." This tool must be brought to an edge very much from the inside, the edge being strengthened in the manner just described. If it is to work easily in a hollow, but a little larger than its own size, it must be sharpened on the back with a very long angle; the handle in this case will be inconveniently near the wood, but this inconvenience will be obviated by the use of voluters slightly—only slightly—bent. This tool is made too often, by the absurd manner in which it is sharpened, very much like a wedge. It " binds," and bruises the sides of the hollow in which it works. A third mode in which a scroll tool is often employed is, as in facing the round parts of leafwork. A short tool is perhaps the handiest for this purpose, but no rule can be laid down upon this point. When it is held in position by the left and struck by the right hand, shortness is an advantage, because of the left hand having to rest upon the work at the same time. But it is as often, perhaps, pushed as in moulding, when a longer tool is better. In sharpening, the same attention must be given to the inside as is required for the backs of those just mentioned. If there is any "ridge" near the edge on the inside, there is a constant tendency in the tool to "glance off" the work; and the tool has to be held in a position too nearly approaching the vertical before it can cut at all.

The modes of use just glanced at are the three principal. If the carver has tools well adapted for these, his tools may be described as "handy." The handiness of a tool, then, may be said briefly to consist in the readiness with which it lends itself to any particular purpose. A tool should be made subservient to the requirements of the workman. If a new tool is too long for the purpose for which it is chiefly required, there is no reason why it should not be shortened before being sharpened. It will be for the ingenuity of the workman to surmount the difficulty which arises from the circumstance that the same tool is often required for every purpose. Sometimes, however, it is worth while to have duplicates of certain tools, that they may be kept largely for one particular purpose. A workman's tools are worthy of his most careful study. Enough has been said to show that the manner in which a tool is sharpened has much to do with its utility, and that the subject of sharpening generally is deserving of special notice.

The first essentials for sharpening carving tools are grindstones and oilstones. These have already been described under Carpentry (see pp. 115-18), but more care is needed in choosing them for carving tools owing to the greater delicacy of the edges to be sharpened, so that the least flaw in a stone should suffice to condemn it. The mounted grindstone is used only to take off the thick edge of the tool, as, for instance, when the tool is new. It should be ground back to a breadth of $\frac{1}{8}$ to $\frac{1}{4}$ in., great care being taken to keep the tool cool by the use of abundant water in the trough, to avoid injuring its temper. The coarse edge is next drawn fine by applying oilstones of progressive degrees of fineness. These oilstones are obtained in slips, and their edges are gradually adapted to fit the inner sides of the curved or angular tools, while their sides become recessed and similarly adjusted to the outer side of the tools. The grinding away should be done from the inside, while the "setting" proper is done from the outside. In the rubbing out, it is well to fix the stone in a vice, with pads to protect it from the jaws, and use both hands in manipulating the tool. In sharpening the outside edge, the tool should be held in the left hand, and the stone worked upon it by the right hand. Certain slips should be reserved for certain kinds of tools, and care must be observed to commence with a coarser (generally a darker coloured) and proceed to a finer (whitish and semitransparent) grained stone. The final edge is given to the tool by stropping it on a broad strip of buff leather saturated with tallow and crocus powder rubbed in under the influence of a fire. A well-set tool should pare deal against the grain with a perfectly clean cut. The slips of oilstone will require grinding at the edges to fit the tools. The rubbing out is effected in the case of very small tools by the aid of emery powder and oil applied by a strip of wood. The oil used is generally ordinary machine oil, but petroleum is also in favour. The handles of all tools should be well adapted to the hand using them, and some system should be observed in the style (shape, colour, &c.) of handle, so that the tool may always be immediately recognized by the handle alone.

Operations.—When the carver has made a selection of a design and of a piece of wood to be carved, he proceeds to transfer the design to the wood. There are several ways of performing this. (1) Rub the surface of the wood with chalk, and then sketch the design on it. (2) Cut a piece of paper the right size, sketch the design on it, and paste it on the wood. (3) Sketch the design on paper, lay it on the wood with a sheet of carbon paper intervening, and pass a hard point over the lines, when they will be transferred to the wood. (4) In mouldings, a piece of cardboard may be cut to the design and a pencil drawn round the outline. The wood bearing the design is suitably fixed on the bench or table.

No two carvers work exactly in the same manner, but the object of all is to secure complete command over the action of the tools. In general terms, the tool should be firmly grasped by the left hand, so that the hand reaches to within about 1 in. of the cutting edge, while the right hand encompasses the top of the handle and applies the motive power. It is a great advantage to the operator to be able to reverse this order of things in left-handed work. In diaper carving, commence by cutting out the outline with the parting tool, held slanting in the right hand, with the left hand arched over the tool, and having the wrist and finger-tips resting on the work, as a check to the forward motion of the tool, and a guide in curves. The groundwork of the design is thrown up by punching. In commencing a panel in relief, the outline is gone over with a chisel or gouge held perpendicularly in the left hand, with the middle finger beside the blade, the right hand giving slight blows with the mallet. Small gouges are next used to scoop out the parts to be cut away, and chisels to reduce the ground to a uniform depth. To ensure clean cutting, the grain of the wood must be constantly watched and humoured by altering the direction of the tool. The work consists in the two operations of " blocking out " the design (cutting away the superfluous wood) and " finishing " the details, but every carver has his own way of dividing the work between the two steps. The amateur will find the grounding and bordering punches made by Holtzapffel of the greatest assistance in carving. Their use is described in Leyland's Manual on Carving.'

Fretwork.—Fret or scroll sawing is a modern invention by which much handsome work is now done especially for ornamental cabinet-making. The subject may be divided into woods, tools, and operations.

Woods.—Wood for fret-sawing must be good, free from knots, and perfectly smooth. Soft woods can be hand-planed to a sufficient degree of smoothness; but hard woods require scraping down with a steel scraper, and then sandpapering. The chief woods used are:—

Bird's-eye maple is close-grained, gritty in sawing, and polishes well, but needs much filling.

Black walnut is cheap, goes well under the saw, and is very generally used. Pieces of uniform shade and free from streaks should be chosen, except where the streaks would show up well.

Ebony is well suited for inlaying, and takes a high polish: but it is costly, and the hardness and closeness of grain render sawing difficult without applying olive-oil to the blade.

Mahogany is adapted to almost all work, being easy to saw, yet hard, close-grained, and susceptible of taking a fine polish.

Rosewood is close-grained and as difficult to saw as ebony, but polishes well.

Red cedar, though not hard, is troublesome to saw and liable to split. It is pleasantly fragrant.

Spanish cedar is soft and easily worked. Small articles can be made out of old cigar-boxes, when the paper has been got off and the surface sandpapered.

Satinwood has an elegant colour and lustre, with considerable hardness and a close grain, and polishes well.

Tulipwood has a reddish streaked appearance, a finer and closer grain than satinwood, and is capable of being highly polished, but it is costly.

White holly is very popular in America, being very easy to saw, while possessing a fine close grain.

Tools.—These are very few in number. The first requisite is an ordinary table for supporting the work, which latter is held tight by clamps such as have already been described (p. 71), the jaw of the clamp being prevented from coming into contact with the fretwood by the intervention of a "rest," formed of a slot of deal about 20 in. long, 6 in. wide, 1 in. thick, and having a triangular piece cut out of one end, so as to form a couple of legs: the saw is worked in the crutch of the fork, and thus the "rest" helps to sustain the fretwood against the force of the sawing. For making a hole to admit the saw, recourse may be had to a bradawl (p.121) or to a small archimedean drill (p.123), the latter being preferable, and capable of doing much useful work by the aid of a set of drills.

Of saws there is an endless variety, reaching in price from 1s. 6d. to 5l. or 6l. The small hand-saws with a set of blades are best for beginners; the expensive machine saws, such as the Fleetwood, Challenge or Rival can only be appreciated and used to advantage by skilled manipulators, in whose hands they do wonderful work. A very useful machine, costing 57s. 6d. without or 65s. with drilling attachment, is shown in Fig. 722. These saws are made of iron and steel throughout, except the bows and table. They are very carefully made and fitted, and neatly finished; will hold the finest to coarsest saws, and will cut 1½-in. wood, if desired, but they are recommended for light work principally. The distance from saw to the back of frame is 17 in. The frame is a solid casting, provided with a clamp to secure it to a table or bench. The bows F, of hard ash, are fitted with iron plates on the back end. These plates have knife edges, carefully made, upon which the bows rock with little or no friction. The front ends of the bows are fitted with pivoted steel screw clamps, A, B, for holding all sizes of saws. The plates on which these swing are adjustable, so that the pitch of the saw can be altered if desired, or corrected if it does not run straight. The straining rod D is provided with a cupped nut C containing a spiral spring. This and the stop in the back end of the frame hold the upper saw arm still, and the lower one in place, when from any cause the saw is disconnected. The machine is sold by Churchills, Finsbury, together with many other forms.

722.

The edges left by the saw need filing down, for which purpose the operator will require a round file about 4 in. long, and half-round and flat files each 2 to 4 in. long. The filing is followed by the application of sandpaper. In this there is some art. The sandpaper should never be held in the fingers. If the work is very small, the sheet of sandpaper should be fastened down on a smooth surface and the work be rubbed on it with a circular motion. If larger, the sandpaper may be stretched round a smooth slab of wood 4 in. long, 3 in. wide, and $\frac{3}{8}$ in. thick, and secured by clamping a corresponding slab to the back of the first, making what may be called a "sand board." Or the paper may be glued to a smooth wooden cylinder and used in a lathe if at hand.

Operations.—In fretwork, the design is cut out by means of a saw, instead of by the edged tools used in carving. The mode of working has been made pretty evident in describing the tools. In sawing, care must be taken to give short gentle strokes adapted to the thinness and lightness of the wood dealt with.

One of the most general forms in which fretwork is applied is for forming an ornament called a "gallery," used for the tops of cabinets and other articles of furniture. These galleries vary in size according to the nature of the work for which they are intended. They are generally about $1\frac{1}{4}$ in. to 2 in. wide, and their length is $\frac{1}{4}$ in. to $\frac{3}{8}$ in. less than that of the top upon which they are placed. When getting out the wood, be particular to select as straight-grained a piece as possible ; this is indispensable for all kinds of fretwork. Its thickness should be $\frac{3}{8}$ in. or $\frac{1}{2}$ in. ; for miniature work, $\frac{1}{4}$ in. is sufficient. Before cutting out, consider the kind of gallery you are to have, and the manner in which it is to be finished at the ends, various modifications being adopted. In some, the ends are tenoned into a turned ornament, having a pin fitting into the top. In others, ends are also made at right angles to the back and tenoned into the ornaments. Where it is necessary to have ends, dispense with the turning, and secure them to the back by means of dovetails. It is necessary to have ends where the top is rather wide, and it is better, wherever possible, and where there is sufficient space, to admit one about 3 in. and upwards long. Having considered the kind of gallery, the length it is to be, and the manner of finishing the ends, plane it over, take to a width, and square it. You may with advantage get one piece out long enough to make both ends. You should now mark the gallery and ends. It will be necessary not to allow the fret-cutting to come quite to the ends. Whether it is to be tenoned or dovetailed, you will require sufficient for working; $\frac{1}{2}$ in. or $\frac{5}{8}$ in. should be marked and left plain for this purpose. The bottom must, of course, always be so, because of fitting, and the top is better straight or plain, whether the design is geometrical or otherwise, as a straight or plain top bar protects to a great extent the other fretwork, rendering it less liable to accident, especially if a scrollwork pattern. The bars should be about $\frac{3}{16}$ in. wide, and care should be taken that the cutting is of such a nature as to allow sufficient support to the various parts of the figure, preserving a light appearance with the requisite strength. Galleries are fixed on by means of dowels. When turned ornaments are employed, the pins are usually sufficient, with one dowel or so, to secure it. In other cases, small dowels are placed at a distance of $3\frac{1}{2}$ in. or 4 in. apart in the back, and a little closer in the ends; one or two dowels in the ends acting as a great support to the back. When marking their position, be careful to select the strongest part of the fretwork, that is, the portion connected with the bottom rail, and where you can bore deepest for the dowels. In boring, do it slowly and in the centre; glue and knock in the dowels gently. It is best to cut them in lengths first, and in pressing them into the holes made to receive them in the top, keep the gallery as upright as possible, and allow all the dowels in back and ends to enter together. Do not get one end in first, or the back ones in and not the ends, or you will be likely to break some of them.

It is sometimes required to place a gallery upon a shaped surface, with which it is necessary for it to correspond. It is then got out of thinner material, about half the thickness of that previously given, to enable it to be bent the requisite shape. The method differs from the preceding one, dowels being insufficient to hold it when bent. After the position it is to be in is determined, the thickness of the fretwork is marked bare, and a groove to receive it is cut upon the work. This should be about $\frac{1}{4}$ in. deep and of a uniform depth throughout. The work is carefully bent to this and inserted, afterwards removed and glued. When getting out work of this description, be careful to allow additional width for the bottom bar or rail, so that it will show equal with the top after insertion; that is, add the depth the groove is to be to the width of the bars.

Another application of fretwork is for "stretchers," used principally for the various kinds of tables, and sometimes for other things, both for structural and ornamental purposes. Figs. 723, 724, 725, and 726 are drawings representing forms of stretchers.

723.

724.

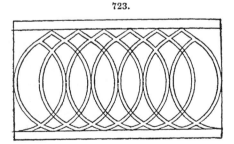
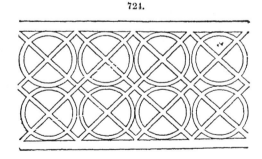

In Figs. 723 and 724 the geometrical designs are intended to be used as shown. This is a form adopted for tables in place of the turned one connecting the front and back legs with a cross one at right angles between. The rails are used diagonally, being tenoned into the alternate legs, and passing through an ornament in the centre. You must allow for the diameter of this when setting out, also a space each side equivalent to that against the legs where tenoned. You will be able to put one rail in in one length, but the other will require to be in two halves, on account of the mortices intersecting in the centre of the ornament. The width of these rails will vary from about 1¼ in. to 2½ in., according to the size of the work; in some of the largest octagon tables this is sometimes exceeded. The material is usually 1 in. thick; in small work ¾ in. is sufficient. The top edges may be moulded. In stretchers of this description the top and bottom bars of the rails

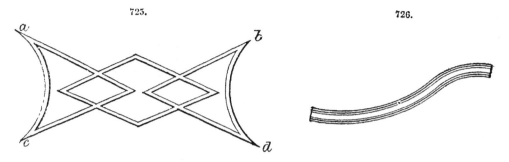

725.   726.

should be always left strong. Fig. 725 is a very good form if used flatways, intended for a large table, being tenoned into legs at *a b* and *c d*. The whole of the wood for this is not, as might be imagined, got out in one, for the obvious reason that the end pieces connecting *a c* and *b d* would be crossways of the grain of the wood and consequently of little use. The stretcher is fret-cut first, the ends being cut separately and afterwards connected. Fig. 726 is a portion of a stretcher where the end is tenoned into a leg and the other into a centre placed rather higher, the edges being either plain-shaped or moulded. It is sometimes required to have the centre of a stretcher cut with a more elaborate design than the remainder. The thickness of wood required for the general part of the stretcher would not admit, or at least not readily, this kind of work to be executed. The centre may then be got out of thinner material, ¼ in. or ⅜ in., and fitted accurately as a panel to the framing of the stretcher. By adopting this plan, the finest description of work may be employed without affecting the requisite strength.

Outline Cutting.—This variety of work, as its name implies, is used for all purposes where outline shaping alone is required, either applied separately or to work that is to be afterwards carved. The importance of getting all carved work previously shaped by fret-cutting, so far as is possible with the nature of the design, is much greater in some cases than in others; but in all it is sufficient to demand careful consideration. It is advisable to first make a pattern the requisite shape, and to mark out from it. It should not be very thick; about ⅛ in. or ⅛ full will answer best. By placing this upon your wood you will be able to mark out in the best manner. If your work is straight or nearly so, there is not much difficulty; but if it curves considerably, as in some kinds of legs, cabriole, for instance, endeavour to arrange the markings so that they will to a great extent cut out of each other, getting the hollow portion of one against the rounded of another, and *vice versâ*.

Brackets.—Among the varieties of brackets most used may be mentioned the following. First, those which are fitted upon a flat surface or pilaster, the front and sides being carved, like those used for bookcases and wardrobe doors. The wood for these should be got out, and the back planed, fitted, and toothed. One end should also be squared, the one that is to be the top in the upper brackets and the bottom in the lower. After carving they are fixed by simply glueing or by dowelling. Second, brackets having two of their sides straight and at right angles to each other. These have a very extensive application, and numerous forms are employed. Sometimes they are merely cut in outline, the front being moulded; the whole design fret-cut is preferable. These brackets vary in thickness from ⅜ in. to 2 in., and occasionally upwards; they are used for most articles of furniture, the heavier kinds being sometimes employed partly as a means of support for shelves, &c., and the lighter more usually for ornamental purposes. When cutting out brackets like these, it is most convenient to mark the wood so that each piece will make 2, leaving the further cutting to the fret-cutter. The advantages of this are obvious. It is necessary to plane over, and thickness, and to square the edges and ends first ; this can be more easily done with a square or rectangular piece of wood than with one approximating to the shape of the brackets. When marking, you can see the size necessary to get out the shape by drawing a line from the extremities of the brackets. Let these lines be the diagonal of the rectangle, and mark your work, so that there is sufficient space to get out the outline inside it when setting the edges square with the outside. It is sometimes advisable to make a slight difference from the diagonal mark when the spaces between the top, bottom, and centre of the outline are considerable. Brackets are fixed either by dowels or screws, generally by a combination of both methods. For most purposes dowels of $\frac{1}{4}$ in. diameter are sufficient; for the lighter kinds less will do. Consider the most suitable position for them, where the work will afford the best hold, and where they will prevent it from twisting or moving. It is rarely possible to use screws from the front or face, without the work is applied in such a manner that some part is not easily discernible. They may, however, be sometimes used from the back or inside.

Many excellent designs for fretwork will be found in Bemrose's ' Fret-cutting and Perforated Carving.'